THE ILLUSTRATED DIRECTORY OF
BEER

THE ILLUSTRATED DIRECTORY OF
BEER

CHARTWELL
BOOKS, INC.

CONTENTS

INTRODUCTION

Above and below: *The Ancient Egyptians and Sumerians brewed and drank beer.*

The art of beer-making goes back many thousands of years, and beer was mankind's first alcoholic drink. Almost as soon as man started to farm grain, he began to brew. Historians have even suggested that it was humankind's fondness for beer that encouraged hunter gatherers to settle down. Evidence from ancient civilizations around the world proves that simple forms of beer were produced and drunk over ten thousand years ago. Beer is known to have been made and drunk by the ancient Egyptians, Africans, and Sumerians. It is said that Noah's provisions on the ark included beer.

Archeological relics indicate that the people of Sumeria (whose territory included the iconic cities of Babylon and Ur) were the first to discover the secrets of fermentation. The Sumerians were so grateful for the discovery of beer that they consecrated a goddess, Ninkasi, as the deity of brewing. It is very likely that the first beers were made from barley bread being crumbled into water to make a simple mash, which was then left to ferment. Others have suggested that beer may even have been made before bread was baked. The Sumerians celebrated the soothing and elevating qualities of beer and considered the drink to be a gift from the gods. The famous Gilgamesh Epic is one of the earliest surviving works of literature, dating from around three thousand years before Christ. It was written by several different Sumerian poets over several hundred years, and tells how the primitive man, Enkidu, became civilized by eating bread and drinking beer. Having drunk seven cups of the beer, Endiku's heart was said to have "soared" and became a human being.

When the Sumerian empire collapsed (around four thousand years ago), their culture and lands were gradually assimilated by the ancient Babylonians. The Babylonians quickly adopted the tradition of brewing beer and developed at least twenty different beer types. These beers were recognizable to us, but were bitter, cloudy, and unfiltered. Drinkers used a kind of draw to avoid drinking the bitter-tasting sediment. Beer became an important part of the Babylonian way of life, and was used in all great celebrations. For a month after a wedding, the bride's father was obliged to give his new son-in-law all the beer he could drink. So enjoyable was this time that it became known as the honeymoon. The Babylonian King Hammurabi wrote one of the first legal codes, this included a legally-established daily beer ration. This ration was dependent on the social standing of the individual. A working man was entitled to a third of a gallon, civil servants received half a gallon, and administrators and high priests were awarded a gallon of beer per day. This beer was not always drunk, but used to barter. A Babylonian clay tablet has been found from around 4300 B.C. that gives a beer recipe.

The Babylonians exported beer around the Middle East and it became particularly popular in Ancient Egypt. In fact, it became so popular that a new hieroglyph for brewer was created. Beer and malt have been found buried in the tombs of the Pharaohs, to keep them cheerful in the after-life. The

Above: *Beer formed part of the Pharaohs' grave goods.*

Below: *The Babylonians had a legally-established daily beer ration.*

Above: *The Babylonians exported their brewing expertise to Ancient Egypt.*

Egyptians added unbaked bread dough and dates to their beers to impart flavor. Beer was so highly thought of that it was also used as a medicine.

Brewing quickly spread around the globe, with each different culture using its own local materials to make beer. Africans brewed with millet, maize, and cassava. The Chinese used wheat. The Japanese made rice beer. The Egyptians brewed with barley. Persimmon, corn, and black birch sap were used in Native American brewing. Agave was used in Mexico, and corn and sweet potatoes were used in Brazil. Each brewing tradition also added various flavorings to their beers, including balsam, hay, dandelion, mint, wormwood seeds, horehound juice, crab claws, and oyster shells.

The ancient Romans brewed beer, but the ruling classes tended to drink more wine. They called the drink "cerevisia," an amalgamation of Ceres (the goddess of crops and agriculture) and vis (strength in Latin). The Roman philosopher Pliny wrote that beer was popular in the Mediterranean but that it was superseded by wine as the drink of the ruling classes. But it was during the Roman period that bittering herbs and spices were first added to beer. These were probably to keep the drink fresher for longer. As the Roman Empire spread to the north and west, beer became the drink of the conquered races rather than that of the ruling elite. The Roman historian Tacitus wrote that the Teutons (Germans) drank "a horrible brew fermented from barley or wheat" and seemed to consider this as proof of their barbarian ways. The mood-altering properties of the brew were considered to be divine and it was thought that beer contained a spirit or god.

Beer was just as popular in Scandinavia. The Finnish Kalewale saga and the Nordic Edda both praise beer and celebrate its inventions. Beer was especially important in these northern countries where it was very difficult to grow wine grapes.

Hops were not introduced to the beverage until much later. German records first

mention the addition of hops to beer around 822. Hop shoots were also eaten, these taste like asparagus tips. Writing in 1150, the nun Hildegarde of Bingen, wrote that hops were added to beer to "reduce the putrefaction" caused by bacteria. The addition of hops to beer slowly spread throughout Europe and had been adopted in Britain by the middle of the fifteenth century. Other wild herbs such as bog myrtle, lemon balm, borage, St. John's Wort, tree bark, and elderberries were also used to brew various styles of beer. Beers were also brewed with honey.

It was in the Middle Ages that beer became so crucial to the welfare of many European countries. As the cultivation of barley spread north and west, brewing went with it. At this time, many brewers were women, as beer-making was considered a domestic activity.

As centers of science and agriculture, it was inevitable that the great monasteries soon became the most important brewers of this period. Not only did they brew for their own consumption, and to refresh visiting pilgrims, but the monasteries also sold their brews. Monks developed new styles of beer, and honed their brewing techniques and recipes. In this way, brewing became centralized, rather than being a domestic activity. This monastic tradition of beer making continues today, particularly in Belgium. The

Above and left:
Monasteries became the focus of the medieval brewing industry.

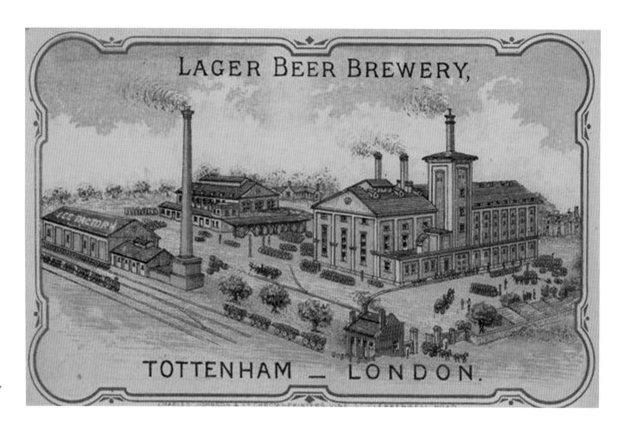

LAGER BEER BREWERY,

TOTTENHAM — LONDON.

Right: *Brewing became industrialized in the nineteenth century.*

Below: *The German Purity Law dates from 1516.*

refreshing beer made a welcome break in a very austere lifestyle and could still be enjoyed during times of fasting. Monks soon acquired a taste for ale and records show that in some monasteries consumption up to almost a gallon a day was allowed. Beer was safer to drink than untreated water, and had nutritional benefits. It is even credited with drawing disparate communities together into village life, and many medieval workers were paid with jugs of beer. Beer was also used to pay tithes and taxes and used as a form of currency.

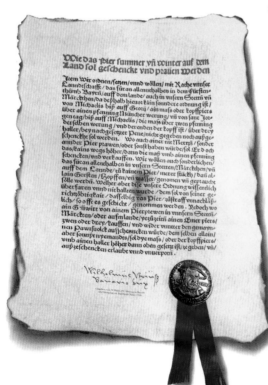

The next important event in the history of beer brewing was the introduction of the Reinheitsgebot or Purity Law of 1516. This was the world's first food regulation. The law was first introduced in the Munich area of Germany and was extended to the whole of Bavaria in 1516. Later, the law was extended to the whole of Germany. The Purity Law stipulated that beer could only be brewed from water, hops, and malted wheat or barley with no additional ingredients. Yeast was added later, when it was identified as being responsible for fermentation. The law is the source of the European disdain for adding adjuncts such as corn, rice, and sugars to beer. It also indicates how, by this time, beer making had become an important commercial enterprise in many countries, including Germany, England, Czechoslovakia, Holland, and Austria. Germany's first brewing guild, the Brauerei Beck, had been established in 1489.

Over the centuries, beer became a hugely important part of German life. The world's oldest operating commercial brewery is Bavaria's Weihenstephan abbey brewery, which was established in 1040. Beck's Brewery was founded in 1553 and also still brews today. German beer making gradually changed to artisan production, with beer halls and monasteries brewing beer for mass consumption. In 1810, German society enshrined its

Opposite: *Lagering became a popular method of storing beer in the fifteenth century.*

appreciation of the country's great brews by establishing the annual Oktoberfest beer festival in Munich. A couple of decades later, two Bavarian brewers developed the world's first lager brews.

The next great development in brewing happened in the mid-nineteenth century, through the work of Louis Pasteur. Pasteur was the first person to explain how yeast worked. He used samples of Bavarian yeast and determined that yeast was required for successful fermentation. His research enabled brewers to control the process much better. German brewers had started to make beer by lagering (storing) beer in the fifteenth century. They couldn't make beer in the warm months because wild yeasts soured the beer. We now know that the winter cold killed the yeast and this could be filtered out of the beer. The invention of pasteurization meant that fermentation could be controlled, and beer could be made year-round. The process also made beer more stable and it became possible to manufacture clearer, more uniform beers on an industrial scale.

The next major even in the history of beer was the introduction of Prohibition in the United States. This was a nationwide ban on the production, sale, and import of alcoholic drinks. It remained in place for thirteen dry years between 1920 and 1933. Some states also banned the personal possession of alcohol. This law was enshrined in the Volstead Act of 1919. The consumption of alcohol halved during the 1920s and remained below pre-Prohibition levels until the 1940s. Prohibition also had a dramatic effect on the American beer industry. This had thrived since Sir Walter Raleigh's men brewed the first European-style beer in the New World in 1587. The first commercial brewery opened in American on the island of New Amsterdam (Manhattan) in 1612, staffed by a group of brewers from London, England. For centuries, beer continued to be an intrinsic part of American life. The staple diet of the poor consisted of bread and beer. William Penn owned a commercial brewery, and both George Washington and Thomas Jefferson had private brew houses. Washington

Above: *Pliny wrote about the popularity of beer in Ancient Rome.*

Below: *Louis Pasteur explained how yeast works in the brewing process.*

Roaring Good Times SAT EDITION

•• GENTLEMEN: STEP OUT IN YOUR FEDORA ••

PROHIBITION ENDS AT LAST!

DECEMBER 5, 1933

Right and below: *Prohibition lasted for thirteen dry years.*

Below: *Food shortages meant that wartime beers were lighter.*

wrote his own recipe for small beer. Beer also became an important Canadian industry. The Molson brewery was founded in Montreal in 1786. The American brewing industry was encouraged by the government, with higher tariffs being levied on malt liquors to encourage beer drinking. In the mid-nineteenth century there was a huge flowering of beer manufacture in America, when many German brewers immigrated to the country and started new brewing enterprises. These included Anheuser-Busch, Miller, Coors, Stroh, Schlitz, and Pabst. German brewers also introduced cold maturation lagers to America.

American breweries greatly benefitted from the technological advances of the late nineteenth century, such as refrigerated transport, and were able to develop their beers as national brands. Busch was one of the first breweries to embrace these advances. It used double-walled railcars and ice houses to establish Budweiser as America's first national beer brand. Pabst was the first American brewer to sell over a million barrels of beer in a year.

The effects of Prohibition were dramatic. Virtually overnight, the American beer business collapsed, and nearly two thousand small-scale brewers closed down. Several large-scale industrial brewers managed to switch production to non-alcoholic goods. This meant that that they were able to stay in business until Prohibition was repealed and they were able to produce beer once more. Even when Prohibition was repealed, War-time food shortages meant that it was difficult to return to the beers of the past. There was an increasing substitution of various adjuncts for malt, resulting in much lighter beers. Ironically, while so many American men were away fighting the war, these lighter beers were popular with the largely female workforce. Prohibition also had a dramatic effect on the American beer market, by ensuring that it was dominated by large-scale brewers of industrial beers.

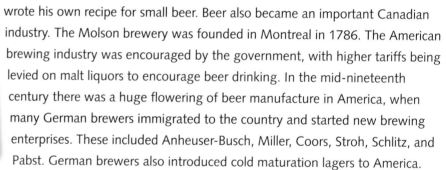

Only 160 breweries survived Prohibition. This domination of the beer market by a relatively small number of brewers persisted for several decades until the explosion of craft brewing in the 1970s and 1980s. This led to a great re-diversification of the beer on sale in America and a great interest in the beers of other countries.

On the positive side, the modern era of canned beer began on January 24, 1935 when Krueger Cream Ale became the first-ever canned beer. The beer industry also introduced other industrial processes, like automatic bottling to grow the American beer business. In 1966 Budweiser became the first beer brand to sell ten million barrels in a year.

In the late 1970s, the craft brewing movement began to offer an alternative to highly uniform industrially-produced beers. The 1976 opening of the New Albion brewpub and micro brewery in 1976 by Jack McAuliffe in Sonoma, California. New Albion is acknowledged as the first American microbrewery of the modern era. The brewery had a huge influence on the subsequent microbrewery and craft beer movements of the late twentieth century. Although New Albion failed to survive, the brewery laid out a blueprint that inspired the craft beer, and micro brewery movements. Like New Albion, many of these small beer-making enterprises have their roots in home brewing, and many also have a community-based agenda. The movement gathered pace in the 1980s and continues to the present day. New micro breweries and pubs open in all kinds of communities every year, answering a need for good beer. The craft brewing movement has also had a great influence on the variety and quality of beers on offer in America. Not only are many old-style brewing techniques used to construct a huge range of brew-styles, but a plethora of new ingredients are also trialed by these small breweries.

The craft brew movement has also raised the profile of beer as an exciting and innovative consumer product. This has had a positive effect on the whole of the beer industry, and has encouraged even large-scale breweries to make craft-style beers. Despite this, America's five largest brewers (Anheuser-Busch, Miller, Coors, Stroh, and G. Heileman) still make around 90% of the country's beer. The craft beer movement has also had a big effect on the cultural function of beer. In the early part of the twentieth century, beer was associated with blue-collar manual workers, college students, and sports enthusiasts. The advent of micro breweries, many of which serve good food, has made beer drinking a more mainstream activity that cuts across class barriers. Many of these beers are marketed to partner food in the place of wine. Some hand-crafted beers have also moved into the luxury drinks market.

By 1991 America was producing a fifth of the world's beer (around 5.89 billion gallons), and was the

Below: *Jack McAuliffe's New Albion brewpub began the modern craft brewing movement.*

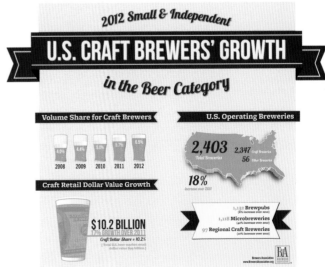

largest global producer. Beer is the world's most popular alcoholic drink and the third most popular drink of any kind after water and tea. The average American drinks around twenty-two gallons of beer each year and beer is a hugely important national commodity. The American brewing industry supports thousands of jobs, and the country's Anheuser-Busch brewing facility is the largest in the world. However, the profile of beers consumed by the American public has undergone a fairly substantial change over the past five years. Overall sales of many popular mass-produced beers have fallen. Sales of the once top-selling Budweiser have declined by more than a quarter since 2008. This has been especially noticeable in light beer sales. The sales of Michelob Light, for example, have declined by almost 70% in the past five years. By contrast, the sales of flavored beers and much more expensive craft beers have been increasing. Specialty beers with creative labels, unusual ingredients, and a higher alcohol content seem to be taking beer to new levels of appreciation. Micro breweries have become leisure destinations, with many offering dining, tours, and merchandise to give their brews a higher profile. This trend has not gone unnoticed by the major brewers, who have been buying up medium-sized craft brewers and absorbing these companies into their brewing portfolio. Big brewers have also been making new beers to compete with craft-brewed ales. Bud Platinum, for example, has a higher alcohol content than most mass-produced beers. The brew sold almost two million cases in 2012, becoming the nineteenth most popular beer in the United States.

The huge upsurge in craft brewing across the world, especially in America, Canada, and Great Britain, has given many new brewers the opportunity to start their own brewing businesses. Many people starting their own breweries have become disillusioned with more main-stream careers and have decided to go it alone to produce a commodity that arouses strong passions. Many of these new businesses are very people-focused enterprises that are in direct contrast to the financial, IT, and big business careers that their founders have abandoned. Many of these new breweries focus on being local rather than international, serving their communities and buying their ingredients locally. But some of these enterprises have gone on to rival the success of the large brewing combines. The Boston Beer Company is now tied with Yuengling for the honor of being the largest American-owned beer maker. Others have been taken over by mass market brewers seeking to broaden their range of beers.

Beer Ingredients

Essentially, beer is an alcoholic beverage produced by changing starch into sugary water, and fermenting the result of this process. The enzymes that achieve this miracle are mostly derived from malted cereal grains. In modern times, barley and wheat are the most popular cereals used in brewing. Since the Middle Ages, most beer has been flavored, or bittered with hops. Hops also act as natural preservatives. In specialty and craft beers, many other flavorings are also added to beers to create a wide range of interesting brews. Some of these ingredients have been added for hundreds of years, but some are completely new and experimental. Brewing is now considered to be a craft, and many school and colleges offer courses in brewing for both amateur and home brewers.

The magic of brewing comes from the combination of a few simple ingredients.

Water

The most voluminous ingredient in beer is water. As the water of each geographical region differs in its mineral composition, this has a huge influence on the taste of beer. This means that almost all beers have a distinct regional character. Many breweries have been deliberately sited near wells, springs, aquifers, and streams to take advantage of pure local water sources. Different kinds of water are suited to making different styles of beer. Dublin, Ireland is a hard water area (the water has a high mineral content) and this is particularly suited to the brewing of stout. By contrast the Pilsner brewing area of Czechoslovakia has soft (low ion) water which makes good pale beers. The English beers made in the famous Burton-on-Trent area reflect the gypsum content of the water there. This is so important to the flavor of the pale ales brewed there that local brewers even add gypsum to their brewing water in a process called Burtonization.

Cereal

All beers are made with some kind of starch, which is almost always derived from cereals. It is this material that is soaked in water and then dried. This process is called malting. This substance (often called the mash) is then fermented to make the alcoholic base of the drink. Different kinds of malt (pale and dark, for example) are made by roasting the grain at different temperatures.

Barley is a very popular cereal used to make beer, but several other grains are also used for this including wheat, oats, rice, corn, sorghum, cassava, and rye. Each produces beers of a different taste and character.

Hops

Hops are now used to flavor, bitter, and preserve almost all beers. Hops are the pretty, cascading flowers of the hop bine (or vine). The monk Adalhard the Elder was the first person to write about the use of hops in beer in 822 A.D., but they did not come into widespread use in brewing until the Middle Ages. Today, the use of hops is almost universal but some specialist craft breweries use other plants to bitter the beer. This hoppy bitterness balances the sweetness of the malt and gives a range of flavoring notes to beer, including citrus, herbal, floral, and pine. Generally speaking, heavier beers need more hops to balance the flavor. The bitterness of beers is measured on the scale of International Bitterness Units. This scale was designed by the American Society of Brewing Chemists. The bitterness is measured with a spectrophotometer. Light beers usually score around 5 IBUs while a strong IPA might score the maximum bitterness score of 100 IBUs. Hops also help a beer's foaming head to be retained for longer.

Yeast

It is yeast that enables the fermentation of beer, when sugar is turned into alcohol. Different yeasts give the beer different flavors, but also influence the density of the beer's body. Different styles of beer are made with different yeasts, and they have a very strong influence on the character of each beer. In early times, natural airborne yeasts fermented simple brews, but as brewing became more sophisticated, the fermentation process itself became better understood and controlled and yeasts were cultured. Airborne yeasts are still used to ferment some craft-style brews, but they can result in quite unstable brews.

BEER STYLES: Ale and Lager

There are now a great number of different beer styles in production around the world, but all beers are either lagers or ales. The difference between lager and ale is largely due to the temperature of the fermentation. Ale yeasts work best between 60 and 72 degrees Fahrenheit, and tend to work at the top of the fermentation tank. Lager yeasts work best at a lower temperature of 46 to 55 degrees Fahrenheit, and work at the bottom of the fermentation tank. The fermentation process for ales and lagers is also different. Ales are usually aged for just a few weeks while lagers are usually aged for months. The lager aging process is called "lagering" and it results in a cleaner flavored beer with a light flavor and aroma, while ales are richer and more complex beers. All early beer types were variants of ale. Lagers are a much more modern style of beer, which relied on the invention of refrigeration to become widely produced. From the 1860s onwards, lagers gradually became the principal beer product of the Czech brewers and the style spread quickly around the world. After working in Czechoslovakia's new lager industry, the brewer Gabriel Sedlmayr took the pale ale brewing techniques he had learned back to the Spaten Brewery in Germany. A wide variety of lager beers is now available. While the classic lager is pale, mild, and quite low in alcohol, darker and higher alcohol lagers are also available. Pale German and Czech-style lagers are described as pilsner or helles, and the darker styles are often known as dunkel. Lagers can range in color from the palest blond to black. Amber colored lagers are also popular.

Altbier

Altbier is German for "old beer" is a German style of beer that is a speciality of the city of Düsseldorf. The beer is produced using the brewing technique of top fermentation, which is typical of lager production. Altbier is usually dark copper in color. It is brewed at a moderate temperature using a top-fermenting yeast. This gives the beer a fruity flavor.

Amber Ale

Amber ales range in color from light golden to deep red. They are slow-fermenting ales with a medium body. The flavor of amber ales comes mostly from the hops from which they are brewed. Amber ales are usually transparent, although some may be slightly cloudy. They usually have a large pale head and are well-carbonated. Some amber ales are also described as West Coast ales, as the style is popular in California, Oregon, and Washington. Darker versions of the style are called red ales. Like all ales, ambers are made with top fermenting yeast.

Barley Wine

Barley Wine is a style that dates from the eighteenth and nineteenth centuries.

Barley Wine is a strong beer style with an alcohol level between 10% and 12%. This meant that the beer could be stored for long periods of up to two years. The beer was often drunk at meals as a replacement for French wine, and was often served in wine glasses. Many micro-breweries now produce their interpretations of this style. The beer usually has strong sweet malt and ripe fruit tasting notes.

Berliner Weisse

Berliner weisse is a refreshing, citrus flavored wheat beer with very little hop bitterness. It is a top-fermented, bottle conditioned style made with both traditional warm-fermenting yeasts and the lactobacillus culture. Berliner weisse beers have a clear, pale golden straw-colored appearance. These beers are often served in wide bulbous stemmed glasses, and may have fruit syrups added to them to counteract their sourness.

Biere de Garde

Bière de Garde or "beer for keeping" is a strong pale ale traditionally brewed in the Nord-Pas-de-Calais region of France. These beers were originally brewed in farmhouses in the winter and spring. Several beers of this type are now made commercially. Typically, beers of this style are copper or golden in color. Once bottled, the beer was matured for a period of time in the bottle.

Bitter

Bitter is an English pale ale. These beers vary in color from pale gold to dark amber. The alcoholic strength of bitters varies between 3% and 7%. The color of bitter may be controlled by the addition of caramel color.

Blonde Ale

Blonde ale is made by warm fermentation using mostly pale malt. This results in a lighter colored beer. The style was introduced around 1703 when it was realized the using coke to roast the beer malt resulted in a lighter brew.

Bock

Bock is a strong, dark, malty, and lightly hopped German lager. The style was first brewed in the fourteenth century in the German city of Einbeck. There are also several variants of this style including maibock, doppelbock, eisbock, and helles bock. Doppelbock is stronger and maltier, while eisbock is a strong beer made with a freezing process. Although bocks were originally dark, they now vary from light copper to brown in color. It is a popular style and many variants are brewed around the world.

Brown Ale

Brown ale is an increasingly popular beer style brewed in America, England, and Belgium. These beers are dark amber or brown in color. The term was first used by London brewers in the late seventeenth century. These original brown ales were brewed from brown malt and were lightly hopped.

California Common

California common beers were originally produced in San Francisco and along the West Coast. These beers were made with lager yeast and without any refrigeration. Modern steam beer was re-introduced during the craft beer revolution. The first and most influential of these was Anchor Steam Beer which was launched in 1981.

Cream Ale

Cream ales are American beers, similar in style to pale ales. They are light and refreshing and very pale gold in color. Hop and malt flavors are both subtle. They are produced with top fermentation and are cold-conditioned to give the beer a clean flavor. It is a style now favored by many craft breweries.

Doppelbock

Doppelbock (literally "double bock") is a stronger and darker version of the German Bock beer style. Doppelbock is exceptionally malty, with very little bitterness. Standard Doppelbocks may have as much as 7% alcohol by volume but the strongest versions can have an alcohol level of up to 13%. Doppelbock emerged in the late eighteenth century as a powerful lager variant of the old monastic strong beer.

Dortmunder Export

Dortmunder Union is a lager beer that originated in Germany's steel and coal district along the River Ruhr in the nineteenth century. Dortmunder beers are full-bodied and moderately hopped with an alcohol level of at least 5%. The style is still brewed in Germany and America.

Dunkel

Dunkel means dark, so the term can be applied to any dark beer. Dunkels can generally be divided into dark wheat beers and dark lagers. Dark lagers are brewed with a darker roasted malt than pale lagers and have a distinctive taste.

Dunkelweizen

Dunkelweizen is the dark version of the weissbier, weizenbier, or hefeweizen. Dunkel means dark in German and weizen means wheat. Like hefeweizen, dunkelweizen is made from a mixed mash of wheat and barley malts, but it also contains a large array of caramelized or roasted malts that give it both its color and its complexity.

Eisbock

Eisbock is a traditional German specialty beer. It is made by partially freezing doppelbock beer and removing the ice to concentrate the flavor and alcohol content. Eisbock is clear, and ranges from deep copper to dark brown in color, often with ruby highlights. Eisbock has an intense aroma and little hop presence. It is often quite fruity and has a smooth mouth feel.

Fruit lambic

Fruit lambic beers are characterized by fruit flavors and aromas. The beer color reflects the choice of fruit. Sourness is an important part of the flavor profile, though sweetness may compromise the intensity. These fruit flavored beers may be very dry or mildly sweet and range from a dry to a full-bodied mouth feel.

Golden Ale

Golden ale is a new style of pale, well-hopped and quenching beer developed in the 1980s. The hallmark of golden ales is their biscuity and juicy malt character. This is derived from pale malts. The ale usually have flavor notes of tart citrus fruit, peppery hops, vanilla, and corn flour. Golden ales are pale amber, gold, yellow or straw colored. They are thirst quenching and can be served cool.

Gose

Gose is a top-fermented beer that originated in Goslar, Germany. It is brewed with 50% malted wheat and coriander. The dominant flavors include lemon, herbs, and salt. The salt is the result of either local water sources or added salt. Gose beers have little hop bitterness. Because of the use of coriander and salt, Gose does not comply with the Reinheitsgebot. Gose beer is allowed an exemption on the grounds of being a regional specialty.

Gueuze

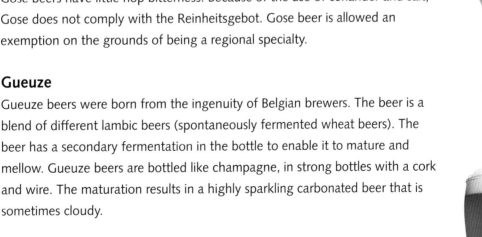

Gueuze beers were born from the ingenuity of Belgian brewers. The beer is a blend of different lambic beers (spontaneously fermented wheat beers). The beer has a secondary fermentation in the bottle to enable it to mature and mellow. Gueuze beers are bottled like champagne, in strong bottles with a cork and wire. The maturation results in a highly sparkling carbonated beer that is sometimes cloudy.

Hefeweizen

"Hefe" means yeast and "weizen" means wheat. Hefeweizen is a top fermented, unfiltered, bottle conditioned wheat beer. The brew has noticeable yeast sediment and a cloudy appearance. Wheat beers are also referred to as weissbiers (white beers). This is because before pale lagers and pale ales were invented, most beers were dark. Wheat beers were the exception as the wheat content lightened the color of the beer.

Helles

Hell is the German word for light, and helles means a light one. This refers to the color of the beer rather than its flavor or level of alcohol. The helles beers were the first blond lagers from Munich. Helles beers are also known as Munich original lagers.

India Pale Ale

India Pale Ale or IPA is a pale ale beer style that was first brewed in England in the nineteenth century. The first known use of the term India pale ale was in an advertisement in the *Sydney Gazette and New South Wales Advertiser* in 1829. This extra strength beer was designed to survive the sea voyage from Britain to India to supply their troops. The term pale ale denoted an ale that had been brewed from pale malt.

Kölsch

Kölsch (also spelled koelsch) is a local specialty beer brewed in Cologne, Germany. It is clear with a bright, straw-yellow hue. The beer has a prominent hoppiness, and is less bitter than standard German pale lager. The beer is warm-fermented at around 55 to 70 degrees Fahrenheit, and then cold-conditioned, or lagered. This style of fermentation links kölsch with some other central northern European beers such as the altbiers of Germany and the Netherlands.

Lambic

Lambic beers are brewed in Belgium. Unlike conventional ales and lagers, which are fermented by carefully cultivated strains of brewer's yeasts, lambic beer is produced by spontaneous fermentation. It is this unusual process which gives the beer its distinctive flavor. This is dry, vinous, and cidery, with a sour aftertaste.

Light Ale

Light ale is a low alcohol style of bitter, which is often bottled rather than being sold on tap.

Maibock

Maibock (May Bock) beer is strong, golden lager brewed in Bavaria. It is made in spring each year. Maibock is brewed with pale malts for a warm golden hue. It is more agressively hopped than others bocks for a refreshing finish.

Mild

Mild ale is a low-gravity beer with a predominantly malty palate. The style originated in Britain in the seventeenth century. Modern mild ales are mostly dark in color with an alcohol level of 3% to 3.6%. Some mild ales are lighter, and some have a higher alcohol level.

Oktoberfest/Marzenbier

Octoberfest or Marzenbiers were originally brewed in March and laid down in caves before the summer weather meant that brewing was impossible. This beer would be drunk during the summer, and finally used up in October. Märzenbier has a malty aroma, and is a medium-strong version of amber-red Vienna beers. The beer is seasonal to the Oktoberfest, where it is offered as a traditional speciality alongside paler beers of a similar strength.

Old Ale

Old ale is a term used to describe England's dark, malty beers. These are usually above 5% alcohol. The term is also applied to dark ales of any strength in Australia. Old ales are sometimes retained by brewery and re-fermented.

Oud Bruin

Oud Bruin (which means old brown in Dutch) is also known as Flanders Brown beer. The style originated from the Flemish region of Belgium. The name refers to the long aging process that the beer is subjected to, which could last for up to a year. The beer is medium bodied, reddish-brown in color. It has a gentle malty flavor and no hop bitterness.

Pale Ale

Pale ale is a generic term for light-colored beers made with pale malts. The style has many different types including amber ale, American pale ale, English bitter, Irish red ale, India Pale Ale, strong ale, Scotch ale, and blonde ale.

Pilsner

Pilsner (also pilsener or pils) is a type of pale lager first brewed in Czechoslovakia in 1842. It was first brewed in the city of Pilsen in Bohemia. The original Pilsner Urquell beer is still produced there today. Modern pilsner has a very light, clear color that ranges from pale to golden yellow. The beer has a distinct hop aroma and flavor.

Porter

Porter is a dark style of beer that originated in London, England in the eighteenth century. Porter is similar to brown beer. It is well hopped and brewed with brown malt. The name is thought to have come from its popularity with street and river porters.

Red Ale

Red Ale refers to any beer paler than a dark ale in color. The color of the beer ranges from amber to deep red. Red ale is brewed with predominant malt. The hop character can range from low to high. These are balanced beers, with toasted malt and light fruitiness.

Roggenbier

Roggenbier is a medieval ale made from barley, wheat, and rye malts. A roggenbier can be either an ale or a lager. Modern renditions of this style have about 5 to 5.5% alcohol by volume. Rye ales are mildly hopped, which allows the grain flavors to dominate. Filtration is optional for this style of beer, and many are "naturtrüb" or unfiltered. These beers are more authentic, considering that the style pre-dates filtration, which was invented in 1878.

Saison

Saison beers are pale ales that are highly carbonated, fruity, and spicy. Spices are sometimes added to the brew. Saison beers were originally brewed in farmhouses in the French-speaking region of Belgium. They were then stored for drinking during the summer months. Modern saisons are brewed in a range of countries, including America. They are often bottle conditioned.

Scotch Ale

Scotch Ale was the name given to strong pale ale brewed in Edinburgh, Scotland in the nineteenth century. The beer is brewed with pale barley malt and moderately hopped. The style is similar to English strong ales and barley wines. Scotch Ales are popular in America, where most examples are brewed locally.

Steam Beer

Steam beer is a highly effervescent beer made by brewing lager yeasts at warm fermentation temperatures. Historic steam beer is associated with San Francisco and the West Coast. The beer was popular with gold miners in the Nevada Gold Rush.

Stout

Stout is a dark beer made using roasted malt or roasted barley, hops, water and yeast. Stout is the generic term for the strongest or stoutest porters. The style has a number of variations, including Baltic porter, dry stout, and imperial stout.

Schwarzbier

Schwarzbier, or black beer, is German dark lager beer. The beer is black and opaque with slight hints of chocolate or coffee. These are much stronger in stout or porter. Unlike dark ales, Schwarzbiers share some lager characteristics. Schwarzbiers are bottom-fermented beers.

Vienna Lager

Vienna lager was first developed by the brewer Anton Dreher in Vienna in 1841. Austrian brewers immigrated to Mexico and brought the style across the Atlantic. Vienna lager is a reddish-brown or copper-colored beer with medium body and slight malty sweetness. The malt aroma and flavor may also be toasted. Vienna lagers are now little known in Europe, but are popular in America, where it is widely known as pre-Prohibition style amber lager.

Witbier

Witbier is a top-fermented wheat beer that is mainly brewed in Belgium and the Netherlands. The beer gets its name from its white and cloudy appearance. This is due to the yeast and wheat proteins that are suspended in the beer. The beer is brewed with gruit. This substance consists of coriander, orange, bitter orange, and hops.

Weissbier

Weissbier or white beer is a Bavarian beer in which a significant proportion of malted barley is replaced with malted wheat. It is a top-fermented beer. Specialized strains of yeast are used to brew the beer, which produce overtones of banana and clove in the brew. Hefeweizen is wheat beer in its traditional, unfiltered form. Kristallweizen beers are filtered to remove the suspended yeast.

Weizenbock

Weizenbock is similar to barley-based bockbier. It is a stronger version of an unfiltered weissbier or hefeweizen. The beer is usually made with mostly wheat malt, and German law requires that Weizenbier is made from at least 50% wheat.

ALBANIA

BIRRA TIRANA

Country of Origin: *Albania* • **Brewery Founded:** *1938* • **Alcohol Content:** *4.1%*

Birra Tirana is brewed by Birra Malto, which is based in Tirana, Albania. Birra Malto is Albania's largest brewery. Birra Tirana was first brewed in 1961. It is a pale lager that is brewed for export. The beer is clear golden in color. It has a very fizzy carbonation with a short-lasting off-white head. The aroma is sharp and malty with hints of grain and fruit. The beer has a fairly watery medium-density body and is generally mild in flavor.

ERENIKU PILSNER BEER

Country of Origin: *Albania* • **Brewery Founded:** *Unknown* • **Alcohol Content:** *4%*

Ereniku is brewed by the Stefani & Co. brewery in Tirana, Albania. The brewery also brews Stella beer for the Albanian market. Ereniku is a pale lager-style Pils with a rich and sour flavor that has hints of grass, corn, orange, and syrup with a touch of crystal malt and fairly low bitterness. This medium-bodied beer has a clear golden appearance with an airy head.

KORCA GOLD PILS

Country of Origin: *Albania* • **Brewery Founded:** *1928* • **Alcohol Content:** *4.5%*

Korca Gold Pils is bottled by the Birra Korca brewery in Tirana, Albania. The beer pours a clear, pale gold with a lively carbonation. It has a white head. The aroma is slightly grainy and dusty, with a hint of hoppy aroma. The beer itself has a watery texture and a light body, with a short, slightly dry finish. The flavor is sweet with a balancing medium bitterness. Korca has always been popular in the South East part of Albania, whereas Birra Tirana is favored in the rest of the country.

NORGA ROSSA

Country of Origin: *Albania* • **Brewery Founded:** *Unknown* • **Alcohol Content:** *4.5%*

Norga Rossa is brewed by Albania's A & B Grup (Norga). It is a Vienna-style amber lager, brewed at Vlore in Albania. The beer has an attractive copper color and has a small beige head. The flavor of the beer is sweet, with hints of raisins, caramel, fruit, and brown sugar. The beer has a medium body and a malty aroma.

ALGERIA

BEAUFORT

Country of Origin: *Algeria* • **Brewery Founded:** *Unknown* • **Alcohol Content:** *4.5%*

Beaufort is a pale lager brewed in Oran, Algeria by the S.N.B. brewery. The beer pours a clear golden, with a brief white head. Beaufort has an aroma of vegetables and malt. The taste is sweetish and the beer is light bodied with a mellow mouth feel. The brew has some late bitterness mixed with slightly metallic notes.

MINI BR

Country of Origin: *Algeria* • **Brewery Founded:** *Unknown*
Alcohol Content: *4.5%*

Mini BR is brewed by E.P.B.R. (Enterprise de Production des Boissons de Reghaia) in Algiers, Algeria. The beer is hazy pale gold with a snow white head and a light honeyish aroma. The texture is fairly grainy. The flavor is a bit herbal and grassy. The finish is fairly bitter and hoppy but with sweet fruity notes.

TANGO BIERE BLONDE

Country of Origin: *Algeria* • **Brewery Founded:** *Unknown* • **Alcohol Content:** *4.8%*

Tango Biere Blonde is brewed by S.A.R.L. Tango a Heineken owned brewery in Algiers, Algeria. The beer has a hazy golden-blond color with high carbonation and a thin white head. The beer has a light texture with low bitterness, tart flavors, and touches of sweetness. The beer has a hop aroma and a herby, almond flavor.

TANGO GOLD

Country of Origin: *Algeria* • **Brewery Founded:** *Unknown* • **Alcohol Content:** *5.2%*

Tango Gold is brewed by Heineken's Algerian brewery, S.A.R.L. in Algiers, Algeria. It is sold in cans. The beer is a bright golden straw yellow with a light ring of foam. The beer has some sweet citric notes, medium bitterness, and malty flavors. The aroma is quite neutral and the body of the beer is malty and grainy. It has a clean mouth feel.

ARGENTINA

ANTARES IMPERIAL STOUT

Country of Origin: *Argentina* • **Brewery Founded:** *1995* • **Alcohol Content:** *8.5%*

Imperial Russian stouts were first developed by English brewers to export to the Imperial Russian court. This deep black stout has aromas of toast, alcohol, soaked raisins. The brew is bitter and smoky. The beer is constructed with Pilsen, Caramel, and chocolate malts blended with European ale hops.

BARBA ROJA BARREL AGED RED ALE

Country of Origin: *Argentina* • **Brewery Founded:** *2001* • **Alcohol Content:** *9%*

This rarity is a smoked and aged strong red ale that is best consumed at a cellar temperature of about 55 degrees. This American-style strong ale is slightly smoky and wood-influenced. It also displays very nice qualities of roasted toffee and caramel-like flavors, but not with any intense sweetness, which make it an ideal food beer. It is particularly good with classic Argentine fare such as grilled steak or burgers, simply-cooked potatoes, and nutty or salty cheeses.

BEAGLE FUEGIAN ALE (RUBIA)

Country of Origin: *Argentina* • **Brewery Founded:** *Unknown* • **Alcohol Content:** *5.8%*

Located in the mountainous seaside city of Ushuaia, Beagle produces artisanal craft beer. The brewery is named after HMS Beagle, Charles Darwin's ship that sailed around South America and performed a variety of scientific surveys. The brewery was born from the simple idea of making beer to share among friends. Beagle's Fuegian Ale is a nice honey color. It has a strong freshly baked bread aroma with fruity notes. The beer is mildly bitter from start to finish with a long yeasty aftertaste. It is unfiltered and finely carbonated.

BERLINA FOREIGN STOUT

Country of Origin: *Argentina* • **Brewery Founded:** *Unknown* • **Alcohol Content:** *6%*

Berlina Foreign Stout is brewed by Cerveceria Berlina in San Carlos de Bariloche, Argentina. The beer pours black with a light brown head. It has an aroma of roasted malt, coffee, and dark chocolate. The flavor is malt, coffee, chocolate, and light vegetables. The beer has a thin body, with soft carbonation and a dry finish.

BERSAGLIER CREAM STOUT

Country of Origin: *Argentina* • **Brewery Founded:** *2003* • **Alcohol Content:** *6%*

Bersaglier Cream Stout is brewed by Bersaglier Cerveza Artesanal in San Martin, Argentina. Bersaglier was founded in 2003 by four cousins who got together to make a craft brewery. They offered their first brews in 2005. This cream stout is black in color with a rich yet dry roasty, burnt aroma which continues into the taste. This turns spicy and bitter although it remains full, roasted and coffee-like. The finish has the same with some additional liquorice. It is a very complex, accomplished, and impressive stout.

BLEST BOCK

Country of Origin: *Argentina* • **Brewery Founded:** *2003* • **Alcohol Content:** *5.8%*

Best Bock is a dunkler bock brewed by Cerveceria Blest in San Carlos de Bariloche, Argentina. This dark burgundy bock has a thin, tan head. The aroma is malty and sweet, full of brown sugar, caramel and has a light fruitiness. The beer has a fairly full body. The flavor is on the sweet side, but not excessively so. The beer has nice malts and a hint of bitterness at the finish. Many beer drinkers rate this as the best beer made by Blest.

CARDOS BARLEY WINE

Country of Origin: *Argentina* • **Brewery Founded:** *1825* • **Alcohol Content:** *12%*

Cardos Barley Wine is brewed by Cerveceria Cardos, based in Los Cardales, Argentina. The beer is fermented twice, which develops the beer's harmony and sweetness. The great Cardos reserve maintains its quality for many years if stored in a dark place and attains a faint and agreeable port flavor.

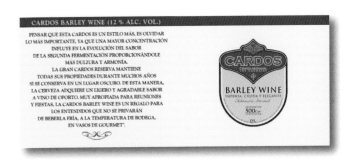

EL BOLSON NEGRA EXTRA XXX

Country of Origin: *Argentina* • **Brewery Founded:** *2003* • **Alcohol Content:** *6%*

El Bolson Negra Extra XXX is a dunkel beer brewed by the Cerveceria Artesanal El Bolson of El Bolson, Argentina. The beer pours a deep dark brown with a thin taupe head. The aroma is full of coffee and bitter nutty chocolate, a little sour. The beer is mildly sweet and acidic and bitter all the way through.

JEROME NEGRA

Country of Origin: *Argentina* • **Brewery Founded:** *2000* • **Alcohol Content:** *6.5%*

Jerome Negra is brewed by the Cerveceria Jerome, based in Potrerillos, Argentina. The beer is a stout with a complex character of dried fruits and raisins and a sweet bouquet of coffee, truffles, and chocolate. The beer has a great body and soft mouth finish. Jerome Negra pours a black pearl color and has a creamy foam head.

KRAKEN AMERICAN IPA

Country of Origin: *Argentina* • **Brewery Founded:** *Unknown* • **Alcohol Content:** *7%*

Kraken American IPA is brewed by the Kraken Cerveza Artesanal. This India Pale Ale pours an unclear, hazy medium amber color and has a large, frothy, and off-white to light beige head. The beer's aroma is moderately malty, with notes of caramel and moderate hops. There are also tasting notes of citrus, pine, spruce, grass, and orange. The flavor is moderately sweet and bitter with hints of hop, pine, grass, and spruce. The body of the beer is medium, the texture is oily, and the carbonation is soft.

KRAKEN GOLDEN ALE

Country of Origin: *Argentina* • **Brewery Founded:** *Unknown* • **Alcohol Content:** *5.6%*

Kraken beers are brewed by the Kraken brewery in Buenos Aires, Argentina. It is a craft brew made without additives or preservatives. The company brews their beers with just water, malt , hops, and yeast. The brand does not filter its beers to avoid stripping the beer of its essential carácter. This beer is popular with craft beer enthusiasts.

LA LOGGIA IMPERIAL STOUT

Country of Origin: *Argentina* • **Brewery Founded:** *Unknown* • **Alcohol Content:** *11%*

La Loggia Imperial Stout is brewed by Cerveza Artesanal La Loggia in Olivos, Argentina. The beer is dark black and oily in appearance with a large, frothy and creamy, light brown head. The aroma is moderate to heavy with malty, roasted, molasses, chocolate, coffee, strong coffee, dark chocolate, raisin, and wood notes. The flavor is moderate to heavy, sweet and moderately bitter with flavors of malt, dark chocolate, dark roasted, tart notes, and licorice. The beer's carbonation is soft.

SIXTOFER OATMEAL STOUT

Country of Origin: *Argentina* • **Brewery Founded:** *Unknown* • **Alcohol Content:** *5.6%*

Sixtofer's Oatmeal Stout is based on English stout beers. The beer pours black with a creamy light brown head. It has an aroma of roasted malt, coffee, milk chocolate, and light spice. The flavor is of malts, roast and dry, coffee, and milk chocolate and has a moderate bitterness. The beer has a medium body, lively carbonation, and a dry roasted finish. Sixtofer's Oatmeal Stout is brewed with the best traditions of this style of beer. Oatmeal stouts usually have oats added during the brewing process, and these may constitute up to 30% of the mash. Although a large proportion of oats beer can lead to a bitter beer, this practice has been popular since the Middle Ages, when oats often made up more than a third of a beer's raw ingredients. Oats are still commonly added to the beers of many European countries, including Norway. There was a revival oat beers in the nineteenth century, when they were thought to be good for the health. By the twentieth century, many oatmeal stouts contained very few oats, but a more authentic style of these beers has now become popular. These brews are notoriously smooth. This comes from the high content of proteins, lipids, and gums that make up the oats.

AUSTRALIA

BOOTLEG BREWERY RAGING BULL

Country of Origin: *Australia* • **Brewery Founded:** *1994* • **Alcohol Content:** *7.1%*

Raging Bull begins with the intense malty flavors ranging from the crystal flavor and all its diversity to the coffee flavors of the roasted barley. A slight bitterness is apparent from the Pride of Ringwood hops but the main essence remains with the intense warming body structure. The Bull finishes with a resounding sweetness. The Bootleg Brewery is a microbrewery in Willyabrup, near the Margaret River in Western Australia, and is set on thirty hectares of land beside a lake.

BOOTLEG BREWERY SOU'WEST WHEAT

Country of Origin: *Australia* • **Brewery Founded:** *1994* • **Alcohol Content:** *4.7%*

Sou'West Wheat beer is a refreshing summer ale. It has a low bitterness threshold and is relatively sweet. The hops used in this wheat ale are aromatic (Hersbrucker & Willamette). This allows for gentle hop flavors to emanate rather than having a distinct bittering flavor. Coupled with this is a residual sweetness which combines with the grassy/floral hop flavors to form a beer that is well rounded, soft and pleasant on the palate. Bottled Sou'West Wheat is bottle conditioned and contains yeast sediment.

BOOTLEG BREWERY TOM'S AMBER ALE

Country of Origin: *Australia* • **Brewery Founded:** *1994* • **Alcohol Content:** *4%*

Tom's Amber Ale is a traditional malty Australian ale. It is based on Australian amber ale. The initial bitterness is quite distinctive and not so overpowering that the other flavors are masked. The bitterness rounds off to reveal malty toasty flavors, offset and balanced by the bite of Australian Ringwood hops. Being profoundly malty in aroma, copper in color, and lightly carbonated makes this a pleasant ale for social occasions.

BOOTLEG BREWERY WILS PILS

Country of Origin: *Australia* • **Brewery Founded:** *1994* • **Alcohol Content:** *4.7%*

Bootleg's premium beer, Wils Pils, is designed to represent the true Pilsener beers of Czechoslovakia. Heavily hopped with imported Saaz and Hersbrucker varieties, the Pils is not only quite bitter but displays an intense herbaceous bouquet imparted by the use of Saaz. Strikingly bitter, the beer softens to a dry cleansing distinct finish. The softness of the rainwater used in the beer creates a silky texture for which this style of beer is renowned.

BURLEIGH BREWING COMPANY 28 PALE ALE

Country of Origin: *Australia* • **Brewery Founded:** *2006* • **Alcohol Content:** *4.8%*

Inspired by the style of the cool 1970s, Burleigh's 28 Pale Ale has a character that's as funky as the times that inspired it. 28 Pale Ale was brewed in honor of the famous 28-day swell at Burleigh, beach back in 1975. This American-style pale ale boasts a deep amber color and a fragrant bouquet. 28 Pale Ale is a medium bodied beer with a well balanced hoppiness. It is a flavorful beer with a complex, fruity character of citrus, grapefruit, passion fruit, and lychee notes. The beer is brewed with malted barley, American hops, yeast, and water.

BURLEIGH BREWING COMPANY BIGHEAD

Country of Origin: *Australia* • **Brewery Founded:** *2006* • **Alcohol Content:** *4.2%*

By respecting age-old craft brewing techniques, Burleigh have managed something no Australian brewer has done before, to create a full flavor beer with zero carbs. The name Bighead honors the history of the town of Burleigh Heads, which was named after the large volcanic headland above the famous surf beach. Bighead is a full-flavored, full-strength beer that is 100% natural. It is smooth, balanced and easy to drink. The beer is brewed from malted barley, hops, yeast, and water.

BURLEIGH BREWING COMPANY BLACK GIRAFFE

Country of Origin: *Australia* • **Brewery Founded:** *2006* • **Alcohol Content:** *5%*

Black Giraffe is a coffee beer brewed with Mexican Arabica coffee beans. The beans are ground on-site at the brewery so none of the fresh intensity escapes, before being added to the brew. Burleigh then adds a unique combination of American hops, caramel, chocolate, and toffee malts before fermenting the blend with their own lager yeast. The result is a sumptuous, black lager that boasts an intense, smooth coffee aroma. Black Giraffe lacks the bitterness and astringency often present in dark beers. It is a beautifully balanced brew that has chocolate and toffee characteristics, rounded out with the richness of mocha.

BURLEIGH BREWING COMPANY DUKE HELLES

Country of Origin: *Australia* • **Brewery Founded:** *2006* • **Alcohol Content:** *3.5%*

Duke Helles is one of Australia's very few mid-strength beers that are brewed the natural way. No artificial ingredients or crafty tricks are used to achieve the alcohol content. Duke Helles was created in honor of Europe's proud brewing history. The beer is a European style lager with a slightly maltier character than the better known pilsner style. The moderate hopping contributes a comfortable bitterness and a clean, refreshing taste. Fine and balanced with fresh floral highlights that hint at a European pedigree. The beer is brewed with malted barley, European hops, yeast, and water.

BURLEIGH BREWING COMPANY DUKE PREMIUM LAGER

Country of Origin: *Australia* • **Brewery Founded:** *2006* • **Alcohol Content:** *4.8%*

Duke Premium Lager was Burleigh's first beer. It is a hand-crafted, traditional, European-style lager, created in honor of Europe's proud brewing history. The beer is a filtered lager that boasts the classic flavors of continental European beers and brewed in the pilsner style. The hop and malt characteristics are finely balanced, providing a clean, refreshing palate with a superb dry, crisp finish. The beer is made with malted barley, European hops, yeast, and water.

BURLEIGH BREWING COMPANY FIGJAM IPA

Country of Origin: *Australia* • **Brewery Founded:** *2006* • **Alcohol Content:** *7%*

An intensive five-stage hopping process delivers a rich, robust character, smooth flavor and an inviting aroma to Figjam India Pale Ale. Although the beer has impact, it is also surprisingly well balanced. The beer is brewed with five malted barley varieties, five natural hop varieties, fruity ale yeast, and water.

BURLEIGH BREWING COMPANY HEF

Country of Origin: *Australia* • **Brewery Founded:** *2006* • **Alcohol Content:** *5%*

The Burleigh Brewing Company is a craft brewery located in Burleigh Heads, Queensland, Australia. It is the only craft brewery on Queensland's Gold Coast. Hef is an unfiltered wheat beer brewed from only malted barley, malted wheat, water, hops, and yeast. The beer boasts the classic German wheat beer characteristics of banana and clove, rich flavors, a bright white head, and a smooth and creamy texture. Hef is a refreshing, flavor-filled beer.

BURLEIGH BREWING COMPANY
MY WIFE'S BITTER

Country of Origin: *Australia* • **Brewery Founded:** *2006* • **Alcohol Content:** *5%*

My Wife's Bitter was inspired by the traditional English bitter that has been drunk in pubs across England for generations; it blends genuine English malt, hops, and yeast. Burleigh's coastal version of a classic English Bitter is brewed with a unique blend of English specialty malts that lend a smooth, malty flavor. The beer has a hint of nuttiness and a soft caramel character.

CARLTON DRAUGHT

Country of Origin: *Australia* • **Brewery Founded:** *1907* • **Alcohol Content:** *4.6%*

Carlton Draught is a pale lager which is sold on tap in its home state of Victoria, and across Australia. It is now one of Australia's most popular selling tap beers. The formulation of Carlton Draught was changed slightly in 2003 to reduce the alcohol content from 5.0% to 4.6% in response to an increase in alcohol taxes by the Federal government. Carlton Draught, like most Australian Lagers, is made using the wortstream brewing process, which uses a portion of cane sugar to thin out the body of the beer.

CARLTON MID

Country of Origin: *Australia* • **Brewery Founded:** *1907* • **Alcohol Content:** *3.5%*

Carlton Mid is a mid-strength pale lager. Carton Mid's use of traditional bittering hops and the finest hop extracts combine to give this brew its delightful hop character. The muted malt flavors in this mid-strength lager give it perfect balance and drinkability. This beer is golden, slightly amber, and clear with a minimal frothy head. The aroma is slightly floral and malty hops, with some dough as it warms up. The beer tastes bitter and sour, with no sweetness.

CARLTON PURE BLONDE

Country of Origin: *Australia* • **Brewery Founded:** *1907* • **Alcohol Content:** *4.6%*

An all-malt lager, Pure Blonde is brewed using the finest pure ingredients; water, hops, barley and yeast. It contains nothing artificial so that it delivers a pure, crisp taste. Pure Blonde was Australia's first, and remains Australia's number one, premium low-carb beer. The beer was first brewed in 2004, and Pure Blonde quickly established itself as the most popular low-carb beer in Australia. Pure Blonde is brewed longer to break down more natural sugars than usual, delivering a refreshing, full-flavored taste with 70% fewer carbs than a standard full strength beer.

CASTLEMAINE XXXX

Country of Origin: *Australia* • **Brewery Founded:** *1878* • **Alcohol Content:** *3.5%*

Castlemaine is brewed by Castlemaine Perkins in Brisbane, Australia. The brewery is a wholly owned entity of the Japanese-controlled Lion Nathan company. Operations began in 1878 and continue today. Castlemaine Perkins is the home of the XXXX (Fourex) beer brand. Taste wise, XXXX is a crisp lager that has a delicate aroma and sweet fruity taste. The blend of hops produces a distinct bitter flavor with a light texture. Not surprisingly, it is perfect for BBQ meats, such as beef and pork. The stronger bitter taste also compliments seafood dishes such as cuttlefish, baby octopus, and battered fish.

COOPERS BREWERY EXTRA STRONG VINTAGE ALE

Country of Origin: *Australia* • **Brewery Founded:** *1862* • **Alcohol Content:** *7.5%*

Coopers introduced their drinkers to the Strong Ale style with the first release of Coopers Extra Strong Vintage Ale (ESVA) back in 1998. ESVA is a high alcohol, high bitterness. It is a flavorsome beer that which may be consumed young whilst holding excellent prospects for developing with bottle age. When young, the beer displays a blend of esters and hop aromatics with some alcohol heat and a firm bitter finish. Aging should see the ester, hop and alcohol meld together, the bitterness soften and toffee/sherry like characters develop. Today, Coopers is Australia's sole remaining family-owned brewery of stature, so it's still an everyday occurrence to meet a Cooper at the Brewery. The fifth and sixth generations of the Cooper family are now acting as custodians of Thomas Cooper's legacy.

COOPERS BREWERY ORIGINAL PALE ALE

Country of Origin: *Australia* • **Brewery Founded:** *1862* • **Alcohol Content:** *4.5%*

The Coopers Beer story began in a newly established colony with a brilliant accident. After turning his hand to a number of trades, Thomas Cooper discovered his talent as a brewer by accident; when he created his first batch of beer as a tonic for his ailing wife Ann. South Australia was only twenty-six years old and most settlers preferred to drink imported beer rather than colonial beer. Thomas Cooper saw the opportunity to create an all-natural beer from the very best ingredients. Coopers Pale Ale has fruity and floral characters balanced with a crisp bitterness. It is naturally brewed in the Burton-upon-Trent style, where a secondary fermentation creates its trademark sediment and gives the beer its cloudy appearance.

EKIM AFTER BATTLE PALE ALE

Country of Origin: *Australia* • **Brewery Founded:** *Recent* • **Alcohol Content:** *5.5 to 5.8%*

Ekim is a small craft brewing company based in Sydney's northern beaches. Their Battle Pale Ale is an American-style pale ale. The beer is a pale ale, honey like in color. Ekim use hops which present a citrus character particularly late in the boil as well as dry hopping during fermentation. This beer packs a fresh hop punch, and is best enjoyed "after battle" or a hard day's work. This beer is both unfiltered and unpasteurized. Ekim use only natural ingredients including malt, hops, yeast, and water.

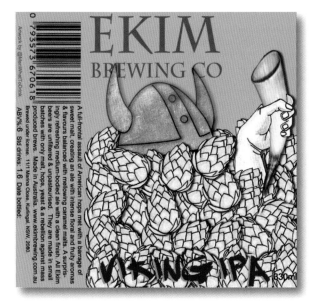

EKIM VIKING IPA

Country of Origin: *Australia* • **Brewery Founded:** *Recent* • **Alcohol Content:** *5.9 to 6.0%*

This beer is a hybrid American-English India Pale Ale, and is amber in color. We use generous amounts of predominantly American hops coupled with a solid malt profile.

The IBU (International Bittering Unit) is around the 50 IBU mark, giving the brew a reasonable bite. This beer is both unfiltered and unpasteurized. Ekim use only natural ingredients including malt, hops, yeast and water.

FERAL BREWING COMPANY FANTAPANTS

Country of Origin: *Australia* • **Brewery Founded:** *2002* • **Alcohol Content:** *7.4%*

Fantapants is an Imperial Red India Pale Ale. It is Feral's most heavily hopped year-round beer. Fantapants is extremely bitter but begins slightly sweet, with an aroma of pineapple and tropical fruits. The finish is full-bodied with a hint of biscuit malt. The beer has a copper body topped with persistent foam. It has wonderful aromas of passion fruit, citrus, and pine. These features are present in the flavors but there is considerable toffee malt to perfectly balance this beer along with its great bitterness.

FERAL BREWING COMPANY GOLDEN ACE

Country of Origin: *Australia* • **Brewery Founded:** *2002* • **Alcohol Content:** *5.6%*

Feral Golden Ace is a refreshing Golden Ale brewed with Japanese-bred Sorachi Ace hops. The beer is lightly filtered and slightly cloudy. The result is a vibrant aroma of hoppy lemon and citrus with a refreshingly clean bitter finish.

FERAL BREWING COMPANY HOP HOG

Country of Origin: *Australia* • **Brewery Founded:** *2002* • **Alcohol Content:** *5.8%*

Feral Hop Hog is an American-style IPA or India Pale Ale. Feral adds a heavy dose of American Hops during both during the boil and late in the fermenting stage to give Hop Hog a strong pine needle and citrus aroma, followed by an aggressive bitterness and a dry finish.

FERAL BREWING COMPANY KARMA CITRA

Country of Origin: *Australia* • **Brewery Founded:** *2002* • **Alcohol Content:** *5.8%*

Karma Citra is an India Black Ale. This relatively new beer style sees a high proportion of dark malt combined with resinous New World hops and results in a beer with chocolate overtones in the flavor. The beer also showcases the tropical fruit character of the Citra hop variety.

FERAL BREWING COMPANY RAZORBACK

Country of Origin: *Australia* • **Brewery Founded:** *2002* • **Alcohol Content:** *10%*

Razorback is an English-style barley wine. The beer has a dense, fruity bouquet, an intense palate and a deep reddish-brown color. Its big stewed fruit flavored maltiness is superbly balanced by wonderfully bittersweet hops.

FERAL BREWING COMPANY RUNT

Country of Origin: *Australia* • **Brewery Founded:** *2002* • **Alcohol Content:** *4.7%*

For those who find Feral Hop Hog too robust, The Runt is more delicate, dry and lightly hopped alternative. However, this description detracts from what is a fantastic beer in its own right. The hop profile is all a beer connoisseur could ask for but at a sensible gravity that can be enjoyed.

FERAL BREWING COMPANY RUST

Country of Origin: *Australia* • **Brewery Founded:** *2002* • **Alcohol Content:** *6%*

Rust is a strong Belgian Dubbel Abbey ale style. The aromatic, and is reminiscent of candied banana. Rust is produced from a distinctive imported yeast stain. Rich, opulent malt character is the dominant flavor of the brew and the finish is dry and slightly astringent.

FERAL BREWING COMPANY SMOKED PORTER

Country of Origin: *Australia* • **Brewery Founded:** *2002* • **Alcohol Content:** *4.7%*

Feral Smoked Porter has a very gentle bitterness and combines the classic chocolate malt and coffee characteristics that are true to the Porter style. A subtle smoked hickory flavor comes from the use of German malts smoked over Birchwood chips.

FERAL BREWING COMPANY THE WHITE HOG IPA

Country of Origin: *Australia* • **Brewery Founded:** *2002* • **Alcohol Content:** *5.8%*

The White Hog IPA is Feral's Ten-year anniversary celebration beer. It is an amalgamation of Feral's flagship Belgian White and their multi award winning American IPA, Hop Hog. The resulting beer has all the bitter hoppiness of Hop Hog and the smooth mouth-feel of their Belgian White beer.

FERAL BREWING COMPANY WATERMELON WARHEAD

Country of Origin: *Australia* • **Brewery Founded:** *2002* • **Alcohol Content:** *2.9%*

Feral Watermelon Warhead is a Berlin Weisse, a light sour German wheat beer infused with half a metric tonne of local Swan Valley watermelons. These are added to the end of primary fermentation leaving a fresh, spritzy, and refreshing beer.

FERAL BREWING COMPANY WHITE

Country of Origin: *Australia* • **Brewery Founded:** *2002* • **Alcohol Content:** *4.6%*

The Feral Brewing Company is a proudly family owned and operated hand-crafted microbrewery situated in the heart of Perth's premier food and wine tourism precinct, the Swan Valley. The brewery holds the current title as the best medium-sized Australian Brewery. Feral handcrafts a world class range of awarded beers. Feral's brewers are well known for pushing the boundaries of their craft, experimenting with all types of exotic hops, spices, and fruits to create unique, full flavored beers. They maintain around sixteen beers on tap, which are constantly changing to satisfy the thirst of visiting beer enthusiasts. Feral's White beer is a witbier produced in the true Belgian style with 50% wheat, 50% barley, and a Belgium yeast strain. The beer is cloudy and unfiltered with coriander and orange peel added during the boil to contribute to a unique spicy citrus finish.

FOSTER'S BREWERY COMPANY GOLD

Country of Origin: *Australia* • **Brewery Founded:** *1888* • **Alcohol Content:** *4.8%*

Foster's was founded in 1888 by William and Ralph Foster. The hot dry summer inspired them to create a beer whose main function was to refresh. They established their brewery on Rokeby Street in Melbourne, Australia. Gold pours a medium white head over a light golden body. The aroma is lager malts with a slight citrus hint. The lager has a sweet fizzy finish.

FOSTER'S BREWERY COMPANY LAGER

Country of Origin: *Australia* • **Brewery Founded:** *1888* • **Alcohol Content:** *5.2%*

Foster's Lager is an internationally distributed Australian brand of pale lager. The beer is brewed under license in several countries, including the United States and Russia. The European rights to the beer are owned by Heineken. Foster's is a well-balanced lager with vanilla tasting notes. It has no hard edges or bitter aftertaste.

FOSTER'S BREWERY COMPANY RADLER

Country of Origin: *Australia* • **Brewery Founded:** *1888* • **Alcohol Content:** *2%*

Foster's Radler combines Foster's lager with lemon. It combines refreshment with a cloudy appearance. It is a refreshing mixed drink that combines 60% citrus-flavored soft drink with 40% Foster's lager. The most refreshing option of this summer's new drinks, the refreshing Foster's Radler is a low-alcohol content alternative for cooling off after the heat.

HARGREAVES HILL
EXTRA SPECIAL BITTER

Country of Origin: *Australia* • **Brewery Founded:** *2004* • **Alcohol Content:** *5.4%*

Hargreaves Hill's cult beer, Extra Special Bitter is a New World interpretation of the classic English-style ale. This beer features considerable crystal malt character, as a backbone to carry the hefty bitterness. It is substantially dry hopped with carefully selected hops from the United States, New Zealand, or Australia. Currently, the Nelson Sauv variety from New Zealand is being used. This adds aromatic and flavor notes of ripe passion fruit to the brew.

JAMES SQUIRE
FOUR WIVES PILSENER

Country of Origin: *Australia* • **Brewery Founded:** *1798* • **Alcohol Content:** *5%*

Four Wives Pilsener is brewed by Australia's Malt Shovel Brewery. Owned by Lion Nathan, the brewery is located in Sydney, Australia. The key to the beer's distinctive flavor is the use of quality ingredients. Using a much higher hopping level than most Australian Lagers, James Squire Pilsener is brewed with Czech Saaz and New Zealand Belgian Saaz aroma hops to produce the pronounced floral spicy finish and the wonderful herbaceous aroma.

JAMES SQUIRE SUN DOWN
AUSTRALIAN LAGER

Country of Origin: *Australia* • **Brewery Founded:** *1798* • **Alcohol Content:** *4.4%*

James Squire Sundown is an Australian craft lager and the latest edition to the permanent James Squire range of beers. It is a crisp drinking beer with fresh grassy aromas, and a hint of citrus. The beer pours a clear pale golden amber color with a white foamy head. The beer is moderately carbonated and has an aroma of mild sweet malt, a trace of hops, and a trace of yeast. The taste is of sweet malt followed by a hint of mildly sour yeast then mild bitterness. The beer has a light body.

JAMES SQUIRE THE CHANCER GOLDEN ALE

Country of Origin: *Australia* • **Brewery Founded:** *1798* • **Alcohol Content:** *4.5%*

James Squire was a convict transported to Australia. He is credited with the first successful cultivation of hops in Australia around the start of the nineteenth century, and is also considered to have founded Australia's first commercial brewery in 1798. The Chancer Golden Ale is a fruit-driven beer that is light in texture but full on flavor with a well rounded style. It is a fresh and fruity brew with a dry finish that makes it the ideal thirst quencher.

KNAPPSTEIN RESERVE LAGER

Country of Origin: *Australia* • **Brewery Founded:** *1850* • **Alcohol Content:** *5.6%*

Knappstein Reserve Lager is brewed in Australia by the Clare Brewery. The beer has a full round palate with intense citrus and melon fruit with subtle pine flavors. It has a honeyed malt and hop finish. The beer is golden straw in color and pours with a bright creamy head. The beer was first launched in 2006.

KOOINDA AMERICAN PALE ALE

Country of Origin: *Australia* • **Brewery Founded:** *2008* • **Alcohol Content:** *4.7%*

Kooinda Boutique Brewery currently produces 400 liter batches of their handcrafted pale ale using only the freshest available hops, barley, and yeast. The ale is brewed in accordance with the German Purity Law of 1516, which states that only malt, water, yeast, and hops can be used in brewing. Kooinda'a beer is non-filtered and contains no artificial preservatives. Kooinda American Pale Ale is a full bodied brew with a copper hue and hints of citrus in its aroma. The ale combines three specialty malts and finishes with a touch of bitterness on the palate.

KOOINDA BELGIAN WITBIER

Country of Origin: *Australia* • **Brewery Founded:** *2008* • **Alcohol Content:** *5.5%*

Kooinda's traditional Belgian Witbier is a delicate ale brewed with wheat and pilsner malt, then lightly hopped to provide a low bitterness which allows the yeast flavors and spices to shine through. Brewed with coriander and sweet orange peel, this cloudy witbier is flavorsome and refreshing.

KOOINDA BLACK IPA

Country of Origin: *Australia* • **Brewery Founded:** *2008* • **Alcohol Content:** *7%*

This new world beer is beautifully balanced and boasts a fairly heavy body. It uses de-husked malt to provide its black color and combines six specialty malts for the body and flavor of a traditional India Pale Ale. The predominant hop aroma is provided by late additions of hops in the kettle and dry hopping for seven days. It has a rich malty taste and a resinous hop flavor.

KOOINDA ENGLISH RED ALE

Country of Origin: *Australia* • **Brewery Founded:** *2008* • **Alcohol Content:** *4.7%*

This traditional English Red Ale has a deep ruby red color and pure white head which laces the glass. The beer combines a variety of caramel and biscuit malts to produce a complex, malt driven ale which is full bodied and rich in malt flavor. The ale is brewed with traditional Fuggles and Goldings hops from the United Kingdom. These hops provide an earthy flavor and aroma with a moderate to low bitterness. This beer is all about the rich malt flavor.

KOOINDA MILK PORTER

Country of Origin: *Australia* • **Brewery Founded:** *2008* • **Alcohol Content:** *4.7%*

Kooinda'a traditional Porter is black in color and boasts a thick, rocky, brown head which laces the glass. The ale is brewed with a combination of dark, roasted and chocolate malts and is hopped with Northern Brewer hops from the United Kingdom. This beer has flavors of chocolate, roasted coffee, and a delicate milk sweetness. The subtle bitterness cuts through the rich, sweet malt flavors.

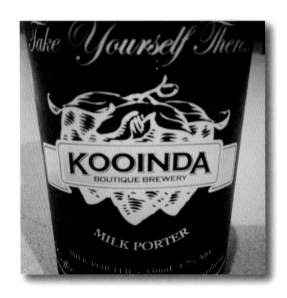

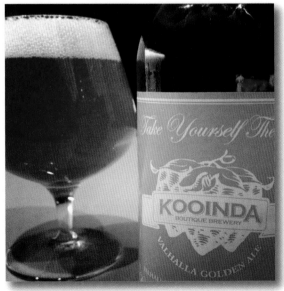

KOOINDA VALHALLA GOLDEN ALE

Country of Origin: *Australia* • **Brewery Founded:** *2008* • **Alcohol Content:** *4.6%*

Kooinda'a Valhalla Golden Ale really is golden in color. This ale is delicately hopped with American hops and has a sweet malt finish and low bitterness. The brew commemorates Valhalla, the heaven of the Vikings. In legend, when the Viking warriors entered Valhalla, they received a horn full of golden ale.

LITTLE CREATURES BRIGHT ALE

Country of Origin: *Australia* • **Brewery Founded:** *2000* • **Alcohol Content:** *4.5%*

This bright filtered ale takes inspiration from both the new and old worlds of brewing. It may be a hybrid ale in origin, but it is a truly Australian style ale. Using four gentle malts including Pale, Carapils, Munich, and Vienna and whole hop flowers, ensures that Bright Ale is clean, crisp, and refreshingly balanced.

LITTLE CREATURES IPA

Country of Origin: *Australia* • **Brewery Founded:** *2000* • **Alcohol Content:** *6.4%*

For the past decade Little Creatures have poured much of their passion into brewing the best Pale Ale possible. Sitting alongside their Pale Ale, Little Creatures' IPA will deliver the big, rugged hop flavors and the citrusy nose that characterise India Pale Ales. The beer has aniseed and savory notes, balanced out with a long firm bitterness to finish.

LITTLE CREATURES ORIGINAL PILSNER

Country of Origin: *Australia* • **Brewery Founded:** *2000* • **Alcohol Content:** *4.6%*

As much as Little Creatures loves to brew ales there is something special about the classic pilsners of Europe. With that in mind, they have taken this classic style and made it their own. With Tasmanian Helga, New Zealand Pacifica, and Saaz hops are added throughout the brewing process to give this beer a light, fresh flavor, and a crisp bitterness.

LITTLE CREATURES PALE ALE

Country of Origin: *Australia* • **Brewery Founded:** *2000* • **Alcohol Content:** *5.2%*

Little Creatures is an Australian brewing company based in Fremantle, Western Australia. It was established in 2000 by the original brewers of the Matilda Bay Brewing Company. Little Creatures adds bag loads of whole hop flowers to their Pale Ale throughout the brewing process. These hops provide intense citrus and stone fruit characters, which are carefully balanced with speciality malts and local pale malt. It's a beer that's ultimately refreshing with a distinct bitterness. The beer is preservative and additive free, and is live-yeast conditioned for unmatched freshness and character.

LITTLE CREATURES PUFFING BILLY

Country of Origin: *Australia* • **Brewery Founded:** *2000* • **Alcohol Content:** *6.5%*

Little Creatures launched their latest Single Batch beer, Puffing Billy in 2012. It is a lavishly hopped rich, dark lager with a gentle hint of smoked malt. Modeled from the traditional Bocks of Germany but with a natural twist, the brewery has challenged this traditional style with the addition of smoked malt. This gives the beer a subtle hint of beech wood smoked malt, with lasting peat-like characters on the finish, and a full load of hops throughout. Puffing Billy had all been sold by December 2012.

LITTLE CREATURES ROGERS' BREW

Country of Origin: *Australia* • **Brewery Founded:** *2000* • **Alcohol Content:** *3.8%*

With this beer, Little Creatures salutes two great men and legends of Australian brewing; Roger Bailey and Roger Bussell. With a nod to fine English Ales and a distinctive Little Creatures hop driven slant, Rogers' beer has notes of roasted toffee and caramel malt flavors. Light citrus hop notes and a gentle bitterness define this unique, easy-drinking amber ale.

LITTLE CREATURES SINGLE BATCH

Country of Origin: *Australia* • **Brewery Founded:** *2000* • **Alcohol Content:** *Various*

From time to time Little Creatures offers one of their Single Batch beers. These brews may be the brewery's interpretation of an old classic style or something a little bit different. One thing is for sure, they are always a very limited release, and be available at just a few great beer loving venues and retailers around Australia. Shepherd's Delight is one of these rare brews.

MATILDA BAY BREWING COMPANY ALPHA PALE ALE

Country of Origin: *Australia* • **Brewery Founded:** *1984* • **Alcohol Content:** *5.2%*

Matilda bay's Brewers Reserve Alpha Pale Ale is very much in line with the beers from America's North West. It has an assertive bitterness together with a distinctive fruit and citrus aroma. The beer has a big hop nose with citrus notes derived from the use of Cascade hops imported from North America.

MATILDA BAY BREWING COMPANY BEEZ NEEZ

Country of Origin: *Australia* • **Brewery Founded:** *1984* • **Alcohol Content:** *4.7%*

Matilda first created Beez Neez in 1996 as a Christmas surprise for staff at honey-makers Capilano. It is a handcrafted wheat beer, with the addition of pure light amber honey. This unique brew has a light malt palate with a distinct honey aroma and flavor plus a hint of bitterness. The beer is clean, crisp, and dry on the palate and surprisingly refreshing. Matilda Bay brews Beez Neez with a blend of premium pale malted barley and malted wheat, and adds Pride of Ringwood hops and pure light amber honey to the kettle to produce a light golden colored beer.

MATILDA BAY BREWING COMPANY BOHEMIAN PILSNER

Country of Origin: *Australia* • **Brewery Founded:** *1984* • **Alcohol Content:** *4.7%*

Ever since Matilda Bay first started brewing beer, they have had a great respect for brewing tradition. That's why they brew a classic pilsner-style lager, highly hopped, crisp and golden, and true to the style. Bohemian Pilsner has a light, golden color and a distinctive hop character with spicy and peppery notes. Importantly, its bitter finish is balanced across the palate with a clean mid-palate and a full malty flavor. Powerful

aromatics in the beer are driven by 100% premium pale malts and a late kettle hopping of authentic Saaz hops from the Czech Republic. Matilda Bay ferments and stores their Bohemian Pilsner longer than most other pilsners to allow for the complexities of its unique flavor to fully develop. Bohemian Pilsner works perfectly with roast meats, such as pork or crispy duck, and with spicy dishes like salt & pepper chili squid or Thai curries.

MATILDA BAY BREWING COMPANY FAT YAK PALE ALE

Country of Origin: *Australia* • **Brewery Founded:** *1984* • **Alcohol Content:** *4.7%*

Matilda Bay wanted to create an easy drinking craft beer in the traditional North American pale ale style and fat Yak was the result. The beer first impresses with its golden color, and its distinctive, hop driven, fruity and herbaceous aromas, giving characteristic passion fruit and melon notes. These are followed by a hit of hop flavor at the finish. The taste is refreshingly clean on the palate. Fat Yak is created from natural ingredients, including premium malts, American Cascade hops and a hint of New Zealand Nelson Sauvin hops. The beer pairs well with almost any food, but particularly with spicy wedges, chorizo, tomato pizza, or antipasto.

MATILDA BAY BREWING COMPANY HELGA

Country of Origin: *Australia* • **Brewery Founded:** *1984* • **Alcohol Content:** *4.7%*

Helga is a Munich-style dry lager launched in 2010. It is malty, full bodied and well rounded. Helga is a beer that is easy to drink, but still has a level of complexity. Helga was inspired by the Munich Oktoberfest lagers are also known as Helles lagers. Helga pours to a golden amber hue, slightly deeper than mainstream lagers and is capped with a densely packed white head. The malt driven flavors are well balanced by the dry hopping process used in the late fermentation. The Pacifica hop used produces a refreshing fruit aroma and leaves the palate dry and crisp. The beer is a perfect accompaniment to a mixed plate of Spanish tapas, and continental sausages.

MATILDA BAY BREWING COMPANY I.G.P.

Country of Origin: *Australia* • **Brewery Founded:** *1984* • **Alcohol Content:** *4.7%*

Matilda bay brew this Australian Cloudy Ale. I.G.P. is Matilda Bay's handcrafted take on the classic Australian Ale. Launched in 2012, the brew is characterized by its cloudy, yeast sediment. The beer is well balanced with late hopped Galaxy & Summer Saaz resulting in a zesty clean finish. The Galaxy hops provide a fruity note while Summer hops (a local Saaz variety) provide subtle spice and pepper flavors. The resulting beer is refreshing, naturally cloudy, cleansing Australian ale. This full-flavored beer with its fruity aromas goes nicely with marinated BBQ meats. The beer is also a great match with light Asian dishes containing chili and lime.

MATILDA BAY BREWING COMPANY REDBACK BEER

Country of Origin: *Australia* • **Brewery Founded:** *1984* • **Alcohol Content:** *4.7%*

The Matilda Bay Brewing Company is an Australian brewery. It was the first new brewery opened in Australia since World War II and the country's first craft brewery. It is based in Port Melbourne, Victoria. Launched in 1988, Redback's innovation and unique style took an Australia starved of beer diversity by storm. Styled on the traditional German wheat beer or weizen, Redback has a fruity/clove aroma, a generous creamy mouth feel, and refreshing hop finish. The beer is made with both malted wheat and barley, and then hopped with Pride of Ringwood hops. Fermentation is produced with a specially developed yeast strain.

McLAREN VALE BEER COMPANY VALE ALE

Country of Origin: *Australia* • **Brewery Founded:** *2008* • **Alcohol Content:** *4.5%*

McLaren was founded in South Australia by two local men in 2008. The brewery is still locally owned. Vale Ale is an Australian pale ale. Bottle-conditioned the beer is full, fruity, and hoppy. The beer has a balance of malt, hops, and yeast character. Amarillo and Cascade hops give a wonderful fresh and crisp finish. The beer has lingering flavors of citrus, passion fruit, and peaches. The hop flavors and aromas are beautifully matched with the sweet honey finish given by the Crystal malt hops.

McLAREN VALE BEER COMPANY VALE DARK

Country of Origin: *Australia* • **Brewery Founded:** *2008* • **Alcohol Content:** *4.5%*

Vale Dark is an American-style dark lager. The beer was designed using pale, Munich, Crystal, and Carafa roasted malts. This results in a filtered beer with brilliant clarity, dark brown in color with ruby and garnet highlights. The flavor has a strong malt backbone with hints of coffee, chocolate, and cocoa that perfectly balance the use of Falconer's Flight hops. The beer has citrus, pine, and vanilla flavors and aromas. The combination of dark malt and hops with lager yeast develops a crisp, clean, dark beer.

McLAREN VALE BEER COMPANY IPA

Country of Origin: *Australia* • **Brewery Founded:** *2008* • **Alcohol Content:** *5.5%*

Vale IPA is an Australian interpretation of an American IPA. The beer is brewed with a combination of hops from three countries: Galaxy from Australia, Nelson Sauvin from New Zealand, and Citra from the United States. Malt flavors are derived from the combination of pale, wheat, and Crystal malts. The aroma has strong pine and citrus notes combined with stone fruit and passion fruit characters. The malt structure is combined with dry hopping, which gives the beer a refined balance.

McLAREN VALE BEER COMPANY VALE LAGER

Country of Origin: *Australia* • **Brewery Founded:** *2008* • **Alcohol Content:** *4.5%*

Vale lager is the McLaren Vale Beer Company's interpretation of a New World craft lager. The beer is filtered for smooth and refreshing crispness and has medium carbonation. The 100% malted grain profile is a combination of Pilsner, Carapils, and Light Munich malts. The beer is hopped with German Tettnang, Australian Helga, and New Zealand Pacifica varieties. The sweet malt characters are balanced by the earthy spice and fresh citrus kick from the hops.

MOO BREW BARREL AGED IMPERIAL STOUT

Country of Origin: *Australia* • **Brewery Founded:** *Unknown* • **Alcohol Content:** *8.5%*

Moo Brew represents a challenging beer experience for all beer lovers. Moo Brew produces five core beers: a Pilsner, a German-style Hefeweizen, a Belgian Pale Ale, an American Pale Ale, and an American Dark Ale. Moo Brew is best stored cold as it contains only the essential ingredients: malt, hops, yeast and water. No preservatives are added. The brewery also releases a range of small batch beers throughout the year. Barrel Aged Imperial Stout pours black with small tan head. The aromas of the beer are chocolate and espresso with some vanilla sweetness. The beer has flavors of roasted dark chocolate, with hints of espresso, and a lingering sweetness.

MOO BREW BELGO

Country of Origin: *Australia* • **Brewery Founded:** *Unknown* • **Alcohol Content:** *4.5%*

Moo Brew's Belgo is a light Belgian ale with a seamless blend of yeast and hop aroma, so that it's impossible to tell where one ends and the other starts. The palate is dry and slightly tart, with a moderate Belgian texture. The beer pours an amber golden color and has a foamy white head. It has a strong flavor despite the low alcohol level. The aromas are of stone fruit, banana, and yeast. The beer has low carbonation.

MOO BREW DARK ALE

Country of Origin: *Australia* • **Brewery Founded:** *Unknown* • **Alcohol Content:** *5%*

This Dark Ale is an American brown ale with hues of brooding sherry red. Moo Brew is located at the Moorilla Estate Brewery in Hobart, Australia. The beer has a nice light brown head and sweet, grainy, and fruity scent. The beer is sweet, with a malty and bitter taste. It has a metallic, grainy aftertaste. The brew has a medium mouth feel and medium bitterness.

MOO BREW HEFEWEIZEN/ WHEAT BEER

Country of Origin: *Australia* • **Brewery Founded:** *Unknown* • **Alcohol Content:** *5.1%*

A classic German Hefeweizen beer, this is naturally cloudy Wheat Beer has a vibrant yellow color and a strong foam head. The aroma features some clove, spice and some earthy yeast. The flavor is fairly typical for a hefeweizen beer, with banana, clove, some spicy notes, and a touch of lemon. The beer has a medium body and lively carbonation.

MOO BREW PALE ALE

Country of Origin: *Australia* • **Brewery Founded:** *Unknown* • **Alcohol Content:** *4.9%*

This is an American style hop driven ale. Strong hopping leads to a pungent floral and citrus aroma, with a pleasant late bitterness. The beer pours a clear orange/amber with a small but lasting white head and generous carbonation. The aroma is peach, lemon, flowers, spice, and passion fruit with a hint of malt sweetness coming through. The taste starts off with peach and apple, before a zesty grapefruit bitterness kicks in. This pale ale is medium bodied. It has a mostly clean finish but leaves a pleasant citrus aftertaste.

MOO BREW PILSNER

Country of Origin: *Australia* • **Brewery Founded:** *Unknown* • **Alcohol Content:** *5%*

Moo Brew have created a Czech Pilsner style beer with a crisp, noble hop aroma and light malt and honey flavors. The beer pours a light, clear, golden yellow with a finger of fluffy white head. It has a slightly floral and fruity nose with a bit of spice. Its taste is fruity, with a bit of citrus and peach, and a very spicy noble hop bitterness on the finish. The carbonation is spot on, and its mouth feel is the fuller side of light.

MOUNTAIN GOAT BEER HIGHTAIL ALE

Country of Origin: *Australia* • **Brewery Founded:** *1997* • **Alcohol Content:** *4.5%*

The Hightail is an English inspired amber ale. It has a rich malt body and floral hop aroma. Mountain Goat handcrafts their ales with the utmost care and avoids all preservatives, additives, and pasterization. Highland ale has a mixture of toffee and fruit aromas with an aromatic lift. It has a complex palate with burnt phenolic characters that are complemented by fresh slightly sweet flavors. It has plenty of grassy and floral tones with a robust, fruity flavor.

MOUNTAIN GOAT BEER INDIA PALE ALE

Country of Origin: *Australia* • **Brewery Founded:** *1997* • **Alcohol Content:** *6.2%*

Mountain Goat's IPA is the brewery's newest beer to find its way into a 330ml bottle. Ale, wheat, and crystal malts upfront blended with Citra and Galaxy hops combine to make a strong, smooth beer.

**Mountain Goat Beer
India Pale Ale**
6.2% alcohol – 330ml
Brown bottle – Twist top
www.beeradvice.com.au

MOUNTAIN GOAT BEER RARE BREED

Country of Origin: *Australia* • **Brewery Founded:** *1997* • **Alcohol Content:** *Various*

Rare Breed Goats come out pretty regularly. These beers are generally higher in alcohol and bigger in flavor and aroma than the Steam and Hightail ales. Regular Rare Breed beers include Double Hightail, Rye IPA, and Surefoot Stout along with some rarer Rare Breeds like Rapuzel and Black IPA.

MOUNTAIN GOAT BEER STEAM ALE

Country of Origin: *Australia* • **Brewery Founded:** *1997* • **Alcohol Content:** *4.5%*

Mountain Goat Beer is a microbrewery in Richmond, Victoria, Australia. The brewery was founded in 1996 by Cam Hines and Dave Bonighton, who continue to manage the company. Steam Ale is a crisp, certified organic ale. Mountain Goat incorporates a slap of wheat malt in the grist make-up and use Cascade and Citra hops to give it a fresh finish.

PURRUMBETE RED DUCK AMBER ALE

Country of Origin: *Australia* • **Brewery Founded:** *2005* • **Alcohol Content:** *4.5%*

Scott and Vanessa Wilson-Browne are another couple of 'ale changers' who swapped busy Melbourne careers to move to the country, bring up their young family, and brew and market craft ales. Along the way, they also helped restore the historic Purrumbete. The brewery's core range of ales includes an amber ale, pale ale and porter. The brewery was relocated from Purrumbete to Ballarat in 2011. Purrumbete's beers are mostly flavorsome, bottle-conditioned ales. Red Duck Amber Ale is full flavored ale, copper colored with rich malt flavors.

PURRUMBETE RED DUCK PALE ALE

Country of Origin: *Australia* • **Brewery Founded:** *2005* • **Alcohol Content:** *4.5%*

Red Duck Pale Ale is a golden/blonde ale made by Purrumbete Brewing of Camperdown, Victoria, Australia. The beer is a refreshing, sparkling ale that is clean and crisp. The beer pours clear golden yellow and has Citrus and melon aromas. The beer is hoppier than usual for basic Australian ale, with very little malt character other than a little cereal grain. The ale has a light body and a clean finish.

STONE & WOOD PACIFIC ALE

Country of Origin: *Australia* • **Brewery Founded:** *2008* • **Alcohol Content:** *4.4%*

Stone & Wood Brewing Company was established in Byron Bay, which is located at the eastern tip of Australia. Pacific Ale was inspired by the brewery's location on the edge of the Pacific Ocean. It is brewed using all Australian barley, wheat, and Galaxy hops. Pacific Ale is cloudy and golden with a big fruity aroma and a refreshing finish. After being dry hopped at the end of fermentation, the brew is then drawn straight from the storage tank at the brewery into kegs and bottles. Bottling the beer without filtering or pasteurizing it means that the beer can be enjoyed fresh.

STONE & WOOD LAGER

Country of Origin: *Australia* • **Brewery Founded:** *2008* • **Alcohol Content:** *4.7%*

When it came to developing their lager, the brewery used the inspiration of memories of sunny afternoons spent in the beer gardens of Munich drinking steins of the local full flavored pale lagers. Stone & Wood saw the parallel with what they were trying to achieve and what the Bavarian brewers had mastered. Good quality grain adds both softness to the palate and a full bodied malt character. Stone & Wood Lager has a sparkling light color, and a flavor that strikes a fine balance between its subtle hop aroma and full malt palate with a soft clean finish.

STONE & WOOD JASPER ALE

Country of Origin: *Australia* • **Brewery Founded:** *2008* • **Alcohol Content:** *4.7%*

In Australia, there are only a few weeks of the year where it gets really cold in the hills. So winter beers are unusual. Jasper Ale is designed for drinking in the winter months. Stone & Wood brewed their Jasper Ale to reflect the red volcanic soil of our hinterland and it is brewed from a blend of pale and Crystal malts. Jasper Ale is deep red, has a rich malt character and is well balanced with a firm spicy hop bitterness. The inspiration behind the ale comes from German Ale, American Amber Ale, and English Brown Ale styles.

TOOHEYS EXTRA DRY

Country of Origin: *Australia* • **Brewery Founded:** *1869* • **Alcohol Content:** *4.6%*

Tooheys Extra Dry is a crisp-tasting dry style lager. It is sold throughout Australia. The beer was originally sold in bottles and cans, but it began to be sold on tap in late 2005. Extra Dry is popular with young people, and Tooheys Extra Dry sponsors music festivals and many surfing events around Australia. In May 2006, Toohey's Extra Dry Platinum, a beer with increased alcohol content of 6.5%, was launched, with the first shipment selling out in days.

TOOHEYS NEW

Country of Origin: *Australia* • **Brewery Founded:** *1869* • **Alcohol Content:** *4.6%*

Tooheys dates from 1869, when John Thomas Toohey obtained his Australian brewing license. John and his brother James Matthew started their business by brewing Tooheys Black Old Ale. Tooheys New is a pale lager and is the most popular of the brewery's beers. It can be found on tap at almost any bar in New South Wales. The beer was first brewed in 1930 it was first sold as Tooheys Draught but the beer's name was changed to Tooheys New in 1998.

VICTORIA BITTER

Country of Origin: *Australia* • **Brewery Founded:** *1907* • **Alcohol Content:** *4.9%*

Victoria Bitter is actually a lager. It is produced by Carlton & United Breweries, a subsidiary of Foster's Group in Melbourne, Victoria. The beer was first brewed by renowned Melbourne brewer's Thomas C. Moore and Henry F. Baxter in the early 1900s. It is now one of the highest selling beers in Australia and was the country's highest selling beer until 2012.

WHITE RABBIT DARK ALE

Country of Origin: *Australia* • **Brewery Founded:** *2009* • **Alcohol Content:** *4.9%*

White Rabbit's Dark Ale is an intriguing beer that is rich, dark, and flavorsome. The beer is malt driven but with the aromatic lift of generous doses of hops. With the help of traditional open fermentation tanks White Rabbit lets their Dark Ale yeast work without any inhibition. The raisin-like esters bind a balancing act of flavor with malt and a rich dark color. The brew is hopped with whole hop flowers prior to a liberal dry hopping regime during open fermentation.

WHITE RABBIT WHITE ALE

Country of Origin: *Australia* • **Brewery Founded:** *2009* • **Alcohol Content:** *4.5%*

The white ale story starts in medieval times when Belgian monks played with flavor enhancing ingredients and spices such as wheat, coriander, orange peel, and suspended yeast in their ales to create a cloudy white appearance. This is White Rabbit's Australian interpretation of these white ales. White Rabbit White Ale delivers refreshing hints of coriander, juniper berry, and bitter orange, blended with un-malted wheat. Light citrus aromas round out a classic, cloudy white ale with just a gentle hint of bitterness.

AUSTRIA

FOHRENBURGER BOCK

Country of Origin: *Austria* • **Brewery Founded:** *1881* • **Alcohol Content:** *7.2%*

Ferdinand Gassner founded the Fohrenburg F. Gassner & Company brewery in 1881, along with eleven associates. The brewery started with twenty-one employees in February 1881. Half a year later the company expanded the brewery and beer production hit 800,000 liters per year. Fohrenburger Bock is a small but strong specialty beer. Its special brewing process uses dark roasted brewing and caramel malt. This gives its characteristic amber color and its distinctive taste. The special feature of this brew is its full-bodied taste, which is perfect for special occasions.

FOHRENBURGER DUNKLES

Country of Origin: *Austria* • **Brewery Founded:** *1881* • **Alcohol Content:** *5.5%*

Fohrenburger Dunkles (Dark) gets its rich deep brown color from a special brewing process that uses dark roasted hops and caramel malt. The beer presents itself to a beer connoisseur as a spicy and aromatic brew that has a dry first sip and a pleasantly light, mildly tart finish. The unique thing about the beer is its dark and velvety hue combined with its deep and aromatic flavor.

FOHRENBURGER ENGELBURG BRAU

Country of Origin: *Austria* • **Brewery Founded:** *1881* • **Alcohol Content:** *4.2%*

Engelburg Brau has been brewed at the Fohrenburger brewing facility at Bludenz, Austria since 1978. It is a simple and uncomplicated beer, with a classically tart and fresh flavor. Engelburg Brau is usually sold on draught at inns and hostelries in the western part of Austria.

FOHRENBURGER FESTBIER

Country of Origin: *Austria* • **Brewery Founded:** *1881* • **Alcohol Content:** *5.7%*

Fohrenburger Festbier (celebration beer) is a special edition beer that was first made for the third Fohrenburger Beer Festival. The special roasted malt that is used to produce this celebration beer its bright and cheerful amber color. The fine hops and the original wort of 13.5 degrees offer an unusual and unforgettable beer experience. Fohrenburger offer several tips to help you pour a perfect glass of beer. The glass should first be rinsed with cold water, and should be held at a slant. The beer should then be poured in three stages so that the head can settle. This process shouldn't be hurried, and will take around three minutes.

FOHRENBURGER JUBILAUM

Country of Origin: *Austria* • **Brewery Founded:** *1881* • **Alcohol Content:** *5.5%*

This is a special brew created for the beer connoisseur. Jubilaum is made from the best raw materials. These and crystal clear Alpine spring water from the high mountain region of the Arlberg-Silvretta massif give the beer its distinctive fresh and aromatic taste. It is the most popular specialist beer in the west of Austria and is a unique combination of being both widely drunk and niche.

FOHRENBURGER KELLER NATURTRUB

Country of Origin: *Austria* • **Brewery Founded:** *1881* • **Alcohol Content:** *5.3%*

Fohrenburger's Keller Naturtrub is one of the company's original beers and has a traditionally full flavor. After an extensive maturing process, bottles are filled directly from the storage tanks without the beer going through a filtration process. This means that natural yeasts and proteins stay in the beer. They give the brew its natural cloudy texture and its unique full-bodied taste. The unique feature of Keller Naturtrub is that it is brewed in a highly traditional way: organically and unfiltered, so that its unique flavor and cloudy appearance is preserved.

FOHRENBURGER MARZEN

Country of Origin: *Austria* • **Brewery Founded:** *1881* • **Alcohol Content:** *4.8%*

Fohrenburger Marzen is a modern addition to the Fohrenburger family of beers. It has a new, light enjoyable beer flavor with an aroma of fine hops and a malty smell. It is brewed for the discerning beer drinker. The special feature of this modern beer is that it is a lighter alternative for drinkers that don't want to give up classical beer enjoyment. The Fohrenburger brewery made 19.3 million liters of beer in 2011, and offers thirteen specialty brews to its customers in the Tyrol and Vorarlberg regions of Austria.

FOHRENBURGER NO. 1

Country of Origin: *Austria* • **Brewery Founded:** *1881* • **Alcohol Content:** *5.5%*

The Fohrenburger brewery created Fohrenburger No. 1 especially for their overseas markets. It is a classic Austrian lager-type beer which is brewed using the finest Austrian materials and crystal clear Alpine spring water from the Arlberg-Silvretta massif. This careful brewing process produces a great drinking beer with a distinctive fresh and spicy taste.

FOHRENBURGER OHNE

Country of Origin: *Austria* • **Brewery Founded:** *1881* • **Alcohol Content:** *0%*

Frohrenburger Ohne("without") is a unique proposition from this traditional brewing house; an enjoyable beer brewed to contain no alcohol. Dry-sweet in flavor with a delicious beery taste, it is a fabulous low-calorie thirst quencher, ideal after sports or any exertion. Fohrenburger Ohne tastes best when chilled and served between six and eight degrees centigrade. The special feature of this particular beer is that it has only twenty-five calories per hundred milliliters of beer, which makes it lower calorie than most ordinary alcohol free beverages.

FOHRENBURGER PARTY BEER

Country of Origin: *Austria* • **Brewery Founded:** *1881* • **Alcohol Content:** *4.9%*

Fohrenburger Party Beer has been specially brewed to be a light, fresh tasting beer with a pleasant fizziness and a delicate hoppy aroma. It is sold in a practical ring pull cap bottle for convenience of opening. The company markets Party Beer as being ideal to take to a concert, party, or outdoor gathering. The Fohrenburger brewery now brews 145,000 liters of beer each year and fills 200,000 beer kegs annually.

FOHRENBURGER PILS

Country of Origin: *Austria* • **Brewery Founded:** *1881* • **Alcohol Content:** *4.8%*

The Fohrenburger brewery founder Ferdinand Gassner must have been impressed by the qualities of the fabled unicorn to make it the symbol of his brewery. The mythical beast was attributed with energy, strength, purity, and uniqueness, just like Gassner's beer! The unicorn was first connected with the beer's hometown of Bludenz in 1260, when it appeared on its coat of arms. According to the legend, real unicorns lived in the mountain forests above the town. Fohrenburger Pils is a sparkling light beer that has a dry-sweet aromatic flavor due to the carefully blended hops it is brewed from.

FOHRENBURGER RADLER

Country of Origin: *Austria* • **Brewery Founded:** *1881* • **Alcohol Content:** *2.7%*

Fohrenburger Radler is a shandy-styled drink that consists of 50% of Fohrenburger Special beer and 50% sparkling lemonade. It is a classic thirst quencher with a beery taste, cut with the freshness of lemons. It is particularly nice to drink on a hot day, after work or sports. Fohrenburger also makes a beer-based drink mixed with Alpine water rather than lemonade for a less sweet taste. These mixed beer drinks are widely drunk in Austria and Germany. The Fohrenburger brewery fills 50,000 bottles of beer an hour, and uses 3,000 metric tonnes of brewing malt each year.

FOHRENBURGER STIFTLE

Country of Origin: *Austria* • **Brewery Founded:** *1881* • **Alcohol Content:** *4.8%*

Fohrenburger Stiftle is a finely hopped beer that is perfect for a refreshing drink at any time. It is sold in the smaller third liter bottle in line with modern preferences. The beer is a fine light golden color and pours with a foamy, snow white head. The Fohrenburger brewery now employs 120 beer makers and has thirty-seven dedicated Fohrenburger wagons to deliver its products around western Austria.

FOHRENBURGER WEIZEN

Country of Origin: *Austria* • **Brewery Founded:** *1881* • **Alcohol Content:** *5.2%*

Fohrenburger Weizen is a naturally cloudy top-fermented wheat beer. It is brewed from wheat and barley malt and the unmistakable taste of the grain combines with that of fine natural yeast. The mild hopping and the subtly sparkling carbonation give this naturally cloudy beer a fizzy, fruity flavor. Typically, wheat beers are very pale in color, and Fohrenburger's Weizen is no exception. The beer is the first true Weizen brewed in Austria's Vorarlberg region.

GÖSSER BEER

Country of Origin: *Austria* • **Brewery Founded:** *1860* • **Alcohol Content:** *5.2%*

Gösser beer is the main brand of the Göss brewery in the Austrian town of Leoben. Goss is one of the largest and most-well known Austrian beer breweries. Leoben is located in the Austrian federal state of Styria, and many see it as the heart of the region. The green color of the Gosser trademark is symbolizes the heart of Styria. Gösser represents the epitome of Styrian brewing skills, and is considered by many to be Austria's best-known beer brand. This bottom fermented, light, lager-style beer pours a pale orangey gold. It has a moderate white head that lasts quite well. Its aroma is mildly malty and a nutty, with a creamy background. Its refreshingly sharp tang derives from balanced hopping. The beer tastes quite strong and alcoholic, with more malt-derived flavors than hoppiness.

GOSS BRÄU MARZEN

Country of Origin: *Austria* • **Brewery Founded:** *1860* • **Alcohol Content:** *5.5%*

The color of Goss Bräu's Marzen beer is bright clear amber with lots of with orange hues. It has a strong off-white foam head. The aroma is of toasty malts and is very aromatic with a hint of hop bitterness. The flavor of the beer is sweet and malty, with a strong hint of roasted caramel malts and an intense sweetness. The front of the beer has a light sourness, but the sides and middle are all syrupy malt flavors. The aftertaste is all sweet malts with a slightly hoppy floral flavor. The beer won Gold (2008) and Silver (2004) in the Beer World Cup. Unusually, this March beer would partner with cake or torte deliciously.

HIRTER 1270

Country of Origin: *Austria* • **Brewery Founded:** *1270* • **Alcohol Content:** *4.9%*

Hirter 1270 is a traditional, natural full-bodied beer. Although it is derived from a traditional recipe, it suits the modern taste. Hirter 1270 gets its distinctive color from gently toasted, caramelized malt. Brewed with Hirter's famous spring water, it is subjected to an extremly long storage and ripening time before it finally becomes a GMO-free, non-pasteurized, and completely natural specialty beer. It has a finely tuned, malty flavor that is enhanced by the finely-bound carbonic acid. Hirter 1270 is a full-bodied and spicy treat for lovers of beer. This bottom-fermented beer goes well with roast chicken, and strong and spicy dishes like peppered steak.

HIRTER BIOBIER

Country of Origin: *Austria* • **Brewery Founded:** *1270* • **Alcohol Content:** *4.8%*

Building on Hirter's tradition of brewing natural and untreated beers, Hirter Biobier goes one step further. Hirter Biobier was Austria's first completely organic beer, with all of its ingredients sourced from Austrian organic farmers, combined with local spring water. Naturally, this full-bodied, bottom-fermented beer is also GMO-free, non-pasteurized and completely natural. It is mildly carbonated and has sweet and fruity notes. Hirter Biobier goes well with tasty main courses, vegetable dishes, and creamy soups (such as pumpkin and parsley). In 2013, the beer was awarded Gold at the DLG Awards. The DLG (Deutsche Landwirtschafts- Gesellschaft, or German Agricultural Society) was founded by the engineer and author Max Eyth in 1885. It has over 22,000 members and is a leading organization in the agricultural and food sector. It awards Gold, Silver and Bronze medals to the best German-style beers each year. Winners must all abide with the German Reinheitsgebot (purity law) of 1516 that ensures that only natural ingredients are used to brew beer.

HIRTER BIOHANFBIER

Country of Origin: *Austria* • **Brewery Founded:** *1270* • **Alcohol Content:** *4.8%*

Hirter Biohanfbier is brewed using only exclusively selected raw materials, which are all sourced in Austria. The distinctive herby and fruity taste of Carinthian hemp perfectly integrates into the overall character of the beer and makes for a lovely, sweet finish in its finely carbonated structure. Brewed with soft mountain spring water and completely natural ingredients, Hirter Biohanfbier is characterized by its sweet, fruity, and very drinkable flavor. The beer goes well with flavorsome main courses, vegetable dishes, and creamy soups.

HIRTER KRAUTER RADLER

Country of Origin: *Austria* • **Brewery Founded:** *1270* • **Alcohol Content:** *2.5%*

Hirter Krauter Radler consists of equal parts of multi-award winning Hirt beer and refreshing herbal lemonade. The herbal lemonade contains Alpine herbs such as gentian, sage, and local elder in its delicious recipe. Coriander and ginger are also added. Hirt makes all its beers with soft spring water from the Hanslbauer mountain streams that are located in the water protection area opposite the brewery. The beer is GMO-free, has no artificial sugar additives, and is unpasteurized. Even the carbonic acid used is derived from the brewing process itself. The crowning glory of this natural beverage is the full, slightly sweet-tart taste of herbs. The drink goes especially well with desserts, salads, and white meats.

HIRTER MARZEN

Country of Origin: *Austria* • **Brewery Founded:** *1270* • **Alcohol Content:** *5.0%*

Marzen (March) beers are pale lagers that originate from Bavaria,Germany. In 1553, it was decreed that beer could only be brewed between September 29 and April 23 each year. Bottles of beer were needed to drink at the annual Oktoberfest, and needed a good wort gravity and alcohol content to last this long. Hirter Märzen is completely GMO-free, non-pasteurized and natural. A high degree of fermentation results in a lighter, but full-bodied taste and a mature, round, supple finish. The beer goes well with local dishes such as Bernese sausages, Vienna cutlets, and rumpsteak. The beer was awarded Silver at the 2010 European Beer Star Award, and Gold at the 2012 DLG Awards.

HIRTER MORCHL

Country of Origin: *Austria* • **Brewery Founded:** *1270* • **Alcohol Content:** *5.0%*

Hirter Morchl is a unique dark beer that is quite different from other beers produced by Hirt. The dark malt, hops and caramel malts give it a seductive color, while the soft mountain spring water does the rest. Particularly long matured, GMO-free, non-pasteurized and natural, Hirter Morchl tastes rather dry, and has a slim, slightly bitter finish. It is a bottom fermented beer that goes very well with rich meats such as game, cheese (especially spicy soft cheese), creamy desserts, and souffles. In 2010, the beer was awarded Silver at the European Beer Star Awards, and won Gold in 2012. Hirter describe thier Morchl as their dark secret.

HIRTER FESTBOCK

Country of Origin: *Austria* • **Brewery Founded:** *1270* • **Alcohol Content:** *7.0%*

Hirter Festbock is a specialty beer with centuries of heritage. It differs from other beers by having a higher alcohol content, produced by a long maturation period of at least five months. GMO-free, non-pasteurized, and completely natural, the water used in brewing Hirter Festbock comes from the soft mountain spring water next to the Hirt brewery. With its exceptionally clear color and the beery smell, Festbock is extremely tasty, almost sweet. The finish is bittersweet and harmonious. Characteristic of this bottom-fermented specialty beer from Hirt is the mild carbonic acid structure. It is a great accompanyment to rich foods like stew, venison steak, and spicy sausages.

HIRTER PRIVAT PILS

Country of Origin: *Austria* • **Brewery Founded:** *1270* • **Alcohol Content:** *5.2%*

Hirter Privat Pils is brewed by the Brauerei Hirt in Austria. It is a German-style pilsner lager that is available all year round. This special beer is bottom-fermented and brewed in accordance with an ancient Bohemian recipe. The soft mountain spring water from the water conservation area surrounding the brewery and the finest aromatic hops result in Privat Pils' unique taste. The beer has the character that beer connoisseurs describe as "semi-dry." This full-bodied pilsner has a bittersweet aftertaste combined with its soft character. It goes well with carpaccio, fish, baked chicken, cheese, and pasta. Privat Pils won a DLG Gold medal in 2012.

HIRTER TWIST OFF

Country of Origin: *Austria* • **Brewery Founded:** *1270* • **Alcohol Content:** *5.0%*

Hirter Twist Off beer is a full-bodied, bottom-fermented beer, brewed with the pure spring water of the Hanslbauer mountain springs. As well as being a delicious lager-style beer of character, Hirter Twist Off is also easy to open, thanks to its handy screw cap. GMO-free, non-pasteurized and completely natural, Hirter Twist Off is given a very mild degree of carbonation. The beer is highly fermented and this results in a full-bodies and mature finish. It is a great gastronomic partner for German specialities such as Bernese sausages, Vienna cutlets, and rumpsteaks.

HIRTER WEISSBIER

Country of Origin: *Austria* • **Brewery Founded:** *1270* • **Alcohol Content:** *5.4%*

Hirter Weissbier is a typical German-style white beer. It is brewed with selected barley and wheat malts and Hallertau hops. The beer is not pasteurized, is GMO free, and is made from only natural ingredients. This top-fermented brew has a typical, subtle smell of banana caused by the fermenting yeast. This yeast is also responsible for the mildly spicy flavor and fruity aroma of the beer. This weissbier is delightfully fresh and full-bodied and has the round taste of wheat on the palate. The beer is a great dining partner for grilled, white meats, poultry, fish, and fruity desserts.

HIRTER ZWICKL

Country of Origin: *Austria* • **Brewery Founded:** *1270* • **Alcohol Content:** *5.2%*

Hirter Zwickl beer is distinguished by its natural yeastiness, which perfectly complements the other flavors in the drink. Unfiltered, the beer has a naturally cloudy appearance, and the residual yeast is perfectly integrated into the full-bodied overall character of the brew. Brewed using soft mountain spring water, the beer has a tasty, low carbonated character. This bottom-fermented beer is also GM-free, non-pasteurized, and completely natural. It goes well with salads, full-flavored dishes and fruit salads. It also works well when served with multi-course meals as you will not need to change beers to go with each different dish.

KECKEIS STILL MAN'S

Country of Origin: *Austria* • **Distillery Founded:** *2003* • **Alcohol Content:** *High*

Keckeis Still Man's beer is brewed by the Distillerie Harald Keckeis using whisky malt to give the final brew a hint of whisky. The result is a strong and spicy beer with the smoky taste of real whisky malt. Keckeis only bottles a small amount of this special brew. Their distillery and brewing facility is based at Rankweil in Austria.

KELLERBRAUEREI RIED NATURTRÜB

Country of Origin: *Austria* • **Brewery Founded:** *Fifteenth century* • **Alcohol Content:** *5.3%*

Ried's Keller (basement) brewery was located in the town of Ried im Innkreis, in Upper Austria. It was first written about in the fifteenth century, and was considered to be the oldest brewery in the country. Privately owned, Ried distributed their beers around Austria. Unfortunately, the brewery hit hard times in recent times, and closed down in July 2013. Naturtrüb was one of the brewer's most well known beers. A classic March beer, it received a Gold medal at the 1994 Monde Selection in Paris, France. The beer was unfiltered, and cloudy in appearance, and a pale straw color. It tasted dry, with a hoppy bitterness and a light malt.

MURAUER BLACK HILL

Country of Origin: *Austria* • **Brewery Founded:** *1495* • **Alcohol Content:** *5.1%*

Murauer Black Hill is a fine and full-bodied beer brewed in a small private brewery in the town of Murau in the Styrian region of Austria. The crystal clear water of the local mountain springs make this a pure and special brew. It has a naturally fresh, malty scent, and a slender and delicately tangy taste. This newly created beer has an original wort gravity of 11 degrees. Black Hill is distributed by Murauer beer in returnable third-liter bottles and is a produced exclusively for the catering and beverage trade.

MURAUER BOCK BEAT

Country of Origin: *Austria* • **Brewery Founded:** *1495* • **Alcohol Content:** *7.3%*

Murauer Bock Beat is a strong, full-bodied and very drinkable stout-style beer. The beer has a very high wort gravity of 16.4 degrees and a calorific value of 600 calories per liter. Bock is usually a strongly brewed beer which was originally developed in monasteries. Bock beer helped the monks survive the long Lenten days because its high alcohol content makes it very filling. Murauer's Bock Beat is delivered during the festive season.

MURAUER DUNKEL

Country of Origin: *Austria* • **Brewery Founded:** *1495* • **Alcohol Content:** *5.4%*

Murauer Dunkel (dark) is a full beer with a sweet dark character. With an original wort gravity of thirteen degrees, this beer has a relatively low alcohol content of 5.4% and a moderate calorific value of 500 calories per liter. As the name suggests, the beer is a dark amber-colored beer in the Munich style that contains little alcohol because of its low attenuation (conversion of sugar to alcohol). It is well suited for mixing with light beers.

MURAUER HOPFENGOLD

Country of Origin: *Austria* • **Brewery Founded:** *1495* • **Alcohol Content:** *5.7%*

Murauer's Hopfengold or Hop Gold is a full-bodied and spicy beer. Hopfengold's wort has an original gravity of 13.4 degrees, which distills to an alcohol content of 5.7%. The beer has a calorific value of 520 calories per liter. Murauer Hopefengold is an unusual beer that has a higher than usual proportion of hops. Due to its strong taste, the beer is often served as a partner to spicy food. Hopfengold is an alternative beer with a character between that of Pils and Bock. Murauer bottles this beverage in half-liter bottles.

MURAUER MÄRZEN

Country of Origin: *Austria* • **Brewery Founded:** *1495* • **Alcohol Content:** *5.2%*

Murauer Märzen beer is mild and harmonious, with balanced malt and hop bitterness. It also has the characteristic golden yellow color common to March beers. Murauer Märzen has a original wort density of 12.2 degrees. Murauer's March beer constitues 90% of the company's total beer production and is their "star" beer. In 1994 the beer was awarded the coveted title of The Best Beer in Austria. The term March beer comes from a time when the wort was made using ice and snow. This cooled the yeast so that it could ferment properly. Beer makers were obliged to store ice and snow in thier cool cellars to keep brewing after the winter months. This usually lasted until March, when the final beers of the spring were made. Murauer packs its Marzen in 15 and 30 liter kegs, and 50 liter barrels. The beer is also bottled in third-liter and half-liter bottles.

MURAUER PILS

Country of Origin: *Austria* • **Brewery Founded:** *1495* • **Alcohol Content:** *5.1%*

Murauer Pils is a refreshing premium beer. It tastes very light, but is a little malty with a pleasant hop bitterness. The color of the beer is one of the lightest yellows Pils known. The Murauer Pils has an original wort density of 12.2 degrees and a calorific value of 450 calories per liter. The beer has a fine bitter taste and is often served as an aperitif, or lightly-flavored dishes. The term Pils comes from the beer-brewing Czech city of Pilsen. The city is world–renouned for its access to the beer-brewing trinity of soft water, good hops, and excellent barley. Today, the term is used for a beer with twelve degrees of gravity and a high degree of bitterness.

MURAUER PREISELBEER

Country of Origin: *Austria* • **Brewery Founded:** *1495* • **Alcohol Content:** *Low*

Murauer Preiselbeer, which mixes Murauer beer and cranberry juice is one of the world's first mixed berry-beer drinks. These drinks are becoming increasingly popular in Austria and Germany, where drinkers are looking for a low-alcohol alternative. The drink consists of sixty percent of Murauer Märzen beer mixed with forty percent cranberry lemonade. Together, the two drinks make a really special treat: with a bittersweet cranberry taste and the pleasant hoppy bitterness of the Murauer March beer.

MURAUER WEISSBIER

Country of Origin: *Austria* • **Brewery Founded:** *1495* • **Alcohol Content:** *5.6%*

Since 2011, Murauer's brewmaster has been making unusual Styria-style white beers. Murauer's Weissbier (white beer) has an exceptionally fruity flavor with a fine and delicate tanginess. Combined with the centuries-old Murauer brewing tradition, this results in a unique new style of beer that is best served at a temperature between 8 and 10 degrees centigrade. Murauer brewer Günter Kecht says that his new Weissbier has wonderful aromas, reminiscent of cloves, combined with good fruit sweetness and a harmonious and subtle hoppy bitterness.

MURAUER ZWICKL

Country of Origin: *Austria* • **Brewery Founded:** *1495* • **Alcohol Content:** *5.2%*

This hefetrübe (cloudy yeast) specialty beer keeps fresh for only a short time. The taste of the residual yeast is perfectly integrated into the overall character of the beer and the slightly lower proportion of carbonation gives the Zwickl beer an extremely round and tasty finish. Unlike conventional beers Murauer Zwickl is unfiltered and it is this that results in a limited shelf life of around three weeks. Zwickl is bottled directly from the storage tank, and this is where its name comes from. The storage tank's sample valve is opened with a special tap, the "Zwickl." Brewing the beer fresh in the barrel means that the Zwickl beer retains all the precious flavors and ingredients (yeast, vitamins, minerals, and trace elements) of a completely natural beer to make a rich and indulgent tipple.

OTTAKRINGER GOLD FASSL BOCK

Country of Origin: *Austria* • **Brewery Founded:** *1837* • **Alcohol Content:** *7.6%*

Gold Fassl Bock special brew is one of Ottakringer's most popular beers. It is also the brewery's strongest offering. The Bock has an individual character and a perfect balance of malty flavor and hoppiness, together with a rich and full-bodied character that stems from its high wort gravity of seventeen degrees. This beer is only produced at specific times of year to serve at festive occasions such as Christmas or Easter.

OTTAKRINGER GOLD FASSL DUNKLES

Country of Origin: *Austria* • **Brewery Founded:** *1837* • **Alcohol Content:** *5.2%*

Ottakringer's Gold Fassl Dunkles is an aromatic dark beer that is brewed using four different kinds of malt, which gives this special brew a unique flavor and aroma. It has an intense malty flavor with hints of chocolate, caramel and a whiff of coffee. The beer engenders more sophisticated tasting notes than many wines! The wort that goes to make this dark beer has a gravity of 12.2 degrees.

OTTAKRINGER GOLD FASSL PILS

Country of Origin: *Austria* • **Brewery Founded:** *1837* • **Alcohol Content:** *4.6%*

Ottakringer's Gold Fassl Pils is a light, pilsner-style lager. It has a wonderfully hoppy aroma and is brewed from fresh water. It has a pearly and elegant carbonation, together with a perfect beer garden feel! Its fresh and intense Pils taste is made from the finest Austrian hops. For a Pils, the beer has quite a high original gravity of 11.2 degrees. Even before the annexation of Austria by Nazi Germany, brewer Moriz von Kuffner was forced to sell Ottakringer because of his Jewish background. The brewery went to Gustav Harmer for the low price of fourteen million Austrian schillings.

OTTAKRINGER GOLD FASSL PUR

Country of Origin: *Austria* • **Brewery Founded:** *1837* • **Alcohol Content:** *5.2%*

Ottakringer's Gold Fassl Pur draft beer is a modern bio-beer (organic brew). These have been embraced by connoisseurs of gastronomy and fine dining. Pur is a bio-beer because it is made with organic ingredients taken directly from nature. The beer has a wort gravity of 11.8 degrees. Ottakringer produces Pur in co-operation with the WWF, partnering them to bring clean water to countries where this is at a premium. The company donates 5 Euros to their charity, H2Ottakringer, for each Hectoliter of Gold Fassl Pur sold.

OTTAKRINGER GOLD FASSL SPEZIAL

Country of Origin: *Austria* • **Brewery Founded:** *1837* • **Alcohol Content:** *5.6%*

This premium lager is typical of twenty-first century beer. Spezial is a Vienna-malt beer with light caramel notes and good hoppy bitterness. It is very carefully made and highly drinkable, a harmonic composition of the best beer flavors. After the liberation of Germany by the Allies, the Ottakringer brewery was temporarily managed by the Russians, before Gustav Harmer's family managed to prove their ownership and take control of the brewery once more. By 1955, Ottakringer was manufacturing 150,000 hectoliters of beer a year.

OTTAKRINGER GOLD FASSL ZWICKL

Country of Origin: *Austria* • **Brewery Founded:** *1837* • **Alcohol Content:** *5.2%*

Ottakringer's Zwickl is a creamy, fresh and mild unfiltered light draft beer. Zwickelbier is essentially an effervescent form of Keller bier that is slightly weaker and less hop-accented. (A Zwickel is the sampling cock or tap that is mounted on a cask or tank so that the beer can be tasted at various stages as it ferments.) Like Keller bier, Zwickelbier originated in small artisanal breweries and is rarely exported internationally. This is because it has less hop acidity than Keller bier and doesn't keep for very long. Ottakringer's Zwickl beer is unfiltered and unpasteurized. It has good effervescence and a nice creamy head when poured into a glass.

OTTAKRINGER GOLD FASSL ZWICKL ROT

Country of Origin: *Austria* • **Brewery Founded:** *1837* • **Alcohol Content:** *5.2%*

Ottakringer's Gold Fassl Zwickl Rot (red) beer is a darker colored, unfiltered brew. In style, the beer is a Vienna stock. This modern beer is probably the closest to the tradition that established the reputation of the Vienna stock beers in the nineteenth century. Ottakringer's Zwickl Rot is a light reddish brown color, and is not particularly turbid. It is a refreshing drink with fruity, peach-like aromas and a cocoa-like bitterness that comes from the blend of roasted malts and yeasts. It also has a little caramel sweetness, but the aftertaste is balanced and fairly dry.

OTTAKRINGER HELLES

Country of Origin: *Austria* • **Brewery Founded:** *1837*
Alcohol Content: *5.2%*

The Ottakringer Brewery was opened in 1837 by the master miller Heinrich Plank under the name of the Planksche Brauerei, when the ruling diocese of Klosterneuburg granted him permission to brew beer. In 1850, the brewery was taken over and expanded into a larger business by the cousins, Ignaz and Jakob Kuffner. Ottakringer Helles is now the company's most popular brand. It is a beer with a wort gravity of 12 degrees Plato. Ottakringer also uses their Helles beer to make their Ottakringer Radler which is 50/50 Helles beer/lemonade.

SCHLOSS EGGENBERG DOPPELBOCK DUNKEL

Country of Origin: *Austria* • **Brewery Founded:** *1681* • **Alcohol Content:** *8.5%*

Schloss Eggenberg offer several unusual beers, but Doppelbock Dunkel is a fairly straight proposition. This darker beer has a full and pleasant body with a malty, toffee sweetness, balanced with a hoppy bitterness in the finish. It has a very nice complexity and a balance of malty flavors and no cloying sweetness. The beer is deep reddish brown in color, with a slightly cloudy appearance. Doppelbock Dunkel won the Silver Medal at the 2007 World Beer Cup.

SCHLOSS EGGENBERG HOPFENKONIG

Country of Origin: *Austria* • **Brewery Founded:** *1681* • **Alcohol Content:** *5.1%*

Schloss Eggenberg's Hopfenkonig (Hop King) is an excellent lager-style beer brewed from the world famous Saazer hops. Saazer is a "noble" variety of hops, named for the Czech city of Žatec. This hop is used extensively in Germany and Austria to flavor beer styles such as the Czech pilsner, and is often used in premium beer production. Schloss Eggenberg's Hopfenkonig has a crisp, clean, and dry hoppy nose and aromatic flavors, and makes a perfect aperitif.

BANKS LIGHT

Country of Origin: *Barbados* • **Brewery Founded:** *1961* • **Alcohol Content:** *3.8%*

Banks has evolved into an icon of the Barbadian manufacturing industry. Banks Light Beer was brewed by the Banks Barbados Brewery in St. Michael, Barbados. The beer is a light pilsner lager with a clean smooth flavor and lower alcohol content. The beer is light and refreshing, a little malty and quite watery. Very little hop flavor. The beer has now been retired.

BANKS SEVEN STRONG LAGER

Country of Origin: *Barbados* • **Brewery Founded:** *1961* • **Alcohol Content:** *7%*

Among the newest beer creations to come out of the Banks Brewery, Seven Strong Lager debuted in 2010. It's already impressing beer-loving visitors to Barbados. The beer also took the gold medal at the 2011 Caribbean Rum & Beer Festival in the "Strong Beer" category. Seven Strong pours like a regular lager, gold and frothy. But the flavor is a breed apart, with a heavy alcohol element overwhelming everything else. The effect breeds a distinctive flavor bordering on sour, especially if it's not ice-cold.

BANKS STALLION MILK STOUT

Country of Origin: *Barbados* • **Brewery Founded:** *1961* • **Alcohol Content:** *5%*

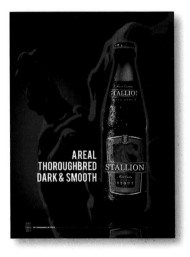

Banks Stallion Milk Stout is a sweet stout brewed by Banks Barbados Brewery in St. Michael, Barbados. The beer is dark brown with a tan-colored head. Its aroma is of coffee, and it has floral, grassy, toast, chocolate, vanilla, and vinous notes. The taste is medium sweet, with bitterness and sourness. The body of the beer is smooth with thick texture, with a light to medium body. The beer has average carbonation and is slightly astringent.

BANKS TWIST SHANDY

Country of Origin: *Barbados* • **Brewery Founded:** *1961* • **Alcohol Content:** *0.9%*

Banks offer their Twist Shandy in three different flavors, sorrel, lemon, and ginger. Lemon flavor Twist has a fresh lime-lemon flavor and a smooth taste. The drink is a blend of Banks Beer and lemonade to produce a clean fresh shandy. Twist shandies enjoy popularity as thirst quenchers and like most shandies worldwide, are consumed predominantly as an alternative to beverages with high alcohol content.

BELGIUM

BRUGGE TRIPEL

Country of Origin: *Belgium* • **Brewery Founded:** *1597* • **Alcohol Content:** *8.2%*

Brugge Tripel is a famous Belgian triple ale. It is known as the unsurpassed city beer of the people of the Belgian city of Bruges. The beer has a well-rounded malt character, an aromatic hop flavor, and a great complexity of tasting notes that include malt and spice. The beer is golden brown with a white head. The taste is said to evoke the beautiful city of Bruges, which is known as the Venice of the North. The beer is brewed by the Palm Brewery.

CHIMAY BLUE CAP

Country of Origin: *Belgium* • **Brewery Founded:** *1862* • **Alcohol Content:** *9%*

Chimay Blue Cap, or Grande Reserve is a dark Trappist beer with a powerful aroma. It has a complex flavor that develops over several years of maturation. Blue Cap was first brewed as a Christmas beer. This authentic Belgian beer, whose tinge of fresh yeast gives the beer a light rosy flowery touch that is particularly pleasant. This relatively dry beer has a lightly caramelized note, and a creamy brown head. Ideally, the beer should be served at cellar temperature (ten to twelve degrees centigrade).

CHIMAY GOLD

Country of Origin: *Belgium* • **Brewery Founded:** *1862* • **Alcohol Content:** *4.8%*

A short time before the construction of the Trappist brewery in 1862, the monks at Chimay set about brewing small quantities of an easily digestible, low alcohol beer for members of their own monastic community. Despite Gold's low alcohol content, it is still a highly fermented Trappist beer with a touch of hops and a spicy aroma. This exclusive brew, with its snow-like head, is only sold at a few local hostelries. Chimay is one of only six Belgian beers that are allowed to describe themselves as Trappist products.

CHIMAY RED CAP

Country of Origin: *Belgium* • **Brewery Founded:** *1862* • **Alcohol Content:** *7%*

The Cistercian Trappist monks of Chimay have, since 1862, brewed their Trappist beers. These beers continue to be extremely popular in Belgium and abroad. Chimay Red Cap is the oldest of the Chimay beers, and the first brewed at the Notre-Dame de Scourmont Abbey in 1862. This Trappist beer possesses a beautiful coppery color that makes it particularly attractive. Topped with a creamy head, it gives off a slight fruity apricot smell from the fermentation. The aroma felt in the mouth is a balance of fruity notes. This traditional Belgian beer is best savored at cellar temperature (ten to twelve degrees centigrade).

CHIMAY TRIPEL

Country of Origin: *Belgium* • **Brewery Founded:** *1862* • **Alcohol Content:** *8%*

Chimay Tripel was the last-born of the Chimay Abbey beers. It has a golden color, and this Trappist beer combines sweet and bitter flavors in a rare balance. The beer's aroma is derived from the perfumes of the hops. These fruity hints remind the drinker of Muscat grapes and raisins, and ripe apples. This traditional Belgian beer is best savored fresh at a temperature between six and eight degrees centigrade.

DIKKENEK GRAND CRU

Country of Origin: *Belgium* • **Brewery Founded:** *1878* • **Alcohol Content:** *5.1%*

Dikkenek is a renowned Belgian ale that is now discontinued. It was originally brewed by the Brouwerij Affligem De Smedt, but the beer was made by the Kerkom brewery from 2005. The beer was a deep ruby brown with a short, lasting beige head. The beer had a taste of raisins in the nose, with a slight acidity and a big prune flavor. Dikkenek had a smooth body, and was intensely sweet with minimal bitterness.

DUVEL

Country of Origin: *Belgium* • **Brewery Founded:** *1871* • **Alcohol Content:** *8.5%*

Duvel is a strong pale ale with a subtle bitterness, a refined aroma and a pronounced hop character. The brewing process, which lasts about ninety days, guarantees a pure style, a delicate sparkle and a pleasant sweet taste. Malted barley is the most important ingredient of Duvel, but the beer gets its typical bitterness by adding several varieties of aromatic hops from Slovenia and the Czech Republic. Duvel's yeast strain comes from a local brewery in Scotland, Victor Moortgat. The first part of the fermentation takes place in in warm cellars (24 ° C) and lasts two weeks. The beer is then taken to cold cellars, where it matures for a further six weeks.

DUVEL TRIPEL HOP

Country of Origin: *Belgium* • **Brewery Founded:** *1871* • **Alcohol Content:** *9.5%*

Duvel Tripel Hop is brewed with three different hop varieties. Each year, Duvel's brewers select the third interesting hop variety. Thus the final flavor profile changes from year to year so that the beer remains surprising and interesting to true beer lovers. In 2013, Duvel's brewers selected an exotic hop variety, Sorachi Ace from Japan. By brewing Tripel Hop with three varieties instead of two, Duvel achieves intense hop aroma and increased bitterness. 2013's Tripel Hop brew, enriched by the Sorachi Ace hop has fresh notes of grapefruit and tropical fruit. This beer's higher aromatic intensity also translates into a high final alcohol content of 9.5%.

FLOREFFE BLONDE

Country of Origin: *Belgium* • **Brewery Founded:** *1876* • **Alcohol Content:** *6.5%*

Floreffe Blonde is brewed by the Lefebvre Brewery in Belgium. It is made with well water and malted spring barley. Candy sugar is added during the boiling phase. After fermentation and storage, the beer is mechanically purified in a centrifuge. Even when served very cold, the beer may be slightly cloudy. In this way, Floreffe Blonde maintains its inimitable bouquet and aroma of malt and fruit. The bitterness comes from a subtle mix of the best hop varieties. The first sip is powerful but is transformed into a taste of softness and ends with a finale of liquorice root.

FLOREFFE DUBBEL

Country of Origin: *Belgium* • **Brewery Founded:** *1876* • **Alcohol Content:** *6.5%*

Floreffe Dubbel beer is brewed using a clever mixture of special malt varieties that give the beer its brown color and malty flavor. During the boiling process, Dubbel is enriched with a mixture of flavorings. Its main fermentation takes a week. After cold sedimentation and clarification, the beer is then bottled without being filtered, following the traditional method used by the monks of the Floreffe Abbey.

FLOREFFE PRIMA MELIOR

Country of Origin: *Belgium* • **Brewery Founded:** *1876* • **Alcohol Content:** *8%*

Floreffe Prima Melior was a special brew that the Floreffe Abbey's Father Superior would serve his guests and visitors. The beer is brown and dense and is strengthened with powerful flavorings such as aniseed and coriander. After fermentation and sedimentation, the beer is given a dose of yeast and sugar for re-fermentation in the bottle. This maturation method was inherited from the monks of the abbey. Prima Melior is ideal as an accompaniment to mature cheese and rabbit stew.

FLOREFFE TRIPEL

Country of Origin: *Belgium* • **Brewery Founded:** *1876* • **Alcohol Content:** *8%*

Floreffe Tripel beer owes its name to its high density and strong taste. A splendid mixture between bitterness and caramel characterizes this beer. Like other beers made in the Floreffe Abbey, it is not filtered. It may therefore be slightly cloudy if served cold. As the monks' recipe specifies, it is re-fermented in the bottle with the addition of yeast and sugar. As a terrible punishment, monks at the Floreffe Abbey who arrived late for prayers did not get their beer ration.

HOEGAARDEN

Country of Origin: *Belgium* • **Brewery Founded:** *1965* • **Alcohol Content:** *4.9%*

The Hoegaarden brewery was founded by local milkman Pierre Celis. He used a traditional wheat beer recipe that had been first brewed by Belgian monks in the fifteenth century. The brewery was a great success and it now makes 90% of all the wheat beer sold in Belgium. Orange peel, coriander, and herbs go into this unique light yellow, cloudy brew.

HOEGAARDEN CITRON

Country of Origin: *Belgium* • **Brewery Founded:** *1965* • **Alcohol Content:** *3%*

Hoegaarden wheat beer is often drunk with a lemon wedge. Hoegaarden Citron is the brewery's attempt to re-create that drinking experience. The beer is a clear light blond beer, which pours with a tall, snowy-white hear. It is only available in the Benelux countries.

HOEGAARDEN FORBIDDEN FRUIT

Country of Origin: *Belgium* • **Brewery Founded:** *1965* • **Alcohol Content:** *8.5%*

Hoegaarden's Verboden Vrucht, or Forbidden Fruit beer is a strong dark ale. The beer is available year-round. The beer has a dark amber hue and has a medium body that is quite highly carbonated. It has an off-white head. The brew smells of yeast and is both tart and sweet with caramel malts and sour banana tones. The beer is brewed with roasted malt and hops, and has a herby aroma.

HOEGAARDEN ROSEE

Country of Origin: *Belgium* • **Brewery Founded:** *1965* • **Alcohol Content:***3%*

Although Hoegaarden Rosee is pink, it is still very much a wheat beer. The fruity brew features the soft taste and subtle color of raspberries. As the beer is low alcohol, it is a great refreshing beverage for drinking in the sun. The beer has a low carbonation and is sweet, with very little aftertaste. The beer is only distributed in the Benelux countries. Hoegaarden also make a no alcohol version of Rosee.

HOEGAARDEN SPECIALE

Country of Origin: *Belgium* • **Brewery Founded:** *1965* • **Alcohol Content:** *5.7%*

Hoegaarden Speciale is a seasonal beer that is brewed for the festive season, and available only between December and January. It is only distributed in Belgium. The clear, golden blond beer is quite bitter with a ripe taste and a prolonged aftertaste.

KERST PATER

Country of Origin: *Belgium* • **Brewery Founded:** *1897* • **Alcohol Content:** *9%*

Kerst Pater is a Belgian strong ale that is brewed by the Van Den Bossche brewery, which is based in at St. Lievens-Esse in Herzele, Belgium. Brown in color, the beer has a creamy beige head. The beer has the aroma of the dark Belgian abbey beers, with hints of dark caramel, cherries and overripe bananas. It has a round body with a slick texture. The beer's aftertaste is complex, and the beer is quite heavily carbonated.

KERKOM ADELARDUS DOUBLE

Country of Origin: *Belgium* • **Brewery Founded:** *1878* • **Alcohol Content:** *7.0%*

Kerkom first brewed this special Abbey beer at the request of the Abbey of the Belgian town of Sint-Truiden, on the occasion of the first open days at the Abbey in 2002. What makes Adelardus Double so special is its flavoring with 'gruut.' Gruut is a mixture of about ten different local herbs. The beer is a dark brown high fermentation beer that is unfiltered, unpasteurized, and is given a secondary fermentation in the bottle. It is made from five types of malts, two varieties of Belgian hops, brewing water, dark sugar candy, yeast, and gruut.

KERKOM ADELARDUS TRIPLE

Country of Origin: *Belgium* • **Brewery Founded:** *1878* • **Alcohol Content:** *9.0%*

Kerkom first brewed their Adelardus Triple brew on the occasion of the opening of Sint-Truiden's Abbey tower on May 1, 2005. The beer has a somewhat darker (orange like) colour and a slightly fuller taste than the brewery's Kerkomse Tripel. What makes Adelardus Triple so special is the use of 'gruut' to flavor the beer. Gruut is a mixture of about ten different local herbs.

KERKOM BINK BLOND

Country of Origin: *Belgium* • **Brewery Founded:** *1878* • **Alcohol Content:** *5.5%*

The brewing farm of Kerkom was founded by Evarist Clerinx in 1878. Around 1936, his son Paul took charge and, in 1952, it was taken over by Jean Clerinx. Jean was forced to close the brewery in 1968, but he re-started the business in 1988. As of that moment, Bink Blond was born. This easy-drinking beer has a really hoppy character and is the perfect thirst-quencher. It is made with two types of malt, two types of Belgian hops, brewing water, and yeast. It has a hoppy nose and an aftertaste of bitterness.

KERKOM BINK BLOESEM

Country of Origin: *Belgium* • **Brewery Founded:** *1878* • **Alcohol Content:** *7.1%*

Kerkom Bink Bloesem (blossom) was the third beer to be brewed by the revived Kerkom brewery, and was introduced to the market in the blossom time of spring 2000. Kerkom brew this seasonal beer in the spring and summer months of each year, so it is only available from April to October. The beer is brewed using five types of malts, one variety of Belgian hops, brewing water, yeast, honey from Sint-Truiden (a town in Flemish Belgium), and pear syrup from Vrolingen, Belgium. Bloesem has a fruity taste with a slightly sweet tone with a long fruity and softly bitter aftertaste.

KERKOM BINK BRUIN

Country of Origin: *Belgium* • **Brewery Founded:** *1878* • **Alcohol Content:** *5.5%*

Bink Bruin was the second beer to be brewed by the re-started Kerkom brewery. It is an easy-drinking brown beer popular with adherents of this style of brew. The beer is made from four types of malt, one variety of Belgian hops, brewing water, and yeast. Bink Bruin is a full, softly bitter beer with a sweetish malty aftertaste. It is sold in small quarter-liter bottles.

KERKOM WINTERKONINKSKE

Country of Origin: *Belgium* • **Brewery Founded:** *1878* • **Alcohol Content:** *8.3%*

As well as Kerkom's Blossom Bink, drinkers can also enjoy a second seasonal beer from the brewery, Winterkoninkske. This is the ideal beer to make a cold and chilly winter evening cosy. It is brewed from seven types of malt (including rolled oats), two varieties of Belgian hops, brewing water, and yeast. Kerkom's winter brew is strong, dark, and heart-warming with a full pure, slightly sweet taste and a long, softly bitter aftertaste.

KERKOM WINTERKONINKSKE GRAND CRU

Country of Origin: *Belgium* • **Brewery Founded:** *1878* • **Alcohol Content:** *13%*

Kerkom's Winterkoninske Grand Cru was launched in December 2009. It is a strong dark beer that (because of its high alcohol content) should be enjoyed with moderation. The use of different dark malts results in tones of chocolate, coffee and sherry. This makes the beer a perfect match for game dishes and chocolate desserts. The brew is the strongest winter beer brewed in the Limburg region of Belgium.

LA CHOUFFE

Country of Origin: *Belgium* • **Brewery Founded:** *1982* • **Alcohol Content:** *8%*

La Chouffe is a blond ale from the Ardennes region of Belgium. It is an unfiltered blonde beer, which is re-fermented in the bottle as well as in the keg. It is pleasantly fruity, spiced with coriander, and with a light hop taste. It has a high wort density of sixteen degrees Plato, and should be served at a temperature between four to ten degrees centigrade. Made by the Achouffe Brewery, La Chouffe is the brewery's most popular beer.

LA CHOUFFE BOK 6666

Country of Origin: *Belgium* • **Brewery Founded:** *1982* • **Alcohol Content:** *9%*

La Chouffe's Bok 6666 is a seasonal amber beer especially brewed for the Dutch market. Bok beers are season. Traditionally, they appear on the Dutch market at the end of September each year. Chouffe Bok 6666 stands out from other beers due to its lovely copper colour, its fresh and fruity scent and a pleasant full-bodied feeling in the mouth, which ends in an aftertaste with a hint of bitterness.

LA CHOUFFE McCHOUFFE

Country of Origin: *Belgium* • **Brewery Founded:** *1982* • **Alcohol Content:** *8%*

The Belgian Brasserie D'Achouff was founded in 1982. It is nestled in the green heart of the Belgian Ardennes, and specializes in brewing high quality specialty beers. La Chouffe beers are easily recognizable due to the friendly elf logo used to decorate its labels. Elves and other goblins feature heavily in the myths and legends of the Belgian Ardennes. Mc Chouffe is an unfiltered dark beer, which is re-fermented in the bottle as well as in the keg. Behind its fruity flavour is a slight hint of bitterness.

LA CHOUFFE N'ICE CHOUFFE

Country of Origin: *Belgium* • **Brewery Founded:** *1982* • **Alcohol Content:** *10%*

La Chouffe's N'Ice Chouffe is a strong dark beer designed to warm you up during the winter months. It is spiced with thyme and curaçao and has a light hop taste that produces a well-balanced beer. N'Ice is unfiltered and is re-fermented in the bottle as well as in the keg. The original wort gravity of the beer is very high at twenty degrees. The beer should be served at between four and ten degrees centigrade.

LEFEBVRE BARBAR

Country of Origin: *Belgium* • **Brewery Founded:** *1876* • **Alcohol Content:** *8%*

Barbar takes the beer drinker back to the roots of the craft of brewing. For centuries, the only known sweetener in Europe was honey. The beer is brewed with extremely pure well water and honey, which is added to it instead of sugar. Since 2009, this beer has been marketed in third-liter bottles with a swing-top cap which emphasizes the strength and ancient character of the beer. Barbār is golden in color with a generous head. The mead aroma immediately reveals its origin. After shaking, the taste becomes more complex with a hint of milk, candied lemon peel, coriander, and ginger. This acidity strengthens the beer and gives it a lovely balance and freshness. The aftertaste is smooth and refined, spicy and slightly sweet.

LEFEBVRE BARBAR BOK

Country of Origin: *Belgium* • **Brewery Founded:** *1876* • **Alcohol Content:** *8%*

Lefebvre's Barbār Bok is adorned with dark colors and has a ruby reflection. It undergoes secondary fermentation in the bottle and merges the softness of honey with the strength of alcohol. The honey originates from Yucatan in Mexico. This is a splendid and uncompromising beer. Originally, it was only brewed in the winter and was called Barbār Winter Bok. However, since 2008 the beer has been brewed year-round. Since 2009, the beer has been marketed in third-liter bottles with a swing-top cap, highlighting the strong and ancient character of this beer.

LEFEBVRE BELGIAN KRIEK

Country of Origin: *Belgium* • **Brewery Founded:** *1876* • **Alcohol Content:** *3.5%*

Brewed by the same brewery that makes the Floreffe Abbey beers, Belgian Kriek is one of the popular Belgian fruit beers. Since as long as people can remember, the brewers from Belgium's Senne Valley mixed their old beer with cherries. This Belgian Kriek (cherry beer) is part of this tradition, but the beer has been adapted for the modern taste. It is soft and very fruity, while being relatively low in alcohol.

LEFEBVRE BELGIAN PECHES

Country of Origin: *Belgium* • **Brewery Founded:** *1876* • **Alcohol Content:** *3.5%*

Brewed by the same brewery that makes the Floreffe Abbey beers, Belgian Peches (peach beer) is one of Belgium's popular fruit-flavored beers. Belgian Peches is a fun mélange of beer and peach juice. This produces a harmonious beverage that has a symphony of flavors and aromas. It is both soft and very fruity, while also being relatively low in alcohol.

LEFEBVRE BLANCH DE BRUXELLES

Country of Origin: *Belgium* • **Brewery Founded:** *1876* • **Alcohol Content:** *4.5%*

Blanche de Bruxelles is a Belgian white beer or Witteke. Originally, these beers were typical of farm-based breweries where craft brewers used the best ingredients from their own harvest. Blanche de Bruxelles owes its natural cloudiness to the presence of wheat. During the boiling process, natural aromas are added to the wort, including coriander and dried orange peel. The brewing method, which includes the gradual addition of hot water, is a particularly long process. The beer is unfiltered and if it is served correctly, it is a cloudy beer with a white head. Blanche de Bruxelles is fresh and refined, typical for this extraordinary kind of Belgian white beer.

LEFEBVRE HOPUS

Country of Origin: *Belgium* • **Brewery Founded:** *1876* • **Alcohol Content:** *8.3%*

Hopus is one of Lefebvre's specialty beers. The flavor of the beer is shaped by the selection of the hops and by a production process that has its roots in the Belgian brewing tradition. After two years of research, five hop varieties from the best regions were chosen to be used in the beer. The selection was based on their taste and their harmonious fusion. Hopus has a lovely white, creamy head while the beer itself has a deep golden hue. The brewer's yeast adheres to the bottom of the bottle and is released in the form of tiny particles. Hopus is both strong and bitter, with a high degree of carbonation.

LEFEBVRE MANNEKEN PILS

Country of Origin: *Belgium* • **Brewery Founded:** *1876* • **Alcohol Content:** *5%*

Due to its passion for good beers, the Brewery Lefebvre also wanted to make its own Pils and has done so since 2004. Fresh and tasty, their Manneken Pils proves that with good ingredients and talent, a small brewery can produce a Pils of supreme quality. Originally, the beer was marketed as a local specialty, and was called "The Quenast." But due to its growing success, in both Brussels (the capital of Belgium) and abroad, the brew was renamed Manneken Pils in 2010.

LEFEBVRE MOEDER OVERSTE

Country of Origin: *Belgium* • **Brewery Founded:** *1876* • **Alcohol Content:** *8%*

Lefebvre's Moeder Overste (Mother Superior) is a triple beer with a full, strong taste. It may be one of the best brews produced by Lefébvre. Beer drinkers in Flanders and the Netherlands have been able to appreciate this heavenly beer for the last fifteen years. Moeder Overste has a golden hue and is perfumed with spices, wood, and fruit flavors mixed with malt to produce a fine bitterness. The beer can be served cold at five degrees centigrade or with the chill taken off at ten degrees centigrade, depending on one's preference.

LEFEBVRE SAISON 1900

Country of Origin: *Belgium* • **Brewery Founded:** *1876* • **Alcohol Content:** *5.4%*

Saison is an old beer recipe originating from the Belgian region of Hainaut. The beer was commonly brewed in the last century. In honor of the founder of the Lefebvre brewery, who produced Saison for the local quarrymen, this beer was brewed once again in 1982. It is a golden colored beer with an impressive head. The hop aroma is dominant with hints of flowers, resin and spices. Its density makes it a beer for special occasions and celebrations.

LEFFE BLOND

Country of Origin: *Belgium* • **Brewery Founded:** *1240* • **Alcohol Content:** *6.6%*

In 1250 the Abbey Notre-Dame de Leffe bought the Saint Medart brewery. The brewery was situated on the opposite bank of Belgium's Meuse River. There, the monks brewed beer for the community as well as for passing travelers and pilgrims. At the top, the only known method of beer production was the top fermentation process, which Leffe still uses today. Leffe Blond has a lovely golden color and is brewed using pale malt, water, hops, and yeast. It is brewed as an aperitif beer, but also partners well with many dishes. Leffe Blond is now one of Belgium's most internationally well-known beers.

LEFFE BRUIN

Country of Origin: *Belgium* • **Brewery Founded:** *1240* • **Alcohol Content:** *6.5%*

Leffe Bruin can trace its origins right back to the thirteenth century. This elegant brown beer is most attractive poured slowly into a traditional beer chalice. Beneath a smooth creamy beer head, this top fermented dark brown beer shows its centuries of brewing heritage. Leffe Bruin is rich and smooth, sweet and bitter, with hints of caramel, coffee, vanilla, and cloves. The beer pairs well with cheese and spicy dishes.

LEFFE NECTAR

Country of Origin: *Belgium* • **Brewery Founded:** *1240* • **Alcohol Content:** *5.5%*

Leffe Nectar is a blond, honey-flavored, orange-colored Abbey beer. It has a floral bouquet of several notes, including field flowers, acacia, lime blossom, and sunflower. It also has the aromas of vanilla, cloves, and fruit. The beer is delicious with rich foods like foie gras or baked goat's cheese. Serving the beer in a wide beer chalice allows all of its complex flavors to develop.

LEFFE RADIEUSE

Country of Origin: *Belgium* • **Brewery Founded:** *1240* • **Alcohol Content:** *8.2%*

Leffe Radieuse is a top-fermented Abbey beer that has been developed from several centuries of brewing expertise. As well as having a rich and balanced flavor, the beer also has a pronounced bitterness to it, which is due to the use of several varieties of hop. Hints of citrus, coriander and clove provide a pleasant counterbalance to Leffe Radieuse's character. Its unique golden amber brown color is a pleasure to the eye, and a temptation to the taste buds. Leffe Radieuse is delicious with refined dishes such as grilled lamb fillet and soft cheeses.

LEFFE RITUEL 9°

Country of Origin: *Belgium* • **Brewery Founded:** *1240* • **Alcohol Content:** *9%*

Leffe Rituel 9° is a top-fermented beer with a deep golden color. Its strong flavors give this beer plenty of character. Brewed according to age-old traditions, this deep-gold blond Abbey beer derives its flavor from its superior ingredients. This is elegant and distinguished, with bitter and fruity spices balancing each other out. Thanks to its elevated alcohol percentage, Leffe Rituel 9° is the perfect beer to accompany dishes with a smoky aftertaste, such as charcuterie, cheese or tapas. It is the strongest beer in the Leffe range.

LEFFE ROYALE

Country of Origin: *Belgium* • **Brewery Founded:** *1240* • **Alcohol Content:** *7.5%*

Leffe Royale is a top fermented beer made with three different hop varieties. It provides the perfect balance between bitterness and sweetness. The beer has tones of clove, vanilla, and banana, with a clear citrus character. The beer works well with fish, shellfish, sea food, and cheeses. Royale is traditionally served in a twisted stem glass chalice.

LEFFE RUBY

Country of Origin: *Belgium* • **Brewery Founded:** *1240* • **Alcohol Content:** *5%*

Leffe Ruby has the taste of sunshine. It is a red and refreshing beer that combines the flavors of Abbey beer with delicate notes of forest fruits. Fruity, spicy, and soft, the flavors of the beer are light and refreshing. This fruity brew pairs well with tasty appetizers such as blue cheese and cured ham.

LEFFE TRIPEL

Country of Origin: *Belgium* • **Brewery Founded:** *1240* • **Alcohol Content:** *8.5%*

Leffe Tripel is an authentic blond Abbey beer full of character. It is given a secondary fermentation in the bottle, and due to the presence of unfiltered yeast particles, its flavor is robust and refined. It has a great balance between being bitter and sweet and has a magnificent bouquet. This contains magical flavors such as banana, peach, ripe pineapple, and a variety of spices, including coriander and orange. To obtain an even more pronounced flavor, pour the beer at an angle to the glass, to mix in the sediment at the bottom of the bottle. If you prefer your beer sweeter and softer, don't pour the entire contents into the glass.

PALM ESTAMINET

Country of Origin: *Belgium* • **Brewery Founded:** *1597* • **Alcohol Content:** *5.2%*

Estaminet is the latest example of Palm's brewing craftsmanship. The results are available to be seen, smelled, and tasted in the finished product. This yellow-gold pilsner-style beer has a subtle hop aroma and a distinctly fruity flavor. The beer is a refreshing, relatively low alcohol beer, designed to quench the thirst.

PALM SPECIALE BELGE

Country of Origin: *Belgium* • **Brewery Founded:** *1597* • **Alcohol Content:** *5.4%*

Palm Speciale Belge is still one of the most popular Belgian beers launched in the early twentieth century. It is a smooth-drinking, top-fermented pale ale with relatively modest alcohol content. The amber-colored beer has a honey-like mellow taste, fused with a fruity aroma that is derived from the use of Palm's own selected yeasts. Palm markets the brew as being Belgium's number one amber beer.

RODENBACH ALEXANDER

Country of Origin: *Belgium* • **Brewery Founded:** *1597* • **Alcohol Content:** *6%*

Rodenbach Alexander is brewed by Belgium's well-known Palm brewery. It is a sour-tasting red-brown beer, and is usually served in a typical tulip-shaped glass. Alexander is an extra-fermented brew that is matured for two years in oak casks to develop its flavor. It has a fruity bouquet and a sharp, sweet and sour taste and a pure white head of foam.

STEENBRUGGE ABBEY BEER

Country of Origin: *Belgium* • **Brewery Founded:** *1597* • **Alcohol Content:** *8%*

In 2003, the Prior of the Sint Pietersabdij Abbey authorized the long-established Palm brewery to brew the famous Steenbrugge Abbey beer. In doing so, he instructed Belgium's leading family brewery to preserve the legacy of the Abbey's Saint Arnoldus beer for future generations. Palm had to undertake to safeguard the religious order's unique and ancient beer recipe.

TRAPPIST WESTVLETEREN 8

Country of Origin: *Belgium* • **Brewery Founded:** *1838* • **Alcohol Content:** *8%*

Westvleteren's 8 is a fairly typical Belgian Dubbel beer. It is easy-to-drink and rather sweet, with notable fruity flavors. The character of the beer borders more on the side of Belgian strong dark ale, and does not widely differ in flavor or quality from many other Dubbels. The beer has a good head of beige foam, made up of small-sized bubbles, which creates a frothy appearance. The body of the beer is a dark garnet color, nearly black-brown, with light bringing out garnet-amber hues and orange tints. The substantial carbonation is visible throughout the slightly transparent body and the aroma is sweet, slightly fruity with hints of grape.

TRAPPIST WESTVLETEREN 12

Country of Origin: *Belgium* • **Brewery Founded:** *1838* • **Alcohol Content:** *10.2%*

Westvletern 12 is known to many beer lovers as the Holy Grail of beer. It pours chocolate brown and cloudy out of the bottle with a modest, light tan head. Its dominant aromas are of caramel, malt, and yeast. It tastes of sweet malt, dark fruit, with a subtly bitter after taste. Despite its relatively high alcohol level, it is smooth and well balanced.

TRAPPIST WESTVLETEREN BLONDE

Country of Origin: *Belgium* • **Brewery Founded:** *1838* • **Alcohol Content:** *5.8%*

This blond Belgian beer is produced on a small-scale basis by the monks of the Saint Sixtus Abbey of Westvleteren. The Cistercian monks of this Trappist Abbey sell their beer direct to the public to help fund their contemplative lifestyle. They only sell their beer to members of the public (in crates of twenty-four plain, brown glass bottles), who are forbidden to sell the beer on to anyone else.

BOLIVIA

CERVEZA POTOSINA NEGRA MALTA

Country of Origin: *Bolivia* • **Brewery Founded:** *1907* • **Alcohol Content:** *Unknown*

Cerveza Potosina Negra Malta is brewed by Cerveceria Nacional Potosi, located in Potosi, Bolivia. The beer is a dunkler bock. The beer is a dark brew with a smoky blackcurrant aroma and flavor. Chocolate comes though in the end but the beer is too sweet and syrupy to be served at room temperature.

CERVEZA TAQUIÑA

Country of Origin: *Bolivia* • **Brewery Founded:** *1895* • **Alcohol Content:** *4%*

This pilsner beer is brewed by Cerveceria Taquiña in Cochabamba, Bolivia, the oldest brewery in the country. The beer is brewed at 2986 meters above sea level with natural materials of the finest quality and pure water from the Tunari Mountains. It is a crystal clear golden colored beer with a smallish white head. It has an aroma of pale malt, light hops, caster sugar, corn, and some light citrus. The beer is medium-bodied with a sharp taste of oranges and lemons with hints of peaches, malt, sugar, and wheat. The aftertaste shows the freshness of a light lager, but it has the flavors of a nice ale.

CRUCEÑA CERVEZA TIPO PILSENER

Country of Origin: *Bolivia* • **Brewery Founded:** *Unknown* • **Alcohol Content:** *4.8%*

Crucena Cerveza Tipo Pilsener is a pilsner style lager. From 2011, the lager has been sold in 330ml cans. The beer is brewed by Cerveceria Boliviana Nacional in La Paz, Bolivia. The beer is a pleasant light lager with a light body and a medium carbonation.

DUCAL

Country of Origin: *Bolivia* • **Brewery Founded:** *Unknown* • **Alcohol Content:** *5%*

Ducal beer is a pale lager brewed by Cervecería Santa Cruz (Bolivia), which is located in Santa Cruz, Bolivia. The beer has a crystal clear yellow colored body with a light white head and tons of bubbles that rise from the bottom. The aroma is of metal and fruit. The beer is light to medium-bodied. It tastes of malt, wheat, and metal. The aftertaste is very bitter, of pale malt.

EL INCA BI-CERVECINA

Country of Origin: *Bolivia* • **Brewery Founded:** *Unknown* • **Alcohol Content:** *3%*

El Inca Bi-Cervecina is brewed by Cervecería Boliviana Nacional. The brewery is located in La Paz, Bolivia. It brews the most popular Bolivian beers and several international brands for their home market. El Inca is a low alcohol beer. It pours clear dark brown with a medium, fizzy light tan head. The aroma is of lightly toasted malt. The flavor is highly sweet, with tones of toast and caramel malt with a sweet finish. The beer has a light body and carbonation.

HUARI PILSENER

Country of Origin: *Bolivia* • **Brewery Founded:** *Unknown* • **Alcohol Content:** *5%*

Huari Pilsener is a pale lager and is one of Bolivia's most popular beers. It is brewed by Cervecería Boliviana Nacional (AB-InBev) in La Paz, Bolivia. The beer pours a clear golden straw color with a frothy white head. It is a pretty standard South American lager offering notes of corn, grain, lemon, and a gentle hop presence in the finish. It is a light-bodied beer with medium carbonation.

JUDAS CERVEZA FUERTE

Country of Origin: *Bolivia* • **Brewery Founded:** *Unknown* • **Alcohol Content:** *7%*

Judas Cerveza Fuerte is a malt liquor brewed by Cerveceria Crucena Boliviana in El Alto, Bolivia. The beer is clear yellow with a creamy off-white head. The aroma is very fruity, with hints of ripe fruits, oranges, and yeast. The beer is quite highly carbonated and has a medium to full body. The taste is fruity and sour, with flavors of very ripe fruit, banana, and some spices. The beer has a bitter aftertaste.

PACENA RED LAGER

Country of Origin: *Bolivia* • **Brewery Founded:** *Unknown* • **Alcohol Content:** *4.8%*

Pacena Red Lager was a popular Bolivian beer, which has now been retired. It was brewed by Cervecería Boliviana Nacional (AB-InBev) in La Paz, Bolivia. The beer was a Vienna-style amber lager. The beer was bottled. It poured a light red, an almost orange color, with a thin bubbly head. It had a lightly toasted aroma, with a sweet candy-like fruit. The beer had a bitter palate with a slightly sweet malty flavor.

PACENA TROPICAL EXTRA

Country of Origin: *Bolivia* • **Brewery Founded:** *Unknown*
Alcohol Content: *5%*

This pilsner-style beer is brewed by Cervecería Boliviana Nacional (AB-InBev) in La Paz, Bolivia. The beer has a crystal clear colored body with a thin white head. It has an aroma of faint fruit, light malt, and a tiny amount of hops. It has a light to medium body. The beer has a strong malty taste with a bit of sugar and a little fruitiness. Its aftertaste is clean, tart and malty.

REINEKE BRAU

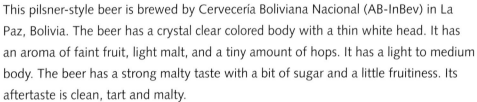

Country of Origin: *Bolivia* • **Brewery Founded:** *Unknown* • **Alcohol Content:** *4.8%*

Reineke Brau is the first German beer brewed in Bolivia. Reineke Brau is a pilsener and has some sediment. The beer has a pleasant flavor although it is a little pale and cloudy. The beer has a stable foamy head. It has moderate carbonation.

TAQUIÑA STOUT

Country of Origin: *Bolivia* • **Brewery Founded:** *1886* • **Alcohol Content:** *5.8%*

Taquina Stout is brewed by the CBN Brewery in Bolivia. The brewery was founded in 1886. The beer has a very dark brown colored body with a thin tan head. The aroma is of roasted malt, coffee, chocolate, pit fruits and a very light caramel scent. The beer is medium-bodied with a strong malt flavor with plenty of chocolate tastes along with hints of nut.

BOSNIA

CRNI DORDE

Country of Origin: *Bosnia* • **Brewery Founded:** *1873* • **Alcohol Content:** *5%*

Nektar Pivo is a dunkel beer brewed by Banjalu ka Pivara in Banja Luka, Bosnia. The brewery was founded in 1873 by Trappist monks. The beer is a clear amber-brown color with a big light brown, lasting head. The aroma has some caramel, roasted malt, herb, and grass notes. It has a light sweet caramel taste at the start, which turns into a moderate bitter aftertaste. The beer is medium bodied and oily with a soft carbonation.

ERSTER

Country of Origin: *Bosnia* • **Brewery Founded:** *1884* • **Alcohol Content:** *4.3%*

Erster is a pale lager brewed by Pivara Tuzla in Tuzla, Bosnia. The beer has a clear straw color with a large frothy white head and soft visible carbonation. The aroma is of fresh hay, grassy hops, grainy malt, and citrus. The taste starts mildly malty, with fresh grainy and grassy notes. This becomes tart, while the aftertaste is very light bitter. The beer has a light body, thin texture, and soft carbonation.

KASTEL

Country of Origin: *Bosnia* • **Brewery Founded:** *1873* • **Alcohol Content:** *4.7%*

Kastel is a pale lager brewed by the famous Bosnian brewery Banjalu ka Pivara. The beer pours with a golden body and a small head. The beer has a weak and grainy aroma. The flavor is a little acidic with tones of corn, grain, and honey malt. This is more pronounced toward the end.

NEKTAR PIVO

Country of Origin: *Bosnia* • **Brewery Founded:** *1873* • **Alcohol Content:** *5%*

Nektar Pivo is a dunkel beer brewed by Banjalu ka Pivara in Banja Luka, Bosnia. The brewery was founded in 1873 by Trappist monks. The beer is a clear amber-brown color with a big light brown, lasting head. The aroma has some caramel, roasted malt, herb, and grass notes. It has a light sweet caramel taste at the start, which turns into a moderate bitter aftertaste. The beer is medium bodied and oily with a soft carbonation.

BODEBROWN/STONE CACAU IPA

Country of Origin: *Brazil* • **Brewery Founded:** *2009* • **Alcohol Content:** *6.1%*

Cervejaria Bodebrown brew this India Pale Ale in Curitiba, Brazil . The beer pours clear amber with a big white head. The aromas are sweet, of cocoa, caramel, malt, pine, grapefruit, and hops. The taste is sweet cocoa, mixed with bitter herbs, caramel malts, bitter herbs, and pine hops. The body is quite fizzy. The beer is quite sweet for an India Pale Ale, where most of the sugars are fermented into alcohol.

BODEBROWN PERIGOSA IMPERIAL IPA

Country of Origin: *Brazil* • **Brewery Founded:** *2009* • **Alcohol Content:** *9.2%*

India Pale Ale is an American ale. The aroma is of citrus hops, passion fruit, and guava. The beer has a high bitterness. The beer is a copper color. It was developed in 2010 by Bodebrown Brewery in partnership with the Homebrewers, Paulo Cavalcanti, Rafael Samuel, and David Cavalcanti. Their Imperial IPA joins Bodebrown's line of extreme beers. The brew is the first Imperial IPA beer to be produced in Brazil.

BODEBROWN WEE HEAVY

Country of Origin: *Brazil* • **Brewery Founded:** *2009* • **Alcohol Content:** *8%*

Bodebrown's Wee Heavy is a classic Scotch ale. The brew is high in alcohol, and is full bodied with dominant residual malty sweetness. The beer's aromas are of malt and toast. The beer has a good bitterness and a medium/low body. The brew is a reddish copper color. Wee Heavy was one of the first beers from Bodebrown, and Brazil's first Scotch ale. The beer was awarded a Gold Medal at the Mondial de la Bière in Canada in 2011.

BOTTO BIER ZOONTJE

Country of Origin: *Brazil* • **Brewery Founded:** *Unknown* • **Alcohol Content:** *6.6%*

Botto Bier is a Brazilian microbrewery. Zoontje is a Belgian-style strong ale. The beer pours a deep red color with an off-white head. The aroma is of sweet malt, and fruits like tangerine, raisins, and plums. There are also notes of citrus, caramel, and dry hops. The taste is also of sweet malt, with plenty of fruit. The beer is full of notes of raisins and plums with some caramel and yeast with dry hoppy bitterness.

COLORADO DEMOISELLE

Country of Origin: *Brazil* • **Brewery Founded:** *1995* • **Alcohol Content:** *6%*

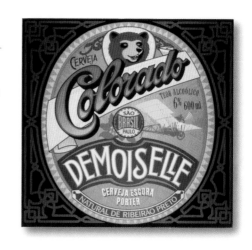

This beer is made with imported malts of the highest quality and the best Brazilian coffee from the Upper Mogiana region. The coffee is purchased directly from the producer, roasted, ground, and macerated in cold water. It is then added to the beer mash. The Demoiselle name is an homage to the great Brazilian Alberto Santos Dumont, whose family owned coffee plantations in the region of Ribeirão Preto.

COLORADO INDICA

Country of Origin: *Brazil* • **Brewery Founded:** *1995* • **Alcohol Content:** *7%*

This India Pale Ale pours a nice clear golden orange with some golden hues. It has a nice creamy white head. The aroma is fruity, with orange and a slight touch of caramel. The flavor is really balanced with an orangey and tea hoppiness. It also has caramel maltiness and a touch of toffee with a nutty finish. The beer has a medium to heavy mouth feel. It is a nice strong English ale.

COLORADO VINTAGE BLACK RAPADURA

Country of Origin: *Brazil* • **Brewery Founded:** *1995* • **Alcohol Content:** *10.5%*

Colorado was one of the first craft breweries founded in Brazil. Rather than trying to make copies of American beers, the brewery embraces its Brazilian heritage to make beers from special local ingredients. These include Brazilian coffee, unrefined cane sugar, cassava flour, honey, and Brazil nuts. Vintage Black Rapadura is a classic Imperial stout. The beer has a strong taste of sugar.

COLORADO VIXNU IMPERIAL IPA

Country of Origin: *Brazil* • **Brewery Founded:** *1995* • **Alcohol Content:** *9.5%*

Colorado's Vixnu Imperial IPA is an Imperial/Double IPA brewed by Cervejaria Colorado in Ribeirão Preto, Brazil. The beer pours a moderately hazy amber color with a dense cream head. The aromas are of grapefruit, tangerine, orange peel, lemongrass, peach, papaya, candied sugar, floral, light pine, caramel, bread, and a floral earthiness. The taste has all of these flavors with the addition of bread and floral earthiness. The beer has a medium carbonation and is medium bodied.

WALS DUBBEL

Country of Origin: *Brazil* • **Brewery Founded:** *1999* • **Alcohol Content:** *7.5%*

Wals Dubbel is a dark Belgian-style ale. The beer is dark brown in color and has a dense and durable foam. The beer has an aroma of dried fruit, with notes of spice and malt. The taste is slightly spicy and quite dry. The beer goes well with red meat, wild game, and fowl. It also complements chocolate desserts.

WALS PETROLEUM

Country of Origin: *Brazil* • **Brewery Founded:** *1999* • **Alcohol Content:** *12%*

Wals Petroleum is produced by one of Brazil's microbreweries. The beer is a Russian Imperial Stout. It is produced with several different types of dark grains. It has the deep velvety body of a liqueur. The beer has complex aromas of Belgian chocolate, coffee, caramel, and toffee. The beer also has a balanced bitterness.

WALS QUADRUPPEL

Country of Origin: *Brazil* • **Brewery Founded:** *1999* • **Alcohol Content:** *11%*

Wals Quadruppel is a Belgian-style strong ale, made with four types of malt, a noble strain of yeast, hopes, and several spices. The beer has a ruby brown color, a balanced bitterness, and velvety foam. It has an intense aroma and malt flavor. The beer is matured in French oak casks which have been marinated with rum.

WALS TRIPPEL

Country of Origin: *Brazil* • **Brewery Founded:** *1999* • **Alcohol Content:** *9%*

Wals Trippel is a strong Belgian-style ale. The beer is orange-colored with dense foam. It is made with malts, hops, yeast, coriander, orange peel, and other spices. The beer has citrus aromas, and has a fruity and spicy taste. The beer is a great partner for white meat, spicy sauces, blue cheese, and citrus desserts.

WAY BELGIAN DARK ROLLER COASTER IPA

Country of Origin: *Brazil* • **Brewery Founded:** *2011* • **Alcohol Content:** *6.2%*

The Way Brewery is a micro craft brewery located in the Brazilian pine forests. Way now manufactures five different beers; American Pale Ale, Lager Amburana, Cream Porter, and Irish Red Lager American Ale. Way Belgian Dark Roller Coaster IPA is a re-interpretation of this Trappist Belgian wheat beer.

WAY CREAM PORTER

Country of Origin: *Brazil* • **Brewery Founded:** *2011* • **Alcohol Content:** *5.6%*

The Way Cream Porter is a full bodied beer that is inspired by the Porters of the eighteenth century. These beers were reinforced to survive the long sea voyages across the Baltic Sea. The caramelized malt and toasted aromas are enriched with selected oats. These give the Porter Cream complexity and a unique creaminess. The dark colored beer has aromas reminiscent of coffee, chocolate, and dried fruit.

WAY DOUBLE AMERICAN PALE ALE

Country of Origin: *Brazil* • **Brewery Founded:** *2011* • **Alcohol Content:** *8.8%*

Like Way's American Pale Ale, their Double American Pale Ale is a high fermentation beer that takes caramelized malt and a double amount of hops imported from America (including Cascade, Citra, and Amarillo varieties). In addition, two dry hoppings are made to the fermentation of the beer. This guarantees a more intense aroma which is very characteristic of this beer. Way's Double American pale ale is a stronger version of the traditional American pale ale. These beers were first developed in the early 1980s, by American West Coast micro brewers. These pioneers used significant quantities of American hops in their experimental brews and were credited with constructing the first modern American ales. These beers were inspired by the robust pale ales brewed in the British breweries of London, Yorkshire, and Burton upon Trent. American versions of the style are often brewed with just malt rather than the malt and sugar combination common in British pale ales. They also feature the American-grown hop, Cascade. The style soon became popular. American Pale Ales are close in style to American India Pale Ales (IPAs), but IPAs are stronger and more assertively hopped than APAs. These are also close in style to amber ales, although these are darker and maltier.

CANADA

ALLEY KAT AMBER

Country of Origin: *Canada* • **Brewery Founded:** *1994* • **Alcohol Content:** *5%*

Alley Kat Amber is Alley Kat's version of the original London-style Brown Ale. Amber pours a nice reddish hue, accompanied with a nose of caramel malts and floral hops. Golding hops are used in this brown ale to give it that light floral hoppiness and slight bitterness. Brown ales like Alley Kat Amber are full bodied and tend to be slightly maltier and sweeter on the palate. They are typically made with darker roast and chocolate malts.

ALLEY KAT APRIKAT

Country of Origin: *Canada* • **Brewery Founded:** *1994* • **Alcohol Content:** *5%*

Aprikat, is an apricot flavored beer with a filtered wheat ale base. The beer is a Canadian twist on the traditional German style wheat ales. Alley Kat's style of wheat ale is brewed with 50% wheat, but fermented with the brewery's regular ale yeast. The result is a crisp, light, ale with the fresh aroma and flavor of apricots substituted for the banana and clove accents of a German wheat beer. Aprikat's subtle apricot aroma contrasts nicely with its big fruity mouth feel. The beer pours a nice straw color and its medium carbonation keeps it light and refreshing, perfect for a hot day or as an after dinner drink.

ALLEY KAT CHARLIE FLINT'S LAGER

Country of Origin: *Canada* • **Brewery Founded:** *1994* • **Alcohol Content:** *5%*

Alley Kat's lager is named after the famous Albertan brewing pioneer, Charles Flint. It is the brewery's first beer brewed with organic malts. The beer is a crisp and easy drinking European style lager. Brewed with Sterling hops and organic malts, Charles Flint's organic lager is extremely smooth. The lager is aged to perfection, staying in the brewery's tanks for a minimum of four weeks before being filtered and packaged. The result is a lager that provides a perfect dry finish with moderate maltiness and a lingering bitterness from the hops.

ALLEY KAT FULL MOON PALE ALE

Country of Origin: *Canada* • **Brewery Founded:** *1994* • **Alcohol Content:** *5%*

Alley Kat's Full Moon is a West Coast style pale ale that is both kettle hopped and dry hopped with Centennial and Cascades varieties. The hops provide this ale with a nice citrus-like taste to balance out the caramel malts. West Coast style pale ales are from a larger category of brews that are collectively known as American Pale Ale (APA). APA is a cleaner and slightly hoppier version of British Pale Ales brewed with North American hop varieties.

ALLEY KAT MAROON DRAGON

Country of Origin: *Canada* • **Brewery Founded:** *1994* • **Alcohol Content:** *7.5%*

Alley Kat's Maroon Dragon is a new single hopped Double IPA. It was released on October 1 2013. Brewed with Centennial hops, this Centennial hopped double IPA has floral and citrus aroma with notes of light malt and loads of citrus hop. Brewed in limited quantities, each Dragon brew is sold for only two months. Alley Kat Brewing Company was established by its co-owner Neil Herbst.

ALLEY KAT PUMPKIN PIE SPICED ALE

Country of Origin: *Canada* • **Brewery Founded:** *1994* • **Alcohol Content:** *5.4%*

September marks the return of Alley Kat's Pumpkin Pie Ale. This delicious full-bodied beer is infused with pumpkin, ginger and cinnamon. Pumpkin Pie Spiced Ale is like the season of Fall bottled! The beer is brewed with Northern Brewer hops, water, malt, yeast, real pumpkin, and spices.

BEAU'S ALL NATURAL BREWING COMPANY BEAVER RIVER

Country of Origin: *Canada* • **Brewery Founded:** *2006* • **Alcohol Content:** *5.6%*

Beau's Beaver River beer marries the typical flavor profiles of the British and American interpretations of an India Pale Ale. The brew blends a bold and yet balanced blend of hop bitterness, yeasty character, and citrus and earthy hop aromas. The origins of the India Pale Ale are as exciting as the flavors themselves. During Britain's occupation of India, British soldiers were guaranteed a ration of six pints of beer a day. However the beer would spoil on the long sea voyage to India, so brewers were forced to make a few adaptations to give the beer a better chance of surviving. The essential oils of the hop plant are a natural preservative, as is alcohol. To help the beer stay fresh for longer, it was brewed with more hops (which increased the bitterness of the beer), and at a higher strength. This also helped to keep the beer tasting balanced, as the extra malts needed to increase the level of alcohol added sweetness. The resulting beer was both strong and flavorful. The innovative pioneers of craft brewing in the United States and Canada began by brewing flavorful, high quality beer that was intended to provide an alternative to bland, mass produced beer. Inevitably, their experimentation led them to the traditional IPA style. They also began to use North American hops, which have a more assertive flavor and aroma. This led to the origination of the American-style IPA.

BEAU'S ALL NATURAL BREWING COMPANY BOG WATER GRUIT ALE

Country of Origin: *Canada* • **Brewery Founded:** *2006* • **Alcohol Content:** *6.6%*

The inspiration for Bog Water Gruit Ale came from the Alfred Bog, a 10,000 year old peat bog located in Eastern Ontario. The bog is home to many rare or endangered plants and animals. Like its namesake, the gruit style of beer is rare and endangered. Bog Water's malt and yeast profile is that of a Belgian Dubbel beer, with the addition of spice and fruit notes. Beau's also add an interesting twist to the beer: instead of hops they brew the beer with wild bog myrtle (which is also known as sweet gale). The result is a completely unique style of beer, an Eastern Ontario Gruit. Before the introduction of the Bavarian Purity Act of 1516, many herbs and spices were used to flavor and preserve beer. Bog myrtle (sweet gale) was one of the popular herbs used in brewing. While the purity laws had a positive effect on the quality of German beer, it also had the unfortunate consequence of destroying many traditional brews that used herbs as aromatics and preservatives. Bog Water is a spicy and fruity interpretation of the gruit style. It has a good malty taste, laced with a plum-like fruitiness that is offset by an earthy bitterness.

BEAU'S ALL NATURAL BREWING COMPANY FESTIVALE ALTBIER

Country of Origin: *Canada* • **Brewery Founded:** *2006* • **Alcohol Content:** *4.7%*

Eastern Ontario's outdoor festival season launches with the first long weekend in May, and so does Beau's our summer seasonal beer, Festivale Altbier. Beau's created this tasty, quaffable beer to enjoy at the many festivals and special fundraisers of the summer. Festivale is based on a rare German style of ale, know as Alt, or old, which refers to how long this style has been in existence. The beer originated from the northern part of the German Rhineland. Festivale is an amber ale, with balanced high-intensity maltiness and good hop presence. Caramunich malts give the beer Festivale its color and a rich caramel sweetness. Festivale bucks the trend of pale summer beers, offering up amber hues and tastiness for a unique result that is both quaffable and refreshing.

BEAU'S ALL NATURAL BREWING COMPANY HOGAN'S GOAT SPICED BOCK

Country of Origin: *Canada* • **Brewery Founded:** *2006* • **Alcohol Content:** *6.9%*

Beau's Hogan Goat Spiced Bock is one of their Wild Oats series of beer. This series is the brewery's attempt to explore the bold flavors and exciting aromas of different styles of beer. Hogan's Goat Spiced Bock is number 15 in the Wild Oats series. It is an experimental spiced beer. This amber bock-style beer with added rye malt is infused with peppermint, orange peel and juniper berries. The beer pours a deep orange. Its malty, sweet taste is given a pleasant cleansing lift from cooling peppermint and herbal juniper flavors. Light orange peel adds a citrus note to the flavor undertones. The beer would be an ideal accompaniment to traditional festive foods.

BEAU'S ALL NATURAL BREWING COMPANY LUG TREAD LAGERED ALE

Country of Origin: *Canada* • **Brewery Founded:** *2006* • **Alcohol Content:** *5.2%*

Available year-round, Beau's All Natural Lug Tread Lagered Ale is this organic brewery's award winning, flagship beer. In developing it, brewmaster Matthew O'Hara, aimed to produce a hand-crafted beer with a unique style and history. He had to use only natural ingredients and certified organic malts & hops to brew a beer that would be incredibly tasty and very drinkable. Beau's brew this tasty golden ale and then lager it to create a beer like nothing else in Ontario. Golden-hued, crisp, and finely balanced, Lug Tread is Beau's tribute to the classic beer of Cologne, Germany. The beer is top fermented (like an ale) and then cold aged (like a lager) for a lengthy period. This gives the beer some light ale notes complemented by a lager-like crispness. Lug Tread displays interwoven malt and hop flavors, subtle fruit flavors and has a crisp, lingering finish. It is the perfect year-round beer with thick, chewy malts to warm in the colder months and a refreshing, crisp finish to quench a summer's thirst. It is well suited for lighter foods like chicken, salads, salmon, seafood and bratwurst.

BEAU'S ALL NATURAL BREWING COMPANY NIGHT MARZEN OKTOBERFEST LAGER

Country of Origin: *Canada* • **Brewery Founded:** *2006* • **Alcohol Content:** *5.5%*

Märzen is the traditional Oktoberfest style of beer, and the brew is Beau's only regularly produced lager. This orangey-amber, malty beer has just the right amount of Noble hops to balance the Munich malts that Beau's uses to make the brew. Beau's first brewed Night Märzen in 2008 to welcome harvest time in Ontario, Canada. Their intention was to create a beer that reflected the tradition, heritage, and sense of promise that is felt in the local farming communities at that fruitful time of year. A small gathering to celebrate the harvest has now grown into Beau's annual Oktoberfest. Märzen is a traditional German lager style that takes its name from the month of March when it was historically brewed. The beer would then be lagered in cellars through the summer and then released for the local Oktoberfest celebrations. Beau's brew is bready and biscuity with a malt backbone complemented by a firm hop presence that lends balancing bitterness.

BEAU'S ALL NATURAL BREWING COMPANY OISEAU DE NUIT PUMPKIN GRUIT

Country of Origin: *Canada* • **Brewery Founded:** *2006* • **Alcohol Content:** *5.1%*

Beau's Oiseau de Nuit Pumpkin Gruit is one of their Wild Oats series of beer. This series is the brewery's attempt to explore the bold flavors and exciting aromas of different styles of beer. It is number 29 in the Wild Oats series. The beer was brewed in collaboration between Beau's and Seattle's Elysian Brewing. This pumpkin gruit, brewed without hops, has a similar malt base to Beau's award-winning fall seasonal, Night Märzen and the generous addition of pumpkin was inspired by the fall harvest. The Oiseau de Nuit collaboration blends Elysian's experience in producing pumpkin beers and Beau's experience in producing gruits together into one tasty beer. Malt and pumpkin blend harmoniously and provide medium body to this gruit, which displays restrained earthy, herbal bitterness. Floral and herbal aromatics are complemented by intriguing cumin spice notes.

BEAU'S ALL NATURAL BREWING COMPANY THE TOM GREEN BEER!

Country of Origin: *Canada* • **Brewery Founded:** *2006* • **Alcohol Content:** *5%*

Beau's All Natural Brewing Company and Canadian actor and comedian Tom Green have collaborated to create The Tom Green Beer! A milk stout, The Tom Green Beer! has flavors of chocolate and coffee, while delivering a creamy, velvety texture, and finishing with a mild sweetness. Milk stouts were first patented in 1907. The use of milk sugar helped with the popularity of the beer due to its nourishing attributes. The Tom Green Beer! is a slightly more robust interpretation of the style and showcases the appeal of a milk stout's silky mouth feel. The beer has a dark malt complexity with a complex aroma and roasted malt character, featuring notes of espresso and

chocolate. Roasted elements dominate the flavor, but it also has subtle notes of slightly burnt caramel, and nuts. The strength of both the flavour and aroma is contrasted by an approachable mouthfeel. The inital dryness of the beer is subdued by a gentle flourish of increased body and sweetness in the finish. The end result is a flavorful and robust stout.

BIG ROCK BREWERY ANTHEA WET HOP ALE 2013

Country of Origin: *Canada* • **Brewery Founded:** *1984* • **Alcohol Content:** *6%*

Anthea Wet Hop Ale is a very unusual brew, made with fresh hops taken straight from the vine. It is autumn orange in color and has a fresh and intense flavor of hops. Wet hop beers are only brewed once a year immediately after the annual hop harvest in late summer or early fall. This is unique because the fresh hops are a very delicate ingredient and once they are picked from the vine they have to be used as soon as possible in order to prevent them from spoiling. The result is an extraordinary seasonal brew. Only 3,600 numbered bottles were produced in 2013, and will be distributed in Alberta and British Columbia.

BIG ROCK BREWERY BLACK AMBER ALE

Country of Origin: *Canada* • **Brewery Founded:** *1984* • **Alcohol Content:** *6%*

Black Amber Ale is a stout, black in color with a deep amber hue. It is brewed using pale malt, a healthy dose of caramel and black malts, and two hop varieties. The result is a brew with the aromas of black malt, coffee, and chocolate. The brew is also hoppy in character. Big Rock's brew master Bernd has choreographed barley malt sugars in a delicate dance. He transformed some into spirits, others into texture, flavor and sweetness. In this beer, the sweetness is center stage.

BIG ROCK BREWERY GERSTEMEISTER MARZEN

Country of Origin: *Canada* • **Brewery Founded:** *1984* • **Alcohol Content:** *5.5%*

Gerstemeister Marzen is a deep golden color in the Marzen tradition. It is brewed with four different malts, Pale, Munich, Biscuit, and Vienna. Big Rock's brew master Paul Gautreau is a student of beer history. He culls the past for inspiration, and uses Big Rock's award-winning panache, quality ingredients, and careful craftsmanship to make some memorable beers. Marzen beer was traditionally brewed in March then cooled in caves to be savored in the fall. Two varieties of authentic German hops, Hallertau from Bavaria and Tettnanger from Baden-Württemberg, are woven into Big Rock's exquisite lager yeast. The end result has a true German flavor.

BIG ROCK BREWERY GRASSHOPPER WHEAT ALE

Country of Origin: *Canada* • **Brewery Founded:** *1984* • **Alcohol Content:** *5%*

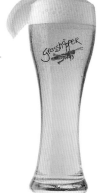

Grasshopper is a filtered wheat ale. Golden yellow in color, it is brewed with three types of pale and wheat malts. The beer is light on the palate, but packed with flavor and European hop aroma and notes of fruit and citrus. The beer was inspired by the wheat of the great Alberta prairie and is designed to be a Canadian wheat beer in the Belgian and German tradition. The beer was named after a grasshopper that met his end on Ed McNally's windshield.

BIG ROCK BREWERY HONEY BROWN LAGER

Country of Origin: *Canada* • **Brewery Founded:** *1984* • **Alcohol Content:** *5%*

Big Rock brew this honey beer as a dark lager, using a blend of pale and caramel malts. The slow lager maturation process develops the subtle molasses notes of the barley sugars. These are balanced a dry note of hops and a very light touch of Alberta honey. The first keg of the beer was brewed in 1998.

BIG ROCK BREWERY LIFE OF CHAI

Country of Origin: *Canada* • **Brewery Founded:** *1984* • **Alcohol Content:** *6%*

Big Rock's Life of Chai is a very unusual beer. Amber-colored spiced ale, the beer has a selection of very unusual ingredients: Galena and Willimette hops and nine spices including Masala Chai, rose petals, and strong cardamom. The beer is the newest jewel in Big Rock's collection. It is a complex yet whimsical blend of spices with a quartet of superlative malts. Everything combines to make a perfectly-balanced beer. The beer's carbonation is low, its mouth feel is a perfect medium, and the flavor is delightfully high. Life of Chai is the perfect blend of sensory stimulation and polished refreshment.

BIG ROCK BREWERY LIME LIGHT LAGER

Country of Origin: *Canada* • **Brewery Founded:** *1984* • **Alcohol Content:** *4%*

Big Rock's Lime Light Lager is a soft gold beer with a light body and a slight aroma and flavor of lime. The beer is made using smooth Alberta barley malt and the zest of citrus with malty notes and a touch of hops and natural lime essence. The beer is a marriage of the prairie sun and the Mexican sun. Brewer Ed McNally fell in love with the flavors of Mexico in the 1970s and this inspired Big Rock Lime.

BIG ROCK BREWERY MONKEY'S FIST ROYAL IPA

Country of Origin: *Canada* • **Brewery Founded:** *1984* • **Alcohol Content:** *7.5%*

Monkey's Fist is a Royal IPA (India Pale Ale). Amber in color, it is brewed from a variety of hop strains including Whitbread golding, East Kent Golding, Challenger, and Progress combined with a blend of Maris Otter barley and caramel malts. The result is a beer of a medium to full-bodied character with medium carbonation. The beer's flavors are rich and complex with spicy and earthy notes.

BIG ROCK BREWERY SAAZ REPUBLIC PILZ

Country of Origin: *Canada* • **Brewery Founded:** *1984* • **Alcohol Content:** *4.9%*

This light and crisp brew is made with authentic Czech Saaz hops that impart an earthy yet floral character balanced by a soft malty flavor. The beer has a distinct but mild bitterness on the front end followed by a slight hop middle and a clean, refreshing finish. Poured in a glass, SAAZ Republic Pilz has a dense, white head atop a golden yellow body. The beer was inspired by the creation of the first Pilsner beer created in Plzen, Bohemia in 1840.

BIG ROCK BREWERY SCOTTISH STYLE HEAVY ALE

Country of Origin: *Canada* • **Brewery Founded:** *1984* • **Alcohol Content:** *7%*

Big Rock's Scottish Style Heavy Ale is a lovely bronze color with toffee tones. The main ingredients of the brew are pale malt, caramel malt, peated malt, Munich malt, and hops. Brewed together, they combine into a beer of character, strong and full-bodied with a complex mix of toffee, caramel, vanilla, and a hint of peat. The beer is slowly aged in oak and emboldened with strong flavors.

BIG ROCK BREWERY TRADITIONAL ALE

Country of Origin: *Canada* • **Brewery Founded:** *1984* • **Alcohol Content:** *5%*

Big Rock Brewery's Traditional Ale is a brown ale in the English style, deep copper in color with flashes of garnet. The ale's three primary ingredients are three different varieties of hops, brewed with pale and black malts. The big character of this medium-bodied ale fills the mouth with a fusion of toasty malt and sweet caramel flavor. It has a creamy carbonation and has a mild, hoppy bitterness. The brew was inspired by brewery fonder Ed McNally and brew master Bernd Pieper.

BIG ROCK BREWERY WARTHOG

Country of Origin: *Canada* • **Brewery Founded:** *1984* • **Alcohol Content:** *4.5%*

Warthog is a brown ale that is a warm reddish brown in color. Big Rock's brew master blended the beer with roasted pale and caramel malts to bring out their hazelnut and chestnut flavors. This is balanced it with a generous measure of spicy, aromatic hops, giving the brew a bright personality. The ale has a crown of cream. Unlike its namesake, Warthog is a handsome ale that was first brewed in 1993.

CAMERON'S AMERICAN WHISKEY BARREL

Country of Origin: *Canada* • **Brewery Founded:** *1997* • **Alcohol Content:** *7.2%*

Cameron's American Whiskey Barrel brew was the very first offering of their oak-aged series of beers. The beer is aged in American whiskey barrels for months. Its complex character evokes notes of caramel, chestnut, strong malt, vanilla, subtle hops and of course, whiskey. It has a surprisingly smooth quality and goes well with barbequed food, a rich Holiday season turkey dinner. Of course, it can also be drunk by itself. The beer won the People's Choice Award at the 2012 Ontario Brewing Awards.

CAMERON'S AUBURN ALE

Country of Origin: *Canada* • **Brewery Founded:** *1997* • **Alcohol Content:** *5%*

Cameron's Auburn Ale is the brewery's most-awarded beer. Deliciously complex, this West Coast style ale uses an abundance of citrus and aromatic American hops. Named after its unique rich color, this beer offers a full body that evokes a multitude of different flavors. Watch for the generous hop aroma and smooth maltiness, followed by a deep smooth finish. Auburn Ale is a perfect complement for red meat, fish or a spicy food.

CAMERON'S CREAM ALE

Country of Origin: *Canada* • **Brewery Founded:** *1997* • **Alcohol Content:** *5%*

Cameron's Cream Ale is the beer that started the Cameron Brewery. Hailed by *Toronto Life* in 1998 as "best new beer of the year", this elegant golden ale is crisp, refreshing and balanced with a fruity backbone. It also has a strong malty taste and a clear British hop presence, but with a clean taste that is reminiscent of lager. The beer is brewed with two-row malted barley and specialty hops from the UK.

CAMERON'S DARK 266

Country of Origin: *Canada* • **Brewery Founded:** *1997* • **Alcohol Content:** *4.5%*

Cameron's Dark 266 is a rare breed of dark lager that was originally brewed as a one-off draught for one of Cameron's specialty beer bars. Specialty imported hops and dark malts result in a chestnut-colored lager with a wonderful lacy head. The result is a beer with the deliciousness of a North American Lager combined with the complexity of a German Schwarzbier (black beer).

CAMERON'S DEVIATOR DOPPELBOCK

Country of Origin: *Canada* • **Brewery Founded:** *1997* • **Alcohol Content:** *7.1%*

Cameron's Deviator Doppelbock is a Teutonic-inspired dark lager featuring imported German malt. Doppelbocks were originally served to the Bavarian monks during times of fasting as liquid bread. Deviator Doppelbock has a deep dark amber color. Its aroma is full of sweet toffee and caramel and its body brings out hints of coffee and freshly baked bread. The finish is deliciously complex with a full mouth feel, followed by lasting sweetness.

CAMERON'S DEVIATOR DOPPELBOCK BOURBON BARREL AGED

Country of Origin: *Canada* • **Brewery Founded:** *1997* • **Alcohol Content:** *8.6%*

Cameron's Deviator Doppelbock Bourbon Barrel Aged is a unique brew that is based on the brewery's previous award-winning Doppelbock. Doppelbocks are Teutonic-inspired dark lagers that feature imported German malt. This version of Cameron's Deviator Doppelbock has been aged for six months in Kentucky bourbon barrels. This process lends to a smooth, toasted vanilla notes, and layered upon the complex malty body. Chris Schryer, from *The Toronto Beer Blog*, described it as follows "This produced an aroma which is huge, with clear bourbon notes… vanilla and oaky but without significant alcohol heat. The bourbon is fragrant, but very much in the background. As the beer warms, everything becomes more pronounced, but especially the vanilla, which becomes an enticing perfume when poured into the glass. Just a magnificent beer, clean and complicated. Great as an after-dinner brew, or while sitting around a campfire."

CAMERON'S LAGER

Country of Origin: *Canada* • **Brewery Founded:** *1997* • **Alcohol Content:** *5%*

Cameron's Lager is pale golden in color. This European-style lager is brewed with noble hops. This term refers to traditional hop varieties that have low bitterness and high aroma and have been grown for hundreds of years. Only the finest two-row malted barley is used to brew the lager. Never rushed, this beer is fermented cold and long, to create a crisp, fresh beverage that is perfect for easy-drinking occasions. Amazingly, the beer was voted the best German Pilsner in the World in 2012.

CAMERON'S OBSIDIAN IMPERIAL PORTER

Country of Origin: *Canada* • **Brewery Founded:** *1997* • **Alcohol Content:** *9.2%*

Cameron's Obsidian Imperial Porter is the next beer in their successful oak-aged series of beers. Obsidian Imperial Porter is as dark and intriguing as the midnight sky. The beer is loaded with magnificent and robust flavor. Aged for seven months in Caribbean rum barrels, roasted malt and chocolate character abound in this velvety, nectarous ale. The beer won Bronze at the 2013 Ontario Brewing Awards.

CAMERON'S RESURRECTION ROGGENBIER

Country of Origin: *Canada* • **Brewery Founded:** *1997* • **Alcohol Content:** *5.2%*

Roggenbiers (rye beers) were declared illegal in 1516 with the passing of the Reinheitsgebot (Bavarian Purity Law). After a series of poor harvests, the use of rye was forbidden for use in brewing beer so that it could be reserved for making bread. Cameron have resurrected this lost style to create a very refreshing and smooth rye ale. Resurrection Roggenbier is brewed with a combination of German rye, malted wheat, and two-row barley and is fermented with a German Hefeweizen yeast strain to create a beer with hints of banana, clove, and light black pepper.

CAMERON'S RYE PALE ALE

Country of Origin: *Canada* • **Brewery Founded:** *1997* • **Alcohol Content:** *6.6%*

Cameron's Rye Pale Ale is one of the breweries year-round beers. It is made of a combination of seven different floral British and pungent American hops, some which are added in a dry hopping process. This involves adding hops directly to the fermented beer in the fermenter. The hops are well supported by a large malt bill of five character malts with a massive portion of rye which contributes to a rich mouth feel and Cameron's Rye Pale Ale's own special character.

CAMERON'S SIRIUS WHEAT ALE

Country of Origin: *Canada* • **Brewery Founded:** *1997* • **Alcohol Content:** *4.2%*

Cameron's Sirius Wheat Ale is an interpretation of the American wheat ale style. It is brewed with Canadian malted wheat and two-row malted barley, and the newest breeds specialty hops. This all-natural, unpasteurized, and unfiltered wheat ale has a distinct, citrusy aroma and a taste that is smooth and drinkable. The beer is light, rounded, thirst-quenching, and refreshing. Sirius Wheat Ale is a seasonal lager perfect for the warm days of fall.

CAMERON'S VERY SPECIAL PALE ALE COGNAC BARREL AGED

Country of Origin: *Canada* • **Brewery Founded:** *1997* • **Alcohol Content:** *7.7%*

Cameron's Very Special Pale Ale (VSPA) Cognac Barrel Aged is a unique, first-time creation for the brewery. Cameron's VSPA is aged for six months in French cognac barrels. This maturation process delivers a delicate fruity pear character and an oaky flavor derived from long aging in toasted barrels. Cameron's version of the pale ale style is brewed with warm fermentation with a predominantly British malt blend that is well balanced with specially imported hops. Cognac is a variety of brandy that must meet strict legal production requirements to carry the name. The brandy must be twice distilled in copper pot stills and be aged at least two years in French oak barrels from Limousin or Tronçais. Cognac matures in the same way as whiskies and wine when aged in barrels, and most cognacs are aged considerably longer than the minimum legal requirement. The resulting flavor that resides in the oak barrels has contributed to Cameron's VSPA Cognac Barrel Aged's spectacular taste.

CENTRAL CITY BREWING RED RACER EXTRA SPECIAL BITTER

Country of Origin: *Canada* • **Brewery Founded:** *2003* • **Alcohol Content:** *6.5%*

The use of crystal malt gives the Red Racer Extra Special Bitter its color and flavor profile. An original twist on the classic English bitter beer, ESB is brewed with hops from England's North West region. The beer is constructed with several malts including Maris Otter, Superior Pale Ale, and crystal malt, blended with the German Magnum, Horizon, Centennial, and Cascade varieties of hops. The beer is matured for five weeks.

CENTRAL CITY BREWING RED RACER IPA

Country of Origin: *Canada* • **Brewery Founded:** *2003* • **Alcohol Content:** *6.5%*

Central City Brewing has a range of Red Racer beers, including their India Pale Ale. IPAs were brewed to survive the long voyage from England to India during the British colonization. Part of this process was the addition of lots of hops to preserve the beer. Red Racer IPA has an intense hoppy aroma and a long lingering finish. The beer combines Maris Otter, Superior Pale Ale, Carastan, and Crystal malts with German Magnum, Centennial, Amarillo, and Simcoe hops to make this amber colored brew.

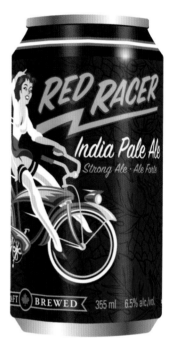

CENTRAL CITY BREWING RED RACER WHITE ALE

Country of Origin: *Canada* • **Brewery Founded:** *2003* • **Alcohol Content:** *5%*

Traditionally cloudy, this unfiltered Belgian-style white ale is brewed with coriander seed and dried orange peel to produce a beer with a light body and a refreshing citrus-spice aroma. The beer is brewed using malted wheat and Superior Pilsen malt, combined with Cascade hops to produce a pale yellow, opaque brew.

DIEU DU CIEL! ANNEDD'ALE

Country of Origin: *Canada* • **Brewery Founded:** *1998* • **Alcohol Content:** *4.4%*

Dieu du Ciel!'s Annedd'ale ale is an unusual brew flavored with light balsam fir. The beer was first brewed in May 2011. It is a blonde beer that is straw-colored and slightly cloudy with a delicate white foam. On the nose, the brew has hints of pine with a hint of lemongrass. With very little bitterness, Annedd'ale offers a silky texture on the palate, and is slightly resinous and spicy, with good malt sweetness. The beer is fermented with wild yeast.

DIEU DU CIEL! APHRODISIAQUE

Country of Origin: *Canada* • **Brewery Founded:** *1998* • **Alcohol Content:** *6.5%*

Dieu du Ciel!'s Aphrodisiaque beer is a stout with added cocoa and vanilla. This black ale has heady aromas and flavors of vanilla, dark chocolate, bourbon, and roasted malt. Surprisingly, the beer has a good balance. The beer is also quite hoppy, but the cocoa introduces some bitterness and it is not too sweet. This beer was first brewed in 2003.

DIEU DU CIEL! PECHE MORTEL

Country of Origin: *Canada* • **Brewery Founded:** *1998* • **Alcohol Content:** *9.5%*

Since the 1998 opening of the Dieu du Ciel! (God in heaven) brewery in Laurier Avenue, Montreal, its aim has been to brew original and satisfying beer. With high standards of employee welfare and respect for the environment, the brewery has become known for its innovative and creative attitude to quality beers, and brews a wide range of unique brews. Péché Mortel (French for "Mortal Sin") is an intensely black and dense beer with very pronounced roasted flavors. Fair trade coffee is added during the brewing process, intensifying the bitterness of the beer and giving it a powerful coffee taste. Péché Mortel is a stout style beer that is high in alcohol and bitterness. Historically stouts were brewed to support the long and arduous voyage necessary to export the beer from England to Russia. The word Imperial comes from the fact that the beer was specially brewed for the Russian court.

DIEU DU CIEL! SOLSTICE D'HIVER

Country of Origin: *Canada* • **Brewery Founded:** *1998* • **Alcohol Content:** *10.2%*

Solstice d'hiver (Winter Solstice) is a barley wine. This beer offers a complex aroma of fruit, alcohol, and hops. Its taste is slightly sweet and syrupy, with a hint of burnt caramel. It is very bitter, and has a profile of aromas and very fruity flavors. Solstice d'hiver is brewed once a year in July so that is can be matured for five to six months before being put on sale on December 21. This maturation is necessary to achieve an ideal balance between the pronounced bitterness and other flavors in the beer.

DRIFTWOOD CROOKED COAST AMBER ALE

Country of Origin: *Canada* • **Brewery Founded:** *2008* • **Alcohol Content:** *5.1%*

Driftwood's Crooked Coast Amber Ale was inspired by the original Alt-style beer of Dusseldorf, Germany. Crooked Coast brings together the aromas of German noble hops and Munich malt in a delicate malt-hop balance. The beer is great as an accompaniment to celery, fennel, parsnips, German-style sausages, and pork dishes.

DRIFTWOOD FARMHAND SAISON

Country of Origin: *Canada* • **Brewery Founded:** *2008* • **Alcohol Content:** *5.5%*

Driftwood's Farmhand Saison is the brewery's interpretation of the farmhouse ales of the southern region of Belgium. The beer is brewed with a partial sour-mash with the unusual addition of freshly ground black pepper. Driftwood uses a Belgian yeast to add further layers of spice to this rare style of beer. The beer is ideal drunk with walnuts, pecans, and ripe cheeses such as Trappist, Livarot, or Comte. It also complements beef, venison, and mussels.

DRIFTWOOD FAT TUG IPA

Country of Origin: *Canada* • **Brewery Founded:** *2008* • **Alcohol Content:** *7%*

Fat Tug is a northwest style India Pale Ale with an intense hop profile with notes of grapefruit, mango melon and passion fruit. Sufficient malt is there to provide support. The beer is available in government and private liquor outlets and is served on tap in select pubs and restaurants. The beer can be drunk as an aperitif, or with spicy and pungent dishes.

DRIFTWOOD PALE ALE

Country of Origin: *Canada* • **Brewery Founded:** *2008* • **Alcohol Content:** *5%*

Driftwood's Pale Ale has a dry and restrained malt character that allows the hops to shine through in this quintessential example of a beer style that Canada is famous for. Ideal food pairings for the beer are salads with plenty of bitter greens, grassy cheeses like Bleu d'Auvergne, Reblochon and Gruyere, and seafood.

DRIFTWOOD LUSTRUM WILD SOUR ANNIVERSARY ALE

Country of Origin: *Canada* • **Brewery Founded:** *2008* • **Alcohol Content:** *9.4%*

Driftwood is an independent brewery located in British Columbia, Canada. Lustrum Wild Sour Anniversary Ale is an American Wild Ale that was launched to commemorate Driftwood's fifth anniversary (or Lustrum).   Aged for over a year in French Oak barrels, this blood red beer has an amazing depth of color, flavor and aroma. The beer is fermented with locally sourced wild yeast and copious black currants.

DRIFTWOOD SARTORI HARVEST IPA

Country of Origin: *Canada* • **Brewery Founded:** *2008* • **Alcohol Content:** *7%*

This wet hopped India Pale Ale can only be brewed once a year, immediately following the hop harvest, when fresh wet Centennial hops are brought from the Sartori Cedar Ranch near Chilliwack, British Columbia to the Driftwood brewery. Centennial wet hops have a very unique and rich profile that is allowed to shine through the 100% Canadian malt base used to brew the beer.

DRIFTWOOD WHITE BARK WITBIER

Country of Origin: *Canada* • **Brewery Founded:** *2008* • **Alcohol Content:** *5%*

This traditional Belgian-style wheat ale is brewed with the addition of freshly ground coriander and curacao orange peel. Hops are outshone by the wonderful floral aromas that dominate the nose of this dry and quaffable beer. Gastronomically, the beer is a great accompaniment to duck, goose, and port, Thai and Indian curries, sweet potatoes, carrots, ginger, and bell peppers.

FLYING MONKEYS CRAFT BREWERY HOPTICAL ILLUSION ALMOST PALE ALE

Country of Origin: *Canada* • **Brewery Founded:** *2008* • **Alcohol Content:** *5%*

The Flying Monkeys Craft Brewery is locally run by a small group of beer lovers in the heart of downtown Barrie. Their goal is to brew edgy brews and creative ales for Ontario beer lovers, and to keep the microbrewery revolution going. Hoptical Illusion is an American pale ale but is hoppier than most commercial beers. The beer's main aroma is of the privately grown Amarillo hop. Beyond the provocative citrus and floral essences of the hop is a subtle but unique maltiness blended from amber kiln and roasted specialty malts.

FORT GARRY BREWING COMPANY DARK ALE

Country of Origin: *Canada* • **Brewery Founded:** *1930* • **Alcohol Content:** *5%*

Fort Garry's Dark Ale is a chestnut colored English Mild Ale that boasts caramel, coffee, and chocolate flavors and has a balanced hop finish. The beer has excellent drinkability and pairs well with hard cheeses.

FORT GARRY BREWING COMPANY FRONTIER ORIGINAL PILSENER

Country of Origin: *Canada* • **Brewery Founded:** *1930* • **Alcohol Content:** *5%*

Fort Garry's iconic Frontier Original Pilsener was first brewed in 1930. Frontier Pilsener is a classic North American lager made with premium two-row Canadian barley and Pacific Northwest hops. It is one of the Fort Garry Classics. The beer pours a cloudy gold color, and its aromas are malty and sweet and the flavor is not as bitter as many pilseners.

FORT GARRY BREWING COMPANY PALE ALE

Country of Origin: *Canada* • **Brewery Founded:** *1930* • **Alcohol Content:** *5%*

Fort Garry's IPA is a refreshing amber hued British Ale with a clean hoppy character. The beer is one of the Fort Garry Brewing Company Classics. The company was established in 1930 by B.W. Hoeschen. At that time, the company produced two brands: Frontier Beer and Frontier Stout.

FORT GARRY BREWING COMPANY PORTAGE AND MAIN IPA

Country of Origin: *Canada* • **Brewery Founded:** *1930* • **Alcohol Content:** *6.5%*

The Fort Garry Brewing Company is Manitoba's oldest microbrewery, having been established in 1930. The brewery's recipes and brewing techniques have been passed down through the generations. Fort Garry uses only the finest raw ingredients to brew their fine ales and lagers. Portage and Main IPA is one of Garry's Brewmaster Series beers. This is a group of limited edition small-batch beers that explore the boundaries of craft beer making. The beer is a West Coast-style India Pale Ale, brewed with high quality malted barley, and whole West Coast and Manitoba flower hops. The brew has a solid body and a strong, refreshing aroma of citrus fruits.

FORT GARRY BREWING COMPANY ROUGE

Country of Origin: *Canada* • **Brewery Founded:** *1930* • **Alcohol Content:** *5%*

Fort Garry's Rouge is an amber ale brewed by them in Winnipeg, Canada. The beer is amber in color and has a strong carbonation. The beer has aromas of caramel malt, burnt sugar, and wet grains. The beer's flavors are a mix of caramel sweetness and more wet grain. The beer has a mouth coating of sweetness.

FORT GARRY BREWING COMPANY ST. NICK'S PORTER

Country of Origin: *Canada* • **Brewery Founded:** *1930* • **Alcohol Content:** *6.5%*

St. Nick's Porter is one of Fort Garry's Brewmaster series of beers. These are limited edition small-batch beers that explore the boundaries of craft beer making. This festive porter is designed to warm up the frostiest of winter nights. The beer is spiked with cinnamon, nutmeg, and all-spice and then aged on oak chips that give it a subtle vanilla flavor and aroma.

GARRISON BREWING COMPANY BLACKBERRY WHEAT ALE

Country of Origin: *Canada* • **Brewery Founded:** *1997* • **Alcohol Content:** *4.6%*

The seasonal Blackberry Wheat ale perfectly balances refreshment with natural fruit flavors. The beer is light amber in color and crisp in body, perfect with earthy cheeses such as Camembert, Fontina, salads, and poultry. The all-natural beer is brewed with 2-row pale, wheat, and dextrin malts and Pilgrim hops.

GARRISON BREWING COMPANY GLUTENBERG BLONDE

Country of Origin: *Canada* • **Brewery Founded:** *1997* • **Alcohol Content:** *4.5%*

Garrison's Glutenberg Blonde is a completely gluten-free ale brewed from millet. The beer has notes of floral hops, white pepper, and has aromas of lemon zest. The beer is constructed without any malt, just raw millet and corn grits, and Styrian Golding and Northern Brewer hops. The beer won Bronze at the 2012 World Beer Cup.

GARRISON BREWING COMPANY GRAND BALTIC PORTER

Country of Origin: *Canada* • **Brewery Founded:** *1997* • **Alcohol Content:** *9%*

Garrison's traditional Grand Baltic Porter is based on a beer style that was originally brewed in the Baltic Sea countries. Although the beer is derived from the later English porters, it was also influenced by Russia's imperial stouts. The beer is brewed with two malts, roasted barley, molasses, and brown sugar with German Spalt hops. This is one of Garrison's seasonal brews.

GARRISON BREWING COMPANY HARVEST WHEAT ALE

Country of Origin: *Canada* • **Brewery Founded:** *1997* • **Alcohol Content:** *4.7%*

Garrison's harvest Wheat Ale is a refreshingly smooth North American style wheat ale, brewed with 40% wheat malt for a light bodied and a deliciously tart and fruity finish. Garrison suggests drinking the beer garnished with a slice of lemon. The beer is brewed with 2-row pale, wheat, and dextrin malts and Pilgrim hops.

GARRISON BREWING COMPANY HOPYARD PALE ALE

Country of Origin: *Canada* • **Brewery Founded:** *1997* • **Alcohol Content:** *5.3%*

Garrison's Hopyard Pale Ale is a deep golden, medium bodied and nicely bitter brew, brewed in the classic West Coast style. The beer is generously hopped in the boil and dry-hopped to produce a fruity and floral aroma with a refreshingly bitter finish. The beer is made with 2-row pale and Crysal malts combined with Nugget, Amarillo, and Cascade hops.

GARRISON BREWING COMPANY IMPERIAL IPA

Country of Origin: *Canada* • **Brewery Founded:** *1997* • **Alcohol Content:** *7%*

The Garrison Brewing Company has been brewing in Halifax, Nova Scotia since 1997. Since the first brewery opened there in 1754, Halifax has always been at the center of the Canadian Maritime brewing tradition. Garrison produces premium ales of distinction for the local market. Imperial IPA was launched in 2007 and is now known as the hoppiest beer in Atlantic Canada.

GARRISON BREWING COMPANY IRISH RED ALE

Country of Origin: *Canada* • **Brewery Founded:** *1997* • **Alcohol Content:** *5%*

This classic beer style was inspired by centuries of Celtic brewing tradition. It is constructed from specially kilned malts such as dark caramel and Munich. These malts dominate Garrison's Irish Red, resulting in a ruby red color and a smooth malty taste.

GARRISON BREWING COMPANY MARTELLO STOUT

Country of Origin: *Canada* • **Brewery Founded:** *1997* • **Alcohol Content:** *4.8%*

Garrison's Martello Stout is one of Garrison's seasonal brews. The beer is a bold and unfiltered ale characterized by heavily roasted malts that give this dark brew its essential character. Martello Stout is made with six malts including black, chocolate, and dark caramel malts. It is brewed with Fuggle and Pilgrim hops.

GARRISON BREWING COMPANY NUT BROWN ALE

Country of Origin: *Canada* • **Brewery Founded:** *1997* • **Alcohol Content:** *5%*

This ale-style beer is a traditional ale that is modeled on the rich, dark brews of southern England. The beer is constructed from specialty malts such as chocolate, caramel, and black patent blended with 2-row pale malt and Pilgrim hops. The beer is a deliciously flavorful dark beer like those popular in early Nova Scotia.

GARRISON BREWING COMPANY OKTOBERFEST BRAU

Country of Origin: *Canada* • **Brewery Founded:** *1997* • **Alcohol Content:** *4.9%*

This seasonal lager-style beer is based on Germany's iconic Oktoberfest beer, which is brewed in the traditional Marzen style of the famous march beers. The brew has lovely toffee-like flavors, with a medium body, and low hopping. Garrison brews the beer with Munich malts and German Brewers Gold hops.

GARRISON BREWING COMPANY RASPBERRY WHEAT ALE

Country of Origin: *Canada* • **Brewery Founded:** *1997* • **Alcohol Content:** *4.6%*

Garrison's Raspberry Wheat Ale is a golden amber brew infused with all-natural raspberry flavor. The beer has a crisp, refreshing taste that is perfect for year-round drinking. The beer is made with 2-row pale, wheat, and dextrin malts, combined with Pilgrim hops.

GARRISON BREWING COMPANY SPRUCE BEER

Country of Origin: *Canada* • **Brewery Founded:** *1997* • **Alcohol Content:** *7.5%*

Garrison's Spruce Beer is a strong ale brewed in the style of North America's oldest beer. It is brewed with local spruce and fir tips, three different malts, oat flakes, dates, molasses, and Citra hops. Dark amber and brown in color, the beer has an unusual aroma of spruce boughs, caramel malts, molasses, and dates. The beer had a medium bitterness.

GARRISON BREWING COMPANY SUGAR MOON MAPLE ALE

Country of Origin: *Canada* • **Brewery Founded:** *1997* • **Alcohol Content:** *7%*

Sugar Moon Maple Ale is a truly Canadian ale brewed with Nova Scotia syrup from the Sugar Moon farms. This term was originally coined by Native Americans for the sugaring season, and this is certainly a beer to be enjoyed under a cold summer moon. The beer is made with four different malt and Millenium and Willamette hops.

GARRISON BREWING COMPANY TALL SHIP AMBER ALE

Country of Origin: *Canada* • **Brewery Founded:** *1997* • **Alcohol Content:** *4.6%*

Tall Ship Amber is a refreshing premium ale. Golden-amber in color, the beer has a light maltiness, a crisp hoppy aroma, and a smooth clean finish. It is made from 2-row pale, caramel, and dextrin malts combined with Fuggle and Pilgrim hops. The beer celebrates the proud nautical history of the Canadian Maritime.

GARRISON BREWING COMPANY TILFORD'S NIT-WIT

Country of Origin: *Canada* • **Brewery Founded:** *1997* • **Alcohol Content:** *4.8%*

This Belian-style Witbier (wheat beer) is named in honor of Scott Tilford, the winner of the 2010 Ultimate Brew-Off. Garrison has scaled up the brewing process to brew this tasty Belgian Witbier for general enjoyment. The beer is brewed with German Hallertau and Cascade hops. The beer won Silver at the 2012 Canadian Brewing Awards.

GARRISON BREWING COMPANY WINTER WARMER

Country of Origin: *Canada* • **Brewery Founded:** *1997* • **Alcohol Content:** *6.8%*

This seasonal brew is a strong dark amber beer, brewed with spices evocative of the holiday season. Garrison brews the beer with 2-row pale, Munich, caramel, and chocolate malts and brown sugar, combined with Brewers Gold hops. The beer has a low bitterness. The beer won Silver at the 2010 World Beer Championships.

GREAT LAKES BREWERY CRAZY CANUCK PALE ALE

Country of Origin: *Canada* • **Brewery Founded:** *1987* • **Alcohol Content:** *5.2%*

Great Lakes Brewery is independently owned by the Bulut family. The brewery makes beers in the traditional way using an open fire, copper brew house that was built in Germany in the early 1900s. Their small-batch brewing process allows them to blend local fine ingredients to produce award-winning beers. Crazy Canuck Pale Ale is the brewery's version of a west coast pale ale. The result is a wildly hoppy aroma with a lingering bitterness complemented by a soft bready malt flavor.

GREAT LAKES BREWERY DEVIL'S PALE ALE

Country of Origin: *Canada* • **Brewery Founded:** *1987* • **Alcohol Content:** *6%*

Released in the fall of 2006, Devil's Pale Ale was the brewery's first seasonal ale. A favorable reception prompted Great Lakes to make it available all year long both on draught and in cans. Brewed with six select malts and four premium hops, the beer has a rich mahogany color, reminiscent of early English pale ales. The wonderful hoppy aroma is revealed even before the first sip, and is followed by a hearty malty body. The flavor culminates with a pronounced bitterness.

GREAT LAKES BREWERY GOLDEN HORSESHOE LAGER

Country of Origin: *Canada* • **Brewery Founded:** *1987* • **Alcohol Content:** *5%*

Golden Horseshoe Premium Lager was Great Lakes Brewery's first brew. Initially, the beer was only available on draught in the Toronto area. Great Lakes's extended aging process results in a lager with an incredibly smooth and refreshing taste with little bitterness or aftertaste. The beer is great for the warm weather or for those who prefer a light bodied beer. This premium golden lager is thirst-quenching and flavorful. Golden Horseshoe is a perfect companion to lighter fare, such as fish or salads, or spicy dishes like wings or sausages. I

GREAT LAKES BREWERY GREEN TEA ALE

Country of Origin: *Canada* • **Brewery Founded:** *1987* • **Alcohol Content:** *4.2%*

Great Lakes brews Green Tea Ale in the spring. The beer is handcrafted with specialty malts and hops and is flavored with selected Organic Gunpowder Green Tea and fresh Ontario-grown ginseng. These unusual ingredients are added directly to the brew. The beer has a green and slightly herbal flavor that is reminiscent of the green leaves of spring. The brew is a good pairing for lobster, pad Thai, spring rolls, and sesame chicken.

GREAT LAKES BREWERY ORANGE PEEL ALE

Country of Origin: *Canada* • **Brewery Founded:** *1987* • **Alcohol Content:** *5.3%*

In their quest to offer the most flavorful and unique beers possible, Great Lakes brewed their Orange Peel Ale as a seasonal beer for the spring and summer. The beer is handcrafted with five specialty malts and five varieties of hops, along with just a touch of honey. Great Lakes add heaps of fresh oranges and peels into the boil. Orange Peel Ale balances the unique flavor of oranges with generous amounts of hops to achieve a slightly fruity and refreshing taste. The beer won the People's Choice Award in the fruit beer category at the 2008 Ontario Brewing Awards.

GREAT LAKES BREWERY PUMPKIN ALE

Country of Origin: *Canada* • **Brewery Founded:** *1987* • **Alcohol Content:** *5.5%*

In Great Lakes's avowed intent to offer the most flavorful and unique beers possible, the company brews this tasty autumn ale. Handcrafted with an assortment of specialty malts and hops, the brewery adds a generous amount of pumpkin directly into the brew. This is combined this with hints of cinnamon, clove, nutmeg, and allspice. The beer is rich, satisfying, and slightly spicy. This seasonal ale goes perfectly with desserts.

GREAT LAKES BREWERY RED LEAF

Country of Origin: *Canada* • **Brewery Founded:** *1987* • **Alcohol Content:** *5%*

Great Lakes Smooth Red Lager has hints of caramel, nuts, and toasted malt. This results in a fully flavored and yet deceptively smooth lager. A well balanced body makes Red Leaf a perfect year-round beer. The beer is an ideal match with burgers, stews, sandwiches and similar fare.

GREAT LAKES BREWERY WINTER ALE

Country of Origin: *Canada* • **Brewery Founded:** *1987* • **Alcohol Content:** *6.2%*

Inspired by the long, cold and seemingly endless Canadian winter, Great Lakes's Winter Ale is a true winter warmer. Handcrafted with specialty hops and malts, which are combined with generous amounts of cinnamon, honey, ginger and orange peel, this unique beer is brimming with flavor. Winter Ale is a seasonal beer that is only available in the chilly months of the year. The beer won the Gold medal at the 2008 Canadian Brewing Awards in the Honey/Maple lager/ale category.

KISSMEYER BEER NORDIC PALE ALE

Country of Origin: *Canada* • **Brewery Founded:** *2010* • **Alcohol Content:** *5.6%*

Kissmeyer Nordic Pale Ale is an imaginative interpretation of the Pale Ale style and features a unique northern-inspired medley of ingredients. Sweet gale, yarrow, dried heather flowers, rose hips, and cranberries comprise its balanced fruit-and-herb bouquet, while a maple syrup addition rounds out the complex character of the beer. The Nordic pale ale features intricate herbal nuance, moderate hop presence, pleasant dryness, and a crisp finish. Described as a one-man gypsy brewing company, Kissmeyer Beer creates innovative beers with a distinct personal and unique character, brewed to an exemplary degree of technical quality, inspired by and often brewed in collaboration with world-class brewer friends and colleagues. Nordic Pale Ale is a pioneering style for micro brewery Kissmeyer, intended to fuse the best in modern brewing techniques with ingredients that reflect Nordic and Canadian traditions.

LABATT 50

Country of Origin: *Canada* • **Brewery Founded:** *1847* • **Alcohol Content:***5%*

John and Hugh Labatt, grandsons of Labatt founder John K. Labatt, launched Labatt 50 in 1950 to commemorate 50 years of partnership. The beer was the first light-tasting ale introduced in Canada, It was Canada's best-selling beer until 1979 when, with the increasing popularity of lagers, it was surpassed by Labatt Blue. Labatt 50 is fermented using special ale yeast, which Labatt have used since 1933. Specially-selected North American hops and a good balance of dryness, complemented by a fruity taste, provide Labatt 50 with all the distinguishing features of true ale.

LABATT ALEXANDER KEITH'S DARK ALE

Country of Origin: *Canada* • **Brewery Founded:** *1847* • **Alcohol Content:** *5%*

Labatt's Alexander Keith's Dark Ale is based on the authentic recipe from Alexander Keith's brewery dating back to the late 1800s. Keith's Dark Ale is crafted using roasted specialty malts to create a dark mahogany colored ale with distinctive notes of chocolate and coffee. This smooth tasting dark beer is brewed to the same uncompromising standards as all Alexander Keith's fine beers.

LABATT ALEXANDER KEITH'S INDIA PALE ALE

Country of Origin: *Canada* • **Brewery Founded:** *1847* • **Alcohol Content:** *5%*

Alexander Keith's India Pale Ale is now Nova Scotia's most popular beer. The brew is fully fermented and mellow-aged for smoothness. It is made with balanced North American flavor and bittering hops to create a unique, malty flavor. Alexander Keith's India Pale Ale is a smooth beer with a slightly floral hop character and a sweet flavorful taste.

LABATT ALEXANDER KEITH'S PREMIUM WHITE

Country of Origin: *Canada* • **Brewery Founded:** *1847* • **Alcohol Content:** *5%*

From the first glimpse of the intriguing cloudy appearance to the surprisingly crisp finish, it's obvious that this isn't your typical white beer. A new addition to Labatt's Alexander Keith's selection, this unfiltered ale is best enjoyed with a slice of orange for a uniquely refreshing, subtly citrus taste. Brew master Alexander Keith began brewing operations in Halifax, Nova Scotia in 1920 and Labatt acquired the business in 1971.

LABATT ALEXANDER KEITH'S RED AMBER ALE

Country of Origin: *Canada* • **Brewery Founded:** *1847* • **Alcohol Content:** *5%*

Alexander Keith's Red Amber Ale is a smooth, well-balanced beer. It is dark amber in color with rich, red overtones. Brewed to the exacting standards first laid out by Alexander Keith in his Halifax, Nova Scotia brewery 185 years ago, Red Amber Ale is rich in every sense of the word: rich in color, rich in heritage, and rich in taste.

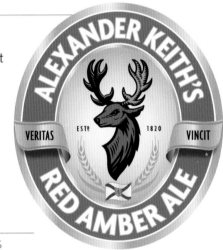

LABATT BLUE

Country of Origin: *Canada* • **Brewery Founded:** *1847* • **Alcohol Content:** *4.9/5%*

Labatt Blue is a pilsner-style Lager and is the best-selling Canadian beer in the world. Introduced in 1951 as Labatt Pilsner, the beer was named for the color of its label by fans of the Winnipeg Blue Bombers football team. Blue was the first beer brand in Canada to have a twist-off cap. The beer won the silver medal in the International Lager category at the 1998 *Brewing Industry International Awards*. Labatt Blue, is brewed with specially selected aromatic hops, to produce a well-balanced, fully matured, full-flavored beer with a fruity character and a slightly sweet aftertaste.

LABATT BUSCH

Country of Origin: *Canada* • **Brewery Founded:** *1847* • **Alcohol Content:** *4.7%*

Labatt Busch is a popular American-style lager that was first introduced back in 1955. Busch is brewed, fermented, and aged to create a smooth, refreshing taste that has just 133 calories. The beer reflects Labatt's development of national domestic beer brands that are respected across Canada for their refreshment and value.

LABATT EXTRA DRY

Country of Origin: *Canada* • **Brewery Founded:** *1847* • **Alcohol Content:** *5.5%*

Labatt Extra Dry was the first national launch of a new dry beer in Canada. Labatt Extra Dry is mashed longer than regular beers to leave less carbohydrate in the finished product, giving a lighter flavor with little aftertaste. Labatt was first founded by John Kinder in 1847 just a few years after arriving in Canada from Ireland.

LABATT GENUINE LAGER

Country of Origin: *Canada* • **Brewery Founded:** *1847* • **Alcohol Content:** *5%*

Originally introduced in 1992, Labatt's Genuine Lager has evolved into a truly definitive Canadian Lager. Balancing a blend of quality aromatic and bittering hops with a medium body, Genuine Lager is a smooth, refreshing and easy-drinking beer with a subtle hop aroma and a hint of malty sweetness in its pleasant flavor.

LABATT ICE

Country of Origin: *Canada* • **Brewery Founded:** *1847* • **Alcohol Content:** *5.6%*

Labatt Ice, introduced in 1993, was the world's first ice-brewed beer and the most successful new brand introduction in Canadian brewing history. Labatt Ice is a fully fermented strong beer that is allowed to mature at cold temperatures. Labatt Ice uses selected North American hops to develop its smooth and full flavour.

LABATT KOKANEE

Country of Origin: *Canada* • **Brewery Founded:** *1847* • **Alcohol Content:** *5%*

Kokanee beer has been brewed at the Columbia Brewery in Creston, British Columbia since 1959. In 1974, the brewery was taken over by the Labatt Brewing Company. Kokanee is a light, pilsner-style beer that is the best seller in British Columbia. Naturally aged, the beer is marketed for its glacier-fresh taste. The beer is constructed from mountain spring water, three varieties of malt, and a blend of North American hops.

LES BRASSEURS DU NORD BORÉALE 25

Country of Origin: *Canada* • **Brewery Founded:** *1988* • **Alcohol Content:** *6.1%*

Boréale 25 is a limited edition beer brewed to celebrate the brewery's 25th anniversary. The brew is wheat beer packed with flavor, perfect to enjoy in the summer sun. The ale is both bright and cloudy. With its abundant, clinging, white head, candied orange aroma, and smooth wheat taste, Boréale 25 offers an exceptional sensory experience. 25 is an all-natural ale brewed from superior ingredients: pale and caramel malts, raw Québec wheat, hops, coriander, and orange zest. The flavor has a high degree of carbonation. This ale is unfiltered and unpasteurized to preserve its unique taste. The beer should be served well-chilled at 40 degrees fahrenheit. Boréale 25 is the perfect complement to summer dishes, such as salmon tartar or chicken teriyaki. It also enhances the flavor of various cheeses, including the Quebec cheese Ménestrel. Boréale 25 also stands out when paired with after-dinner bitter orange chocolates

LES BRASSEURS DU NORD BORÉALE BLANCHE

Country of Origin: *Canada* • **Brewery Founded:** *1988* • **Alcohol Content:** *4.2%*

Boréale Blanche was first brewed in 2004. With its notes of citrus and spices, Boréale Blanche is a velvety, easy-drinking ale of wheat, oats and malted barley. The brewery bottles it unfiltered to preserve its natural cloudy appearance. You can bring the lees into suspension by turning the bottle gently upside down before serving. The beer is an all-natural ale brewed from superior ingredients: water, wheat, malted barley, oats, hops, yeast, zest of orange, coriander, and other spices. A treat on any occasion, Boréale Blanche is best served well-chilled at around 6° centigrade. Blonde is delicious with a wedge of orange. The beer complements white meat or fish, enhances the flavors of sushi.

LES BRASSEURS DU NORD BORÉALE BLONDE

Country of Origin: *Canada* • **Brewery Founded:** *1988* • **Alcohol Content:** *4.5%*

Boreale Blonde has been brewed from 1990 for lovers of pale beers with character. Refreshing and flavorful, Boréale Blonde is an excellent introduction for newcomers to specialty beers. Its crisp velvety taste harmonizes the bitter notes of the hops with the mellowness of the malt. It is an all-natural ale brewed from superior ingredients: water, pale malt of two-row barley, caramel malt, hops, and yeast. The beer won the Gold Medal for North American-style blonde/golden ale at the 2012 Canadian Brewing Awards. The beer is a beer for all occasions. It is best served well-chilled at 40 degrees fahrenheit.

LES BRASSEURS DU NORD BORÉALE CUIVRÉE

Country of Origin: *Canada* • **Brewery Founded:** *1988* • **Alcohol Content:** *6.9%*

Boréale Cuivrée is perfect for fans of strong beers such as Belgian beer. It was first introduced in 1993 as Boréale Forte. A strong ale, Boréale Cuivrée is the one Boréale that is just as enjoyable well-chilled as at cellar temperature. A smooth, richly flavored beginning of caramel and fruit gives way to riffs of bitterness, alcohol, and heat. Cuvree is an all-natural ale brewed from superior ingredients: water, a double ration of pale malt from two-row barley and of caramel malts, hops, and yeast. The brewery suggest two ways of serving the beer, well-chilled at 40 degrees fahrenheit to bring out its bitter side, or allow it to warm a few degrees to around 55 degrees fahrenheit to accentuate its mellow and fruity character. The beer is an excellent foil for full-flavored fine cheeses.

LES BRASSEURS DU NORD BORÉALE DORÉE

Country of Origin: *Canada* • **Brewery Founded:** *1988* • **Alcohol Content:** *4.8%*

Boreale Doree has been brewed since 1999. The beer is ideal for lovers of light, refreshing beers. Silky but not sweet, Boréale Dorée is an easy-drinking ale of complex flavors resulting from the fermentation of Quebec honey in addition to malt sugars. The beer is an all-natural ale brewed from superior ingredients: water, pale malt, roasted barley, hops, yeast, and honey. The beer won the Silver Medal in the special honey/maple lager or ale at the Canadian Brewing Awards of 2012.

LES BRASSEURS DU NORD BORÉALE IPA

Country of Origin: *Canada* • **Brewery Founded:** *1988* • **Alcohol Content:** *6.2%*

Boréale IPA is an amber-colored brew brimming with hops that will make your pallet discover the characteristic bitterness of hops, as well as its floral aromas. Upon tasting, this bitterness blends beautifully with the delicate malt flavors and alcohol to produce a complex yet integrated beer. This India Pale Ale is unfiltered in order to maintain maximum flavor. Boreale's IPA is an all-natural beer brewed from superior-quality ingredients: water, malted barley, hops, and yeast. More hops are added in a final dry-hopping stage. This ale features a consistent and bitter flavor, which complements spicy and savory dishes.

LES BRASSEURS DU NORD BORÉALE NOIRE

Country of Origin: *Canada* • **Brewery Founded:** *1988* • **Alcohol Content:** *5.5%*

Pioneers in the renaissance of the brewer's art, Laura Urtnowski, Bernard Morin, and Jean Morin were still in their twenties when they founded Les Brasseurs du Nord. As students, they had perfected their own beer recipe. The homebrew met with such success, that they decided to start a brewery. Les Brasseurs du Nord is now one of Quebec's leading microbreweries. Boreale Noire was first brewed in 1990. "The World's Best Dry Stout" has a smooth head and its rich velvety taste suggests roasted coffee and dark chocolate. Boréale Noire is a creamy beer that will appeal especially to lovers of British ales. It is an all-natural ale brewed from superior ingredients: water, dark malt, roasted barley and chocolate malts, hops and yeast. The beer is ideal as an aperitif, and delightful with chocolate cake at the end of a meal. Boréale Noire is best allowed to warm a few degrees before serving at around 55 degrees fahrenheit.

LES BRASSEURS DU NORD BORÉALE ROUSSE

Country of Origin: *Canada* • **Brewery Founded:** *1988* • **Alcohol Content:** *5%*

Boreale Rousse was the first Rousse beer brewed in Quebec. Its inimitable style, distinctive taste and even its name are all Boréale creations. An ale of character, the beer has caramel malt aromas, subtle bitter notes and a full mellow taste. It is an all-natural ale brewed from superior ingredients: water, malted barley, caramel malt and roasted malt, hops and yeast. Rousse contains no coloring agents or preservatives. The beer won the Bronze medal for pale/amber beers at the 2012 Brussels Beer Challenge. The beer is delicious before, during and after meals or for evenings with friends. Boréale Rousse is best served chilled at 50 degrees fahrenheit. The beer is an excellent accompaniment to sharp cheeses or grilled game.

McAUSLAN BREWING ST. AMBROISE APRICOT WHEAT ALE

Country of Origin: *Canada* • **Brewery Founded:** *1989* • **Alcohol Content:** *5%*

Natural apricot flavor is married to barley and wheat malts to give St. Ambroise Apricot Wheat Ale its uniquely delicious, subtly sweet taste. The beer is a natural and delightfully refreshing choice for adventurous palates that appreciate a light ale with a playful twist. Willamette and Golding hops is used to brew the beer.

McAUSLAN BREWING ST. AMBROISE CREAM ALE

Country of Origin: *Canada* • **Brewery Founded:** *1989* • **Alcohol Content:** *5%*

McAuslan's St.Ambroise Cream Ale boasts a luxurious, thick head thanks to the nitrogen injected into every pint. These fine bubbles are a contrast to the harsh carbonation found in many North American draft beers. That silky, long-lasting head caps an irresistibly smooth and yet muscular ale. The beer is constructed from Cascade, Willamette, and Golding hops.

McAUSLAN BREWING ST. AMBROISE DOUBLE INDIA PALE ALE

Country of Origin: *Canada* • **Brewery Founded:** *1989* • **Alcohol Content:** *8%*

McAuslan's master brewer uses the word "intense" to describe St. Ambroise Double India Pale Ale. This is a good brew for beer lovers that like strong hoppy and malty aromas. This unfiltered beer also has strong citrus aromas and a full body. The beer is brewed with a combination of Chinook and Cascade hops.

McAUSLAN BREWING ST. AMBROISE GREAT PUMPKIN ALE

Country of Origin: *Canada* • **Brewery Founded:** *1989* • **Alcohol Content:** *5%*

McAuslan brews its Great Pumpkin Ale (Citrouille) each year as the leaves fall and the north wind blows. This pumpkin ale, St-Ambroise Pumpkin Ale makes its return. This magical potion is brewed with a blend of blond and caramelized malts, gentle hops (Cascade and Willamette), cinnamon, ginger, nutmeg, cloves, and pumpkin. Its delicate malty character and hint of sweetness will satisfy anyone looking for easy-drinking refreshment.

McAUSLAN BREWING ST. AMBROISE INDIA PALE ALE

Country of Origin: *Canada* • **Brewery Founded:** *1989* • **Alcohol Content:** *6.2%*

McAuslan's St. Ambroise India Pale Ale is the brewer's New World interpretation of the classic India Pale Ales of the nineteenth-century England. In those days, the ale was brewed extra-strong and generously hopped to help it survive the long journey to India. Inspired by that history and today's blonde American IPAs, McAuslan has married Cascade, Golding, and Chinook hops to a subtle blend of malts to make a strong ale. This IPA has both hop bitterness and malt smoothness.

McAUSLAN BREWING ST. AMBROISE MAPLE ALE

Country of Origin: *Canada* • **Brewery Founded:** *1989* • **Alcohol Content:** *4.5%*

McAuslan's St. Ambroise Maple Ale or Érable celebrates Quebec's unique sugaring-off tradition. With its combination of the finest Golding and Willamette hops, crystal malt, roasted barley, and real Quebec maple syrup, this red ale is the perfect beer to drink in the sugar shack.

McAUSLAN BREWING ST. AMBROISE OATMEAL STOUT

Country of Origin: *Canada* • **Brewery Founded:** *1989* • **Alcohol Content:** *5%*

McAuslan Brewing began operations in January of 1989. Located at 4850 St. Ambroise Street in Montreal's St-Henri district, it soon established itself as one of Quebec's foremost micro-breweries. The brewery launched its first beer in February 1989, St. Ambroise Pale Ale. St. Ambroise Oatmeal Stout soon followed. The beer's expert blend of deeply roasted malts has made it an international medal winner. It won a Platinum medal at the 1994 World Beer Cup. The beer is a rich brew punctuated by espresso and chocolate notes, topped with a thick, creamy head with just a hint of mocha.

McAUSLAN BREWING ST. AMBROISE PALE ALE

Country of Origin: *Canada* • **Brewery Founded:** *1989* • **Alcohol Content:** *5%*

McAuslan's St. Ambroise Pale Ale is the brewery's flagship beer. It was the first beer that the brewery offered after it opened. St. Ambroise Pale Ale is a golden, generously hopped brew, and a perennial favorite of the many pale ale drinkers who have enjoyed its rich, fruity flavor since 1989. The beer is brewed with a blend of Cascade, Willamette, Golding, and Hallertau hops.

McAUSLAN BREWING
ST. AMBROISE RASPBERRY ALE

Country of Origin: *Canada* • **Brewery Founded:** *1989* • **Alcohol Content:** *5%*

St. Ambroise's Raspberry Ale is made with carefully selected fresh raspberries and top-quality sun-ripened hops. This raspberry ale is the perfect thirst quencher for sundrenched summer days. It is full of delicate fruitiness and crisp hoppiness from its Willamette and Golding hops.

McAUSLAN BREWING
ST. AMBROISE RUSSIAN
IMPERIAL STOUT

Country of Origin: *Canada* • **Brewery Founded:** *1989* • **Alcohol Content:** *9.2%*

St. Ambroise Russian Imperial Stout is McAuslan's tribute to the brawny black beers crafted for the Russian Imperial household back in the eighteenth century. Made from a blend of barley malts infused with Cascade, Golding, and Willamette hops, this extra strong ale is aged in bourbon oak, giving it seductive vanilla, espresso, and chocolate notes.

McAUSLAN BREWING
ST. AMBROISE SCOTCH ALE

Country of Origin: *Canada* • **Brewery Founded:** *1989* • **Alcohol Content:** *7.5%*

McAuslan have brewed their St-Ambroise Scotch Ale to celebrate four centuries of Scottish heritage in Canada. Behind its deep ruby color and amber head is a strong beer with a robust flavor. The ale has a smooth, malty taste with hints of vanilla and caramel, rounded out by a long, hoppy finish. McAuslan brew the beer with Golding and Willamette hops.

McAUSLAN BREWING
ST. AMBROISE VINTAGE ALE

Country of Origin: *Canada* • **Brewery Founded:** *1989* • **Alcohol Content:** *10%*

McAuslan brew their St. Ambroise Vintage Ale just once a year, but it has earned a bushel of international medals and praise. This extra strong ale is a masterful blend of barley and wheat malts, including Munich malt. This gives the unfiltered beer an appealing orange glow and a superb malty flavor. Cascade and Golding hops combine with the malts to give the brew notes of caramelized fruit, evoking memories of seasonal plum pudding. Despite this richness, the ale has a refreshing, hoppy finish.

MILL STREET BREWERY COFFEE PORTER

Country of Origin: *Canada* • **Brewery Founded:** *2002* • **Alcohol Content:** *5.5%*

Mill Street's Coffee Porter is a highly unusual beer, made in the tradition of British porters, but with a unique twist. The beer is rich and robust, and full of rich coffee flavor that comes from real roasted Balzac coffee beans. The beer has an aroma of dark malt and dark roast coffee, with notes of chocolate, coffee, and toasted malt with a light bitterness. It is a good food partner for shrimps, oysters, chocolate desserts, and mascarpone cheese.

MILL STREET BREWERY STOCK ALE

Country of Origin: *Canada* • **Brewery Founded:** *2002* • **Alcohol Content:** *5%*

Mill Street's Stock Ale is a thirst-quenching export-style brew. It is crafted in the same way that domestic blonde ales were made a century ago. The natural sweetness of the malt dominates the smooth ale. The beer has a light dusting of hops on the nose, and a light malt flavor that is in perfect balance with its hop bitterness. The beer goes well with chili, oven-roasted turkey, and strong cheddar cheese.

MILL STREET BREWERY TANKHOUSE ALE

Country of Origin: *Canada* • **Brewery Founded:** *2002* • **Alcohol Content:** *5.5%*

Like traditional pale ales, Mill Street's Tankhouse Ale has a deep copper-red color. Brewed with five different malts and an abundance of Cascade hops, this well-balanced and satisfying ale is the brewer's pride and joy. The beer has aromas of citrus and spice with roasted notes. The beer has a complex malty texture with a snappy bitterness from the Cascade hops. The beer partners well with quesadillas, curries, pad Thai, spicy crab cakes, and provolone cheese.

MILL STREET BREWERY WIT

Country of Origin: *Canada* • **Brewery Founded:** *2002* • **Alcohol Content:** *5.2%*

Mill Street's Belgian Wit (white) beer is a refreshing beer made with a unique blend of ingredients. The pale color and soft texture comes from the use of wheat, coriander, orange peel, and Mill Street's special yeast. The unfiltered beer has a complexity and a depth of fruity flavors that include citrus, banana, coriander, and cloves. The beer's cloudy appearance gave rise to its name, Wit or white beer. Mill Street recommends serving the beer with a slice of orange to intensify the citrus flavor of the beer.

MOLSON COORS CANADIAN LAGER

Country of Origin: *Canada* • **Brewery Founded:** *2005* • **Alcohol Content:** *5%*

Molson Coors Canadian is a pale lager that was first introduced to the Canadian market in 1959. It is now brewed by the Canadian division of Molson Coors. The beer has won several awards including a Silver Medal in the North American Style Lager category in the 2002 World Beer Cup. The beer also inspired the Molson Canadian Mega Keg monument, which is the height of a three story building. If it was a real keg, the Mega Keg monument would be large enough to hold the equivalent volume of over half a million cans of Molson Canadian.

MOLSON COORS CANADIAN WHEAT

Country of Origin: *Canada* • **Brewery Founded:** *2005* • **Alcohol Content:** *4.5%*

Molson Coor's Canadian Wheat beer is made with soft white spring wheat that is grown on the Canadian prairie. It is the company's premium unfiltered wheat lager and is brewed to have a smooth and refreshing taste.

MOLSON COORS CARLING LAGER

Country of Origin: *Canada* • **Brewery Founded:** *2005* • **Alcohol Content:** *4.9%*

Molson was founded in 1786 and Coors in 1873. The two companies were merged in 2005, and their Canadian headquarters is in Montreal, Quebec. On May 26, 2011 seventh-generation family member Andrew Molson succeeded Pete Coors as the acting Chairman of the company. Carling Lager is an easy-drinking beer brewed with Canadian 2-row barley. It is a pale Canadian lager in style that uses Canadian barley malt to produce a clean and refreshing beer.

MOLSON COORS CREEMORE SPRINGS COLLABORATION ALTBIER

Country of Origin: *Canada* • **Brewery Founded:** *2005* • **Alcohol Content:** *5%*

Collaboration Altbier was launched in 2012 to celebrate Creemore's 25th anniversary. Creemore Brewmaster Gordon Fuller and head brewer Bryan Egan travelled to Düsseldorf to immerse themselves in German brewing culture, and this brew was the result. They use pale, Melanoidin, and Carafa Special Type 2 malts and combine them with Perle and Hallertau Tradition hops to create this mahogany-hued beer. It is clean tasting with a noble hop bitterness and rich maltiness, and has a lingering hop finish.

MOLSON COORS CREEMORE SPRINGS KELLERBIER

Country of Origin: *Canada* • **Brewery Founded:** *2005* • **Alcohol Content:** *5%*

Kellerbier is an unfiltered, medieval German beer known for its naturally cloudy appearance. It was served straight from the brewmaster's cellar. Creemore Sprigs first brewed their Kellerbier in 2009, using pale, and Cara-Munich malts and Saaz, Spalt, Sladek, and Tettnang Leaf hops. The result is a cloudy, amber-colored brew with a generous fresh hop aroma with hints of citrus and spice. The beer has a dry, hoppy finish.

MOLSON COORS CREEMORE SPRINGS PREMIUM LAGER

Country of Origin: *Canada* • **Brewery Founded:** *2005* • **Alcohol Content:** *5%*

Creemore Springs was a microbrewery located in Creemore, Ontario, Canada, which first opened in 1987. In 2005 it was acquired by Molson, a subsidiary of the seventh largest brewery corporation in the world, the Molson Coors Brewing Company. Creemore Springs Premium Lager was first brewed in 1987 using pale and caramel malts and Saaz, Spalt, and Sladek hops. The beer has a honey-copper color and an aroma of fresh malt. It has a lightly nutty body and a hoppy dryness.

MOLSON COORS CREEMORE SPRINGS TRADITIONAL PILSNER

Country of Origin: *Canada* • **Brewery Founded:** *2005* • **Alcohol Content:** *5.3%*

Creemore Springs first brewed their Traditional Pilsner in 2007, twenty years from when the brewery was founded. It is a traditional golden pilsner in the tradition of Czech pilsners. Creemore uses only four natural ingredients to make the beer, including clear flowing spring water. They combine this with pale malt, and Saaz, Spalt, and Sladek hops to make a sweet, rich, malty brew with a bitter hoppy finish.

MOLSON COORS REEMORE SPRINGS URBOCK DARK BEER

Country of Origin: *Canada* • **Brewery Founded:** *2005* • **Alcohol Content:** *6%*

Bock beers first gained notoriety in Munich back in 1612. Creemore Springs first brewed their Urbock Dark Beer in 1997, using pale, caramel, black, and Munich malts combined with Saaz, Spalt, and Sladek hops. The beer has a rich, ruby hue and subtle, dark roasted flavors. It has a biscuit aroma with a hint of molasses and deep maltiness.

MOLSON COORS GRANVILLE ISLAND MAPLE CREAM ALE

Country of Origin: *Canada* • **Brewery Founded:** *2005* • **Alcohol Content:** *5%*

Granville Island Maple Cream Ale is brewed by the Granville Island Brewery in Kelowna, Canada. The concern is now part of the Molson Coors brewing empire. The beer is bronze-colored amber ale that is brewed using traditional Tettnang hops. A hint of Canadian maple syrup is added for a smooth and creamy taste that is not too sweet. The beer has a sweet malt aroma and low carbonation.

MOOSEHEAD ALPINE LAGER

Country of Origin: *Canada* • **Brewery Founded:** *1867* • **Alcohol Content:** *5%*

Moosehead's Alpine Lager is brewed in New Brunswick, Canada, where it is very widely drunk. It is an American Adjunct lager in style. The beer pours a clean, clear yellow and has a modest head. It smells pleasantly of corn and malt. It also` has a hoppy aroma and a touch of lemon in the background.

MOOSEHEAD LAGER

Country of Origin: *Canada* • **Brewery Founded:** *1867* • **Alcohol Content:** *5%*

Moosehead Breweries' flagship brand is a premium quality pale golden lager that is light in body and highly refreshing, offering a fine balance between malt sweetness and hop bitterness. Made from an age-old yeast culture, Moosehead Lager is brewed longer to impart its unique flavor. It is brewed with 100% Canadian barley malt, specially blended hops, and pure Spruce Lake water.

MOOSEHEAD MOOSE LIGHT

Country of Origin: *Canada* • **Brewery Founded:** *1867* • **Alcohol Content:** *4%*

Moosehead is Canada's oldest independent brewery, brewing craft beers since 1867. Moose Light is a light lager beer with a medium straw color and a foamy white head. The smell of the beer has a pleasant light adjunct malty sweetness with a light grassy hop. For a light beer, Moose Light has quite a full mouth feel.

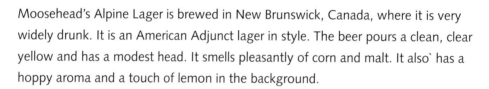

MOOSEHEAD PALE ALE

Country of Origin: *Canada* • **Brewery Founded:** *1867* • **Alcohol Content:** *5%*

Moosehead Pale Ale is the beer that built the brewery. Moosehead Pale Ale was the first beer brewed by the brewery in the 1860s. The beer is also known as 'Moose Red' in Canada's Maritimes. The beer has a loyal following who appreciate its remarkably smooth, European-influenced taste.

PADDOCK WOOD BREWING COMPANY 606 INDIA PALE ALE

Country of Origin: *Canada* • **Brewery Founded:** *2004* • **Alcohol Content:** *5.4%*

The Paddock Wood Brewing Company is Saskatchewan's first microbrewery and Canada's first "indie" beer. The company prides its beers on their unique flavor and refreshing taste. The company was started by brewmaster, Stephen Cavan. Paddock Wood's pure brews can be found bottled and on-tap in some of the finest independent establishments and beer stores in Canada. 606 is a prototype IPA which features a huge malt profile from Maris Otter malt as a backbone, and massive amounts of Cascade & Amarillo hops. The beer's hop flavor, bite, and aroma dominate this beer of character.

PADDOCK WOOD BREWING COMPANY BETE NOIRE

Country of Origin: *Canada* • **Brewery Founded:** *2004* • **Alcohol Content:** *5.4%*

Paddock Wood's Bete Noire is a dry oatmeal stout. The Oatmeal Stout is a traditional English style stout, created before Arthur Guinness established the Dry Irish Stout style. Oatmeal Stout gets its dark profile from chocolate malt which has not been roasted as long or as strongly as the barley used in dry stouts. The chocolate malt gives notes of coffee or chocolate, and the oatmeal has softened the background even further for smooth, easy drinking ale. The stout pours an almost opaque black with a small brown head. Its aroma is roasted malts, coffee and notes of cocoa and dark fruits. The beer's flavor is made up of bitter and dry roasted malts, espresso, cocoa, and a nice velvety mouthful.

PADDOCK WOOD BREWING COMPANY BLACK CAT LAGER

Country of Origin: *Canada* • **Brewery Founded:** *2004* • **Alcohol Content:** *5.4%*

Paddock Wood's Black Cat Lager is a German-style schwarzbier. The beer is a dark beer that has light coffee tasting notes. The beer pours a clear black color and has a small off-white head. The aroma is of roasted malt, coffee, wood, and some sweet chocolate. Black Cat tastes of roasted malts and coffee. This clean and crisp beer has classic pilsner qualities and good hop bitterness on the finish. Spalt and Marynka hops are used to brew the beer.

PADDOCK WOOD BREWING COMPANY HEARTSTOPPER

Country of Origin: *Canada* • **Brewery Founded:** *2004* • **Alcohol Content:** *7.5%*

Paddock Wood's Heartstopper is a rich hot chocolate stout with a medium bitterness and a sweet finish. The brewery uses five different malts to construct the brew: pale malt, wheat malt, roasted barley, chocolate malt, and Crystal 150. Paddock Wood's most recent specialty beer is flavored with chocolate, vanilla and cayenne pepper. Paddock Wood brews the beer for the Sherbrooke Liquor Company by Paddock Wood.

PADDOCK WOOD BREWING COMPANY CZECH MATE

Country of Origin: *Canada* • **Brewery Founded:** *2004* • **Alcohol Content:** *5.2%*

Czech Mate is Paddock Wood's Czech Pilsner. This microbrewery brews Czech mate in a very authentic Czech style to produce a creamy and crisp beer. The brew has a soft and herbal hop profile that carries through in a delicate spicy floral bouquet. Czech Mate pours deep amber, with an ample white head that subsides quickly. It has a delicate citrusy aroma, malty sweetness, and a lasting crisp bitterness.

PADDOCK WOOD BREWING COMPANY LOKI

Country of Origin: *Canada* • **Brewery Founded:** *2004* • **Alcohol Content:** *8.7%*

Paddock Wood's Loki is a Double Imperial India Pale Ale. The beer has a very well balanced malt to hops ratio and is dry-hopped for extra depth and flavor. Paddock Wood uses four different malts to make the ale: pale malt, Vienna Malt, Crystal 240, and Cara Munich I. These are blended with Cascade, Columbus, and Willamette hops.

PADDOCK WOOD BREWING COMPANY MAI BOK

Country of Origin: *Canada* • **Brewery Founded:** *2004* • **Alcohol Content:** *7.5%*

This German-styled Bock is full of complex malt flavors, supported by a light hoppy bitterness. Paddock Wood use lager malt, Munich malt, and Crystal malt combined with Spalt and Hallertau hops. The beer pours a clear deep gold with a small creamy head. The aroma is a clean and malty with lightly toasted malts and some melanoidins. The taste is dominated by malty sweetness complimented by a spicy and peppery hop flavor. Mai Bock has a medium dry finish.

PADDOCK WOOD BREWING COMPANY MELON HEAD

Country of Origin: *Canada* • **Brewery Founded:** *2004* • **Alcohol Content:** *5.2%*

Paddock Wood's Melon Head is a Kolsch beer. It is a pale and yet full-flavored session beer. The beer is brewed with five different barley malts: pale malt, wheat malt, Cara Foam, Cara Hell, and acid malt. These are combined with two European hop varieties, Hallertau and Saaz. Melon Head is a limited release, light ale that is perfect for the summer. This brew has a perfect balance and is pulled to a clean dry finish. Traditionally, Kölsch is a specialty beer that is brewed in Cologne, Germany. It is clear with a bright, straw-yellow hue, and has a prominent but not extreme hoppiness. It is less bitter than the standard German pale lager. The beer is warm-fermented and then cold-conditioned, or lagered.

PADDOCK WOOD BREWING COMPANY RED HAMMER

Country of Origin: *Canada* • **Brewery Founded:** *2004* • **Alcohol Content:** *6%*

Red Hammer is an Oktoberfest Marzen-styled beer. The microbrewery takes its Vienna Red beer and bumps up the alcohol level for the Oktoberfest, although the beer is available year-round. The beer pours a clear amber/toffee color and has a bubbly white head. The aroma has a hint of malty sweetness, and a strong citrus, floral hoppy aroma. The beer has a medium carbonation. The bubbly beer has a dry mouth feel and is medium-bodied. The beer has a light bitterness in the finish and is quite smooth.

POWELL STREET CRAFT BREWERY DIVE BOMB PORTER

Country of Origin: *Canada* • **Brewery Founded:** *2012* • **Alcohol Content:** *5%*

The Powell Street Craft Brewery Dive Bomb Porter is an explosive bomb of dark beer flavor. Hidden beneath a slight hoppy bitterness is a deep roasted malt character with hints of toffee, caramel, chocolate, and nuts. The beer is a seasonal treat in a glass. Opened in 2012, the brewery is one of Vancouver's newest nano-breweries. Powell focus on brewing small, hand-crafted batches and use all-natural ingredients in their beers.

POWELL STREET CRAFT BREWERY OLD JALOPY PALE ALE

Country of Origin: *Canada* • **Brewery Founded:** *2012* • **Alcohol Content:** *5.5%*

The Powell Street Craft Brewery is located in Vancouver, Canada. Their Old Jalopy Pale Ale is a twist on an English-style pale ale. Caramel and English pale malts combine with North American hops to give the beer floral, citrus, and grapefruit tasting notes. The beer has a mahogany color with a small head. It is a nutty, malty mouthful.

PRINCE EDWARD ISLAND BREWING COMPANY BEACH CHAIR LAGER

Country of Origin: *Canada* • **Brewery Founded:** *2012* • **Alcohol Content:** *4.5%*

The Price Edward Island Brewing company was established in 2012 under the leadership of Jeff Squires. Squires immediately supervised the building of a new brewery in Charlottetown, Price Edward Island. The brewery was immediately successful in winning several medals for its products. It also started to brew Beach Chair Lager, which was the first canned craft beer in Atlantic Canada. The lager combines Canadian pilsner malt and the subtle spicy aroma of noble hops.

PRINCE EDWARD ISLAND BREWING COMPANY GAHAN 1772 IPA

Country of Origin: *Canada* • **Brewery Founded:** *2012* • **Alcohol Content:** *6.5%*

Prince Edward Island's Gahan 1772 India Pale Ale pours a copper color and has an attractive foamy white head. It is a medium bodied ale. It has the classic India Pale Ale attributes of being high in alcohol with a very bitter finish.   The aroma has a subtle hint of pine and a strong citrus flavor. The beer has great carbonation and pleasant floral aroma to balance it out.

PRINCE EDWARD ISLAND BREWING COMPANY GAHAN ISLAND RED

Country of Origin: *Canada* • **Brewery Founded:** *2012* • **Alcohol Content:** *5.3%*

Prince Edward Island Brewing Company brews and distributes the Gahan line of handcrafted ales. The beers are served at the Gahan House Pub on Prince Edward's Island's Sydney Street. Island Red is a premium red ale. The Gahan ales are brewed in the old fashioned way with malted barley, hops, water, and yeast. Island Red is an amber ale with a medium body. It has a caramel overtone and a bitter finish.

PRINCE EDWARD ISLAND BREWING COMPANY GAHAN SYDNEY STREET PREMIUM STOUT

Country of Origin: *Canada* • **Brewery Founded:** *2012* • **Alcohol Content:** *5.2%*

Gahan's Sydney Street Stout is a full-bodied stout with roasted barley overtones and a dark creamy head. The beer is virtually black and pours with a small, chocolate-brown head. The aroma of the beer is of roast coffee and caramel. The beer tastes very roasty, with the coffee bitterness covering most of the sweetness. The body is quite thin for a stout.

PRINCE EDWARD ISLAND BREWING COMPANY GAHAN SIR JOHN A'S HONEY WHEAT ALE

Country of Origin: *Canada* • **Brewery Founded:** *2012* • **Alcohol Content:** *5%*

This unusual beer is a wheat ale with a twist. It is made with the finest Prince Edward Island honey. The beer pours a light yellow pour with a faint haziness. It has a fizzy white head with not much lace in the glass. The aroma has a touch of honey sweetness and some light bread and wheat notes. The taste is also wheaty with a bit of honey, light bread, grass, and some mineral notes. The beer has a dry finish.

PRINCE EDWARD ISLAND BREWING COMPANY LOBSTER ALE

Country of Origin: *Canada* • **Brewery Founded:** *2012* • **Alcohol Content:** *6.5%*

Prince Edward Island's Lobster Ale is a strong English-style ale. The beer is refreshingly dry and effervescent and displays notes of fresh lemon. This ale pairs well with rich foods, and cleanses the palate. It is a great partner for island sea food. The ale is brewed with simple and all-natural ingredients: malted barley, hops, water, and yeast. It is unpasteurized.

PROPELLER BREWERY COMPANY BOHEMIAN STYLE PILSENER

Country of Origin: *Canada* • **Brewery Founded:** *1997* • **Alcohol Content:** *6.5%*

Pilsner is a style of lager that originated in Czechoslovakia in 1842. The resulting brew, Pilsner, was a refreshing golden and bright beer that has now been adopted by breweries all over the world. Propeller Bohemian Style Pilsener, is a refreshing brew in the classic lager style of Bohemia. Made with a blend of Canadian and European malts and prized Noble hops, Propeller Bohemian Style Pilsener displays classic European lager characteristics such as a slightly sulphurous nose, distinctive Continental hop aroma, a light malt sweetness, and a refreshing bitter finish.

PROPELLER BREWERY COMPANY HEFEWEIZEN

Country of Origin: *Canada* • **Brewery Founded:** *1997* • **Alcohol Content:** *5.3%*

Nothing refreshes more than this naturally cloudy wheat beer with a yeasty aroma and flavors of banana and clove. Propeller's summer seasonal is made with special Weizen yeast, German Noble hops and equal amounts of barley and wheat malts and is finished with higher than normal carbonation. The yeast sediment is typical in this unfiltered classic German style.

PROPELLER BREWERY COMPANY HONEY WHEAT ALE

Country of Origin: *Canada* • **Brewery Founded:** *1997* • **Alcohol Content:** *5%*

Propeller's Honey Wheat Ale is brewed with a blend of barley and wheat malts, with just a hint of Nova Scotia honey. The honey used is high quality fruit blossom and wildflower honey made in Canada's Annapolis Valley. This honey is gently blended into the kettle late in the boiling process. Propeller Honey Wheat is fermented at a slightly lower temperature than most other Ales. This provides a cleaner, smoother beer and also ensures the delicate flavors provided by the addition of Honey are uninhibited.

PROPELLER BREWERY COMPANY INDIA PALE ALE

Country of Origin: *Canada* • **Brewery Founded:** *1997* • **Alcohol Content:** *6.5%*

Propeller's IPA won Gold at the World Beer Championships of 2006, 2007, and 2008. The beer is made in the style of the true India Pale Ales, which had to withstand long sea voyages before quenching the thirst of British troops stationed in India. Propeller's IPA is a bracing and bitter, made with Warrior and Amarillo hops and pale, Crystal, and wheat malts. It's full-bodied ale for true beer lovers.

PROPELLER BREWERY COMPANY LONDON STYLE PORTER

Country of Origin: *Canada* • **Brewery Founded:** *1997* • **Alcohol Content:** *5%*

The Propeller Brewing Company is one of the best known and loved craft breweries in Atlantic Canada. The brewery was founded by John Allen in 1997 and is based in Halifax, Nova Scotia. Porters are named for the hardworking porters of London England's Covent Garden market. It is a dark full-flavored beer but smoother and less bitter than stout. Made with softened water, Propeller London Porter is a blend of pale, roasted and chocolate malts, hopped with English and North American varieties.

PROPELLER BREWERY COMPANY PUMPKIN ALE

Country of Origin: *Canada* • **Brewery Founded:** *1997* • **Alcohol Content:** *5%*

Propeller first brewed their Pumpkin ale in the fall of 2004 at the request of the Town of Windsor's Pumpkin Festival. A fall classic was born. Propeller brew the beer with Howard Dill's world famous Atlantic Giant Pumpkins and a special blend of spices. This is in addition to the usual beer ingredients, which include high quality malted grains, hops, water, and yeast. The ale is like a pumpkin pie in a glass. The ale is available from October each year.

PROPELLER BREWERY COMPANY REVOLUTION

Country of Origin: *Canada* • **Brewery Founded:** *1997* • **Alcohol Content:** *8%*

Sent by English brewers via the Baltic Sea to the court of the Czars, Russian Imperial Stout was brewed to very high gravities and allowed to ferment on the long voyage. The result is a dark, strong, and bracing brew. Propeller's version has a deep, rich, black color. The taste of alcohol is well masked by the intense hop bitterness, extreme roasted malt, and dark fruit notes. This seasonal beer was first brewed in 2006.

PUMP HOUSE BREWERY BLUEBERRY ALE

Country of Origin: *Canada* • **Brewery Founded:** *1999* • **Alcohol Content:** *5%*

This brew is Pump House's refreshing ale served with blueberries. The beer pours golden-orange with a fine white head. It has an aroma of fresh blueberries, blueberry bread, crystallized sugars, and pepper. The beer's sweet flavors are dominated by mild blueberries with a malty background, and the beer has a sweet fruity aftertaste with hints of pepper. The brew has a light to medium body, and is creamy and refreshing. This Blueberry Ale is best enjoyed as an aperitif or with dessert.

PUMP HOUSE BRAUNSCHWEIG WICKED WHEAT

Country of Origin: *Canada* • **Brewery Founded:** *1999* • **Alcohol Content:** *5%*

Pump House's ambition behind creating this beer was to achieve a superb blend between established German brewing techniques and local Braunschweig (German for Brunswick) flavor. The beer is both unfiltered and unpasteurized which gives the beer a high level of freshness and an intentionally cloudy appearance. The beer is made with 50% wheat malt and 50% barley malt combined with Noble hops.

PUMP HOUSE BREWERY CADIAN CREAM ALE

Country of Origin: *Canada* • **Brewery Founded:** *1999* • **Alcohol Content:** *5.5%*

Pump House Cadian Cream Ale is a golden colored cream ale-style beer that has malty aromas layered with a hint of spicy hops for a clean, smooth finish. The beer is brewed in Moncton, New Brunswick, Canada.

PUMP HOUSE BREWERY FIRE CHIEF'S RED ALE

Country of Origin: *Canada* • **Brewery Founded:** *1999* • **Alcohol Content:** *5.5%*

The Pump House poured its first beer on September 3, 1999. Since then, brewery owners Shaun and Lilia Fraser have received many awards and accolades while working hard to keep the brewery and Pump House Restaurant moving forward. A deep tawny reddish hued Irish-inspired ale with a lingering nut-like maltiness. Fire Chief's Red Ale is a very lightly hopped beer with a pleasant estery fruitiness and a wonderfully smooth finish.

PUMP HOUSE BREWERY PREMIUM LAGER

Country of Origin: *Canada* • **Brewery Founded:** *1999* • **Alcohol Content:** *5%*

Every bottle of Pump House Premium Lager is brewed using just barley, hops, water yeast in accordance with the Reinheistsgebot, the German beer purity law of 1516. The beer is cold aged and matured for more than six weeks, there are no additives, adjuncts, or artificial carbonation added to the brew. This results in a 100% natural lager.

PUMP HOUSE BREWERY S.O.B.

Country of Origin: *Canada* • **Brewery Founded:** *1999* • **Alcohol Content:** *4.8%*

Pump House's special Old Bitter is a deep honey-colored unfiltered West Coast-style session beer with the classic fresh aromatic hop bouquet that mingles with malty undertones for an excellent balanced finish. The beer has a pleasant lingering bitterness. This is a great thirst quencher or the perfect partner with spicy foods.

PUMP HOUSE BREWERY SCOTCH ALE

Country of Origin: *Canada* • **Brewery Founded:** *1999* • **Alcohol Content:** *4.8%*

The Pump House Brewery makes this Scottish Ale in their Canadian brewery. The beer pours auburn brown (a very similar color to an Irish stout) with a thick peaky head. Its aroma is smoky and malty with a little fruit. The taste is smoky, of caramel and dark fruit. The beer is reasonably light-bodied and bitter at the finish.

QUIDI VIDI BREWING COMPANY 1892

Country of Origin: *Canada* • **Brewery Founded:** *1996* • **Alcohol Content:** *5%*

1892 is brewed with the finest two-row malt and a generous helping of hops. This is a full bodied, reddish amber ale that is enjoyed by those who prefer European-style beers with substantial flavor. It has a sweet malt character with hop overtones. The flavor is rich and hearty. 1892 Traditional Ale commemorates the year of the great fire in St. John's, Newfoundland.

QUIDI VIDI BREWING COMPANY ERIC'S CREAM ALE

Country of Origin: *Canada* • **Brewery Founded:** *1996* • **Alcohol Content:** *5%*

Eric's Cream Ale is crafted with the finest two-row pale, Crystal, and Carastan Malts. The beer is moderately hopped, and imparts a substantial but creamy taste with a truly satisfying finish. Previously known as Eric's Red, Eric's Cream Ale was the Silver Medal Winner at the 2001 World Beer Championships in Chicago, Illinois. The beer pours with a reddish color and has an aroma of light malt and gentle hop.

QUIDI VIDI BREWING COMPANY HONEY BROWN ALE

Country of Origin: *Canada* • **Brewery Founded:** *1996* • **Alcohol Content:** *5%*

Quidi Vidi Honey Brown Ale is created with a precise combination of chocolate and Crystal malts. These are embellished with the richness of honey and gentle hopping to create a rich brown ale that is well balanced and smooth. The beer is golden brown in appearance with an aroma of sweet honey and a mild, sweet, smooth flavor. The beer is brewed with no additives or preservatives.

QUIDI VIDI BREWING COMPANY ICEBERG BEER

Country of Origin: *Canada* • **Brewery Founded:** *1996* • **Alcohol Content:** *4.5%*

Quidi Vidi Brewing Company Limited was established by David Rees in 1996. It is a Newfoundland-based independent brewing company focused on producing world-class quality beers for the mainstream, specialty, and premium segment of the beer market. Quidi Vidi's premium Iceberg Beer is brewed with glacial water from icebergs, some of purest waters on the planet. The appearance of the beer is clear and golden. It is a gently hopped, light-bodied brew with a clean, sparkling finish. It is crisp with no aftertaste.

QUIDI VIDI BREWING COMPANY PREMIUM

Country of Origin: *Canada* • **Brewery Founded:** *1996* • **Alcohol Content:** *5%*

Quidi Vidi Premium lager is brewed with the finest malt and is gently hopped so that is has a smooth and crisp taste. It is brewed the way that beer used to be made in the past using just water, malt, hops, and yeast. No additives or preservatives are used in its production. The beer is clear and golden in appearance with an aroma of low maltiness and hops. The flavor is light bodied and crisp.

SLEEMAN CLEAR 2.0

Country of Origin: *Canada* • **Brewery Founded:** *1834* • **Alcohol Content:** *4%*

Sleeman introduced the first low-carbohydrate beer in Canada when it launched Sleeman Clear 2.0. With only 2g of carbohydrates and 80 calories per half pint serving, the beer is the answer to a modern dietary trend. An easy-drinking beer with a light straw color, Sleeman's Clear has a light body that complements its soft citrus aromas. The beer had a refreshing finish and no aftertaste

SLEEMAN CREAM ALE

Country of Origin: *Canada* • **Brewery Founded:** *1834* • **Alcohol Content:** *5%*

Created by George Sleeman in the late 1800s, Sleeman Cream Ale was the first beer produced by the two Guelph breweries, and still remains their most recognized brand. Made from a variety of five imported hops, Sleeman Cream Ale's authentic North American style combines the easy drinking nature of a lager and the rich fruity character of an ale. Crafted from page 64 of the original Sleeman family recipe book, Sleeman's Cream Ale has rich golden hue. The beer has a slight fruity aroma, of pear or apple, with a medium body.

SLEEMAN FINE PORTER

Country of Origin: *Canada* • **Brewery Founded:** *1834* • **Alcohol Content:** *5.5%*

Sleeman's Fine Porter is straight from page 68 of the Sleeman family recipe book. The company first brewed its Fine Porter in the later nineteenth century. The original Porters were the drink of the working class in 1700s England where they were seen to be more nutritious. Fine Porter's deep mahogany color is topped by a rich tan foam. The beer has aromas of dark chocolate, coffee, and licorice. Fine Porter boasts fully rounded roast malt flavors. Its long finish is true to the original Porter style.

SLEEMAN HONEY BROWN LAGER

Country of Origin: *Canada* • **Brewery Founded:** *1834* • **Alcohol Content:** *5.2%*

The Sleeman family brewing tradition in Canada extends back to 1834 when John H. Sleeman arrived in Ontario from Cornwall, England. He started the first Sleeman brewery in 1851, brewing small hundred-barrel batches of beer. Sleeman's Honey Brown boasts a rich copper color with a creamy, off-white foam, creating a full-bodied lager with a touch of natural honey and a slightly sweet finish. The distinctive clover honey notes in this fine brew accent the aromas of toasted grain and caramel.

SLEEMAN INDIA PALE ALE

Country of Origin: *Canada* • **Brewery Founded:** *1834* • **Alcohol Content:** *5.3%*

The heritage of Sleeman India Pale Ale reaches back all the way to eighteenth century England, where it was first brewed to export to thirsty English troops in colonial India. The Sleeman family personalized the recipe back in the 1800's with a brewmaster's special attention to detail, and the brewer now presents the ale again. Sleeman India Pale Ale's distinctive amber color is a perfect partner to its bold, spicy hop nose and slightly fruity aroma. This ale is characterized by a malty sweetness at the beginning that finishes up with an authentic IPA hoppy bitterness at the end.

SLEEMAN LIGHT

Country of Origin: *Canada* • **Brewery Founded:** *1834* • **Alcohol Content:** *4%*

When an increasing number of Canadians began asking for a light beer that didn't compromise on premium taste, Sleeman answered by introducing Sleeman Light. The first impression that the beer presents is its beautiful light gold color with a dense white foam head. The beer has an exceptionally smooth body with hints of fresh citrus. This gives way to a subtle malt character and ends in a very clean finish.

SLEEMAN ORIGINAL DARK

Country of Origin: *Canada* • **Brewery Founded:** *1834* • **Alcohol Content:** *5.5%*

An all malt ale, Sleeman Original Dark is brewed from a combination of roasted barley malts, English Aroma hops, and deep well water. Its unique flavor has become a trademark in the Sleeman lineup. Original Dark's ruby red-brown hues are accented by dense tan foam. The medium body features roasted malt flavors, with hints of caramel and toasted grains showing through. The beer's taste is balanced and aromatic with a surprisingly clean finish.

SLEEMAN ORIGINAL DRAUGHT

Country of Origin: *Canada* • **Brewery Founded:** *1834* • **Alcohol Content:** *5%*

Sleeman Original Draught combines the company's traditional brewing heritage with the freshness and sociability of a draught beer. This unpasteurized lager has a golden color and concentrated white foam collar. Original Draught is well balanced and easy to drink. The lager also has a distinctive floral hop aroma with a refreshing finish.

SLEEMAN SILVER CREEK LAGER

Country of Origin: *Canada* • **Brewery Founded:** *1834* • **Alcohol Content:** *5%*

Sleeman Silver Creek Lager is brewed in the brewery's copper kettles for a traditional pilsner style. The beer is brewed with extra body and smoothness. Silver Creek Lager has a light golden color with an ample white foam collar. A noble hop character is prominent in the taste, along with balanced malt sweetness. Overall, this pilsner style has a very clean finish.

STEAM WHISTLE BREWING PILSNER

Country of Origin: *Canada* • **Brewery Founded:** *2000* • **Alcohol Content:** *5%*

Steam Whistle Brewing is a located in Toronto, Canada. The company produces a single premium pilsner lager packaged in distinctive green glass bottles and a non-twist cap. Steam Whistle use just four natural ingredients to brew their single product, spring water from Caledon, Ontario, German hops, two-row barley malt, and yeast. Steam Whistle's Pilsner is brewed using traditional European brewing standards. It is cold-aged for twenty-eight days, and is naturally carbonated. The beer is not heat pasteurized, but micro filtered for a lasting shelf life. Steam Whistle's three founders are all former employees of the Upper Canada Brewing Company before it was bought by Sleeman's. They originally planned to call their new venture the Three Fired Guys Brewing Company.

UNIBROUE BLANCHE DE CHAMBLY

Country of Origin: *Canada* • **Brewery Founded:** *1990* • **Alcohol Content:** *5%*

Unibroue introduced the first bottle-refermented white ale crafted in North America. Taking inspiration from Quebec history, Unibroue created Blanche de Chambly in honor of the volunteer militiamen who fought and died under Captain De Salaberry. This Belgian-style white ale was first brewed in 1992. It is pale golden in color and is cloudy with a white and creamy head. It has a subtle bouquet of spice, citrus, and aromas of yeast, bread, coriander, and cloves.

UNIBROUE DON DE DIEU

Country of Origin: *Canada* • **Brewery Founded:** *1990* • **Alcohol Content:** *9.5%*

Don de Dieu (Gift of God) was the name of the ship that Samuel de Champlain sailed on his mission to explore America in the name of the King of France. His travels led to the founding of Quebec in 1608. Unibroue created Don de Dieu to commemorate this adventure. It is an abbey-style triple wheat ale, which is re-fermented in the bottle. First brewed in 1998, the beer is orange-golden in color and is lightly cloudy with a creamy white head. It has a complex aroma of vanilla, fruitcake, flowers and honey. The flavor is smooth with fruity and malty notes.

UNIBROUE LA FIN DU MONDE

Country of Origin: *Canada* • **Brewery Founded:** *1990* • **Alcohol Content:** *5.5%*

From the very beginning, Unibroue has carved out a special niche in the beer world with top quality products and a brand rooted deep in Quebec culture. This craft brewer made history by becoming the first North American beer maker to use the brewing techniques of the Belgian Trappist monks. Unibroue was founded in 1990 by André Dion and Serge Racine. La Fin du Monde has been brewed since 1994. It is Triple-style golden ale, and is blonde with a golden hue. The beer is cloudy and has a creamy white head. The beer has aromas of honey, spice, coriander, and malt. The flavor is mildly yeasty with a complex palate of malt, fruit, and spice, followed by a smooth, dry finish.

UNIBROUE NOIRE DE CHAMBLY

Country of Origin: *Canada* • **Brewery Founded:** *1990* • **Alcohol Content:** *6.2%*

Unibroue's Noire de Chambly is a dark ale that was created in honor of the soldiers of the Carignan-Salières Regiment. Many French Canadians are the direct descendants of these intrepid forebears. The beer was first brewed in 2005, and is a Belgian-style black ale, opaque dark brown in color, with shades of mahogany. The beer has a dense beige-colored head with aromas of wood, smoke, roasted coffee, and licorice. The flavor is of smooth roasted grains and spice with a chocolaty finish.

UNIBROUE RAFTMAN

Country of Origin: *Canada* • **Brewery Founded:** *1990* • **Alcohol Content:** *5.5%*

Unibroue introduced Raftman to the Québec market in March 1995. This coral-hued beer has a unique taste that combines the smooth character of smoked malt whisky with the flavors of fine yeast. With this product, Unibroue commemorates the legendary courage of the lumberjacks and log drivers of yesteryear. During their long months away from home, these hardworking men would settle their differences over beer and whisky, both of which are made with malted barley. Unibroue had a great idea when it decided to bring the two together in a peat-smoked whisky malt ale. The beer is a cloudy amber red in color, with a complex blend of smoke, apples, caramel, and whisky malt. The flavor is of smoked malt whisky, apples, and caramel.

Une bière au malt de whisky refermentée sur lie.

UNIBROUE TROIS PISTOLES

Country of Origin: *Canada* • **Brewery Founded:** *1990* • **Alcohol Content:** *9%*

Unibroue's Trois Pistoles (Three Coins) beer is named after a small village in Quebec that was founded over three hundred years ago. Trois Pistoles is a cloudy dark brown top-fermented beer that has been brewed from 1997. It is an Abbey-style strong dark ale with a strong malt flavor, and roasted aromas of chocolate, rum, and spice. The beer has a medium body and is slightly sweet, enhanced by accents of roasted malt, cocoa, ripe fruit, and dark spices.

WELLINGTON BREWERY ARKELL BEST BITTER

Country of Origin: *Canada* • **Brewery Founded:** *1985* • **Alcohol Content:** *4%*

Wellington Brewery is Canada's oldest independently owned microbrewery. Based in Guelph, Ontario, they craft their award-winning beers in small batches using the freshest all-natural ingredients. Since the brewery was founded in 1985, it has been a pioneer in the craft brewing scene; producing timeless, traditional style ales as well as experimenting with new recipes as part of their Welly One-Off Series. First brewed in 1985, Wellington Arkell Best Bitter is an amber session ale with a mild, caramel malt body and a subtle hop aftertaste. Arkell Best Bitter is an incredibly flavorful light bitter that is the perfect session ale for any occasion.

WELLINGTON BREWERY SPECIAL PALE ALE

Country of Origin: *Canada* • **Brewery Founded:** *1985* • **Alcohol Content:** *4.5%*

Wellington Brewery's most popular beer is a refreshingly smooth pale ale that is deep gold in color and notably full of flavor. With a balance of malt and hops that is patterned after traditional British pale ales, Wellington's Special Pale Ale has an aroma of caramel and toasted grain followed by a delicate hop aftertaste.

WELLINGTON BREWERY COUNTY DARK ALE

Country of Origin: *Canada* • **Brewery Founded:** *1985* • **Alcohol Content:** *5%*

Wellington Brewery's County Dark Ale is their most celebrated beer. This beer is a rich, dark ale that is handcrafted to deliver exceptional smoothness and balance. Modeled after a traditional English brown ale, County Dark Ale uses roasted malts and English hops to create a beer of timeless distinction. It is amber brown in color.

WELLINGTON BREWERY IMPERIAL RUSSIAN STOUT

Country of Origin: *Canada* • **Brewery Founded:** *1985* • **Alcohol Content:** *8%*

The year 2000 brought big changes at Wellington Brewery, when long-time employees Doug Dawkins and Michael Stirrup took over the business. With nearly twenty-five years combined experience at the brewery; the pair has an intimate knowledge of both Wellington's products and the craft brewing industry. Full bodied and complex, Wellington's Imperial Russian Stout is one of the blackest beers brewed in Ontario. With an inviting aroma of dark chocolate and coffee, the beer has a smooth, full bodied flavor that is patterned after the highly fortified stouts that were exported from Britain to Russia in the nineteenth century.

WELLINGTON BREWERY IRON DUKE STRONG ALE

Country of Origin: *Canada* • **Brewery Founded:** *1985* • **Alcohol Content:** *6.5%*

Founded in 1985, Wellington Brewery was part of the first wave of Ontario microbreweries that began after changes to Ontario law allowed small brewers to operate in the province. Phil Gosling, the founder of Wellington Brewery, envisioned a brewery that would only produce English style Real Ales. These cask-conditioned ales are unfiltered, naturally carbonated and served at cellar temperature. Wellington Brewery was one of the first modern brewers in North America to produce these traditional ales. With the character of barley wine, Iron Duke Strong Ale is dark burgundy in color. It has an enticing aroma of rich malt, chocolate and fruity notes. This complex ale has a smooth full-bodied flavor and is an excellent dessert beer.

WELLINGTON BREWERY TRAILHEAD LAGER

Country of Origin: *Canada* • **Brewery Founded:** *1985* • **Alcohol Content:** *4.5%*

Wellington's Trailhead is a Vienna-style lager that is characterized by a careful balance of malt sweetness and clean, crisp hop bitterness. Brewed using 100% Canadian two-row pale barley malt, this refreshing lager is the perfect beer for any occasion. Wellington celebrated its twenty-fifth anniversary in 2010, a significant milestone for an independently owned craft brewer.

WILD ROSE ALBERTA CRUDE

Country of Origin: *Canada* • **Brewery Founded:** *1996* • **Alcohol Content:** *5.25%*

Wild Rose's Alberta Crude is as black as its namesake and has a creamy tan-colored head. The beer is a creamy oatmeal stout, with low carbonation. The beer is brewed with six different malts, oatmeal, and hops imported from Britain. The beer is a good food partner for smoky blue cheese, smoked salmon, oysters, and chocolate brownies.

WILD ROSE BROWN ALE

Country of Origin: *Canada* • **Brewery Founded:** *1996* • **Alcohol Content:** *5%*

Wild Rose first brewed their Brown Ale in 1996. Now recognized as a modern day classic, this beer successfully pays homage to the time-honored British beer styles of the past. Dark brown and ruby hued, this ale expresses notes of espresso and chocolate. Very approachable, Wild Rose Brown Ale is mildly hopped with a medium body and a clean finish. It partners well with camembert, chili, and grilled portabella mushrooms.

WILD ROSE HOPTIMAL IMPERIAL IPA

Country of Origin: *Canada* • **Brewery Founded:** *1996* • **Alcohol Content:** *8%*

Wild Rose Brewery's Imperial India Pale Ale (IIPA) is brewed with extra malt and added hops to produce a robust and malty ale with a powerful hop flavor. Hoptimal is extremely hoppy with huge floral notes of pine and citrus. This unfiltered ale expertly blends Summit, Newport, Cascade & Columbus hops with the finest Alberta two-row barley and crystal malts. The result is a beer with sweet caramel notes balanced by an intense grapefruit taste. The beer is available between January and March.

WILD ROSE IPA

Country of Origin: *Canada* • **Brewery Founded:** *1996* • **Alcohol Content:** *6%*

India Pale Ales were developed back in the 1700s when British brewers were charged with making a beer that would survive export to India. To keep the beer fresh and delicious on the long and hot boat journey, brewers discovered that using large doses of hops and brewing to a higher alcohol level would keep the beer tasting fresh. Wild Rose IPA (India Pale Ale) is a copper-colored ale, rich in caramel malt character and well balanced with plenty of hops.

WILD ROSE NATURAL BORN KELLER

Country of Origin: *Canada* • **Brewery Founded:** *1996* • **Alcohol Content:** *6%*

Wild Rose Natural Born Keller is a California-style keller bock. It is a strong lager beer that is crisp and yet boldly flavored. This unfiltered, copper-colored ale combines new world innovation with old world brewing tradition. California Style Keller Bock puts a unique twist on the Bock style of beer and combines the crispness of a lager with the bold taste of an ale. Malty, medium bodied and briskly hopped, this beer is truly an original. A seasonal beer, it is available between March and May.

WILD ROSE S.O.B.

Country of Origin: *Canada* • **Brewery Founded:** *1996* • **Alcohol Content:** *4.1%*

S.O.B. stands for Special Old Bitter. Wild Rose's S.O.B. is brewed in the classic English style of an ordinary bitter. The beer is golden-bronze in color and light in body. It is delicately hopped and refreshingly delicious. Very gentle and approachable, this classic English ale is an excellent choice to enjoy as a session beer. It works well with Canadian cheddar, roast beef, wurst, and falafel.

WILD ROSE VELVET FOG

Country of Origin: *Canada* • **Brewery Founded:** *1996* • **Alcohol Content:** *4.5%*

First brewed in 1998, Velvet Fog is an unfiltered Canadian wheat ale. It is a special blend of 50% wheat malt and 50% barley that gives this unique unfiltered ale a distinctive hazy, golden color and a fresh tangy character. To ensure a perfect velvety smoothness in every sip of Velvet Fog, swirl the bottle before pouring. The beer goes well with Edam cheese, sandwiches, sausage, cured meats, quiche Lorraine, and lemon meringue pie.

WILD ROSE WHITE SHADOW

Country of Origin: *Canada* • **Brewery Founded:** *1996* • **Alcohol Content:** *6%*

An amalgamation of two great styles, White Shadow combines the refreshing spiciness of a Belgian style wheat beer with the bold hoppiness of a North American IPA. Brewed with Pilsner malt, wheat malt, and oats, the beer is spiced with sweet orange peel, coriander and chamomile. Cascade and Columbus hops give the beer a nice citrusy bitterness. Finally a Belgian yeast strain is left unfiltered in the final brew to lend notes of clove and bitter fruit. A seasonal beer, White Shadow is available from August to October.

WILD ROSE WRASPBERRY ALE

Country of Origin: *Canada* • **Brewery Founded:** *1996* • **Alcohol Content:** *4.5%*

Wild Rose have been brewing beer in Alberta, Canada since 1996 and their WRaspberry Ale has become a year-round favorite. The tart taste of fresh raspberries provides the perfect finish for our light, crisp, easy-drinking ale. Wild Rose's passion for great beers and an ongoing dedication to using only the freshest ingredients have helped the company to create Alberta's wildest beers. The beer partners well with fresh mozzarella, salad dressed with vinaigrette, fruit salad, and raspberry cobbler.

WILD ROSE WRED WHEAT

Country of Origin: *Canada* • **Brewery Founded:** *1996* • **Alcohol Content:** *5%*

What makes WRed Wheat Ale distinctive? Perhaps it's the combination of six types of malted wheat and barley. Or maybe it's the variety of hop additions that delicately "spice" the brew? From the beer's distinctive red-amber hues, to aromas of biscuits and a sweetness of caramel, this beer is not to be taken lightly. Wild Rose WRed Wheat is hand crafted, striking a fine balance between malt and hops. The final result is a beer that is crisp, clean and refreshing.

YUKON BREWING COMPANY BELGIAN GOTHIC SAISON

Country of Origin: *Canada* • **Brewery Founded:** *1997* • **Alcohol Content:** *Medium*

A Saison beer was traditionally brewed in Belgium in the fall or winter for the consumption of the farm workers the following summer. The 'saisonnieres,' or seasonal workers, were allowed five liters per day. Yukon's version is quite bit spicy as they use cracked peppercorns in the brewing. It is also fruity (they hand peel oranges and grapefruits, then pound up the fruit and put the fruit into the brewing kettle). The result is a thirst quenching beer.

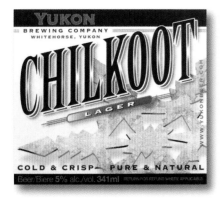

YUKON BREWING COMPANY CHILKOOT LAGER

Country of Origin: *Canada* • **Brewery Founded:** *1997* • **Alcohol Content:** *5%*

Yukon began to offer Chilkoot Lager in May 2000, as a chemical-free alternative to the big brand lagers. The beer is light and effervescent, with no chemical tang. The beer is now one of Yukon's best selling beers. The name Chilkoot harkens back to the Gold Rush days when the world famous Chilkoot Trail was opened between Alaska and the Yukon River.

YUKON BREWING COMPANY DEADMAN CREEK CRANBERRY WHEAT BEER

Country of Origin: *Canada* • **Brewery Founded:** *1997* • **Alcohol Content:** *4.7%*

Yukon's Deadman Creek Cranberry Wheat Beer is unusual to say the least. Yukon makes a wheat ale that combines natural cranberries with the tangy goodness of yeast, as the beer is unfiltered. The brew began as a seasonal beer, using only Yukon berries. But demand for the beer grew until Yukon had to source cranberries from outside the area. The cranberry flavor is quite subtle, and it complements the yeast perfectly. The beer is cloudy and unfiltered.

YUKON BREWING COMPANY
MIDNIGHT SUN ESPRESSO STOUT

Country of Origin: *Canada* • **Brewery Founded:** *1997* • **Alcohol Content:** *6.2%*

Midnight Sun Espresso Stout was launched in the fall of 2003, in conjunction with a local Yukon coffee company. The beer is brewed with eight different malts, oatmeal, and espresso coffee. The result is a beer that is fine yet full-bodied. Midnight Sun is smooth and rich with coffee aromas and flavors.

YUKON BREWING COMPANY
RED, AMBER ALE

Country of Origin: *Canada* • **Brewery Founded:** *1997* • **Alcohol Content:** *5.5%*

Yukon's Red, Amber ale has a deep bronze color, but the beer is crystal clear. The head is an abundant cream-colored mousse and the beer has aromas of clean malty sweetness touched by spicy hop esters. The ale has a full malt body; not sweet, but bold, fruity and persistent. A snap of clean hop bitter blends with caramel flavors, but the beer is clean, almost dry, and leaves only a slight lingering presence of its abundant flavors.

YUKON BREWING COMPANY
THE ANGRY HESSIAN

Country of Origin: *Canada* • **Brewery Founded:** *1997* • **Alcohol Content:** *5%*

Yukon Brewing opened its doors in 1997 under the name Chilkoot Brewing Co. Ltd. Owners Alan and Bob conceived their idea around a campfire on a canoe trip when they came up with the idea of a craft brewery based in the territory. The brewery changed its name to Yukon and their eight beers are now available across Alberta and British Columbia. The Angry Hessian is the brewery's pumpkin beer. It is brewed with pumpkin, molasses, demerara sugar, crushed cinnamon sticks, pureed ginger, crushed whole cloves, whole nutmeg, and oats for body. The result is pretty much pumpkin colored, and is very smooth and creamy.

YUKON BREWING COMPANY
YUKON GOLD

Country of Origin: *Canada* • **Brewery Founded:** *1997* • **Alcohol Content:** *5%*

Yukon Gold English Pale Ale is the Yukon's number one selling draught ale. It is golden in color, brilliantly clear, and clean across the palate. The mix of five malts provides subtle character in the body, and the addition of malted wheat provides a slight, but characteristic citrusy finish. Hopped with noble Saaz, Sterling, and UK Golding, the bitterness is barely perceptible, but mild hop flavors linger in the after-taste. The beer mimics the classic mild ales of the British Isles.

CHILE

AUSTRAL DARK ALE

Country of Origin: *Chile* • **Brewery Founded:** *1896* • **Alcohol Content:** *5%*

Austral Dark Ale is a brown ale brewed by the Cerveceria Austral, which is based in Punta Arenas, Chile. The company was first established in Patagonia, and brews a variety of beers including lagers, dark ale, pale ale, helles, and Calafate ale (which is made with a berry native to Southern Patagonia). The beer is a dark brown color, with a good foam head. It has aromas of malt, dried fruit, raisins, and notes of chocolate. The beer has a medium to light body and complexity. Its immediate sweetness is nicely balanced.

BECKER LAGER

Country of Origin: *Chile* • **Brewery Founded:** *2005* • **Alcohol Content:** *4.5%*

Becker Lager was brewed by the Cerveceria Chile in Quilicura, Santiago, Chile. This Vienna-style amber lager is brewed with Chilean hops. The beer is a clear amber color with an evanescent white head. Its aroma is of malt, with metallic hints and some surprising herbal hops. The brew has notes of apricots, aluminum, and lemongrass. The flavor is bittersweet with a herbal, medicinal note that moderates any malty excess. The body is light to medium with more thickness than the regular lager. The carbonation is fair and the mouth feel is creamy.

CERVEZA GRASSAU PREMIUM LAGER

Country of Origin: *Chile* • **Brewery Founded:** *2005* • **Alcohol Content:** *4.5%*

Grassau's Premium Lager is brewed by Compañia Cervecera Araucania in Temuco, Chile. The beer pours a golden color, slightly cloudy. The beer has a medium white head. The aroma is of malts and citric-herbal hoppy smells, with hints of lemon and pineapple. The flavor is of pale malts quickly balanced by a medium dry hoppipness. The mouth feel is light and the beer has a medium carbonation. This is a pleasant Chilean lager with a hint of pilsner.

COLONOS DEL LLANQUIHUE MAIBOCK

Country of Origin: *Chile* • **Brewery Founded:** *Unknown* • **Alcohol Content:** *6.5%*

Colonos del Llanquihue Maibock is a heller bock brewed by Sociedad Cervecera Totoral. The brewery also brews a pilsner. The maibock style of beer is a helles lager brewed to bock strength, but it is lighter in color than a traditional bock, and has more hop presence. The style is fairly recent compared to other styles of bock beers, and is frequently associated with springtime. The color of a maibock can range from deep gold to light amber with a large, creamy, persistent white head, and moderate to moderately high carbonation.

DEL PUERTO BARBA NEGRA PORTER STOUT

Country of Origin: *Chile* • **Brewery Founded:** *2003* • **Alcohol Content:** *4.5%*

Del Puerto Barba Negra Porter Stout is brewed by Cervecera del Puerto in Valparaiso, Chile. The beer is a porter stout of an intense black color. The beer has an excellent flavor of toasted malts, with smoked hints and a sweet finish. The beer is a full bodied brew. The Del Puerto brewery brings local beer to the streets of Valparaíso, which is situated on Chile's central Pacific coast. The brewery prides itself on using entirely natural ingredients and traditional production methods.

KOLBACH BITTER

Country of Origin: *Chile* • **Brewery Founded:** *2006* • **Alcohol Content:** *5.5%*

Kolbach bitter is brewed by Kolbach in Pirque, Chile. It is one of ten brews manufactured by this brewery. The beer pours a dark amber, almost brown color. The head is huge, frothy and off-white. The aroma is hoppy and flowery with tasting notes of grass, herbs, lemon, grapefruit, apples, and flowers. The malt is subdued. The flavor is bitter with lots of English hops and notes of lime, grapefruit, and grass. The beer has a medium body, a dense smooth mouth feel and high carbonation.

KROSS 5

Country of Origin: *Chile* • **Brewery Founded:** *2003* • **Alcohol Content:** *5.4%*

Kross 5 is a Belgian-style strong ale brewed by the Kross Microbrewery in Curacaví, Chile. Kross brewed this beer to celebrate their fifth anniversary. Kross 5 is a strong ale that has the distinction of being the first Chilean beer to be matured in oak, as well as being bottled in unique packaging. Kross 5 is a very versatile beer that can accompany many different dishes.

KROSS GOLDEN ALE

Country of Origin: *Chile* • **Brewery Founded:** *2003* • **Alcohol Content:** *5.0%*

Kross Golden Ale is an English Pale Ale brewed by the independent Kross Microbrewery, based in Curacaví, Chile. The brewery's objective in making this beer was to develop the pleasant fruity aromas of two different kinds of hops in traditional high heat fermentation. This gives this beer a unique personality. The brew is golden in color, and has aromas of fruit with notes of caramel in the finish and a citrusy, dry bitterness. Kross Golden Ale is ideal for accompanying red meats like lamb.

KUNSTMANN BOCK

Country of Origin: *Chile* • **Brewery Founded:** *1997* • **Alcohol Content:** *5.3%*

Kunstmann Bock is a dunkler bock brewed by Cerveceria Valdivia in Valdivia, Chile. It is a clear dark brown almost black in color with a large, frothy, off-white to light beige head. The aroma is moderately malty, with molasses, caramel, brown sugar, sweet malt, dark malt, and light roasting. The flavor is sweet, laced with dark malt, roastiness, sweet dark malt, brown sugar, and light coffee. The body is medium, the texture is oily, and the carbonation is soft.

QUIMERA AMBER ALE

Country of Origin: *Chile* • **Brewery Founded:** *2007* • **Alcohol Content:** *5.7%*

Quimera Amber Ale is brewed by Casa Cervecera Quinta Normal in Santiago, Chile. The brewery also makes an imperial stout, a sparkling ale, and a regular stout. The beer pours a clear amber color and has a medium-sized white head. Its aroma is soapy, with hints of citrus and earthy hops, complete with light toast, malt, and light peach esters. The flavor is of hops and bitterness with dry malt. The beer has a medium body with moderate carbonation.

PILKA TAMNO PIVO

Country of Origin: *Croatia* • **Brewery Founded:** *2006* • **Alcohol Content:** *4.6%*

Pilka Tamno Pivo is brewed by the Cimper Pub and Brewery, located in Mursko Sredisce. The town is on the border of Croatia, Slovenia and Hungary. This Croatian schwarzbier has a dark brown reddish body with a half white, half ocher head. The aroma is of roasted sugar and caramel, with some faint hoppiness. The flavor is bitter, sour and sweetish. Hints of roasted sugar dominate, with some coffee and acidity. It is a typical schwarzbier in style, but lacks some body. The finish is long and slightly bitter.

SAN SERVOLO PREMIUM CRVENO PIVO

Country of Origin: *Croatia* • **Brewery Founded:** *Unknown* • **Alcohol Content:** *5%*

San Servola Premium Crveno Pivo is brewed by the Bujska Brewery in Buje, Croatia. The beer is a Vienna-style amber lager. Bujska produces beer for the domestic Croatian market that is unfiltered and unpasteurized, and refermented in the bottle. The beer pours a hazy amber color with a thin off-white head and soft visible carbonation. The aroma is yeasty with some caramel. The taste starts with moderate sweet caramel maltiness, followed light sour grains. The finish is pleasantly bitter. The beer has a medium body, and slick texture.

ŠOKAČKO PIVO

Country of Origin: *Croatia* • **Brewery Founded:** *Unknown* • **Alcohol Content:** *5.2%*

Šokačko Pivo is a retired beer that was formerly brewed at the Tivornia Brewery in Solin, Croatia. The beer was a premium lager. The brewery made beer in accordance with the German beer purity laws, The Reinheitsgebot, without any preservatives or manufactured ingredients. The beer was made solely from hops and malt. The beer was a very pale yellow in color with a fluffy white head.

STAROČEŠKO ZIMSKO JAKO PIVO

Country of Origin: *Croatia* • **Brewery Founded:** *1893* • **Alcohol Content:** *6.3%*

This beer is a heller bock, brewed by Staročeško. The brewery is one of the oldest brands in Croatia. The company began by brewing the Staročeško winter beer, which was fermented in wooden barrels. Although the beer is no longer poured from wooden barrels, it remains a characterful brew. The beer pours a nice copper color with a small to medium sized head. The aroma is of malty caramel with a touch of citrus fruits and yeast. The flavor is malty, with wooden, biscuit, and caramel notes. The beer has a medium body.

TOMISLAV

Country of Origin: *Croatia* • **Brewery Founded:** *1892* • **Alcohol Content:** *7.3%*

Tomislav is a Baltic Porter brewed by the Zagreba ka Pivovara, which is owned by Molson Coors. The brewery is located in Zagreb, Croatia. This fruity black beer is made with 17.8% malt extract; Tomislav is the second strongest beer in Croatia. It was introduced in 1925. The use of double malted barley gives this dark lager its full taste and special aroma, which is much appreciated by beer connoisseurs.

VELEBITSKO TAMNO PIVO

Country of Origin: *Croatia* • **Brewery Founded:** *1997* • **Alcohol Content:** *6.1%*

Velebitsko is a popular beer brand from Croatia, which is brewed near Gospic in the Velebit Mountains by the Pivovara Li anka Lake. Velebitsko makes two popular beers. A pale lager that has an alcohol content of 5.1% and a dark lager which has an alcohol content of 6.0%. Known for its high quality brewing, the dark beer has been voted best beer by an English beer fan website.

CUBA

ANTILLANA CERVEZA CLARA

Country of Origin: *Cuba* • **Brewery Founded:** *1985* • **Alcohol Content:** *4.8%*

Antillana Cerveza Clara is a retired pale lager beer that was formerly brewed at the Cerveceria Tinima in Camagüey, Cuba. The brewery was inaugurated in 1985 and was mentioned in a famous speech by Fidel Castro. The beer was a compact brew with a small head of persistent foam. The beer was clear and opaque in color, and had a long-lasting aroma. The brew had a watery flavor with notes of grass and mildew.

BUCANERO FUERTE

Country of Origin: *Cuba* • **Brewery Founded:** *1980s* • **Alcohol Content:** *5.4%*

Bucanero Fuerte is a beer brewed for drinkers who prefer the taste of a full-flavored beer. The beer has a deep amber color and a delicious and refreshing taste. Bucanero Fuerte is made from the most natural and freshest ingredients, with superior malt and blended with just a touch of Cuba's finest sugars. The beer is named after the old legends of the Caribbean pirates. This hidden treasure is truly one of Cuba's best-kept secrets

BUCANERO MAX

Country of Origin: *Cuba* • **Brewery Founded:** *1980s* • **Alcohol Content:** *6.5%*

Bucanero Max is a strong pale lager or Imperial pilsner, brewed by the Cerveceria Bucanero in Holguín, Cuba. The beer pours a clear yellow to light amber color and is a well-carbonated brew. The aroma is muted but there are some noble hops and some sweet corn notes. It has a similar palate with a big carbonated profile giving it more body than it should have. The beer is less agreeable as it warms up but is still one of the better beers brewed in Cuba.

CERVEZA BRUJA CLASICA

Country of Origin: *Cuba* • **Brewery Founded:** *1953* • **Alcohol Content:** *4.5%*

Cerveza Bruja Clasica is a pale lager beer brewed by the Cerveceria Antonio Diaz Santana in Manacas, Cuba. Pale lagers range in color light bronze to nearly transparent and the alcohol level can vary between four and six percent. Adjunct usage may be quite high, though in some cases the beer is all-malt. Carbonation is typically forced, though not always. One thing that doesn't vary is that neither the malt nor the hops make much of an impression on the palate.

HATUEY CUBAN ALE

Country of Origin: *Cuba* • **Brewery Founded:** *1914* • **Alcohol Content:** *5.5%*

Hatuey Cuban Ale is an American pale ale-styled beer brewed by the Barcardi owned Hatuey brewery in Santiago de Cuba. This premium craft beer was first brewed in 1927. The beer has always been Cuba's favorite premium brew and had captured nearly half of the Cuban beer market by the time the brewery was nationalized by Castro in 1959. The beer has a faint aroma and is refreshingly bitter and hoppy. It is also very smooth, with a light malty and fruity sweetness. Carbonation is good and adds to the refreshment. The beer is not watery or thin but has a pleasant medium body.

MAYABE CALIDAD EXTRA

Country of Origin: *Cuba* • **Brewery Founded:** *1980s* • **Alcohol Content:** *4%*

Mayabe Calidad Extra is a pale lager beer brewed by the Cerveceria Bucanero in Holguin, Cuba. The beer pours a pale yellow with a small white head. It has a light nose of malts and some mineral tones. The aroma has light malts, straw, and citrusy notes. The taste is sweet with a pinch of salt. The beer has almost no body and a fizzy carbonation. It is a refreshing and exotic beer.

PALMA CRISTAL

Country of Origin: *Cuba* • **Brewery Founded:** *1980s* • **Alcohol Content:** *4.9%*

Palma Cristal is a pale lager brewed by the Cerveceria Bucanero in Holguin, Cuba. Cristal is the authentic Cuban beer, brewed with the highest quality ingredients. Its personality, light alcohol content and truly refreshing taste has made it the "Preferida de Cuba" which means it is now the most popular beer in Cuba. Each bottle is stamped with the Royal Palm tree, the national tree of Cuba. It is brewed with top quality malt and natural water. The beer has a revitalizing light hop flavor with no after-taste. Cristal is the perfect choice of brew for a hot sunny day, an everyday occurrence in the lives of Cubans.

TINIMA CUBAY CLASICA

Country of Origin: *Cuba* • **Brewery Founded:** *1985* • **Alcohol Content:** *5.3%*

Tinima Cubay Clasica is a pale lager brewed by the Cerveceria Tinima in Camagüey, Cuba. The beer pours a clear and golden yellow and has a fizzy off-white head. The beer's aroma is mild moldy to vegetable, with notes of mild bitter hops and malt. The flavor is sweet and corn-ish, with the same light vegetable note. The beer has a mildly spicy note and a non-bitter finish.

TINIMA SUPERIOR

Country of Origin: *Cuba* • **Brewery Founded:** *1985* • **Alcohol Content:** *3.5%*

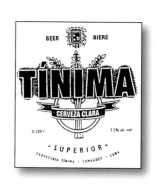

Tinima Superior is a lower alcohol pale lager brewed by the Cerveceria Tinima in Camagüey, Cuba. The beer smells sweet and malty. It is a clear, golden beer that looks very still, amazing considering how fizzy it is. Its flavors are not strong. The slight sourness on the finish is the best aspect of this beer.

CZECH REPUBLIC

BERNARD CERNY LEZAK

Country of Origin: *Czech Republic* • **Brewery Founded:** *1991* • **Alcohol Content:** *5.1%*

The Bernard family brewery uses their own spring water from the Czech Moravian highlands, malt made in their own Brno malt house, high quality Czech hops, and their own yeast culture. The beer is cold fermented rather than being pasteurized. Their dunkel beer is non-filtered and made with four types of malt. It has a distinctive full taste and a fine bitterness. The beer has won the prize of being the best dark lager in the world at the World Beer Awards.

BUDWEISER BUDVAR

Country of Origin: *Czech Republic* • **Brewery Founded:** *1895* • **Alcohol Content:** *4%*

The Budvar brewery produces some of the most popular and widely exported beers in the Czech Republic. Their two most widely-drunk beers are probably their Premium Lager and their Pale Beer. The long tradition of the production of eské Bud jovice beer and carefully selected high quality natural ingredients are a guarantee for the highest quality in both beers. The Pale Beer is ideal for those occasions when several beers will be drunk!

FALKON STALKER IPA

Country of Origin: *Czech Republic* • **Brewery Founded:** *2010* • **Alcohol Content:** *6.9%*

Falkon Stalker India Pale Ale is brewed by the Antos brewery in Slanos in the Czech Republic. The beer is an amber color with a frothy, beige head. It has a fruity nose with citrus, resin, orange peel and mandarin. The taste is fruity and malty with notes of citrus, orange, mandarin, resin, caramel, and a citric bitterness in the finish. It has a medium body with a touch of sweetness and a fresh hop character.

GAMBRINUS ORIGINAL

Country of Origin: *Czech Republic* • **Brewery Founded:** *1869* • **Alcohol Content:** *4.3%*

Gambrinus is a beer brewed in the Czech Republic at the Plze ský Prazdroj brewery. It is one of the most popular beers in the Czech Republic. The beer is named after Gambrinus, a legendary king of Flanders who was known for his mythical brewing abilities. Gambrinus beer sponsors the Gambrinus Liga, the premier Czech football league. The company was founded in 1869. Gambrinus makes two widely drunk beers. Both are derived from the same 13 degree wort, which is watered down post-fermentation. Gambrinus Original is the most widely sold Gambrinus beer in the Czech Republic.

HEROLD CERNY LEZAK 13

Country of Origin: *Czech Republic* • **Brewery Founded:** *1506* • **Alcohol Content:** *5.2%*

Herold Cerny Lezak is a Bohemian dunkel or black lager brewed by the Pivovar Herold in the Czech Republic. The beer is traditionally brewed using four different malts, the finest Saaz hops, and pure spring water. The beer has been lagered for seventy days in the cellars of Herold's five-hundred-year-old castle brewery. Herold is a small brewery in Breznice, a small town sixty kilometers south of Prague.

KOCOUR CATFISH SUMECEK

Country of Origin: *Czech Republic* • **Brewery Founded:** *2007* • **Alcohol Content:** *4.1%*

The Kocour brewery (Kocour is Czech for tom cat) has committed itself to widening the range of Czech beers available. They produce a wide range of beer specials, ranging from strong lagers to top fermented beers including weizens, stouts, saisons, and pale ales. Catfish Sumecek is an american pale ale style of beer. The beer is a hazed amber in color with a moderate off-white head. The aroma is of orange, citrus fruit, and grass, with a juicy hop tang. The taste has notes of orange pith, orange sherbet, grass, and toasted malts. The beer is medium bodied with a fine carbonation.

KOCOUR IPA SUMURAI

Country of Origin: *Czech Republic* • **Brewery Founded:** *2007* • **Alcohol Content:** *5.1%*

Koncour was established with a mission of broadening the range of Czech beers and making alternatives to the traditional Czech pilsner. Kocour's Samurai India Pale Ale is a yellow, and hazy with little yeast particles. It has a thick white head. The aroma is malty and bready, with hop and herbal notes. The taste is malty with a medium bitterness.

KOCOUR KUBIK

Country of Origin: *Czech Republic* • **Brewery Founded:** *2007* • **Alcohol Content:** *5.7%*

Kocour Kubik is an India Pale Ale made by the Kocour brewery at Varnsdorf in the Czech Republic. The beer pours with a clear amber-pale body and a small head. The aroma has a light sweetness of the malt with hints of hops, and the sweeter citrus. The taste is full of hop character, with notes of pine, followed by a very strong bitterness. The body of the beer is full, and the carbonation is fair.

KRUOVICE IMPERIAL AND CERNE BEERS

Country of Origin: *Czech Republic* • **Brewery Founded:** *1581*
Alcohol Content: *5 and 3.8%*

Krušovice's Imperial lager has a slight gold color, a deliciously bitter taste and an excellent foam. Pleasant and significant sharpness is another of its qualities. This product is brewed with superior quality Czech malt, natural spring water, and hops from the Žatec area. Krušovice Dark has been brewed for over a hundred years. The beer has a full, sweet caramel taste, and a light hop flavor. It is brewed with several types of malt, natural spring water, and hops from the Žatec area.

MASTER TMAVY 18

Country of Origin: *Czech Republic* • **Brewery Founded:** *1874* • **Alcohol Content:** *7%*

Master Tmavy 18 is brewed by the Pivovar Velke Popovice. The brewery is now owned by the Czech brewing giant Pilsner Urquell. This dunkler bock-styled beer pours nearly black and has a thick brown head. The beer has a big sweet malty aroma with hints of brown sugar and raisins. The taste is sweet with lots of sugars and dark fruits, including fig and molasses.

MATUSKA CERNA RAKETA

Country of Origin: *Czech Republic* • **Brewery Founded:** *2009* • **Alcohol Content:** *6.9%*

Cerna Raketa means black rocket in Czech. The beer is a black India Pale Ale, the first of this kind to be brewed in the Czech Republic. The beer is black in color. It is produced with intensely roasted malts and hops. The hops are Saaz, Valedictorian, Cascade, and Amarillo. The flavor has traces of coffee, chocolate, berries, and citrus. The beer is intensely bitter.

NOMAD BLACK HAWK

Country of Origin: *Czech Republic* • **Brewery Founded:** *Recent* • **Alcohol Content:** *6.8%*

Nomad is a flying brewery that brews its beers at various locations in the Czech Republic. The Nomad brewers fly around the world tasting brews and re-interpreting them. Black Hawk is a black India Pale Ale made by the cold hopping process. The beer is made with several hops varieties, Columbus, Citra, and Centennial.

NOMAD KAREL CESKA IPA 16

Country of Origin: *Czech Republic* • **Brewery Founded:** *Recent* • **Alcohol Content:** *7.6%*

Nomad's Karel Ceska India Pale Ale pours a clear medium orange color. It has a small to average, frothy, head. The aroma is moderately malty, toasted with notes of malt, moderate hop, grass, pine, citrus, dry, and butter. The flavor is moderately sweet and and bitter. The body of the beer is medium, and its texture is oily. The beer's carbonation is soft to flat.

PILSNER URQUELL

Country of Origin: *Czech Republic* • **Brewery Founded:** *1842* • **Alcohol Content:** *4.4%*

Plze ský Prazdroj beer is better known by its German name, Pilsner Urquell. It is a bottom-fermented beer that has been produced since 1842 in Pilsen, part of today's Czech Republic. Pilsner Urquell was the first pilsner beer brewed anywhere in the world. Today the brand is owned by the global brewer SABMiller. Pilsner Urquell is more strongly hopped than most pilsner beers. Saaz hops, a noble hop variety, are a key element in its flavor profile.

PURKMISTR DARK LAGER

Country of Origin: *Czech Republic* • **Brewery Founded:** *1341* • **Alcohol Content:** *4.8%*

Purkmistr's Bohemian-style dark lager is brewed from four kinds of malt. The beer is brewed by Purkmistr's master brewer Josef Krysl. The beer's pleasant coffee-like flavor blends nicely with hints of genuine Belgian chocolate. The beer is brewed with barley malt, Zatex hops, water, and yeast. The flavor ends in a long, dry fade. The beer is lovely partnered with dessert.

RADEGAST ORIGINAL

Country of Origin: *Czech Republic* • **Brewery Founded:** *1970* • **Alcohol Content:** *4.3%*

Radegast is a Czech beer brewed in Nošovice, in the Moravian-Silesian region of the Czech Republic. The beer is named after the god Radegast. Stemming from the name for the beer is the slogan: "Život je ho ký: Bohudík", a Czech phrase which translates into English as "Life is bitter: Thank God" (in reference to the bitter taste of the beer). The brewery is now owned by Pilsner Urquell.

STAROBRNO PREMIUM LAGER

Country of Origin: *Czech Republic* • **Brewery Founded:** *1325* • **Alcohol Content:***5%*

Starobrno Brewery (the Pivovar Starobrno) is a Czech brewery located in the city of Brno. It was built as a successor of the brewery that was founded in 1325 as a part of the Cistercian convent. The brewery was named Starobrno Brewery in the second half of the nineteenth century. In 2009, Starobrno Brewery produced more than 22 million gallons of beer. The same year, the brewery merged with the Royal Brewery of Krušovice and became a part of the Dutch brewing company Heineken. The brewery makes five different beers ranging from light to dark.

SVATY NORBERT ANTIDEPRESSANT

Country of Origin: *Czech Republic* • **Brewery Founded:** *1629* • **Alcohol Content:** *6.3%*

Svaty Norbert Antidepressant is a dunkler bock. It is a dark brown colored beer with a medium light beige head. It has a strong coffee aroma together with notes of yeast, roasted malt, and red fruits. The taste is of coffee, caramel, dark berries, and black berries. It has a nice coffee bitterness and a fruity finish. The beer is brewed by the Strahov Monastery Brewery.

SVATY NORBERT IPA

Country of Origin: *Czech Republic* • **Brewery Founded:** *1629* • **Alcohol Content:** *6.3%*

Svaty Norbert IPA is brewed by the Strahov Monastery Brewery. The first mention of the monastery brewery dates from the thirteenth century. The construction of the new brewery was instigated by Abbot Kaspar Questenberg in 1629. The brewery's IPA is a recently introduced brew. It is a top-fermented beer brewed from Czech ingredients and two kinds of American hops (Amarillo and Cascade). It combines full a malt body with high hop bitterness and a hoppy aroma.

SVATY NORBERT VELIKONOCNI 13

Country of Origin: *Czech Republic* • **Brewery Founded:** *1629* • **Alcohol Content:** *5.3%*

Svaty Norbert Velikonocni 13 is brewed by the Strahov Monastery Brewery. The beer is the brewery's Easter beer. It is brewed using the three-mash method from a single variety of Czech malt and the famous Czech Saaz hop. The beer is medium fermented, and medium bodied, but has a higher bitterness. This has resulted in the beer's widespread popularity.

SVIJANY KVASNICAK 13

Country of Origin: *Czech Republic* • **Brewery Founded:** *1564* • **Alcohol Content:** *13%*

Svijany Kvasnicak is an unfiltered beer. Established in 1564, Svijany is one of the oldest Czech breweries. It is located in the village of Svijany. The brewery produces an extensive range of unpasteurized lagers, which are mostly light in color and ranging in strength between 3.2% and 6.5% ABV. The aroma is of malt and hops. The beer pours a clear golden color and has a stable head. The flavor is nicely balanced between malt and hops, with notes of grass and light yeast. The finish is bitter hoppy.

SVIJANY RYTIR BITTER

Country of Origin: *Czech Republic* • **Brewery Founded:** *1564* • **Alcohol Content:** *5%*

The Svijany brewery was founded in 1564. It is one of the oldest Czech breweries, located in the village of Svijany. Their Rytir Bitter is a Czech pilsner. The beer pours golden and a little hazy with good head. The aroma has grassy and fruity hop notes. Floral notes are also present. The taste is very grassy and deciduous with forest-like notes. Sweet maltiness and citrus hints are also found. This is a well-hopped pilsner, very similar to pale ale.

U MEDVÍDKU X33

Country of Origin: *Czech Republic* • **Brewery Founded:** *2000s* • **Alcohol Content:** *12.6%*

The U Medvídku mini-brewery is currently the smallest restaurant/brewery in the Czech Republic. Their aim is to brew the strongest beers in the Czech Republic. This is how their X beers were conceived. The beers are produced with traditional technology and Pilze malt. The beer is then fermented in tanks for fourteen days before the beer is fermented in oak barrels for fourteen weeks. A third fermentation takes place after the addition of a special yeast strain. This lasts for another fourteen weeks.

U TŘÍ RŮŽÍ KLASTERNI SPECIAL SV. JILJI NO. 1

Country of Origin: *Czech Republic* • **Brewery Founded:** *2012* • **Alcohol Content:** *7.5%*

U Tří Růží Klasterni Special Sv. Jilji No. 1 is a dunkler bock. U Tří Růží (the three roses) brewery was first established in the middle ages, but was reconstructed in central Prague in 2012. The beer is deep amber colored, and hazy. The aroma is of dry herbal hops with a slightly sweet and caramel nose. The beer has a moderate to distinctive bitter-sweet flavor, and is medium bodied. The finish has a lingering herbal-hoppiness and dark-malt.

ÚNĚTICKÉ PIVO 12°

Country of Origin: *Czech Republic* • **Brewery Founded:** *1710* • **Alcohol Content:** *4.9%*

Únětické Pivo is brewed by the Únětické brewery. The brewery was probably built in 1710, and was owned by the St.Vitus Cathedral in Prague. Each year, the beer was stored in ice in caves near the brewery. Únětické brewed both light and black beers. Pivo 12° is a yellow beer with a yellowish head. The aroma has notes of straw and hops. The flavor is sweet with notes of straw, hops, and malt, leading to a bitter finish.

VELKOPOPOVICKY KOZEL PALE LAGER

Country of Origin: *Czech Republic* • **Brewery Founded:** *1874* • **Alcohol Content:** *4.6%*

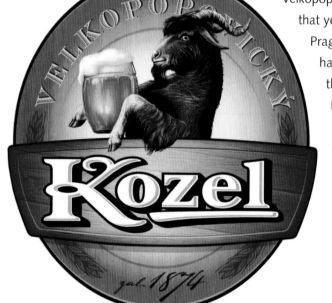

Velkopopovický Kozel is a Czech lager which has been brewed since 1874. In that year, Franz Ringhoffer founded the brewery in Velké Popovice near Prague. The brewery symbol is a goat (kozel is goat in Czech). Kozel has won a lot of different awards including the Australian Beer Award, the Czech Beer of the Year, the World Beer Cup and more. Kozel Premium beer won awards at the World Beer Championships in Chicago in 1995, 1996, and 1997. Kozel beer is now sold in thirty-eight countries worldwide.

VYŠKOV JUBILER IPA

Country of Origin: *Czech Republic* • **Brewery Founded:** *1680* • **Alcohol Content:** *6%*

The Vyškov brewery was built in 1680 on the orders of Bishop Karel of Liechtenstein. But the tradition of brewing beer in Vyškov dates from the medieval ages. This IPA beer has a full, bitter flavor that has hints of citrus fruit. The beer is brewed with a selection of different hops, Kazbek, Premiant, and Cascade. The malts are Czech, Munich, and caramel.

DENMARK

ALBANI GIRAF GOLD

Country of Origin: *Denmark* • **Brewery Founded:** *1859* • **Alcohol Content:** *7.2%*

The Albani Brewery is located in Odense, Denmark, and the vast majority of its customers live on the Danish island of Funen. The brewery was founded by Theodor Schiøtz in 1859. In 2000, the brewery merged with Royal Unibrew, a group of Danish regional breweries. Giraf Beer is a strong pilsner. It was first brewed in 1962, when the Odense Zoo's giraffe, Kalle was found dead. As Albani had previously used this giraffe in its advertising, the brewery decided to create a special beer, whose profits would be spent on purchasing a new giraffe for the zoo. This was a great success and the first year's production of Giraf Gold raised enough money to buy two giraffes for the zoo.

BRØCKHOUSE INDIA PALE ALE

Country of Origin: *Denmark* • **Brewery Founded:** *1995* • **Alcohol Content:** *5.5%*

Brøckhouse was a Danish micro brewery, located in Hillerød, Denmark. It was founded by brewer Allan Poulsen and reached a peak production capacity of 500,000 liters per year. The brewery specialized in brewing beers from Danish history. Brockhouse experienced financial difficulties in connection with the world recession and filed for bankruptcy in 2009. Brockhouse's now retired India Pale Ale was introduced in 2002.

BROCKHOUSE STOUT

Country of Origin: *Denmark* • **Brewery Founded:** *1995* • **Alcohol Content:** *5.5%*

This now retired stout was a round, mellow, and dry beer. The traditional-style beer was brewed with pale ale malt, caramel, and chocolate malts along with roasted non-malted barley. Brøckhouse Stout was top-fermented with fine hop bitterness and a whiff of chocolate. The stout appeared dry and creamy with a thick lush head. It had a moderate content of carbon dioxide. The stout was a good food partner that went well with spicy foods, seafood, and heavy chocolate desserts.

CARLSBERG CARLS PORTER

Country of Origin: *Denmark* • **Brewery Founded:** *1847* • **Alcohol Content:** *7.8%*

J.C. Jacobsen founded Carlsberg in 1847. He located his brewery just outside the Danish capital, Copenhagen. He was a brewing pioneer, and used steam brewing, refrigeration, and a single yeast strain to make his beer. Porter was originally drunk by English railway porters to keep themselves warm. It was a mixture of the sweet English ale and the strong Irish stout. Carls Porter maintains the principles and qualities of the original porter, with a sweet, spicy flavor and a characteristic, coal black color. Carlsberg have brewed their Baltic Porter since 1895.

CARLSBERG ELEPHANT

Country of Origin: *Denmark* • **Brewery Founded:** *1847* • **Alcohol Content:** *7.2%*

Carlsberg Elephant is a strong pilsner beer. First launched in 1959, it is strong in both flavor and alcohol content. The color is light golden amber and the foam white. The ample use of malt gives Elephant a vinous and rich character. The high hop content in Elephant gives a masculine bitter bite to the beer. The elephants on the beer's label are inspired by the two pairs of life-size, elephant statues which form part of the main entrance to Carlsberg's brewery in Copenhagen. The Elephant Gate has become a famous Danish landmark and gives visitors to the brewery a majestic welcome. Carlsberg Elephant received three stars in the prestigious Superior Taste Awards 2006 from the international Taste & Quality Institute in Brussels, Belgium. Carlsberg Elephant goes very well with all spicy dishes, and it is particularly well suited for the Thai kitchen, Cajun dishes and Mexican food. It also goes well with rustic, European dishes.

CARLSBERG EXPORT

Country of Origin: *Denmark* • **Brewery Founded:** *1847* • **Alcohol Content:** *5%*

If you enjoy your premium beer chilled, then the perfect choice is super cool Carlsberg Export Extra Cold. Carlsberg Export was the first leading premium lager to be available in Extra Cold. The stylish Carlsberg Export is a premium strength lager with a refined and satisfying taste. Brewed to the original Danish recipe, it has deep malty notes and a distinct bitterness that that create a full flavored beer.

CARLSBERG JACOBSEN ORIGINAL DARK LAGER

Country of Origin: *Denmark* • **Brewery Founded:** *1847* • **Alcohol Content:** *5.8%*

Jacobsen Original Dark Lager is brewed on the oldest recipe in the Carlsberg archives, J.C. Jacobsen's original recipe of 1854. It is a Munich-style beer. To re-create the original recipe, the Jacobsen Brewhouse focused on one of the key ingredients in beer; water. Water highly influences the taste of beer and by analysing the water used in Jacobsen's time, an exact copy of his original ingredient was created by adding salts and minerals. The beer's main raw material is Münchenermalt from Germany, but a floor malt from England is also added to the brew, just as was done in the 1850s. The beer is fermented at low temperature to give it a special mild and rounded caramel flavor. The beer has aromas of clear bread, malt, and caramel. Original Dark Lager is excellent with the uncomplicated dishes of the typical Nordic kitchen, such as barbequed or roasted meats and vegetables. It also goes well with cheese, lasagne, pizza, and bread.

CERES RED ERIK

Country of Origin: *Denmark* • **Brewery Founded:** *1856* • **Alcohol Content:** *6.5%*

Ceres Brewery was founded by a grocer named Malthe Conrad Lottrup. It was named after the Roman goddess Ceres. The brewery became a supplier to the Royal Danish Court in 1914. Ceres closed in 2008. Red Erik (now retired) got its red ruby color and pink foam from the juices of berries and fruits. Extensive development work has been performed to identify the right berries and fruits, which produce the beer's distinctive color without changing the flavor and smell of the beer. The taste was fresh and sharp balanced with a faint residual sweetness. The beer was brewed from water, malt, maize, hops, and fruit juices.

CERES ROYAL STOUT

Country of Origin: *Denmark* • **Brewery Founded:** *1856* • **Alcohol Content:** *7.7%*

Ceres Royal Stout was one of the (now closed) brewery's oldest beers. This style of beer is sometimes called mild porter. Ceres Royal Stout was made with Pilsen malt, Munich malt, and dark roasted malt. The mild taste was achieved by restricting the malt and using a portion of raw grain. The roasted malt gives the stout a black color and a brown head. Royal Stout was a heavyweight beer, but the Ceres yeast made it more drinkable than other black beers. It was mild and sweet.

FAXE EXTRA STRONG

Country of Origin: *Denmark* • **Brewery Founded:** *1901* • **Alcohol Content:** *10%*

The Faxe Brewery is located in the Danish town of Fakse. The Brewery was founded by Nikoline and Conrad Nielsen and is best known for its strong export beers. In 1989 Faxe Brygeri merged with the Danish brewing group Royal Unibrew. The beer is golden straw yellow and pours with a thin creamy head. The beer has an apple juice aroma with sweet undertones and hints of citrus. The taste is refreshing and has a slight hoppiness.

FAXE PREMIUM

Country of Origin: *Denmark* • **Brewery Founded:** *1901* • **Alcohol Content:** *5%*

FAXE Premium is a classic premium lager with a soft and distinctive flavor. The combination of the finest malt, hops and local water results in a beer with a rich, yet mild and smooth taste. It is an attractive and balanced lager. The beer pours pale gold with a tiny off white head. The aroma is a little malty with a hint of metal. Flavor is mild with a clean finish. Premium is a very refreshing lager.

HANCOCK BREWERY OLD GAMBRINUS DARK BEER

Country of Origin: *Denmark* • **Brewery Founded:** *1935* • **Alcohol Content:** *9.5%*

Hancock's Old Gambrinus is a doppelbock-style dark beer. It pours a dark red-brown with almost no head. It has a sweetish nose with hints of tart cherries, old barrels, golden syrup, and a faint smokiness. The beer has a rich sweet body, with notes of dark dried fruit, dark sugar, old barrel-aged wine, and caramel toffee. The beer's aftertaste is dry-sweet with hop bitterness and a musty note. The forerunner of this beer was first brewed in 1935.

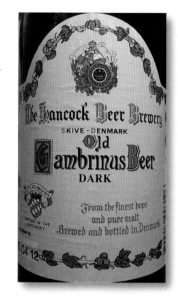

THISTED LIMFJORDSPORTER

Country of Origin: *Denmark* • **Brewery Founded:** *1902* • **Alcohol Content:** *5.8%*

The Thisted Bryghus Brewery is located near Limfjord on Denmark's North Sea coast. The brewery was the first in Denmark to produce ecological beer. Limfjordsporter is a golden pilsner style beer with a steady white head and an aroma of hay, malty sweetness, and hops. The beer has a pleasant caramel-like malty taste and moderate carbonation. The flavor has a good interplay between malt and hops, and a good balance. It has a medium bitterness.

TUBORG PILSNER

Country of Origin: *Denmark* • **Brewery Founded:** *1873* • **Alcohol Content:** *4.6%*

Tuborg was founded by Carl Frederik Tietgen. Since 1970 it has been part of Denmark's largest brewer, Carlsberg. Tuborg initially produced pale lager for the Danish market. It now brews several different styles of beer including Tuborg Green, Tuborg Lemon, Tuborg Christmas beer, Tuborg Gold, Tuborg Red, Tuborg Twist, and Tuborg Black. Tuborg Pilsner lager is bottom-fermented. It is brewed from lager malt. This is a slightly roasted, bright type of malt that results in the well-known mild, fresh taste, and an aroma of flowers and grain. The beer is medium rich and lively with a moderate bitterness in the aftertaste.

WIIBROE IMPERIAL STOUT

Country of Origin: *Denmark* • **Brewery Founded:** *1840* • **Alcohol Content:** *8.2%*

Willbroe's Imperial Stout is pitch black color with a dense brown head. The aroma is sweet, of chocolate, coffee, roasted malts, and a bit of vanilla. The flavor is moderate sweet, of roasted coffee. The body of the stout is on the thin side for the beer's strength and style. Although the beer is brewed by an industrial giant like Carlsberg, it has an excellent hand-brewed presence.

ESTONIA

A. LE COQ PREMIUM

Country of Origin: *Estonia* • **Brewery Founded:** *1807* • **Alcohol Content:** *4.7%*

A. Le Coq was founded by Albert Le Coq in London in 1807. From 1826 the beer was brewed in Tartu, Estonia. The brewery is currently owned by Finnish company Olvi and its best known beer is Premium, which is the most popular beer in Estonia. This mellow light beer is brewed with good quality hops and carefully selected malt.

PULS JOULULEGEND

Country of Origin: *Estonia* • **Brewery Founded:** *1869* • **Alcohol Content:** *5.4%*

Puls Joululegend is brewed by Viru Olu in Haljala, Estonia. Joululegend is as seasonal dunkel or dark beer that is brewed for Christmas. The beer was formerly known as Parnu Joulu Legend. This beer had a higher alcohol level of 5.7%. Production of the beer moved from the Puls Brewery in Parnu in early 2008. The beer pours a dark reddish brown color with a medium beige head. The aroma is of dark plum, spices, and herbal notes. The beer has a smooth, sweet caramel body

SAKU ORIGINAAL

Country of Origin: *Estonia* • **Brewery Founded:** *1820* • **Alcohol Content:** *4.7%*

Saku Brewery is based in Saku, Estonia. It was founded by local landlord Karl Friedrich von Rehbinder. Saku Originaal is Saku's flagship beer. It is made of yeast, water, selected malt, and hops. Brewing of Saku Originaal started in 1993, making it the first Estonian beer to be sold after Estonia regained its independence. According to market research conducted by Emor in 2002, Saku Originaal is now the most recognized and popular Estonian beer.

VIRU

Country of Origin: *Estonia* • **Brewery Founded:** *1807* • **Alcohol Content:** *5%*

Viru is a pilsner-style beer brewed in Tartu, Estonia by the A. Le Coq brewery. The brand is owned by Baltic Beer Company Ltd. which is based in London, England. A. Le Coq is the second largest brewery in Estonia, with a market share of 36.8% in 2005. Viru beer is sold in distinctive tall bottles in the shape of an octagonal pyramid. The beer is brewed with malted barley from Lithuania, well water, and Saaz hops.

FINLAND

HARTWALL LAPIN KULTA ARCTIC MALT DARK LAGER

Country of Origin: *Finland* • **Brewery Founded:** *1836* • **Alcohol Content:** *4.6%*

Hartwall began as a soft drinks company, founded by Victor Hartwall. The company began to brew beer in 1966. It is now the leading beverage company in Finland. Hartwall's Lapin Kulta Arctic Malt Dark Lager is a full-bodied malty and smooth beer, made from barley, hops, and the purest groundwater. It is a great food partner for red meat and game.

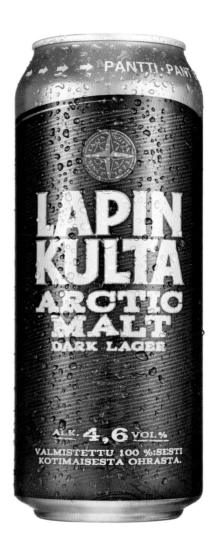

HARTWALL ROGGENBIER

Country of Origin: *Finland* • **Brewery Founded:** *1836* • **Alcohol Content:** *5.7%*

Hartwall's Roggenbier (now retired) was a specialty grain beer brewed in the company's Helsinki brewery. It was a special bottom-fermented beer brewed with respect to tradition on the occasion of the hundred anniversary of the Finnish Breweries' Union. Hartwall Roggenbier's soft malty and aromatic flavor was derived from the balance of rye malt and light hops. A full tenth of rye malt gave this unique full malt beer its beautiful reddish color.

HARTWALL SUKLAA PORTER

Country of Origin: *Finland* • **Brewery Founded:** *1836* • **Alcohol Content:** *4.5%*

Hartwall's Suklaa Porter (now retired) was brewed by Hartwall. The company is now part of Royal Unibrew. Hartwall's Suklaa (chocolate) Porter derived its soft flavor and full nose from the chocolaty aroma and carefully selected special malts. This all-malt porter was brewed by hand from the best ingredients, and it deserved the company's famous seal, a proof of the uncompromised quality of Hartwall's beers.

HARTWALL URHO IV

Country of Origin: *Finland* • **Brewery Founded:** *1836* • **Alcohol Content:** *5.5%*

Hartwall Urho IV is a brewed pale lager brewed in Helsinki, Finland. The beer is strong and rich, smooth and extremely drinkable. It has a pleasant and lingering palate. The beer pours golden and has a small head. The beer has a moderate aroma with malty, grainy, and sweet notes. The beer's body is light to medium, with a malty and sweetish flavor. The finish is average, malty, and sweetish with light caramel and some bread.

LAMMIN SAHTI PUHTI

Country of Origin: *Finland* • **Brewery Founded:** *1985* • **Alcohol Content:** *7%*

Lammin Sahti Oy is the oldest Finnish Microbrewery. It was founded with sixty-eight shareholders and started to sell its beer in 1988. The brewery's main product is Sahti 7,5 %. The brewery makes about 30,000 liters of this brew each year. Lammin Sahti's Puhti is a ruby-red juniper-spiced beer. It is brewed by the Saimaan brewers for Lammin Sahti. This beer is known as Kataja in the United States.

OLVI OYJ SANDELS IVA

Country of Origin: *Finland* • **Brewery Founded:** *1878* • **Alcohol Content:** *5.3%*

Olvi was founded by William Gideon Aberg. The brewery is located on the lonely coast of Iisalmi, Finland. Sandels pours with a large foamy, frothy, white head. The color is a clear, bright yellow with lots of large bubble trails. The aroma is beery with faint hops and malt. The flavor is mostly sweet and tangy with a bit of bitterness. The body is highly dominated by the carbonation which leaves a tingly sensation with some sweetness in the finish.

OLVI TUMMA OLUT

Country of Origin: *Finland* • **Brewery Founded:** *1878* • **Alcohol Content:** *4%*

Olvi's Sandels Tumma Olut (dark lager) has is subtly malty and full-bodied. The flavor comes from selected range of caramelized malts that give this dark lager a festive red to dark brown color. Dark lagers are usually light lagers with a lower alcohol content, and have a surprisingly sweet taste. Sandels Tumma Olut dark lager suits grilled meat and vegetables.

SINEBRYCHOFF KARHU III

Country of Origin: *Finland* • **Brewery Founded:** *1819* • **Alcohol Content:** *4.6%*

Sinebrychoff is a Finnish brewery and soft drinks company. It was founded in 1819 in Helsinki, Finland by Russian merchant Nikolai Sinebrychoff. Today it is one of the largest breweries in Finland. Karhu (bear in Finnish) is a pale lager with a strong taste. The beer was first brewed in 1929 and has become the most popular beer in Finland. There are three Karhu beers in the line-up. Karhu III is the most popular.

SINEBRYCHOFF KAURA

Country of Origin: *Finland* • **Brewery Founded:** *1819* • **Alcohol Content:** *4.5%*

Sinebrychoff Kaura is blond, non-filtered bottom yeast beer, made by combining two rarely used malts, barley and oat. The beer is seasoned with a hint of honey. The taste of Kaura is fresh and fruity and a little sweet, due to the honey. The aftertaste is long and softly refreshing. This honey oat beer is best when served at a temperature of between eight and twelve degrees.

SINEBRYCHOFF KOFF PORTER

Country of Origin: *Finland* • **Brewery Founded:** *1819* • **Alcohol Content:** *7.2%*

Sinebrychoff's Koff Porter is a classic Baltic porter beer. It is a dark unfiltered beer manufactured with top fermentation. It is brewed with Munich malts and plenty of hops that impart a strong flavor to the beer. The beer pours black with dark brown highlights and has a small light brown head. The beer has a nice dark chocolate aroma, a medium body, and low carbonation. The taste is of rich chocolate, roast, earthy hops, and dry coffee.

FRANCE

AGENT PROVOCATEUR

Country of Origin: *France* • **Brewery Founded:** *2000s* • **Alcohol Content:** *6.5%*

Agent Provocateur is brewed by France's Brasserie Craig Allan. Craig started his career brewing beer in several Scottish microbreweries before moving to France. Agent Provocateur is a strongly hopped beer. It is a hybrid of an IPA and a Belgian golden ale. The beer has bright, colorful notes of exotic fruits (pineapple, grapefruit and lime), and spices with a solid bitter finish. This beer is an excellent aperitif and goes perfectly with spicy food and creamy cheese. Agent Provocateur is brewed with pale Ale, crystal, and wheat malts. It is bittered with Amarillo and Cascade hops.

BRASSERIE LEBBE L' AMALTHEE

Country of Origin: *France* • **Brewery Founded:** *Unknown* • **Alcohol Content:** *6%*

Brasserie Lebbe is located at Villefranque in the Hautes-Pyrénées region of France. It produces an excellent beer called L'Amalthée as well as goat cheese. The beer is an orange-tan color with a white head. The beer has a spicy yeasty character, with grainy malt and very light hopping. The flavor is quite subtle but very flavorsome. It is a classic biere de garde.

BRASSERIE DE SAINT-SYLVESTRE BIERE NOUVELLE

Country of Origin: *France* • **Brewery Founded:** *1860s* • **Alcohol Content:** *8%*

Biere Nouvelle is a traditional biere de garde. These beers are strong pale ales from the Nord-Pas-de-Calais region of northern France. They were often brewed by farmers in the winter and spring when cold temperatures enabled them to control their yeasts. The beer is clear orange with medium bubbles and a high nearly white meringue-like head that settles slowly leaving loads of lacing. The aroma is of fruit, ripe apples, pears, pomegranates, earth, and a dash of vinegar. The taste is sweet, with tones of caramelized sugar, lemon curd, vinegar, band bitter lemon zest. The beer has a medium high carbonation.

CASTELAIN BLOND BIERE DE GARDE

Country of Origin: *France* • **Brewery Founded:** *1926* • **Alcohol Content:** *6.4%*

The Brasserie Castelain is a traditional French brewery. The beer pours a pale old gold and has a chunky eggshell head. The beer has an aroma of sweet malt, toast, caramel, cereal, floral, and spicy hops. It has a flavor of cereal, toast, sweet malt, hay, apple skins, light caramel, mineral notes, floral hops, and just a hint of spice, and herbal hops. The beer has a light to medium body with a creamy texture. It has a sharp carbonation and a slightly dry, crisp finish.

CERVOISE LANCELOT

Country of Origin: *France* • **Brewery Founded:** *1990* • **Alcohol Content:** *6%*

The brasserie Lancelot is a French brewery founded by Bernard Lancelot. It is located on the site of a gold mine in Roc-Saint-André in Morbihan, France. The brewery produces seven top-fermented, unfiltered, naturally-produced, and unpasteurized beers. Cervoise Lancelot is a traditional beer that is unfiltered and unpasteurized. Produced with malted barley, it is aromatized with seven different plants and a touch of honey. This gives the beer an exceptional aroma. Serve this luminous amber beer at between 50 and 55 degrees fahrenheit, and remember to let the yeast fall to the bottom of the bottle.

CH'TI BLONDE

Country of Origin: *France* • **Brewery Founded:** *1926*
Alcohol Content: *6.4%*

Ch'ti Blonde is brewed by the Brasserie Castelain, a traditional French brewery. Ch'ti Blonde was first brewed in 1979. It is made using four varieties of hops. The beer was awarded the Silver Medal at the Concours Général Agricole in 2008. In 2003 Ch'ti Blonde was the gold medalist at the World Beer Selection in Brussels, Belgium. In 2009 Brasserie Castelain launched an advertizing campaign to celebrate the thirtieth anniversary of the beer.

FLEURAC LA TRIPLE BRUNE IPA

Country of Origin: *France* • **Brewery Founded:** *2005* • **Alcohol Content:** *8%*

La Triple is a beer of character, slightly amber-blonde in color with a fine white head. It is a tradition abbey triple amber beer. The beer is brewed from water, barley malt, hops, spices, and yeast. The aroma is of honey and nuts. The taste is marked by fermentation esters, with the aroma of hops. The body has a little astringency. The beer should be served at cellar temperature.

GWINIZ DU

Country of Origin: *France* • **Brewery Founded:** *1998* • **Alcohol Content:** *5.4%*

The Brasserie de Bretagne (formerly the Brasserie Britt) is located at Trégunc in the French department of Finistère. Gwiniz Du is an dark amber wheat beer. It pours a dark amber color with an abundant foam head. The aroma is of lightly roasted malt and light notes of wheat and fruit. This amber beer is very slightly tart and bitter. Its sweet flavor and abundant bubbles are very pleasant.

HEINEKEN 33 EXPORT

Country of Origin: *France* • **Brewery Founded:** *19970s* • **Alcohol Content:** *4.8%*

Heineken employs more than 4,150 people in France, where their beer is widely drunk. 33 Export is brewed by Heineken (France). The beer is a light-colored pilsner. 33 Export is quite sweet and refreshing. The beer is a medium gold with a thin white head. The beer smells of pale hops, corn, pale malt, and corn. It has a light thin body with soft carbonation. It has a sweet taste of corn with grass and pale malt with a vegetable center and a bitter sharp dry finish.

JADE BIERE BIOLOGIQUE

Country of Origin: *France* • **Brewery Founded:** *1926* • **Alcohol Content:** *4.5%*

Jade is a "biere biologique" brewed by the Brasserie Castelain. Castelain is a traditional French brewery. Jade was the first French organic beer, created in 1986. The beer is brewed with malted barley (Trémois and Volga malts) and hops (Perle and Aurora varieties). Jade is a light beer and is rich in vitamins (B6, C, PP) and trace elements.

JENLAIN AMBREE

Country of Origin: *France* • **Brewery Founded:** *1922* • **Alcohol Content:** *7.5%*

Felix Duyck's farm-brewery brewed its first beer in 1922. In the 1950s the brewery sold their brews in re-cycled champagne bottles. The brewery's beers were given the name Jenlain in the 1970s. Jenlain Abree (amber) is a high fermentation beer created in 1922, which made the reputation of the brewery. Unpasteurized, it is brewed with three malts and three different hops. It is amber in color. The beer is sometimes used in cooking. The beer received the Diploma of Merit and the National Prestige Award in 1993.

KRONENBOURG 1664

Country of Origin: *France* • **Brewery Founded:** *1664* • **Alcohol Content:** *5.5%*

Kronenbourg Brewery (Brasseries Kronenbourg) was founded in 1664 by Geronimus Hatt in Strasbourg, which is now in France. The company is now owned by the Carlsberg Group. Kronenbourg is the fifth oldest surviving beer brand in the world. The brewer's main brand is Kronenbourg 1664, a pale lager that is the best selling premium lager brand in France and the most popular French beer worldwide. 1664 was first brewed in 1952. Its golden highlights and delicate bitterness come from selecting the best hops, the Strisselspalt.

L'ANGELUS

Country of Origin: *France* • **Brewery Founded:** *1905* • **Alcohol Content:** *7%*

L'Angelus is a biere de garde brewed by the Brasserie D'Annoeullin, located in north France. Their L'Angelus is a blonde beer that pours a very slightly cloudy yellow/golden color, with over an inch of foaming head. The smell is very malty and has a bit of orange, fruit, yeast, and wheat. The beer has a sweet malty taste, with some fruit and a nice bitterness. The beer has decent carbonation and drinkability.

LA CHOULETTE AMBREE

Country of Origin: *France* • **Brewery Founded:** *1895* • **Alcohol Content:** *8%*

The Brasserie La Choulette is a craft brewery located in the village of Hordain in the Nord-Pas-de-Calais region of France. The brewery was founded by Jules Dhassy. The beer is the result of a careful selection of special aromatic malts that give the beer a good taste of caramel. The beer is a redhead with copper highlights, and a dense ivory foam. The beer has a rich aroma with notes of prune. It tastes of coffee and light caramel. The beer has good bitterness with a silky texture.

LA CHOULETTE DE NOEL

Country of Origin: *France* • **Brewery Founded:** *1895* • **Alcohol Content:** *7%*

The Brasserie La Choulette is a craft brewer based in a village in the northern coastal region of France. La Choulette De Noel is a Christmas biere de garde brewed for the festive season. The beer pours fairly dark amber. It smells like a very malty beer, with hints of cinnamon apples. The taste is malty with little sweetness. It has a light spice and a faint suggestion of the apple noted in the aroma. A light hand was used with the spices, they don't overpower the beer.

LES BRASSEURS DE GAYANT LA GOUDALE

Country of Origin: *France* • **Brewery Founded:** *1919* • **Alcohol Content:** *7.2%*

The Les Brasseurs de Gayant Brewery is the second largest independent brewery in France. It was founded in the Norde-Pas-de-Calais region of France that borders Belgium. Les Brasseurs de Gayant specializes in the small batch production of France's unique biere de garde style of beer. La Goudale is brewed using special French malts and hops. La Goudale was awarded the winner of the World's Best Biere de Garde at the 2008 World Beer Awards. La Goudale is a light, golden, and dense ale. It is soft to the palate and provides a long lasting finish.

PAGE 24 BIERE DE NOEL

Country of Origin: *France* • **Brewery Founded:** *2003* • **Alcohol Content:** *6.9%*

A seasonal beer, brewed for the winter months, the Cuvée de Noël is a cordial and convivial biere de garde amber beer. It pours brown in color with a small head. The aromas are of brown bread with some nuttiness and light metallic notes. It has a sweetish taste with some raisins, mud cake, and dough. This is a tasty festive brew. The beer is generally sweetish and slightly nutty in the aftertaste.

PELFORTH BLONDE

Country of Origin: *France* • **Brewery Founded:** *1914* • **Alcohol Content:** *5.8%*

Pelforth is a French brewery founded in Mons-en-Barœul by three Lillois brewers. Production was stopped during World War II, restarting in 1950. In 1972, the brewery name was changed to Pelforth. It was acquired by Heineken International in 1988. The brewery now produces the Pelforth brand of beers. Pelforth Blonde is a pale lager. It pours gold with a medium head. The aroma is of straw, corn, and vanilla. The taste has hints of straw and icing sugar.

PELFORTH BRUNE

Country of Origin: *France* • **Brewery Founded:** *1914* • **Alcohol Content:** *6.5%*

Pelforth brewed their first beer, an ale, in 1935 using two different types of malt and English yeast. The name came from "Pel" for pelican and "forte" for strong. The brewery continues to be famous for strong specialty beers. Pelforth Brune pours a beautiful mahogany with a light tan head. The flavor is initially rich and malty, with a good bit of roastiness. There is no hop balance, but there is a hint of roasty bitterness to balance the malt. It has a distinct grain flavor, and a hint of mild cigar tobacco, and a bit of caramel.

TELENN DU

Country of Origin: *France* • **Brewery Founded:** *1990* • **Alcohol Content:** *4.5%*

Telenn Du is a specialty grain dark lager produced by the Brasserie Lancelot. The brewery is located on the site of a gold mine in Roc-Saint-André in Morbihan, France. The brewery produces seven top-fermented, unfiltered, naturally-produced, and unpasteurized beers. The beer is brown with a tan head. It smells of sweet caramel malt, roast and dark malt, and cocoa with woody tones. The body is medium oily and frothy. Telenn Du tastes of dark and roasted malt without too much bitterness.

THIRIEZ BLONDE

Country of Origin: *France* • **Brewery Founded:** *1996* • **Alcohol Content:** *6%*

Thiriez Blonde is a saison farmhouse ale brewed by the Brasserie Thiriez. The beer is brewed ecologically, from water, wheat and barley malts, hops, spices, and yeast. No additive of any kind or any coloring is added to the beer. The beer is top fermented in stainless steel tanks. It is lagered for at least two weeks and then bottled. The beer is neither filtered nor pasteurized, but is conditioned in the bottle. The beer needs to be drunk within a year of being bottled.

THIRIEZ ETOILE DU NORD

Country of Origin: *France* • **Brewery Founded:** *1996* • **Alcohol Content:** *5.5%*

Etoile Du Nord is a saison or farmhouse ale brewed by the Brasserie Thiriez. All the brewery's beers are brewed ecologically with water, wheat, barley malt, hops, spices, and yeast without any colorings being added. They are top fermented. The beer pours a hazy pale orange with a high white head. The smell is sweet and malty, but also has notes of hops, grass, spices, cloves, and cardamom. The taste is less sweet, with brown sugar, bitter oranges, cloves, and grapefruit peel. The beer has a medium low carbonation and a medium body.

THIERIEZ LA ROUGE FLAMANDE

Country of Origin: *France* • **Brewery Founded:** *1996* • **Alcohol Content:** *5.8%*

La Rouge Flamande is brewed by the Brasserie Thiriez. All the brewery's beers are brewed ecologically with water, wheat, barley malt, hops, spices, and yeast without any colorings being added. They are top fermented. La Rouge Flamande is an amber red beer with a white foam head. The aroma of malt, yeast, and apple with a touch of acidity. The taste is malty, with notes of caramel and hops.

VIVAT TRIPLE STRONG BLOND BEER

Country of Origin: *France* • **Brewery Founded:** *2001* • **Alcohol Content:** *8.3%*

The historic Abbey brewery Du Cateau was established in the heart of a former Benedictine abbey, which is now a World Heritage Site. The first brewery on the site operated until 1926. It then closed for seventy-five years before re-opening. Vivat Triple is a triple fermented golden premium beer, brewed from a unique process that uses two different yeasts. This bière de garde is re-fermented in the bottle and has a rich, copious, and persistent foam. With it slightly cloudy body, Vivat Triple has great aromatic complexity and delivers very good hop bitterness. The beer won a gold medal at the Concours Agricole de Paris in 2008.

YETI BELGIAN STRONG PALE ALE

Country of Origin: *France* • **Brewery Founded:** *2006* • **Alcohol Content:** *8%*

Yeti is a Belgian strong pale ale brewed by the Brasserie Des Cimes. The brewery lies at the heart of the French Alps in Aix-les-Bains. This craft brewery has five main brews. Robust and surprisingly, the Yeti is a strong beer for lovers of great taste sensations. Generous and tasty, it is brewed with the greatest care to give it a rich and unusual aroma. The spicy and floral notes of the aroma and flavor combine with strong hops and malt.

GERMANY

BAMBERGER HERREN PILS

Country of Origin: *Germany* • **Brewery Founded:** *1867* • **Alcohol Content:** *4.6%*

Bamberger Herren Pils is the signature beer of the Brauerei Keesmann. Established opposite the Maria Hilf church in Bamberg, the brewery is still family owned. The brewery brews several different beers all using the Bavarian purity law.   Bamberger's Herren Pils is a bright, light yellow beer with a white, compact head. The sophisticated aroma and taste of this light pils are both very hoppy and the beer has a strong and refreshing taste.

BECK'S

Country of Origin: *Germany* • **Brewery Founded:** *1873* • **Alcohol Content:** *5%*

Brauerei Beck & Co. is a German brewery based in the northern German city of Bremen. Beck's is the world's best selling German beer, sold in nearly ninety countries. The brewery is the fifth biggest in Germany. It was family owned until 2002 when the brewery was sold to Interbrew. Beck's pale lager is the company's best selling beer. It pours with a clear golden color and is topped with a medium foamy head. The aroma is malty and grains are dominant. The taste is slightly sweet with a pleasant bittersweet body.

BERLINER PILSNER

Country of Origin: *Germany* • **Brewery Founded:** *1902* • **Alcohol Content:** *5%*

Berliner Pilsner was founded as a small brewery with an adjoining garden restaurant. Berliner was located in the former East Germany and the East German leader Erich Honecker drank the beer in the 1960s. After German reunification in 1989, the beer was relaunched in 1992. The beer was re-packaged and over three million dollars were spent upgrading the Berliner brewery. This process was accompanied by a new advertising campaign with the slogan "The Beer of here." The beer has a yellow-golden body, and a medium sized white head. The aroma is typical of German pils. The taste is quite bitter, with some maltiness, and mildly salty.

BITBURGER PREMIUM PILS

Country of Origin: *Germany* • **Brewery Founded:** *1817* • **Alcohol Content:** *4.8%*

Bitburger's Pils has a bright, fresh golden color and rich frothy head so typical of an elegant pilsner beer. Its refined herbal notes are delicately poised, followed by a nutty and honeyed aftertaste. The overall impression of this gently sparkling beer is one of deep harmony, with the unmistakeable bitterness of the hops balanced and contained by an agreeable, mellow sweetness in the body.

DIEBELS ALT

Country of Origin: *Germany* • **Brewery Founded:** *1878* • **Alcohol Content:** *4.9%*

Altbier is the dominant beer style in Germany's Lower Rhine region and especially in the towns of Düsseldorf, Krefeld, and Mönchengladbach. The first commercial alt bier was brewed in 1838. Diebels is the market leader in terms of volume sold. The Diebels brewery was founded by the Krefeld brewmaster Josef Diebels. The brewery became a specialist in top fermented dark beer brewing and became a nationally recognized brand. It now has over fifty percent of the German alt bier market.

ERDINGER WEISSBIER

Country of Origin: *Germany* • **Brewery Founded:** *1886* • **Alcohol Content:** *5.3%*

Erdinger is the world's largest wheat beer brewery, located in Bavaria, Germany. Their beer is brewed according to traditional recipes using state-of-the-art technology. It is a family owned business with a strong emphasis on quality. The brewery is the world leader in the sales of traditional weissbier (wheat beer). Erdinger's Weissbier is brewed using fine yeast according to a traditional recipe and in strict accordance with the Bavarian Purity Law. The beer is bottle-fermented in the traditional way for three to four weeks.

FRANZISKANER WEISSBIER

Country of Origin: *Germany* • **Brewery Founded:** *1397* • **Alcohol Content:** *5%*

The Spaten-Franziskaner-Bräu is located in Munich, Germany. It is owned by the Spaten-Löwenbräu-Group which is part of the Belgo-Brazilian company Anheuser-Busch. The brewery makes Spaten (shovel) and Franziskaner (Franciscan) beers. Their Weissbier has an intense aroma with noticeable fruits and some sweetness. The beer's appearance is hazy golden with beautiful white head. The taste is sweet, with notes of fruit, bananas, spice, and sourness. The beer has a medium carbonation, but is very smooth.

FLENSBURGER PILSENER

Country of Origin: *Germany* • **Brewery Founded:** *1888* • **Alcohol Content:***4.8%*

The Flensburger Brauerei (brewery) is located in Flensburg, Germany. It is one of the last independent, country-wide breweries. The company was founded by five citizens of Flensburg and is still owned by two of the founder families, the Petersens and Dethleffsens. Before modern refrigeration, the brewery used to chop blocks of ice from frozen local lakes to keep their underground storage facilities cool in the summer. The brewery still brews with its own well water. Flensburger is known for its technically advanced and highly automated production processes. Flensburger Pilsener has a thin, white head and a hazy, yellow appearance. The aroma is sweet, of crackers and barley malt. The taste is similar with some notes of paper and fairly strong hop bitterness. The beer's mouth feel is light and watery.

FURST WALLERSTEIN CLASSIC

Country of Origin: *Germany* • **Brewery Founded:** *1598* • **Alcohol Content:** *4.9%*

The Princes of Oettingen-Wallerstein have been brewing beer from the days of Tzar Boris Goudonov and continue to do so today. The beer has a classic gold, slightly lemony, color with a hint of haze. The head is white and bright. The nose has some light grass notes and some hop brightness. The aroma is of light malt and is very clean and crisp. The body is quite light. The beer has a malty bread character, crisp and classic, with medium carbonation.

HASSERÖDER PREMIUM PILS

Country of Origin: *Germany* • **Brewery Founded:** *1872* • **Alcohol Content:** *4.8%*

The Hasseröder brewery is located in Wernigerode, Germany. The brewery is the sixth largest in Germany, and is now owned by Anheuser-Busch. The beer has a golden color and a white head that quickly diminishes. The beer's aroma has notes of cereal, hay, and light malt. The flavor is raw cereal with grassy hints. It is slightly sweet. The aftertaste is very light with light sweetness.

HOLSTEN PILSENER

Country of Origin: *Germany* • **Brewery Founded:** *1897* • **Alcohol Content:** *5%*

The Holsten-Brauerei was founded in 1879 in Hamburg's Altona-Nord district. The group now has seven breweries in Germany. Holsten's nationally distributed premium brand is the pale lager Holsten Pilsener. Holsten was acquired by the Carlsberg Group in 2004. Holsten Pilsener is a pale lager first produced in 1953. Holsten's other beer products include Licher Pilsner and Lübzer Pils. The Hamburg brewery exports this popular beer to the whole world.

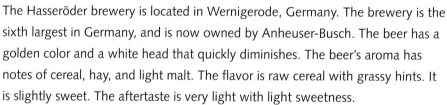

JEVER

Country of Origin: *Germany* • **Brewery Founded:** *1848* • **Alcohol Content:** *4.9%*

Jever is a German beer brand named after the town of Jever where the beer is still brewed. The beer pours a straw yellow in color. It is very clear with a medium white head. The beer has a mild aroma with light floral hops. It has a crisp flavor and medium-dry finish. The beer is light bodied.

KONIG PILSENER

Country of Origin: *Germany* • **Brewery Founded:** *1858* • **Alcohol Content:** *4.9%*

The Konig Brauerei began its business by brewing Pilsener style lager in the nineteenth century, even though this bottom-fermented style of beer was relatively unpopular at the time. Their beer was known for its bitter hoppiness. Konig changed the recipe of the beer to appeal to a mass market. In 2000 the brewery became a subsidiary of the Holsten Group, which is now part of the Carlsberg brewing giant. The beer pours light, clear, gold with a tall white head. The aroma is of honey, lemon malt, and scent. The taste is grainy and moderately sweet, with notes of honeyed barley malt and a slight metallic, grassy bitter.

KÖSTRITZER SCHWARZBIER

Country of Origin: *Germany* • **Brewery Founded:** *1543* • **Alcohol Content:** *4.8%*

The Köstritzer brewery has been owned by the Bitburger Brauerei since 1991. It is located in Bad Köstritz, Germany. The brewery is one of the oldest producers of schwarzbier (black lager) in Germany. One of the most famous drinkers of Köstritzer Schwarzbier was the author Johann Wolfgang von Goethe, who sustained himself on this black beer when he was unable to eat during a period of illness. The beer pours a reddish brown with some bubbles. Its nose is full of sweet herbs, coffee grounds, light sugar, and autumn leaves. The beer tastes of coffee grounds with light milk chocolate, herbs, grains, liquorice, and leaves.

KROMBACHER PILS

Country of Origin: *Germany* • **Brewery Founded:** *1803* • **Alcohol Content:** *4.8%*

Krombacher was founded by Johannes Haas. The water for the brewery was first brought in barrels from a local spring in an ox cart. At the beginning of the twentieth century, Krombacher Pilsener was introduced to the market. Krombacher is now owned by the Schadeberg family. The beer has a distinctive, fine bitter taste and a full-flavored aroma. Krombacher's modern production processes combine the traditional recipe with natural ingredients. Every tenth pils consumed in Germany comes from Krombacher.

KULMBACHER EDELHERB PREMIUM PILS

Country of Origin: *Germany* • **Brewery Founded:** *1895* • **Alcohol Content:** *4.9%*

The Kulmbacher Brewery Corporation was founded by Johann W. Reichel, Johann K. Scheiding, and Johann M. Hübbner. Their brewery was located in the Bavarian town of Kulmbach. The company now produces twenty-two different alcoholic beers. Their Premium Pils is a brilliant straw gold with a fluffy white head. The beer has a mild aroma with a hint of grain. It has a moderate carbonation and a light mouth feel. The flavor is malty with a hint of sweetness and an assertive bitterness. The beer is full-flavored while remaining crisp and refreshing.

LUBZER PILS

Country of Origin: *Germany* • **Brewery Founded:** *1847* • **Alcohol Content:** *4.9%*

Lubzer Pils is a Czech-style pilsner lager brewed by Carlsberg Deutschland, the German division of the Danish brewing giant. The beer was introduced to the market in 1980. It is a bottom-fermented, full-bodied pilsner lager. Pils is Germany's most popular style of beer, and the most widely drunk. Lubzer Pils has a lean, prickly taste, with hops up front, and a creamy foam head. Lubzer is a premium class pilsner that is brewed according to the German Reinheitsgebot Purity Law of 1516.

MAHR'S PILSNER

Country of Origin: *Germany* • **Brewery Founded:** *1670* • **Alcohol Content:** *5.2%*

The Mahr's brewery has been in the hands of the Michel family since 1895. It produces a range of different beers including pilsner, Hell beer (a light full beer), wheat beer, Gig (a malty coachman's beer), a white bock (a strong dark wheat beer), a light bock, and ungespundetes (an unfiltered beer served from a wooden barrel). All of Mahr's beers are brewed according to the Bavarian purity law. Their pilsner is a dark yellow, cloudy beer with a small white head. The beer has a yeasty and malty aroma. The taste is strong with a rounded malty taste. It is pleasantly bitter with a mellow aftertaste.

OETTINGER PILS

Country of Origin: *Germany* • **Brewery Founded:** *1333* • **Alcohol Content:** *4.77%*

Oettinger Brauerei is located in the town of Oettingen in Germany's Bavaria. Since 2004 Oettinger's Pils lager has been the best-selling beer in Germany. Oettinger has an unusual sales strategy. Its remit is to sell the most beer at the lowest possible price. Their Pils is rarely found on tap in pubs and bars; it is mostly sold bottled in supermarkets. Oettinger uses several ways to keep beer prices low. The company does not advertise, it delivers direct to stores, and the brewing process is completely automated. The beer's low price has made this beer brand the most successful in Germany, with an output of 134.2 million gallons in 2011. The beer pours a golden straw color with a soft white head. It has a low carbonation. The inviting aroma is of barley malt, floral hop, and citrus. The taste has notes of citrus zest, malt, and hop bitterness.

PAULANER WEISSBIER

Country of Origin: *Germany* • **Brewery Founded:** *1634* • **Alcohol Content:** *5.5%*

In 1634 the order of the Paulaner monks began brewing beer, laying the foundation stone for today's Paulaner brewery. Paulaner has now been producing excellent beers for 375 years and their beers are considered among the best served in the Bavarian city of Munich. The Paulaner master brewers only use the region's best ingredients. Paulaner get their hops from the Hallertau region of Bavaria. The yeast is their own special culture, and Paulaner uses local brewing malt and the purest, softest brewing water from its own deep wells. Paulaner Weissbier is a natural wheat beer and is the brewery's best-selling product. Specifically cultivated, top-fermented yeast gives the beer its character. The beer is sparkling mild and fruity with a delicate yeast flavor. It pours a gleaming orange color with a uniform cloudiness and a large head. The unfiltered brewing method allows it to retain its yeasty flavor along with many vitamins, minerals, and trace elements.

PINKUS UR PILS

Country of Origin: *Germany* • **Brewery Founded:** *1816*
Alcohol Content: *5.2%*

The Pinkus Müller brewery is located in the Northern Germany town of Münster. Pinkus-Müller traces its origins to the arrival of Johannes Müller in the town. It is now the only brewery left in Münster from 150 that were based in the town. The fifth and sixth generations of the Muller family now operate the brewery. Pinkus is so dedicated to quality that it was the world's first brewery to brew with only organically grown barley malt and whole hop flowers. Pinkus Ur Pils pours with a typical pils appearance. It has an aroma of light malts and grains with spicy hops. The flavor is mild and pleasant.

RADEBERGER PILSNER

Country of Origin: *Germany* • **Brewery Founded:** *1872* • **Alcohol Content:** *4.8%*

Since Radeberger was founded in 1872 the brewery has been seeking "Pilsner Perfection." This is defined as the perfect combination of water, hops, and barley. The brewery in located in Saxony, Germany and it claims to have brewed the first ever pilsner beer in Germany. Radeburger took a recipe from Pilzen in the Czech Republic, and elevated it to the next level by adding the highest quality ingredients, including soft, pure water from Saxony.

TANNENZÄPFLE ROTHAUS PILSENER

Country of Origin: *Germany* • **Brewery Founded:** *1791* • **Alcohol Content:** *5.1%*

Tannenzäpfle is brewed by the Badische Staatsbrauerei Rothaus in the German Black Forest. It is one of Germany's most successful and profitable regional breweries, and in the past decade its beers have become well-known outside its local area. The brewery is owned by the German state of Baden-Württemberg. Tannenzäpfle is a German-style pilsener and it is the brewery's most successful beer. Tannenzäpfle means "little fir cones" and this is a reference to the shape of its bottle. Tannenzäpfle is an excellent pils that pours an incredibly pale yellow. It is an exceptionally clear and bright beer with a stable head. The beer has a floral nose and a very crisp, hoppy taste.

VELTINS PILSENER

Country of Origin: *Germany* • **Brewery Founded:** *1824* • **Alcohol Content:** *4.8%*

Brauerei C. & A. Veltins is based in the West German city of Meschede-Grevenstein. The company is Germany's seventh largest brewer. It was founded by Franz Kramer and taken over by Clemens Veltins in 1852. The Veltins family still run the company. Veltins Pilsener is the brewery's most popular product. The beer is a golden yellow color with a thin head. It has a clear aroma of sweet malt and floral hops. The flavor is of sweet pale malt with notes of herbal hops and vanilla. There is a dry and bitter aftertaste. The beer has a light body with good carbonation.

WARSTEINER VERUM PILS

Country of Origin: *Germany* • **Brewery Founded:** *1753* • **Alcohol Content:** *4.8%*

Warsteiner beer is brewed in the Arnsberg Forest Nature Park in Germany's North-Rhine Westphalia region. Warsteiner has been owned by the Cramer family since the brewery was established in 1753 and is Germany's largest privately owned beer maker. It is also the fourth largest brewery in Germany. Premium Verum, a pilsner style lager, is Warsteiner's most popular beer. The brew is exported to over sixty countries. The ingredients are forest spring water, two-row malted summer barley, and German hops.

WEIHENSTEPHANER PILSNER

Country of Origin: *Germany* • **Brewery Founded:** *1768* • **Alcohol Content:** *5.1%*

The Weihenstephan Brewery can trace its roots at the Weihenstephan Abbey to 768, but the modern brewery was first licensed in 1040. It claims to be oldest working brewery in the world. Their pilsner pours a lovely pale gold color and has a medium to thin head. The beer's aroma is of cereal grain with a touch of hop. The taste is refreshing and light, with clean malt and a slight hop bitterness. The body is very clean with an effervescent carbonation and pleasant hop bitterness. The beer is extremely refreshing.

WERNESGRUNER

Country of Origin: *Germany* • **Brewery Founded:** *1436* • **Alcohol Content:** *4.8%*

The Wernesgrüner Brewery was founded in 1436 when the Schorer brothers acquired the rights to brew beer and open a tavern. It is one of the oldest commercial brewers in the world. The Wernesgruner brewery was located in the former East Germany. The brewer soon established the famous "Wernesgrüner Pils Legend" and the beer was served on the luxurious Hapag-Lloyd vessels that sailed from Hamburg to America. The company was acquired by Bitburger in 2002.

The beer pours a very pale greenish-yellow with a thick frothy white head. The aroma is of faint grass and dough. The taste has notes of hay, and is slightly crisp and astringent.

WURZBURGER HOFBRAU PREMIUM PILSNER

Country of Origin: *Germany* • **Brewery Founded:** *1643* • **Alcohol Content:** *4.8%*

The Wurtburger Hofbrau brewery was founded by the Prince Johan Philipp von Schonborn and is now the oldest business in the German city of Wurzburg. It was originally established to brew beer for the Franconian royal court (Franconia is a German state). The crown on the brewery's logo commemorates this heritage. Wurzburger's Pilsner is a typical Franconian pils with a strong malty flavor. The beer also has an elegant, aromatic hoppy bitterness.

GREECE

ALFA BEER

Country of Origin: *Greece* • **Brewery Founded:** *1961* • **Alcohol Content:** *5%*

The Athenian Brewery is one of the largest breweries Greece. Alfa beer is made from Greek barley. The beer pours a crystal clear medium golden yellow in color with some very light amounts of visible carbonation. The beer has a tall white head. The beer has a very sweet smell of grain, corn, and malt. The taste of this beer is quite sweet with a strong presence of grain, corn, and malt. Grass and hop flavors are present, with very little bitterness. The beer is quite light bodied with moderate to heavy carbonation.

FIX DARK

Country of Origin: *Greece* • **Brewery Founded:** *1864*
Alcohol Content: *5.2%*

Fix Dark is a dunkel-style beer brewed by the Olympic Brewery. Fix Dark is a dark brown beer with red glints and a dark beige head. The aroma is of stale coffee and caramel. The beer has quite a watery body and a lively carbonation. The flavor is predominantly of caramel, with gentle bitter notes and a strong degree of roasted oat. The beer has an aftertaste of caramel.

FIX HELLAS

Country of Origin: *Greece* • **Brewery Founded:** *1864* • **Alcohol Content:** *5%*

Fix Hellas is a pale lager beer brewed by the Olympic Brewery. Olympic was founded by Johann Karl Fuchs in Athens, Greece and it became the first major brewery in Greece. Fix Hellas became synonymous with beer in Greece, and enjoyed a virtual monopoly until the 1960s but lost first place in the Greek market in 1973. The beer pours a light gold with a thin white head. Its aroma is of citrus.

IONIAN EPOS

Country of Origin: *Greece* • **Brewery Founded:** *2009* • **Alcohol Content:** *7.5%*

Ionian Epos is a barley wine brewed by the Corfu Brewery on the Greek island of Corfu. The beer is brewed from water, malt, honey, hop, and yeast. Epos pours an amber color and has a medium body with a creamy head. The aroma is of malt, nuts, spice, honey, and fruit. The taste is also spicy, with notes of malt and honey. The beer has a similar character to red wine.

MYTHOS HELLENIC LAGER

Country of Origin: *Greece* • **Brewery Founded:** *1970* • **Alcohol Content:** *4.7%*

Mythos Brewery is the second largest Greek brewery, and best known for its Mythos brand. The company has been a subsidiary of Carlsberg since 2008. Mythos beer was invented in 1997 and is now the brewery's primary product. Mythos is a light straw-colored lager with a slightly off-white head. The aroma is rich and sweet with notes of barley malt and hops. The flavor is of sweet, sugary malt, light biscuit, and grass with a mellow hop bitterness. The mouth feel is light to medium.

NEDA BEER

Country of Origin: *Greece* • **Brewery Founded:** *2009* • **Alcohol Content:** *5%*

Neda is a pale lager beer brewed by the Messinian Microbrewery located in Messene, Greece. The beer pours a pale golden and bright yellow color, with a white head. The beer has a typical lager aroma, but with a fresh character. The beer has a strong character of malt, hops, and light citrus. The beer has average carbonation.

PIRAIKI BEER

Country of Origin: *Greece* • **Brewery Founded:** *1970* • **Alcohol Content:** *5%*

The Piraiki Microbrewery is situated in Drapetsona, Greece. The brewery produces two types of beer using traditional organic methods and according to the German Reinheitsgebot of 1516. The resulting beers are Piraiki Pils or Piraiki Pale Ale. The Pilsner is a hazy golden color with a small white head. It has a weak malty aroma. The taste is sweet with no bitterness.

ROYAL IONIAN PILSNER

Country of Origin: *Greece* • **Brewery Founded:** *2009* • **Alcohol Content:** *5%*

Royal Ionian Pilsner is brewed by Corfu Beer on the Greek island of Corfu. The beer pours a golden body, with an average white head. It has a malty, floral, and grassy aroma. The flavor is medium bitter, with notes of hops and herbs. The beer is medium bodied, with average carbonation and an oily texture. The Corfu microbrewery is the only brewery in North West Greece and the only Greek brewer that produce real ale. The brewery is very modern and equipped with the latest technology. 220 gallons of beer can be produced in each brew. The brewery produces two real ale beers and a Pilsner, which are produced under the German purity law. Their Royal Ionian Pilsner is a blond lager with a mild bitterness.

SEPTEM PALE ALE

Country of Origin: *Greece* • **Brewery Founded:** *1997*
Alcohol Content: *7%*

The microbrewery Septem is a new addition to the Greek brewing industry. Its beer is stealing the spotlight with its fresh, non-pasteurized quality beers. Septem Pale Ale is made from whole Northern Brewer and Perle varieties of hop. It is a fresh, unpasteurized, filtered beer. It is a golden blonde in color with a firm creamy froth. The beer is distinguished by its aromas of flowers, citrus, caramel, honey, and hops. The beer has a slight sweet flavor, with the discreet presence of malt, a refreshing acidity, and bitterness.

VERGINA LAGER BEER

Country of Origin: *Greece* • **Brewery Founded:** *1998* • **Alcohol Content:** *5%*

Vergina is a pale lager brewed by the Macedonian Thrace Brewery Komotini, Greece. Vergina Premium Lager was the brewery's first product, and has become its signature beer. The brewery now has a line-up of beers including Vergina Red and Vergina Weiss. Vergina Lager pours clear pale gold with a white head. The aroma has hints of fruit and citrus. The beer is medium sweet with notes of acidity and some bitterness.

ICELAND

EGILS GULL

Country of Origin: *Iceland* • **Brewery Founded:** *1913* • **Alcohol Content:** *5%*

The Egill Skallagrímsson Brewery is based in Reykjavík, Iceland. It produces twenty million liters of beer per annum. The brewery is named after the Viking poet and adventurer, Egill Skallagrímsson. The brewery produces pale lager under the Egils brand, including Egils Pilsner, Egils Gull and Egils Premium. It also produced Litli-Jón, which was retired in 2008. Gull is a golden pilsner that pours a straw color with a large white head. The aroma is grassy and grainy and the taste is a grassy, spicy, hoppy, and bitter with a malty sweetness.

GAEDINGUR STOUT

Country of Origin: *Iceland* • **Brewery Founded:** *2011* • **Alcohol Content:** *5.6%*

The Gaedingur (Stallion) brewery is an independent brewery located in the Icelandic countryside outside of the town of Skagafjordur. The brewery makes four different beers that it sells in bottles and on draught in various Icelandic microbars and restaurants. The brewery was founded to diversify the beers available in Iceland. Gaedingur Stout pours deep opaque black with a creamy beige head. The beer's aroma has notes of coffee, roasted malts, and mild chocolate. The brew has a medium carbonation and a creamy mouth feel. The flavor has hints of coffee, cocoa nibs, roast, and nuttiness. It has a long, lingering, malty bitter finish.

GULLFOSS

Country of Origin: *Iceland* • **Brewery Founded:** *Unknown* • **Alcohol Content:** *5%*

Gullfoss is a cascading waterfall located in the canyon of the wide Hvítá River in southwest Iceland. Gullfoss is one of the most popular tourist attractions in the country. Gullfoss is a premium lager brewed at the Reykjavikur brewery. The beer pours a dark straw yellow. The aroma is of almonds with some dried fruit. The taste has some sweet notes of pineapples, cloves, and butter.

ISLENSKUR URVALS STOUT

Country of Origin: *Iceland* • **Brewery Founded:** *1942* • **Alcohol Content:** *5.8%*

Islenskur Urvals is brewed by the Vifilfell Brewery. The brewery's headquarters are in Reykjavik, but the brewing takes place in Akureyri, the largest town in Iceland's northern part. Islenskur Urvals was first produced in 2008. It was the first Icelandic Stout. It has a dark, roasted aroma of espresso beans, dark chocolate, and cocoa. It is intense in texture and character, yet relatively easy drinking and well balanced.

KALDI LAGER

Country of Origin: *Iceland* • **Brewery Founded:** *2005* • **Alcohol Content:** *5%*

Kaldi is an Icelandic beer brewed to a Czech recipe. The company was founded by the couple Agnes Anna and Olafur Trostur, who followed the example of Danish microbreweries. The Trosturs still own 56% of the brewery. Kaldi was created by Czech brewmaster David Masa. All the raw materials are imported from the Czech Republic except for the fresh Icelandic water that comes from the Arskogssandur mountain spring. The beer has no added sugar or any preservatives and is not pasteurized. All this makes Kaldi as fresh and healthy as possible.

SKJÁLFTI PREMIUM LAGER

Country of Origin: *Iceland* • **Brewery Founded:** *2007* • **Alcohol Content:** *5%*

Olvisholt Brugghus is located at an old dairy farm in south Iceland. It was founded by two neighboring farmers who had a true passion for beer. The brewery now exports to Denmark, Sweden, Finland, and Canada. Skjálfti is the brewery's premium lager brewed with a wide variety of five malts and hops (First gold, Cascade, and Celeia) resulting in a complex aroma and taste. Skjálfti Premium Lager is a golden beer with a light to medium body and a good balance between malt and hops. The flavor has a hint of caramel and sweetness and a medium bitter finish. On the nose aroma hops are dominant, with citrus and pine notes and a slight sweetness. Skjálfti means earthquake in Icelandic. The Ölvisholt farm is located directly on top of where the American and European continents meet. In 2000 there was a serious earthquake along the fault line. The beer is named after this quake.

THULE

Country of Origin: *Iceland* • **Brewery Founded:** *1942* • **Alcohol Content:** *5%*

Thule lager is brewed by the Vifilfell brewery. Thule is one of the most widely available brews in Iceland and is quite widely exported. The beer pours a clear golden color with a fluffy white head. It has moderate carbonation. The brew's aroma is mildly floral and coarsely grainy. The taste is mild with some grainy sweetness from the malt, and tea-like floral qualities from the hops. Thule's mouth feel is quite thin and watery.

ULFUR INDIA PALE ALE NR. 3

Country of Origin: *Iceland* • **Brewery Founded:** *1913* • **Alcohol Content:** *5.9%*

Ulfur India Pale Ale Nr. 3 is brewed by the Egill Skallagrímsson Brewery in Reykjavík, Iceland. The beer is brewed with water, malt, American hops, and yeast. Úlfur (wolf in Icelandic) is a powerful clear ale, rich with bitterness. The beer's aroma is of grapefruit rind and pine. It has a hue of golden straw with a bright white head. The taste is mildly piney and citrusy. The beer has a medium body and good carbonation.

VIKING GYLLTUR LAGER

Country of Origin: *Iceland* • **Brewery Founded:** *1942* • **Alcohol Content:** *5.6%*

Víking Gylltur (Golden) Lager is brewed by the Viking Olgerd brewery, which is now part of the Vifilfell group. Viking Gylltur is an internationally recognized quality beer that received Monde Selection gold medals in 1992, 2002 and 2003. It is brewed with a large quantity of hops to give the lager its much coveted bitterness. The beer is a light yellow, with a small fizzy white head. The aroma is of corn syrup, grain, and grass. The flavor has similar notes and is medium sweet with a light bitter. The lager has a light body.

INDIA

ARTOS BREWERY RAJ

Country of Origin: *India* • **Brewery Founded:** *Unknown* • **Alcohol Content:** *5%*

The Artos brewery is in the Andhra Pradesh region of India. The beer pours an ever-so-hazy amber color with a nice fluffy head. The aroma is slightly sweet, of caramel and grain with faint notes of fruit. The flavor is smooth and slightly sweet throughout. It is grainy with some nice floral yeasty notes to balance it. Raj is one of the most highly regarded beers brewed in India.

BOMBAY BEER

Country of Origin: *India* • **Brewery Founded:** *Unknown* • **Alcohol Content:** *4.9%*

Bombay Beer is a pilsner-style lager brewed by India's Hindustan Breweries in Mumbai, India. It is a large company quoted on the Indian Stock Exchange. The beer pours a dull gold color. It has a slight malt aroma, slim flavor, and a thin mouth feel. The beer has very little hop presence. The beer is more like a hot climate pale lager than a strong tasting pilsner.

GODFATHER SUPER STRONG

Country of Origin: *India* • **Brewery Founded:** *1961* • **Alcohol Content:** *7%*

Godfather Strong is one of India's top selling strong beers and is particularly popular in Northern India. It has a smooth, full bodied flavor with a stable head and good mouth fullness. At 7.5% alcohol, Godfather Strong packs a punch for a true beer lover! The beer is a malt liquor brewed by Devans Modern Breweries, located in Jammu, India. The brewery was established by Mr Dewan Gian Chand, a pioneer industrialist of the region. It has a state-of-the-art brewery at Kotputli, Rajasthan which was opened in 2006. Here it manufactures international quality beers.

HAYWARDS 5000

Country of Origin: *India* • **Brewery Founded:** *1961* • **Alcohol Content:** *7.5%*

Haywards 5000 is the one of India's best-selling strong beer brand, which combines strength with quality credentials. Launched in 1983, Haywards 5000 is synonymous with strong beer in India. Haywards 5000 is brewed with the choicest of malts and hops lending itself to a unique flavor profile to suit the Indian taste and preference. Haywards 5000 is a full-bodied malty flavor brewed from Indian malts, and six-row barley malt. The beer is brewed using German hop extract and Indian hops. This bottom-fermented beer pours a golden yellow color.

KALYANI BLACK LABEL

Country of Origin: *India* • **Brewery Founded:** *1857* • **Alcohol Content:** *7.8%*

Kalyani Black Label is brewed by the Indian United Breweries Group in Bangalore, India. Kalyani Black Label Strong, an iconic beer brand whose long history began with its origin in West Bengal. Kalyani Black Strong is now an established brand across the country. It is a typical strong beer brewed in the Indian tradition. It pours a clear gold with high carbonation and a white head. The aroma is of alcohol, rice, straw, and light tropical fruits (mango/pineapple). The taste is very sweet, of sweet corn, and cereal grain. The beer has a watery body.

KINGFISHER PREMIUM

Country of Origin: *India* • **Brewery Founded:** *1857* • **Alcohol Content:** *5%*

Kingfisher is an Indian beer brewed by United Breweries Group, Bangalore. The brand was launched in 1978. It now has a market share of over 36% and is available in fifty-two countries outside India. It is the world's best-selling Indian beer. The brewery makes several Kingfisher beers including Kingfisher Premium, Kingfisher Strong, Kingfisher Strong Fresh, Kingfisher Draught, Kingfisher Ultra, Kingfisher Blue, and Kingfisher Red. The beer pours a clear golden color with a frothy white head. The aroma is of powdered sugar, bubble gum, straw, lemon meringue pie, and light pale malts. The flavor is mostly the same, with heavy lemon zest and straw, and lots of powdered sugar. The beer is medium-bodied with average carbonation.

SUNNY BEACHES

Country of Origin: *India* • **Brewery Founded:** *Unknown* • **Alcohol Content:** *4.8%*

Sunny Beaches is a pale lager beer brewed by India's Som Brewery. Som is a large drinks group that is quoted on the Indian stock exchange. The beer has a very golden color. The aroma is sweet with a little citrus. The taste has notes of malt and hops, with a little sweet grass.

THUNDERBOLT SUPER STRONG LAGER BEER

Country of Origin: *India* • **Brewery Founded:** *1993* • **Alcohol Content:** *9%*

Thunderbolt Super Strong Lager is a super strong pale lager or Imperial Pilsner brewed by the Mount Shivalik Brewery in Delhi, India. Indians prefer stronger alcoholic drinks, like whisky, over beer. Strong beers like Thunderbolt (with an alcohol content in the 5-8% range) account for 83% of the total beer sales in India for 2012. But beer is still only five percent of the total alcohol consumed in India. The beer pours a clear golden body with a small white head. Its aroma is of corn, grass, and sweet malt. The flavor is of toasted grain, light smokiness, and grassy hops with a dry finish.

IRELAND

GUINNESS DRAUGHT

Country of Origin: *Ireland* • **Brewery Founded:** *1759* • **Alcohol Content:** *4.1 to 4.2%*

The Guinness Brewery was founded by Arthur Guinness (1725–1803) at St. James's Gate, Dublin. Guinness is one of the most successful beer brands worldwide, which is now brewed in almost sixty countries and available in over a hundred. Guinness has a roasted malt flavor and hint of chocolate common to most full-bodied beers. It is a rich and creamy Irish favorite that takes around 119.53 seconds a pint to pour. Guiness Draught was the brewery's first beer and it has been brewed for over two-hundred years. The beer has an unmistakeable deep, dark color, the crisp hint of roasted barley, the fresh breeze of hops, and a refreshing, bittersweet bite.

GUINNESS FOREIGN EXTRA STOUT

Country of Origin: *Ireland* • **Brewery Founded:** *1759* • **Alcohol Content:** *7.5%*

Guinness Foreign Extra Stout is the export version of the brewery's famous stout. It is sold in Europe, Africa, the Caribbean, Asia, and the United States. The basis of the beer is an unfermented but hopped Guinness wort extract which is shipped from Dublin and added to local ingredients so that the beer can be fermented locally. The strength of the beer varies from country to country. It is sold at 5% ABV in China, 6.5% ABV in Jamaica and East Africa, 6.8% in Malaysia, 7.5% in the United States, and 8% ABV in Singapore. In its unique brewing process, Foreign Extra Stout is blended with a small amount of intentionally soured beer. The beer was formally known as a porter. The beer was re-launched in the United States in 2010. It was first shipped to America in 1817, when it was known as West India Porter. Foreign Extra Stout is Guinness' strongest beer with a dark color that belies its rich, chocolaty taste. The stout is smoother than Guinness Draught and is less bitter.

HARP LAGER

Country of Origin: *Ireland* • **Brewery Founded:** *1759* • **Alcohol Content:** *4.3%*

Harp Lager is a Vienna-style pale lager brand created in 1960 by the Guinness Brewery in its Dundalk brewery. It is a leading lager brand in Ireland, and is also popular in Australia, Canada, Africa, and the United States. The beer was designed to follow the trend among drinkers in Britain and Ireland towards continental lager. Guinness converted its Dundalk brewery into a modern lager production plant with the guidance of Dr. Herman Muender, a distinguished German brewer. Harp is a crisp summery lager, which has a bitter beginning that quickly turns clean and refreshing. This classic lager is smooth and solid.

KILKENNY IRISH CREAM ALE

Country of Origin: *Ireland* • **Brewery Founded:** *1759* • **Alcohol Content:** *3.8%*

Kilkenny is a nitrogenated Irish cream ale from the brewers of Guinness, which was first brewed in Kilkenny, Ireland. The beer is brewed in Ireland and its heritage dates back to the 14th century. Kilkenny Irish Cream Ale is similar to Smithwick's Draught. But it has less hop finish and a nitrogenated cream head similar to Guinness. Kilkenny is brewed in Ireland's oldest operating brewery. The beer is brewed from water, malted barley, roasted malted barley, hops, and yeast. Although Ireland is the primary market for Kilkenny, Australia and Canada are the two largest importers of Kilkenny. Until recently, the Dubliner Pub in Washington, D.C. was the only place in the United States that served the beer. The amber brew has the rich aroma and flavor of toasted malt. It's all at once sweet and creamy, offset by some bitterness. The beer is available in nitrogen-infused draught and canned forms.

MURPHY'S IRISH RED

Country of Origin: *Ireland* • **Brewery Founded:** *1856* • **Alcohol Content:** *5%*

Murphy's Brewery was founded in Cork, Ireland. It was known as Lady's Well Brewery until it was purchased by Heineken International in 1983. By 1906 Murphy's was Ireland's second largest brewer after Guinness. Murphy's Irish Red was introduced in 1983. The beer gets its reddish hue from the small amount of roasted barley they contain. This true Irish red is dry, crisp, hoppy, and very carbonated with some signs of fruit and caramel.

MURPHY'S IRISH STOUT

Country of Origin: *Ireland* • **Brewery Founded:** *1856* • **Alcohol Content:** *4%*

The lightest and sweetest of Ireland's Big Three stouts, Murphy's Irish Stout is preferred by some drinkers to the offerings of both Guinness and Beamish. Murphy's Irish Stout is dark brown with a medium creamy head. The aroma is slightly smoked and malty. The taste is malty with hints of coffee and chocolate. Since the company's acquisition by Heineken in 1983, Murphy's has been enjoying a reputation as one of the fastest growing stout brands in the world.

O'HARA'S CELTIC STOUT

Country of Origin: *Ireland* • **Brewery Founded:** *1996* • **Alcohol Content:** *4.3%*

O'Hara's Celtic Stout is brewed by the Carlow Brewery. Carlow's is a craft microbrewery. There are now over twenty microbreweries in Ireland, more than half of which opened their doors in the past five years. O'Hara's Celtic Stout is true to the original Irish stout. It's a robust, full-bodied combination of hops and roasted barley. This provides sweetness and a roasty bite with no artificial additives. The beer is brewed with just hops, barley, yeast and water.

O'HARA'S IRISH WHEAT BEER/ CURIM GOLD

Country of Origin: *Ireland* • **Brewery Founded:** *1996* • **Alcohol Content:** *4.3%*

Carlow's wheat beer is named with the old Celtic word for beer and this refreshing wheat beer echoes Ireland's Celtic heritage. Curim has a higher hop rate than mainstream wheat beers. This gives the beer a slightly tart residue that balances the delicate fruity flavors of peach, banana, and plum. The beer is an easy drinking golden ale. Mild and smooth on the palate, the beer's wheaty flavor profile lacks the stronger flavors typical of many American hefeweizens.

PORTERHOUSE BREWING CO. OYSTER STOUT

Country of Origin: *Ireland* • **Brewery Founded:** *1996* • **Alcohol Content:** *4.8%*

Porterhouse Brewing Co.'s Oyster Stout is a superbly balanced brew. The beer is smooth and rounded without being bland. Part of its sweetness is derived from fresh oysters that are shucked into the conditioning tank. Of course this means that the beer is not suitable for vegetarians. It is brewed with pale malt, roast barley, black malt, and flaked barley. The hops are Galena, Nugget, and East Kent Goldings. The Porterhouse Brewing Company is Ireland's largest independent brewery. The company began with a Dublin pub, the company now sells its beers as far afield as New York and London, bringing their craft brews beyond the Emerald Isle's shores. Porterhouse's Oyster Stout is not a typical Irish stout, but it has the characteristic rounded malt flavors with a creamy mouth feel and smooth finish.

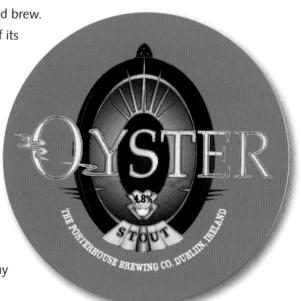

SMITHWICK'S IRISH ALE

Country of Origin: *Ireland* • **Brewery Founded:** *1710* • **Alcohol Content:** *5%*

Smithwick's was founded by John Smithwick. The brewery originally brewed their beers in St. Francis Abbey Brewery in Kilkenny, which is Ireland's oldest operating brewery. Smithwick's Irish Ale is a red ale style beer. It is a clear beer with a rich ruby color and a creamy head. The brewing process depends on four main ingredients, malt, yeast, water, and hops. These contribute to the distinctive aroma and taste of the beer. Smithwick's was originally created as a special brew for the first Kilkenny Beer Festival. Smithwick's is now the major ale producer in Ireland and, along with Guinness, part of the Diageo brewing group. Like Murphy's Irish Red, this is a red ale characterized by caramel malt with a hint of hops.

ISRAEL

ALEXANDER AMBER ALE

Country of Origin: *Israel* • **Brewery Founded:** *2008* • **Alcohol Content:** *5.2%*

Alexander's Amber Ale is the brewery's interpretation of a French biere de Garde. The microbrewery was founded by Ori Sagy a former fighter pilot, who runs Alexander in Emek Hefer, Israel. Sagy studied beer-making at Siebel and brought in Dutch brewmaster Patrick Van Dam, who is responsible for the production process. The brewery makes its brews with minimal impact on the environment. It produces small batches using traditional European techniques on modern equipment. The brewery's hops, malt, and yeast are imported from Europe, while the water is Israeli. Alexander specializes in ale-type beers. Alexander Black is a seasonal beer for the winter with aromas of dark chocolate and espresso. Alexander Ambree is a reddish French-style ale. Alexander Blonde is a low-alcohol Belgian-style ale with a floral and fruity aroma. Alexander Green is a hoppy IPA with an Israeli twist, a fruity aroma of grapefruit, guava, and mango.

DANCING CAMEL PALE ALE

Country of Origin: *Israel* • **Brewery Founded:** *2009* • **Alcohol Content:** *5.2%*

The American-style Dancing Camel brewery in Tel Aviv was the first of Israel's microbreweries. It was founded by U.S. émigré David Cohen and is based in the heart of Tel Aviv, Israel. The brewery produces a variety of carefully crafted kosher brews. These include its Carobbean Stout, Six-Thirteen Pomegranate Ale, Golem beer, and Gordon Beach Blond. The Flying Camel also has its own pub which is closed on Shabbat. Dancing Camel's Pale Ale is a flavorful American-Style Pale Ale. It has a hearty malt character, which is balanced with the finest American West coast hops, and a hint of Israeli date honey. Generously dry-hopped, the beer is bursting with aromas of grapefruit, lemon, and mango, trailing off to a balanced bitterness.

GOLDSTAR DARK LAGER BEER

Country of Origin: *Israel* • **Brewery Founded:** *1952* • **Alcohol Content:** *4.9%*

Goldstar Dark Lager Beer is brewed by Tempo Beer Industries. Tempo is Israel's largest brewer and the country's second-largest beverage company. The brewery produces three brands of pale lager Goldstar, Maccabee, and Nesher Malt. Goldstar is a pale lager which has been produced since the 1950s. It is marketed as a dark lager beer although it is pale golden in appearance. In 2007, Tempo introduced Goldstar Light. The beer is certified kosher by the Chief Rabbi of Netanya, Israel.

JEM'S BEER FACTORY AMBER ALE

Country of Origin: *Israel*   •   **Brewery Founded:** *2008*   •   **Alcohol Content:** *4.6%*

Jem's Beer Factory's Amber Ale is an amber color with medium off-white head. The aroma is of berries, malt, and caramel. The beer has a fruity taste with sweet malt, roasted notes, and caramel. There is a light hoppy bitterness with a fruity finish. The brewery was founded by Jeremy Welfeld. He earned degrees in microbiology and the advanced sciences of brewing from the University of California, and brewing technology from Chicago's Siebel Institute of Technology, before realizing his vision. His unique brewery, which is located in Petah Tikvah, Israel brews several beers that include a clear gold Czech Pils lager, a dark German lager, a copper-colored English-style amber ale, a cloudy light gold Bavarian Wheat ale, a reddish Belgian ale, and a black Irish stout.

MACCABEE

Country of Origin: *Israel*   •   **Brewery Founded:** *1952*   •   **Alcohol Content:** *5%*

Netanya-based Tempo is the largest brewery in Israel. In 1999 Tempo's Goldstar and Maccabee beers accounted for sixty percent all beer sales in Israel. Maccabee is a pale Israeli lager. It is made of 100% European hops. Macabee beer was first brewed in 1968 and has received four medals in international competitions.

MALKA PALE ALE

Country of Origin: *Israel*   •   **Brewery Founded:** *2008*   •   **Alcohol Content:** *5.5%*

Malka Pale Ale pours a dark hazy amber with a lasting beige head. The beer's taste and aroma is of light caramel malt and citrus notes. It is lightly fruity with some yeast and mildly bitter hops. The beer has a medium body with moderate carbonation. It finishes with a good malt character with yeast and bready notes. The Malka brewery, in the picturesque Western Galilee community of Klil, produces three varieties of bottled beers. The owner, Assaf Lavi, maintains a small-scale family-run brewery with a hands-on approach, using only natural ingredients and low-tech equipment.

NESHER MALT

Country of Origin: *Israel* • **Brewery Founded:** *1952* • **Alcohol Content:** *2%*

Nesher Malt is a kvass-style beer, now brewed by the Tempo brewery, but first introduced to the Israel market in 1935. The beer is made from various grains except for barley. White Nesher Malt is a pale lager beer and was the first beer produced in Israel. Black Nesher is a non-alcoholic version of Nesher Malt. It is most commonly referred to as Bira Schora or Black Beer.

SHAPIRO

Country of Origin: *Israel* • **Brewery Founded:** *2008* • **Alcohol Content:** *5.5%*

Shapiro was founded by six Shapiro siblings that run this family-founded brewery. They brew quintessentially Jerusalem beers. Their products are straightforward ales, stouts, and seasonal beers. The Shapiro brewery is located in Beit Shemesh, near Jerusalem. The Israeli beer industry has been dominated by two big commercial companies producing mass produced lagers such as Goldstar and Maccabee. Over the last few years, many microbreweries have sprung up in the country, and made a significant impact on Israel's beer culture. Microbreweries hand-craft small quantities of beer (usually less than 5,000 liters a year) using premium ingredients and classic brewing techniques.

ITALY

32 VIA DEI BIRRAI TRE + DUE

Country of Origin: *Italy* • **Brewery Founded:** *2008* • **Alcohol Content:** *3.2%*

32 Via dei Birrai is an artisan brewery. Its philosophy is embodied by its circular logo; a curved line that represents the on-going craft of brewing. The brewery's ethos is to achieve the perfect balance between taste and design, between research and method, without straying into industrial standardization. Their beer is certified as being 100% Italian. Tre + Due is a highly hopped, spiced, light, top-fermented ale that is given a secondary fermentation in the bottle. The beer has a white head and is a pale straw yellow color. It is cloudy with yeast and has a fine carbonation. The bouquet is intensely fruity and herbaceous with hints of citrus. The flavor is mildly bitter with citrus notes. The finish has the freshness of coriander and hops added to an orange peel sensation.

ALMOND '22 MAXIMA

Country of Origin: *Italy* • **Brewery Founded:** *2003* • **Alcohol Content:** *6.9%*

Almond '22 is named after its brewery's location. It is based in a factory that used to process almonds to create a famous Italian almond confection. The almond factory was founded in 1922. This artisanal brewer creates its beers using the fair trade spices and raw cane sugar, Italian honey, malt, and hops. Almond '22 draws its pure spring water from the mountains of Farindola and adds no chemicals or preservatives to its beers. Maxima is a strong, English-style ale. It is a slight hazy dark yellow with medium off-white head. Its aroma is of malt, fruit, hops, yeast, and citrus. The flavor is malty and medium sweet with hints of citrus, hops, bitterness, and flowers.

BALADIN

Country of Origin: *Italy* • **Brewery Founded:** *1996* • **Alcohol Content:** *Various*

Baladin is one of Italy's largest producers of artisanal beer. It was founded by master brewer Teo Musso in the small village of Piozzo. With the help of Teo's Belgian friend Jean-Luis Dits, Baladin constructed a brewery using old milk vats. The brewery has always been highly experimental and has now brewed over thirty different brews. These have included various different styles of beer. Baladin's spiced beers include Isaac, Wayan, and Nora. Their pure malt beers are Super, Elixir, and Leön. The brewery's hoppy beers include Super Bitter and Nazionale. Their special beers are Mielika, Mama Kriek, Zucca, Nöel Vanille, YI-ER, and Etrusca. They also brew several Open-branded beers, Open, Open Rolling Stone, Open Riserva, and Open Noir. Baladin's cellar beers are Riserva Teo Musso, Xyauyù Oro, Xyauyù Barrel, Xyauyù Fumè, Lune, and Terre. They also brew some beers that are only available only on tap. These include Nelson, Ni a, and Brune.

BEBA BIRRA INTEGRALE

Country of Origin: *Italy* • **Brewery Founded:** *1996* • **Alcohol Content:** *Unknown*

The Beba brewery was founded in 1996. It is an Italian craft brewery. The brewery makes several brews that are crafted according to the dictates of the German Decree of Purity that dates back to 1516. The brewery uses only raw materials for its production of lager beers (water, malted barley grains, hops and yeast). Beba beer is not subjected to any kind of artificial treatment. No carbon dioxide, preservatives, or antioxidants are added to the beer. The beer is unfiltered and unpasteurized. The brewery sources pure mountain water sources at Chisone, Italy. Beba makes both low and high fermentation beers.

BIRRA MESSINA

Country of Origin: *Italy* • **Brewery Founded:** *1873* • **Alcohol Content:** *4.7%*

Birra Messina is owned by the Italian division of the international brewing giant Heineken. The beer is produced in Milan, Italy. This pale lager is a pale yellow color with white head. It has a light malty aroma. The beer is refreshing when cold with a moderate bitterness and a soft, dry, and bitter aftertaste. The taste has notes of grain, cereal, green apples, and ripe berries. Messina is a soft and thin beer.

CASTELLO LAGER BEER

Country of Origin: *Italy* • **Brewery Founded:** *1996* • **Alcohol Content:** *4.8%*

Castello Lager beer is a premium lager brewed by the Castello di Udine brewery based in San Giorgio di Nogaro, Italy. Blond Castello beer has a delicate hop flavor and an attractive golden color blend in an exquisite beer. It is a low fermented premium beer. It has a harmoniously well balanced flavor, with a medium alcohol level. It goes particularly well with pasta.

CITTAVECCHIA KARNERA

Country of Origin: *Italy* • **Brewery Founded:** *1999* • **Alcohol Content:** *Various*

The Trieste-based Cittavecchia brewery is one of the most popular artisanal beer makers in Italy. The brewery makes five basic brews and adds specials from time to time. Their Chiara is a bottom fermented lager and their Rossa is a Vienna-style bottom fermented amber lager. Chiara's Formidable is a dark strong ale that has been highly fermented, while their Karnera is a black double malt stout. They also make a Weizen wheat ale.

DREHER PREMIUM LAGER

Country of Origin: *Italy* • **Brewery Founded:** *1996* • **Alcohol Content:** *4.7%*

Dreher is a pale lager brewed by Heineken Italia. The beer is brewed in Milan, Italy. Dreher has a clear pale golden color with medium frothy white head and average carbonation. The beer has an aroma of adjunct malt, with notes of light grassy hops. The taste starts with moderately sweet malt, followed by hints of vegetable and grain. The beer has a light bitter finish. The beer has a light body, dry texture. It is a classic mainstream lager.

FORST BEER

Country of Origin: *Italy* • **Brewery Founded:** *1857* • **Alcohol Content:** *4.7%*

The Birra Forst is an Italian brewing company, based in Forst, South Tyrol, Germany. The brewery was founded by two entrepreneurs. In 1863, the company was bought by Josef Fuchs, who built the current brewery in Forst, in Italy. The beer is pale gold in color with a fine foamy head. It has an aroma of hay and sweet malts. The strongest flavor is of lager malts with hints of other grains, corn, a touch of honey, and some grassy notes. It is sweet with a very subtle bitterness. It is medium bodied with soft carbonation.

ICHNUSA

Country of Origin: *Italy* • **Brewery Founded:** *1912* • **Alcohol Content:** *4.7%*

Birra Ichnusa is the name of a popular Sardinian-made beer, which is brewed in Assemini, a town near the Sardinian capital Cagliari. The beer is a lager with a hoppy taste. Birra Ichnusa is now owned by Heineken International. The beer is a clear yellow with a small to average, frothy head. The aroma is moderately malty, with hints of grain, grass, toast, and hops. The flavor is moderately sweet with light bitter, toast, and bread. The finish is slightly bitter and grainy.

KIRIN LAGER BEER

Country of Origin: *Japan* • **Brewery Founded:** *1885* • **Alcohol Content:** *4.9%*

The Kirin Brewery Company is based in Tokyo, Japan. It is part of the Mitsubishi Group. Kirin brews two of the most popular beers in Japan, Kirin Lager (the country's oldest beer brand) and Ichiban Shibori. In the happoshu (low-malt) category, Kirin Tanrei is the top selling beer in Japan. The Kirin brewery is named after the Qilin, which are hoofed creatures found in Chinese mythology. The beer pours slightly darker than the average pale lager and has a thin white head. This pale lager has a faint aroma. The flavor is of corn, cereals, apples, herbs, and grass. It is quite sugary, but with a pleasant bitterness in the aftertaste. The mouth feel is thin and fizzy.

KIRIN TANREI

Country of Origin: *Japan* • **Brewery Founded:** *1885* • **Alcohol Content:** *5.5%*

Kirin Tanrei is a happoshu (low malt) style of beer that pours a crystal clear pale golden color with a huge fluffy white head. The beer smells grainy and sweet with some malt. The taste is a bit sweet with a grainy malt edge, light pomme fruit, and floral hops to provide balance. The beer has a medium to thin body with a spirited level of carbonation and a sweet grainy mouth feel. The taste is very clean.

ORION DRAFT BEER

Country of Origin: *Japan* • **Brewery Founded:** *1957* • **Alcohol Content:** *5%*

Orion Breweries, is the fifth largest beer producer in Japan, headquartered in Urasoe, in the Okinawa Prefecture. The company commands approximately one percent of the Japanese beer market. Orion brews around 1.9 million gallons of fresh beer each year. Their beer is characterized by a crisp refreshing feel and a mild taste. Orion Draft is brewed with German Hallertauer hops and the malt is selected from quality European and Australian varieties. The brewery also uses fresh mountain spring water. Orion was founded during the American occupation of Okinawa.

ORION SOUTHERN STAR

Country of Origin: *Japan* • **Brewery Founded:** *1957* • **Alcohol Content:** *5%*

Orion Southern Star is a happoshu (low malt) style beer. It is a very pale yellow beer with a fizzy, white head. The aroma is of light apple and has a soda-like quality. The taste is very mild with a flavor of light hops and club soda. The mouth feel is light with minimal carbonation and a smooth finish. Orion is now a subsidiary of the giant Japanese Asahi chain of brewers.

OTARU PILSNER

Country of Origin: *Japan* • **Brewery Founded:** *1995*
Alcohol Content: *4.9%*

Otaru Beer is based in the coastal city of Otaru which is located on the Sea of Japan. The brewery has been making traditional German-style beers since it opened. Otaru was part of the 1990s boom in craft brewing and its beers are based on recipes which are more than two hundred years old. These beers were first brewed by the family of their German brew master Johannes Braun. Otaru Pilsner is a deep golden-colored beer which is bottom fermented. Otaru's production methods very closely match the production methods used in Bavaria. These include a cold fermentation and a long period of lagering.

SAPPORO BLACK LABEL

Country of Origin: *Japan* • **Brewery Founded:** *1876* • **Alcohol Content:** *5%*

Sapporo is headquartered in Ebisu, Shibuya, Tokyo, Japan. The company has five breweries in Japan as well as the Sleeman brewery in Canada. Sapporo's main brands are Sapporo Draft, Yebisu, and Sleeman Cream Ale. The brewery was founded in Japan's Meiji period. Seibei Nakagawa, a German-trained brewer, became the first brew master of the brewery and he developed the first Sapporo Lager. Sapporo Black Label is made with Japanese hops grown in the Iwate Prefecture is usually only sold in the Tohoku region. The beer has a fresh green hoppy aroma, with a grassy bitterness. It has a nice round flavor with rich malt and bitter hops. The finish is short, but the flavors linger in the mouth.

SANKT GALLEN BREWERY UN, KONO KURO

Country of Origin: *Japan* • **Brewery Founded:** *Unknown* • **Alcohol Content:** *6.5%*

Sankt Gallen has produced several very expensive beers for the luxury market. Their latest offering Un, Kono Kuro is a coffee stout made from coffee beans that have been through the gastric systems of Thai elephants. The digested coffee beans are then harvested from their manure. The beer bottle features a cheeky label showing an elephant pooping out beans. The expensive beer, which sold out within minutes of going on sale on April Fools' Day, has a mellow body with an intense afterglow. It is a combination of bitter and sweet and the body is saturated with the warm scent of coffee.

SUNTORY PREMIUM MALT'S

Country of Origin: *Japan* • **Brewery Founded:** *1899* • **Alcohol Content:** *5%*

Suntory was founded by Shinjiro Torii in Osaka, Japan. The group now makes a range of alcoholic beverages including whiskies, beers, and wines, together with soft drinks, oolong tea, and canned coffee. Suntory's company motto is "Yatte Minahare!" which means "Go for it!" The Premium Malt's is a traditional pilsner has a floral aroma and a rich, quality taste and aftertaste thanks to carefully selected pure ingredients and Suntory's exceptional brewing methods.

TAISETSU JI BIRU

Country of Origin: *Japan* • **Brewery Founded:** *1899* • **Alcohol Content:** *5%*

Taisetsu Ji Biru is a Japanese micro brewery. The brewery has been the winner of many awards including the Japan Beer Grand Prix. Ji Buru is the Japanese word for microbrewery or "local beer." The Japanese phrase for craft beer is "kurafuto bia." There are currently over 200 microbreweries in Japan making Ji Biru brews of various styles including ale, stout, pilsener, weizen, and Kölsch. There are a growing number of regional microbrew festivals held throughout Japan, including the annual Tokyo Real Ale Festival and the Great Japan Beer Festival which are held annually in Tokyo, Osaka, and Yokohama.

YEBISU ALL MALT BEER

Country of Origin: *Japan* • **Brewery Founded:** *1876* • **Alcohol Content:** *5%*

Yebisu is a Dortmuner-style export lager brewed by the famous Sapporo brewery. The beer is one of Japan's most popular brews. The beer pours a light golden color. It is very clear, with bubbles rising from the bottom. The aroma is of grain with a slight hint of hops and light citrus notes. The taste has hints of grain, barley, and hops. It is quite bitter with dominant malt. The flavor is not complex but very refreshing with a high carbonation.

MEXICO

BOHEMIA

Country of Origin: *Mexico* • **Brewery Founded:** *1890* • **Alcohol Content:** *5.3%*

Bohemia is the oldest and most traditional pilsner brewed in Mexico. The beer has a significant hops flavor and is quite dense given its clarity. The beer's name comes from the Bohemia region of the Czech Republic, which is well-known for its beer. It is one of the longest aged products from the Cervecería Cuauhtémoc brewery, and is the only one to use Lepa Styrian hops. There is a dark version of this brew which is a Vienna-style dark beer. In 2009, the company introduced a wheat version of Bohemia called Bohemia Weizen. This is brewed with wheat, Mount Hood hops, coriander, and orange peel. It is the first wheat beer to be produced by a major beer company in Mexico.

CARTA BLANCA

Country of Origin: *Mexico* • **Brewery Founded:** *1890* • **Alcohol Content:** *4%*

Carta Blanca was Cervecería Cuauhtémoc's first premium beer, first marketed in 1890. Technically, Carta Blanca is brewed as a pilsner, but it is marketed as a pale lager. The name means white

card in Spanish. At the time, visiting cards were handed out as a sign of respect. Carta Blanca was successful when it debuted at Chicago's Columbian Exposition of 1893. Since then, the beer has won a number of other awards. The beer has a foamy head and a light gold color. The aroma and flavor are of sweet corn.

CORONA

Country of Origin: *Mexico* • **Brewery Founded:** *1915* • **Alcohol Content:** *4.6%*

Corona lager is one of Mexico's best known Mexican beers. It is the flagship beer of the Grupo Modelo brewing company. Corona is the best-selling beer produced by Mexico and is the best selling nondomestic beer in the U.S. and Britain. It is one of the five most popular beers in the world, and is available in more than 150 countries. The brew was created in 1925 to celebrate Cervecería Modelo's tenth anniversary. The beer is light straw in color with a very mild flavor, with little hop bitterness. Unusually, Corona is bottled in clear glass, which makes it vulnerable to being spoiled by sunlight. This can affect the hop oils in the beer. A draught version of the beer is produced, and the beer is also canned in some markets.

DOS EQUIS SPECIAL LAGER

Country of Origin: *Mexico* • **Brewery Founded:** *1890* • **Alcohol Content:** *4.5%*

Dos Equis was first brewed in Mexico by the German brewer Wilhelm Hasse in 1897. The original name of the beer was Siglo XX (twentieth century). The original version is Dos Equis Ambar, a Vienna-style dark beer. This was Cervecería Moctezuma's best selling beer in the 1940s and 1950s. Demand for the beer has resurged, especially in the United States, where it is now the best-selling imported dark beer. The clear version of this brand is a lager derived from the Ambar. Dos Equis Special Lager is a refreshing, crisp, golden, lager style beer. It is brewed with roasted malts, choice hops, a unique strain of yeast, and purified water.

ESTRELLA

Country of Origin: *Mexico* • **Brewery Founded:** *Nineteenth century* • **Alcohol Content:** *4%*

Estrella (Star) was originally brewed by Cervecería Estrella of Guadalajara at the end of the nineteenth century. This brewery was bought by Grupo Modelo in 1954. The beer is still brewed only in Guadalajara and is a regional brand, mostly sold in Jalisco state and other areas in western Mexico. The beer pours a clear, pale yellow and has lots of tiny bubbles. It has an aroma of green apple, dry cereal, and cooked vegetables. The taste is much like the smell but with a little sour lemon.

INDIO

Country of Origin: *Mexico*
Brewery Founded: *1897* • **Alcohol Content:** *4.1%*

Indio is a Vienna-style amber lager. The beer has an amber hue and a distinctive light caramel-malt taste. Indio was originally named Cuauhtémoc by the brewer Cervecería Cuauhtémoc. However, consumers soon began to refer to it as the Indian for the image of an Indian on what was originally a clay bottle. The beer is now bottled in glass, but still has an image of Cuauhtémoc on the label.

MODELO ESPECIAL

Country of Origin: *Mexico* • **Brewery Founded:** *1922* • **Alcohol Content:** *4.4%*

Modelo Especial is an American-style lager beer. It is Grupo Modelo's second biggest brand after Corona, and was first brewed in 1925. It is a pilsner-style lager that is available in both bottle and cans since 1966. It is the second most popular beer in Mexico and the company's third best seller in the United States. A light version of the beer, called Modelo Light, has been available since 1994.

NOCHE BUENA

Country of Origin: *Mexico* • **Brewery Founded:** *1890* • **Alcohol Content:** *5.9%*

Noche Buena is a bock beer brewed in Mexico by Cervecería Cuauhtémoc Moctezuma. The beer is generally only available around Christmas. For many people, the annual launch of the beer (between the months of October and December) is a sign that Christmas is on the way. Noche Buena is a strong-flavored dark beer named after the poinsettia plant or *noche buena* in Spanish, which decorates the beer's bottles and cartons.

PACIFICO

Country of Origin: *Mexico* • **Brewery Founded:** *1922* • **Alcohol Content:** *4.5%*

Pacífico, a Mexican pilsner beer originally brewed in Mazatlán, Sinaloa, is named after the Pacific Ocean. The picture on the bottle is of the Deer Islands, located off the coast of Mazatlán, surrounded by a lifesaver. Pacífico is Modelo's best-selling beer in northwest Mexico, and it is exported to the southwest United States. A light version of this beer was launched in 2008. The beer is yellow in color with a small white head. The aroma is of hay and the taste is light, bitter, and a little sweet.

SOL

Country of Origin: *Mexico* • **Brewery Founded:** *1890* • **Alcohol Content:** *7%*

Sol was introduced in the 1890s as El Sol. The name came from a ray of sunshine that fell on a pot while beer mash was being prepared. After being off the market for many years, this brand was reintroduced in 1993, and is now exported to Latin America, Europe, and Asia. It is a very light-colored beer with little hop flavor. Sol is known for its sexy advertising and is popular with young people. The beer comes in a number of varieties. Sol 2 is a stronger flavored beer, Sol limón and sal have lime and salt flavors added, and Sol Cero, is a nonalcoholic beer that is also produced in lime and salt versions.

SUPERIOR

Country of Origin: *Mexico* • **Brewery Founded:** *1890* • **Alcohol Content:** *4.5%*

Superior is a pale lager brewed by Cuauhtémoc Moctezuma. As its name implies, it was originally brewed to be a premium beer. Superior's popularity has resurged recently, and the beer received a gold medal at the Monde Selection in Brussels, Belgium. The design of the label has not changed in the fifty years this beer brand has been available. The beer pours a clear golden with a medium off-white head. The aroma is sweet with hints of sweet malt and the flavor has hints of hop. The carbonation is average and the beer has a dry finish with no bitterness.

TECATE

Country of Origin: *Mexico* • **Brewery Founded:** *1890* • **Alcohol Content:** *4.55%*

Tecate is a pale lager. The beer is now brewed by the Cuauhtémoc brewery. The brewer was founded in Monterrey in 1890 by the Muguerza family with a capital of 11,500 dollars. The brewery started by brewing Carta Blanca beer. Tecate was originally brewed by Cerve-cería Tecate, and named after the city of Tecate, Baja California. This local brewery was bought by Cuauhtémoc Moctezuma in 1955. Tecate was the first beer to be canned in Mexico, with Tecate Light launched in Mexico in 1992. Tecate is one of the best-known brands in Mexico due to its patronage of sports teams and events. Pale lager is a very pale to golden-colored beer with a well attenuated body and a varying degree of noble hop bitterness. The brewing process for this style of beer was first developed in the mid nineteenth century when the widely-travelled Gabriel Sedlmayr took pale ale brewing techniques back to his family brew-ery, the Spaten Brewery in Germany's Bavaria. He then applied the technique to the brewery's ex-isting lagering methods. His new recipe greatly improved the brewery's lager and his approach was picked up by other brewers. The most no-table of these was Josef Groll of Bavaria who produced Pilsner Urquell in the city of Pilsen in the Czech Republic. The resulting pale colored, lean, and stable brews became increasingly successful. They gradually spread around the globe to become the most common form of beer consumed in the world today. Pale lagers tend to be dry, clean-tasting, and crisp. Their flavors may be subtle, with no traditional beer ingredient dominat-ing. The hop character of pale lagers can range from negligible to a dry bitterness from noble hops. The main ingredients in these brews are water, Pilsner malt, and noble hops. Some mass market brewers also use adjuncts such as rice or corn to lighten the body of the beer.

NETHERLANDS

ALFA BOKBIER

Country of Origin: *Netherlands* • **Brewery Founded:** *1870* • **Alcohol Content:** *6.5%*

Alfa Bokbier is a ruby red beer. It is brewed in limited quantities in the fall for the winter months. It is brewed with specially selected malt varieties, which give Alfa Bokbier its strong taste. The beer is best enjoyed at a temperature of around 50 degrees fahrenheit.

ALFA EDEL PILS

Country of Origin: *Netherlands* • **Brewery Founded:** *1870* • **Alcohol Content:** *5%*

This pure and natural pilsner is prepared from barley malts, natural hops, and spring water. It is a beer with a character of its own. Edel Pils is generous in taste with a subtle bouquet. Each bottle of Alfa's brew has a unique number printed on its neck label. The ideal drinking temperature for this beer is about 50 degrees fahrenheit.

ALFA SUPER DORTMUNDER

Country of Origin: *Netherlands* • **Brewery Founded:** *1870* • **Alcohol Content:** *7.5%*

Dortmunder is a pale lager that gets its character from being lagered for two months. The aroma has notes of grass, hop, and vanilla. The flavor is sweet and bitter with honey, vanilla, hop, apple, and butter tasting note. It is very bitter finish with grass, hop, and butter aromas. This is an interesting beer that is surprisingly bitter.

AMSTEL 1870

Country of Origin: *Netherlands* • **Brewery Founded:** *1870* • **Alcohol Content:** *5%*

1870 is a pils type of beer with a vanilla aroma and bittersweet taste. The beer has a bitter finish with some biscuity malt flavor. The beer is one of the better commercial Dutch pils-type beers on the market.

AMSTEL BOCK

Country of Origin: *Netherlands* • **Brewery Founded:** *1870*
Alcohol Content: *7.5%*

This extra strong ruby-red Amstel Bock beer has a fine bitterness and a sweet, full taste. Its high alcohol content gives this heritage brew a strong character.

AMSTEL GOLD

Country of Origin: *Netherlands* • **Brewery Founded:** *1870*
Alcohol Content: *7%*

This mass market beer is malty, and roasty with herbal hop notes. It also has tasting notes of dough, alcohol, and a clear, deep golden color. The beer has a frothy white head and a light sweetness. It has a medium body, average carbonation and is clean and smooth. The finish is malty and mildly bitter.

AMSTEL OUD BRUIN

Country of Origin: *Netherlands* • **Brewery Founded:** *1870* • **Alcohol Content:** *2.5%*

Oud Bruin is a dark Lager. The aroma is of toffee, raisin, and metal. The taste is very sweet with hints of toffee and pear. The beer has a sweet finish with a pear aroma. The smell is pleasantly fruity. The beer has a pleasant mouth feel and a fairly lean finish.

BAVARIA PILSNER

Country of Origin: *Netherlands* • **Brewery Founded:** *1719* • **Alcohol Content:** *5%*

The Bavaria brewery produces a range of standard and low alcohol pale lagers under a variety of brand names including Bavaria and Hollandia. The brewery's best-known global product is Bavaria Premium Pils lager.

BRAND URTYP PILSNER

Country of Origin: *Netherlands* • **Brewery Founded:** *1871*
Alcohol Content: *5.5%*

Brand Urtyp Pilsner has an aroma of hop, lemon, and resin. The taste is bitter and sweetish with tasting notes of wood, lemon, tobacco, and vanilla. The beer has a bitter finish with tobacco, hop, and tobacco aromas. This is a nicely hoppy beer that is among the better Dutch beers in the pils style. The use of good-quality hops shines through. This beer was first brewed in 1952.

BUDELS PILSENER

Country of Origin: *Netherlands* • **Brewery Founded:** *1870* • **Alcohol Content:** *5%*

Budels Pilsener is a lager beer that is brewed from biologically-cultivated malt and hops. What is more, Budels Bio-Beer is brewed entirely with green power. The beer reflects Holland's great concern for the environment.

CHRISTOFFEL NOBEL

Country of Origin: *Netherlands* • **Brewery Founded:** *1970* • **Alcohol Content:** *8.7%*

This golden-blond extra strong beer has added fresh noble hop flowers during maturation of at least ten weeks. This unique beer is bottom-fermented, unfiltered, and unpasteurized. Nobel refers to the varieties of the noble hop species. These are selected because of their quality. Traditionally, noble hops are low in bitterness and high in aroma.

DOMMELSCH PILS

Country of Origin: *Netherlands* • **Brewery Founded:** *1744* • **Alcohol Content:** *5%*

Dommelsch Pils is a good and honest Dutch beer. It has a good tap with little carbonation and a nice white head. The beer is dry but also has a smooth taste. The Dommelsch Brewery was founded in 1744 in the village of Dommelen, Netherlands. It is now part of the Anheuser-Busch InBev brewery group. It brews Dommelsch Pilsener for the Dutch market, and makes the global brand Brahma beer for distribution in the European market.

GROLSCH PREMIUM LAGER

Country of Origin: *Netherlands* • **Brewery Founded:** *1615* • **Alcohol Content:** *5%*

Instantly recognizable through the swing-top bottle, Grolsch is a superb continental lager with a full bodied and crisp taste. The beer is brewed to the original recipe that dates back over four-hundred years. Grolsch uses a longer than normal brewing process, and brews its Premium Lager with two different varieties of hops. These factors give Grolsch Premium Lager a wonderful balance of bitter and sweet flavors. This makes a beer that is rich in taste with a savory and spicy character. It has big hoppy aromas and an exceptionally refreshing finish.

GULPENER CHATEAU NEUBOURG

Country of Origin: *Netherlands* • **Brewery Founded:** *1825* • **Alcohol Content:** *5.5%*

This unusual beer is bottled in blue glass flagons. The brew pours a crisp, clear pale gold with a fluffy white head. This dissipates slowly to the edges and it has good lacing. The beer's aroma has a good amount of straw and hay.

HEINEKEN LAGER

Country of Origin: *Netherlands* • **Brewery Founded:** *1873* • **Alcohol Content:** *5.5%*

A world famous brand, Heineken Lager was first brewed by Gerard Adriaan Heineken in 1873. The beer is made of purified water, malted barley, hops, and yeast. In 1886 H. Elion finished the development of the famous Heineken A-yeast, which is still used in the brewing process today.

JOPEN KOYT

Country of Origin: *Netherlands* • **Brewery Founded:** *1994* • **Alcohol Content:** *8.5%*

Koyt is the Old Dutch name for Gruit beer (mulled beer). Jopen Koyt is a heavy variant of this style and has a mellow and spicy character, especially in its aroma and aftertaste. Sweet Gale is the most characteristic of the spices used in the Gruit mixture that is used to brew Koyt. Crafting the beer with darker malts gives the beer its reddish brown hue and a hearty, full-bodied taste. The interaction between the flavors of the three grains and the classic spices gives Koyt an unusual character. Beer connoisseurs praise Koyt for its rich taste and aroma.

KONINGSHOEVEN LA TRAPPE BLOND

Country of Origin: *Netherlands* • **Brewery Founded:** *1884* • **Alcohol Content:** *6.5%*

La Trappe is brewed by Koningshoeven, and is the only Trappist beer in The Netherlands. It is the only Dutch beer brewed in a Trappist monastery under the supervision and responsibility of the monks, and it is this that qualifies La Trappe as a Trappist beer. The beer is brewed according to traditional methods, from a recipe developed by the monks of Koningshoeven. Only natural ingredients, such as hops, barley malt, and yeast are used in the brew. The brewery uses water drawn from its own well. La Trappe Blond is a clear, sparkling lager of high fermentation, attuned to the European taste. It is characterized by the use of refined hops. This gives the beer a slightly bitter aftertaste and a distinctively refreshing but fragrant aroma.

KONINGSHOEVEN DUBBEL

Country of Origin: *Netherlands* • **Brewery Founded:** *1884* • **Alcohol Content:** *7%*

Dubbel is a warm, ruby-red Trappist beer. The beer has a soft, fragrant, but above all refreshing, character. De Koningshoeven Brewery is a Dutch Trappist brewery founded in 1884 within the walls of the abbey Onze Lieve Vrouw van Koningshoeven in Berkel-Enschot, Netherlands.

KONINGSHOEVEN QUADRUPEL

Country of Origin: *Netherlands* • **Brewery Founded:** *1884* • **Alcohol Content:** *10%*

Quadrupel is the heaviest specialty beer available from La Trappe. The taste is full, mild, and pleasantly bitter. This beer is bottled by date. The Onze Lieve Vrouw van Koningshoeven Abbey opened a brewery to finance the monastery and contribute to charitable causes. Despite this goal, the brewery is run as a commercial enterprise. The abbey produces lager under its own Trappist brand as well as contract brewing for several private labels.

KONINGSHOEVEN WITTE TRAPPIST

Country of Origin: *Netherlands* • **Brewery Founded:** *1884* • **Alcohol Content:** *5.5%*

Witte Trappist beer is brewed with especially aromatic hops. This gives the beer a refreshing character. Witte Trappist is neither filtered nor pasteurized and the fermentation process continues in the bottle. In contrast to the other La Trappe beers, this beer should be served cold.

DE LECKERE PILSENER

Country of Origin: *Netherlands* • **Brewery Founded:** *1997* • **Alcohol Content:** *5%*

This Pilsner is packaged in green, long-necked bottles. It pours golden yellow color and has lots of bubbles. The beer is just slightly hazy and has an inch-deep head with good retention. The beer has a soft and very discreet aroma of malts. It has a clear taste that is only slightly bitter. The beer is medium thin in the body and quite carbonated.

DE LEEUW NAJAARSBOCK

Country of Origin: *Netherlands* • **Brewery Founded:** *1997* • **Alcohol Content:** *6.5%*

This beer is a dark bock and is unpasteurized. It is winter seasonal ale. The beer has apple and biscuit aromas. It has a sweet taste with liquorice, smoke, and caramel aromas. It has a bitter finish with toffee and smoke aromas. The beer is a good old-fashioned bottom-fermented bock. The beer has a nice balance of malty sweetness and smoky bitterness.

LINDEBOOM SPELT

Country of Origin: *Netherlands* • **Brewery Founded:** *1870* • **Alcohol Content:** *5%*

This is a Belgian-style ale that doesn't fit neatly into any classic beer style. It is a session ale with a moderate level of alcohol. The brew's color ranges from golden to deep amber, with the occasional example coming in darker. The body tends to be light to medium, with a wide range of hop and malt levels. Yeastiness and acidity are also present.

DE MOLEN AMERIKAANS

Country of Origin: *Netherlands* • **Brewery Founded:** *2004* • **Alcohol Content:** *4.5%*

De Molen beers are not all about heavy flavors and body. This brew is light and refreshing. This light amber colored bitter has an unusual American touch. English Bitters are mild and malty, but American hops give this ale a bitter citrus and grassy character. Amerikaans is a great combination of old and new world beer styles. Brouwerij De Molen is an award-winning small craft brewery, distillery and restaurant located in Bodegraven, a town in the south Netherlands. It is within the rural area known as Het Groene Hart, or Green Heart of Holland.

DE SCHANS VOLLENHOVEN STOUT

Country of Origin: *Netherlands* • **Brewery Founded:** *1791* • **Alcohol Content:** *7%*

This stout pours nearly black with a fine deep fawn head. The beer has a complex fruity dark malt aroma with blackcurrant, coal, chocolate, and vinyl hints. The beer also has a savory smoked bacon bite. The complexity and the bacon hints continue into a sweet dark chocolate, caramel, and raisin palate with brooding fruity tones and a satisfying nuttiness. The beer has a roasty finish with tangy notes of charred wood and mild malt. This stout is notably smoother and less hoppily drying than the brewery's lager.

TEXELS SKUUMKOPPE

Country of Origin: *Netherlands* • **Brewery Founded:** *1999* • **Alcohol Content:** *6%*

Texels Skuumkoppe (Texel Foam Top) is the first top-fermented, dark wheat craft beer brewed in the Netherlands. The brewer uses only natural ingredients, such as malted barley and wheat grown in Texel combined with hops, roasted malted barley, and dune-filtered water. No herbs or spices are added to the brew. The beer is an unfiltered, bottle-fermented beer. The small amount of yeast sediment in the bottle gives the beer its distinctive creamy taste.

US HEIT TWELS BOKBIER

Country of Origin: *Netherlands* • **Brewery Founded:** *1999* • **Alcohol Content:** *6.5%*

This bokbier is a dark bock. It is an autumnal seasonal brew. The beer is mahogany brown with ruby shades. The beer has wheat, coriander, and biscuit aromas. The taste is sweet with malt, coriander, honey, and ginger aromas. It has a bitter finish with burnt, malt, herbal, and coriander aromas. The beer is an unusual bock with lots of spicy flavors. It has a medium body and light carbonation.

NEW ZEALAND

DB BREWERIES EXPORT GOLD

Country of Origin: *New Zealand* • **Brewery Founded:** *1930* • **Alcohol content:** *4.0%*

In 1960, Morton Coutts discovered the Holy Grail of beer, continuous fermentation. Unlike batch brewing, continuous fermentation meant that once the brewing started, the beer never stopped flowing. The process was adopted by the rest of the world and the beer that flowed was Export Gold. The brew is made using only the finest New Zealand hops, barley, and pure spring water. The beer is one of New Zealand's freshest and most refreshing beers. The brew won a Gold medal at the 2011 Monde Selection awards and continues to win awards around the globe.

CANTERBURY DRAUGHT

Country of Origin: *New Zealand* • **Brewery Founded:** *1854* • **Alcohol Content:** *4.0%*

Canterbury Draught is also known as Ward's beer, named after founding brewer James Hamilton Ward. Ward is one of the oldest names in New Zealand's brewing history, first appearing in 1854. The brand was renamed in 1990, but Ward's name remains on the label. Each batch is individually crafted in authentic copper vessels and combines the finest Canterbury malt, pure water from the New Zealand Southern Alps, and choice Nelson hops. This creates a full-bodied, refreshing beer that truly captures the taste of the region.

GALBRAITH BREWERY ANTIPODEAN PALE ALE

Country of Origin: *New Zealand* • **Brewery Founded:** *1995* • **Alcohol Content:** *5.0%*

Antipodean Pale Ale is brewed in the style of Burton-Upon-Trent IPAs. This strong beer uses New Zealand Southern Cross hops which impart a nose of resinous hops and a lighter caramel malt. The beer has a mid-gold color. It first strikes the palate as bitter followed by a rich maltiness balancing the flavor and filling the mouth. The finish is dry and hoppy.

GALBRAITH BREWERY BOB HUDSON'S BITTER

Country of Origin: *New Zealand* • **Brewery Founded:** *1995* • **Alcohol Content:** *4.0%*

This beer was named in honor of Kentish brewer John "Bob" Hudson who passed on the secrets of bitter brewing to the Galbraith brewery. The brew uses floor-malted Maris Otter and Pale Crystal malts with the addition of Styrian and Goldings hops throughout the boil. The local hard water and late hopping provides a tangy and refreshing English style bitter that is an ideal session ale.

GALBRAITH BREWERY BOHEMIAN PILSNER

Country of Origin: *New Zealand* • **Brewery Founded:** *1995* • **Alcohol Content:** *4.3%*

Galbraith's Bohemian Pilsner is a German-style pilsner which uses floor malted Moravian lager and Czech Saaz malts combined with German Hallertau hops. This produces an authentic fresh-tasting and aromatic lager that is a full-bodied example of the type. The beer is also malty and refreshing.

GALBRAITH BREWERY RESURRECTION ALE

Country of Origin: *New Zealand* • **Brewery Founded:** *1995* • **Alcohol Content:** *8.7%*

Galbraith's Resurrection ale is a strong Belgian-style Trappist beer. It pours copper red with a light white frothy head. There are wine-like complexities in the flavor. These include spicy and herbal notes, which impact on the nose and palate. These flavor notes come the use of special yeast in the fermentation process.

HAWKES BAY INDEPENDENT BREWERY AMBER ALE

Country of Origin: *New Zealand* • **Brewery Founded:** *1995* • **Alcohol Content:** *4.0%*

Hawkes Bay Amber Ale has a rich malty body with mild hop characteristic. This adds complex fruitiness and a pronounced bitterness to this deep amber ale. The beer is batch brewed using traditional methods and is cold filtered to give a smooth, crisp finish.

HAWKES BAY INDEPENDENT BREWERY DRAUGHT

Country of Origin: *New Zealand* • **Brewery Founded:** *1995* • **Alcohol Content:** *4.0%*

Hawkes Bay's Draught has a rich malt body with mild hop characteristic. This adds complex fruitiness and a pronounced bitterness to this deep amber ale. The beer is batch-brewed using traditional methods and cold filtered to give a smooth, crisp finish.

STEINLAGER

Country of Origin: *New Zealand* • **Brewery Founded:** *1962* • **Alcohol Content:** *5.0%*

Steinlager was first brewed in response to a challenge issued by the New Zealand Finance Minister Lord Nordmeyer. In his infamous "black budget" Nordmeyer threatened to cut international beer imports to boost the flagging economy, and laid down the challenge for New Zealand's leading brewers to "come up with an International style lager beer." Originally called Steinecker, The beer changed its name to Steinlager in 1962. Steinlager won the Les Amis Du Vin competition four years in a row in the late 1970s. The competition organizers then politely asked if the beer could withdraw to "give the others a chance." At London's 1985 Brewers' International Exhibition, Steinlager was judged the World's Best Lager. In 1998, the beer was awarded two Monde Selection gold medals in Belgium. More recently, Steinlager won a gold medal and Best in Class in the lager division at the 2006 Australian International Beer Awards. Steinlager's worldwide success is credited to its distinctive taste. The beer is brewed with only pure, natural New Zealand ingredients. It has a dry, tangy finish and the green bullet hops deliver a clean, crisp bitterness to the brew.

TUI BLOND LAGER

Country of Origin: *New Zealand* • **Brewery Founded:** *1889* • **Alcohol Content:** *4.0%*

Tui Blond Lager is stored at cool temperatures during the brewing process. This gives the beer a clean, crisp flavor. Tui Blond Lager is a golden, full-flavored beer with European ancestry. The brew has some subtle hopping from classic European hops which adds a refreshing bitterness. The beer is a great thirst quencher on hot summer days.

TUI DARK

Country of Origin: *New Zealand* • **Brewery Founded:** *1889* • **Alcohol Content:** *4.0%*

The Brewers at Tui perfected a blend of five malts to create a distinguished roasted malt flavor. This finely balances the sweetness with some sharp-tasting hops. That's what makes Tui Dark so refreshing for a darker style of beer. Each sip of the beer is smooth without being too filling.

TUI EAST INDIA PALE ALE

Country of Origin: *New Zealand* • **Brewery Founded:** *1889* • **Alcohol Content:** *4.0%*

East India Pale Ale has been one of Tui's award winning ales since 1904. The beer was first brewed in 1889 on the banks of the Mangatainoka River by Henry Wagstaff. The beer is brewed with pale malt. The beer is traditionally brewed to keep it smooth and thirst-quenching. Historically, the brew was shipped to the parched British troops in colonial India. It is now New Zealand's most popular beer.

WAIKATO DRAUGHT

Country of Origin: *New Zealand* • **Brewery Founded:** *1920* • **Alcohol Content:** *4.0%*

Waikato Draught was first brewed in the 1920s. It has been the beer of the Waikato region ever since. Cartoon character Willie the Waiter is the brand's mascot and has become a regional icon. Waikato Draught was recently awarded a gold medal and won best in class in the New Zealand Draught Beer category at the 2005 Brew New Zealand Awards. Waikato Draught has a strong malty flavor and a well-defined bitterness. The beer has a smooth and clean texture and a hoppy and spicy aroma. The beer is brewed by the Lion Group.

WEST COAST BLACK

Country of Origin: *New Zealand* • **Brewery Founded:** *unknown* • **Alcohol Content:** *4.0%*

West Coast Black is a rich and full flavored brew. It has the up-front boldness of fresh roasted coffee and dark chocolate combined with a crisp, subtle hop finish. The brewery blends a truckload of roasted and Crystal malts to give this beer a unique and intense flavor profile.

WEST COAST DRAUGHT

Country of Origin: *New Zealand* • **Brewery Founded:** *Unknown* • **Alcohol Content:** *4.0%*

This beer is a New Zealand classic. The beer has a rich malt body with mild hop characteristics. Using generous amounts of Canterbury malts and Nelson hops gives this classic Kiwi brew a truly unique taste. With a subtle nose of Caramel, Malt & Butterscotch, this Kiwi favorite is a great session beer.

WEST COAST INTERNATIONAL PALE ALE

Country of Origin: *New Zealand* • **Brewery Founded:** *Unknown* • **Alcohol Content:** *5.0%*

West Coast takes English Pale & Crystal malts and adds layers of Nelson Sauvin and New Zealand Cascade hops throughout the boil. The brew is also dry hopped in the fermentation tank. This is where the fruity American ale yeast works its magic. The beer is then cold conditioned for two weeks. It is at this point that the original brewers decided on the dry hop formula to be added to the beer tank. The beer is a combination of the finest English malt, American yeast, and the best Kiwi hops. All these ingredients combine to create a fine international Pale Ale.

SINGAPORE

ADSTRAGOLD RED ALE

Country of Origin: *Singapore* • **Brewery Founded:** *2010* • **Alcohol Content:** *4%*

Red Ale is crafted with lightly roasted barley malt and aroma hops. It is a mellow non-bitter ale, with a slight dash of roasted aroma. It is very similar to English Bass Ale. The brew is an enjoyable and highly drinkable light dark ale.

ADSTRAGOLD GOLDEN ALE

Country of Origin: *Singapore* • **Brewery Founded:** *2010* • **Alcohol Content:** *3%*

The beer is crafted with Liberty hops from Yakima, Washington and East Kent Goldings hops from England. The beer is brewed with 2-row brewers malt with a small amount of roasted barley to give the beer a well-rounded, malty character. This light ale is refreshing, flavorful, and not too filling. This ale is cloudy when it is young, but its character changes over time.

ADSTRAGOLD INDIA PALE ALE

Country of Origin: *Singapore* • **Brewery Founded:** *2010* • **Alcohol Content:** *3%*

This IPA is crafted with specially aged malt and extra multi-hops. This gives the beer a strong flavor. It also has a full body and good bitterness. The beer gets smoother as it continues to mature. The beer is great for ale drinkers who love beers with good bitterness and hoppy flavors.

ADSTRAGOLD ROASTY STOUT

Country of Origin: *Singapore* • **Brewery Founded:** *2010* • **Alcohol Content:** *3%*

Roasty Stout is a rich dark beer crafted with Minnesota 2-row brewers malt, English chocolate malt, black malt, and roasted barley. These malts give the brew a pleasant coffee, nutty character and aroma. The beer is hopped with Liberty and East Kent Goldings hops. This is one of the most drinkable stouts in the micro brewery category.

ARCHIPELAGO EXPLORER

Country of Origin: *Singapore* • **Brewery Founded:** *1931* • **Alcohol Content:** *5%*

This premium ale has a hazy gold body, with an average sized white head. It has a very strong and malty, bread, and biscuit aroma, with an additional slight citrus element to the taste. The beer has medium body.

BREWERKZ GOLDEN ALE

Country of Origin: *Singapore* • **Brewery Founded:** *1997* • **Alcohol Content:** *5%*

Golden Ale is one of the Brewerkz most popular beers. The brew is a light golden color with a slightly malty character, and a subtle floral cascade hop aroma. The beer has low bitterness, a light body, and typical ale fruitiness.

BREWERKZ IPA

Country of Origin: *Singapore* • **Brewery Founded:** *1997* • **Alcohol Content:** *6%*

Brewerkz's best-selling brew is malty, full-bodied, and full of hop character. The beer is a clear copper color, with an off-white head. It has a malty, sweet taste. The brew also has a smooth mouth feel and medium bitterness. It is malty, with a good hoppy scent.

LEVEL 33 BLOND LAGER

Country of Origin: *Singapore* • **Brewery Founded:** *Unknown* • **Alcohol Content:** *Unknown*

The world's highest urban craft brewery is situated in Singapore's MBFC Tower 1. Level 33's Blond Lager is crafted from the brewery's original 1841 Vienna Blond Lager. This refreshing Blond Lager has a slight hint of fruit. It pours a smooth sunshine gold hue.

HANSA PILSENER

Country of Origin: *South Africa* • **Brewery Founded:** *1895* • **Alcohol Content:** *4.5%*

In keeping with the Hansa promise to brew beer styles beyond regular lager, this is the first pilsner style beer brewed in South Africa. The beer was first launched in 1975. Hansa is now part of the South African Breweries Group.

JACK BLACK'S BREWERS LAGER

Country of Origin: *South Africa* • **Brewery Founded:** *2007* • **Alcohol Content:** *5.4%*

This flagship Pre-Prohibition style lager is inspired by the malt beers of the early 1900s. It is a session lager brewed with Pale Malt, Southern Promise, and Saaz hops. The beer achieves a great balance between hop bitterness and malt sweetness. The beer has notes of citrus and malt. It is a full-bodied lager that is crisp and refreshing.

JACK BLACK'S BUTCHER BLOCK

Country of Origin: *South Africa* • **Brewery Founded:** *2007* • **Alcohol Content:** *5.4%*

Butcher Block is an American-style award winning pale ale. The beer is smooth in the body with a distinctive flavor profile, and a decidedly fresh taste. The beer has refreshing characteristics, balanced with rich malt complexity and a bitterness that lingers on the finish. The beer has floral flavor notes with a touch of honey. The beer is well-rounded and perfectly balanced.

JACK BLACK'S LUMBERJACK

Country of Origin: *South Africa* • **Brewery Founded:** *2007* • **Alcohol Content:** *6.0%*

Lumberjack is medium to full bodied with a deep dark red-brown hue. This award winning beer has complex malt character derived from loads of dark roasted Crystal Malt. Black Jack's brewer uses mountains of hops to balance this malt. This makes Lumberjack an outstanding beer to savor with richer foods. The beer has flavor notes of dark malt, roasted flavors, pine aromas, and hops. The beer has a great full body.

JACK BLACK'S SKELETON COAST INDIA PALE ALE

Country of Origin: *South Africa* • **Brewery Founded:** *2007* • **Alcohol Content:** *6.6%*

The Skeleton Coast is the treacherous coastline that contours southwest Africa. Feared by seafarers, and known as the Gates of Hell, the coastline was on the route to India from Cape Town. Many of these ships sailed with IPA on board. The beer was brewed with extra hops and malt to withstand the epic journey. Skeleton Coast is premium pale ale with full malt flavor and extreme hop character. Dry hopping highlights powerful citrus, floral, and earthy aromas.

MITCHELL'S BOSUN'S BITTER

Country of Origin: *South Africa* • **Brewery Founded:** *1983* • **Alcohol Content:** *3.6%*

South Africa's oldest microbrewery was founded in 1983 and has weathered thirty years waiting for the craft beer boom to begin. Their English-style brews can now be found across South Africa both on tap and in bottles. Bosun's Bitter is full of body and character, but not too bitter. It is modelled on English Yorkshire bitters. Bosun's moderate alcohol level does not sacrifice flavor, making it an ideal session beer.

MITCHELL'S FORESTERS LAGER

Country of Origin: *South Africa* • **Brewery Founded:** *1983* • **Alcohol Content:** *3.6%*

The Forester's Lager is low in alcohol but big in flavor. This is a well-balanced, hoppy beer that is slightly sweet and great on the palate. This lager is a refreshing drink for a hot day. Established in Knysna in 1983, Mitchell's crafts seven natural beers. These are unpasteurized, live ales produced using the finest ingredients and a carefully selected amalgam of British mashing and German lager techniques.

MITCHELL'S MILK AND HONEY

Country of Origin: *South Africa* • **Brewery Founded:** *1983* • **Alcohol Content:** *5.5%*

Milk and Honey is as golden as an African sunset. The beer has a flavor of pure honey and a mild, fresh taste. Milk & Honey is a slightly darker, robust ale with a moderate level of alcohol. It has a touch of lactose and a drop of honey to sweeten it up.

MITCHELL'S RAVEN STOUT

Country of Origin: *South Africa* • **Brewery Founded:** *1983* • **Alcohol Content:** *5.0%*

Raven Stout is as black as a raven's wing. The beer is full-bodied and flavorsome. It has a pronounced bite and well developed hop aroma. Strong and smooth, this distinctive stout is perfect for a cold winter evening but can also be served ice cold on a hot African day.

NOTTINGHAM ROAD PICKLED PIG PORTER

Country of Origin: *South Africa* • **Brewery Founded:** *1997* • **Alcohol Content:** *5.0%*

Pickled Pig Porter is a full, dark beer. It is slightly bitter, and perfect for cold-weather drinking. The beer is brewed with pure spring water and is rich in minerals. The beer has no added preservatives. The brewery claims that this delicious Porter is good for health, saying that the more you drink, the better you feel. They also claim that drinking Pickled Pig doesn't result in a hangover.

NOTTINGHAM ROAD PIE-EYED POSSUM PILSENER

Country of Origin: *South Africa* • **Brewery Founded:** *1997* • **Alcohol Content:** *4.6%*

It took months of careful fermentation and maturation to create this bottle beer. Pie-Eyed Possum has a rich, bitter flavor, and a noble hop bouquet. Designed for serious beer drinkers, this pilsner has a moderately high level of alcohol.

NOTTINGHAM ROAD TIDDLY TOAD LIGHT LAGER

Country of Origin: *South Africa* • **Brewery Founded:** *1997* • **Alcohol Content:** *4.0%*

Tiddly Toad Light Lager is Nottingham Road's lightest beer. But it has nothing in common with mass-produced yellow "lite" lagers. The flavor of the beer has a delicious fullness and is full of fine hops. It is a lighter brew made to please serious beer drinkers.

NOTTINGHAM ROAD WHISTLING WEASEL PALE ALE

Country of Origin: *South Africa* • **Brewery Founded:** *1997* • **Alcohol Content:** *4.5%*

Whistling Weasel Pale Ale is a tasty and invigorating brew. The beer is made with the finest quality hops, malt, barley, and pure spring water. These combine to make a this traditional pale ale a really special brew.

PHOENIX

Country of Origin: *South Africa* • **Brewery Founded:** *1963* • **Alcohol Content:** *5.0%*

Phoenix was first brewed in 1963. It is a polished, golden yellow beer that is popular in South Africa. Phoenix beer is pasteurized after bottling, using natural conservation methods. The quality of the underground water also allows the brewers to produce a beer with no chemicals or additives. The beer is matured before distribution in meticulously controlled conditions.

ROBSON'S EAST COAST ALE

Country of Origin: *South Africa* • **Brewery Founded:** *NA* • **Alcohol Content:** *4.0%*

East Coast Ale is made using a single malt variety and two kinds of hops, Brewers Gold and Challenger. Brewers Gold has a high resin content. This provides an excellent balanced bitterness, especially when combined with a late aroma hop in golden beers. Challenger hops give the brew a crisp, fruity character. This results in a beer with around 25 bitterness units. The beer is fermented using a special ale yeast that imparts its own distinctive character. The beer pours a lively yellow gold color, with a fluffy white head. The aroma is crisp and appetizing with citrus lemon and light floral tones. The palate matches the aroma and is crisp with a good citrus and bitter hop bite. The malt contributes smoothness to the beer, which is balanced with plenty of tangy fruitiness.

ROBSON'S DURBAN PALE ALE

Country of Origin: *South Africa* • **Brewery Founded:** *Unknown* • **Alcohol Content:** *5.7%*

Durban Pale Ale was inspired by the original British IPAs. These were shipped to India for consumption by British soldiers and bureaucrats who were billeted there. The IPA travelled via the South African Cape, and records show that some of the IPA made its way to British soldiers serving in South Africa. Durban was a major shipping port, and IPA may well have been imported through the port. Robsons wanted to revive the old tradition of South African IPAs. The brewery uses the finest Pale Ale malts and packs the mash tun full of grains to achieve a higher level of alcohol in the brew. The beer is also crammed full of hops to achieve the 40 units of bitterness that are required to make this style of beer. Cascade hops are used because they don't leave any lingering bitterness or harshness on the palate. The inclusion of Challenger hops provides the crisp, fruitiness characteristic of IPAs. This is complimented by the special strain of English ale yeast that is used to ferment the beer. Durban Pale Ale matures over time if it is cellared. This produces an even more complex ale.

ROBSON'S WHEAT BEER

Country of Origin: *South Africa* • **Brewery Founded:** *Unknown* • **Alcohol Content:** *5.0%*

Robson's Wheat Beer is inspired by both the German Weissbier tradition and the Witbier beer of Belgium and Holland. These beers are made from un-malted wheat and malted barley. Wheat makes up nearly half of the mash. As this is un-malted, the brew house smell of the mash is very pleasant, having an aroma of fresh pasta. When the Hallertau and Saaz hops are added to the brew the aroma intensifies. The Hallertau hop is delicate and imparts a floral, slightly fruity character. This wheat beer is modelled on some of the oldest brewing recipes known in Europe. At his time, spices and herbs (rather than hops) were used to flavor and preserve the beer. In keeping with tradition, Robson's add coriander to the beer in the brewery copper. This results in a less bitter beer. Robson's also use a special yeast strain imported from Germany to ferment the brew, and this imparts its own special flavor to the beer. In the glass, Robson's Wheat Beer is an attractive caramel color with a light and fluffy off-white head.

ROBSON'S WEST COAST ALE

Country of Origin: *South Africa* • **Brewery Founded:** *Unknown* • **Alcohol Content:** *5.0%*

West Coast Ale was inspired by beers of the American West Coast. Robson's uses two types of malted barley in their West Coast Ale, with a fair proportion of Crystal Barley. Using Cascade and Northern Brewer hops Robson's make four separate hop additions to the boil to ensure that the right balance of aroma and bitterness is achieved. The beer is fermented at a colder temperature than Robson's other brews. It is then matured for at least eight weeks. This results in a balanced, smooth, and easy-drinking beer. The beer has a rich aroma of biscuity malt, complemented by the spicy character of the hops. The beer pours clear with an intense ruby-red brown color. It has a well developed head. The beer is medium bodied, and smooth on the palate. The flavor is initially dominated by characteristic Crystal Malt, followed by a well balanced hop character. The beer has a fruity and spicy hoppiness.

SNEEUBERG BREWERY KAROO ALE

Country of Origin: *South Africa* • **Brewery Founded:** *2003* • **Alcohol Content:** *5.0%*

Sneeuberg Brewery's Karoo ale is a dark golden amber color with a white head. The beer has a wonderfully strong roasted malt aroma. It has a particularly fresh and tasty aroma that is strongly reminiscent of homebrewed beer.

SNEEUBERG BREWERY HONEY ALE

Country of Origin: *South Africa* • **Brewery Founded:** *2003* • **Alcohol Content:** *5.0%*

Sneeuberg's Honey Ale is dry in flavor. It is unfiltered with a good mouthfeel. The beer is smooth but highly carbonated, with a good yeast flavor, due to the presence of live yeast. The beer presents an intriguing hop aroma. The flavor begins with some hoppiness, followed by a smooth malt flavor. The finish is bitter and dry with a touch of apple.

SNEEUBERG BREWERY ROASTED ALE

Country of Origin: *South Africa* • **Brewery Founded:** *2003* • **Alcohol Content:** *5.0%*

Roasted Ale is a translucent medium to dark brown with a light tan head. The aroma and flavor of the beer is of light molasses, chocolate, and nuts. The beer is smooth but dry with a nice nutty aftertaste. It is well hopped and heavily malted. Black or chocolate malts are added to give the beer its dark color. The beer is mildly bitter with a malty sweetness. The beer is drier than most stouts and is somewhere between a stout and an ale in style.

TRIGGERFISH EMPOWERED STOUT

Country of Origin: *South Africa* • **Brewery Founded:** *2010* • **Alcohol Content:** *5.9%*

Empowered Stout is a complex full bodied English sweet stout. The beer gets its malty complexity and color from a combination of five different malts and two hop varieties. The beer has coffee, dark chocolate, dried fruit, raisins, and licorice in the aroma. A detectable sweetness is balanced by the bitterness derived from the hops and roasted malts. This beer is best enjoyed at around fifty degrees Fahrenheit and pairs well with meat dishes or dark chocolate.

TRIGGERFISH HAMMERHEAD IPA

Country of Origin: *South Africa* • **Brewery Founded:** *2010* • **Alcohol Content:** *6.2%*

Hammerhead is a well-balanced IPA with a distinct hop character that imparts mild citrus and pine aromas. The significant bitterness is balanced with a solid malt backbone. Caramel, raisin, and dried fruit are characteristic of the malts used in Hammerhead. The working name for the beer was Hammer(ed) (Hop)Head. This gives an idea of the true character of the beer.

TRIGGERFISH ROMAN RED

Country of Origin: *South Africa* • **Brewery Founded:** *2010* • **Alcohol Content:** *5.2%*

Roman Red is a full bodied red or amber ale. The beer has a fuller body and more hops than most brews. The beer strikes a good balance between sweetness and caramel flavors from the Crystal Malts. The beer has plenty of hop bitterness with typical pine and citrus aromas associated with Pacific North Western hop varieties.

TRIGGERFISH SWEETLIPS

Country of Origin: *South Africa* • **Brewery Founded:** *2010* • **Alcohol Content:** *4.5%*

Sweetlips is a light blonde ale and is brewed with two malt varieties. The flavor is light, dry, and refreshing with some sweet biscuit malt and a subtle fruit tang. The beer is very lightly hopped and has very little bitterness. This makes the beer a refreshing choice on an African summer day. It has a light golden hue with a white frothy head and good lacing.

SPAIN

CRUZCAMPO

Country of Origin: *Spain* • **Brewery Founded:** *1904* • **Alcohol Content:** *4.8%*

Cruzcampo is Spain's biggest beer producer in Spain. The brewery was founded in 1904 by Roberto Osborne and Agustín Osborne in Seville, Spain. It is now owned by the Heineken Corporation. Cruzcampo can be found anywhere in Spain, but it is in its home region of Andalusia where it is most popular. Cruzcampo has breweries in Seville, Madrid, Valencia, Jaén, and Arano. Its logo features Gambrinus, the legendary creator of beer. The brand also sponsors the Spanish national football team. Cruzcampo is a straw colored beer with a large frothy head. Its aroma has hints of corn and metallic. The taste has notes of grain, pale malts, and peppery hops. The beer has a medium level of carbonation.

ESTRELLA DAMM

Country of Origin: *Spain* • **Brewery Founded:** *1876* • **Alcohol Content:** *5.2%*

Estrella Damm is a pilsner beer, brewed in Barcelona, Spain. It was founded by August Küntzmann Damm founded his brewery in Barcelona. Estrella Damm is the flagship beer of S.A. Damm and is the oldest beer brand in Spain. The beer's brand name means "star" in Spanish. This pilsner lager is an iconic Spanish beer. It is made with high quality raw ingredients and has been perfected over many years of brewing. The beer pours a clear golden yellow and has a medium head. The beer has a malty aroma, and is a refreshing brew.

SAN MIGUEL

Country of Origin: *Spain* • **Brewery Founded:** *1890* • **Alcohol Content:** *5%*

Grupo Mahou-San Miguel is a Spanish brewing company. It was founded in Spain's capital, Madrid by the Mahou family. The brewery's first product was Mahou beer. This was first produced in 1891 at the brewery on Amaniel Street, Madrid. Its San Miguel brew is now the leading brand in the Spanish beer market. It is an authentic Spanish lager in the pilsner style. It is golden in color with a creamy white head. The taste is full bodied with a refreshing balance of hop bitterness and malty sweetness.

XIBECA

Country of Origin: *Spain* • **Brewery Founded:** *1876* • **Alcohol Content:** *4.6%*

Xibeca or Xibeca-Damm is brewed by Spain's S.A. Damm brewing group. Its name means "owl" in Spanish. The Damm brewery produce Xibeca for the Spanish Catalan region and most of the beer is distributed there. The beer is a low-alcohol, pale lager-style, table-beer that is offered for sale in large (liter) bottles. The beer was designed to be drunk with meals, as an inexpensive alternative to red table wine. Xibeca pours pale golden with a small white head. It has a slightly fruity aroma with notes of ripe pears, vegetables, and grain. The beer is medium sweet with little bitterness. It has a light body with an average level of carbonation.

SWEDEN

FALCON PILSENER

Country of Origin: *Sweden* • **Brewery Founded:** *1896* • **Alcohol Content:** *4.8%*

Falcon Bryggeri was founded in Falkenberg, Sweden by John L. Skantze. The brewery introduced the Falcon brand name in 1955. In 1996 the company was sold to Carlsberg. Carlsberg Sverige (Sweden)has its headquarters in Stockholm and the Falkenberg brewery continues to produce beer and soft drinks. Carlsberg also owns the Swedish beer brands Pripps Ringnes and Pripps Blå. Carlsberg also brews the local variants of the international beer brands Beck's, Stella, Bass, Brooklyn, and Boddingtons. Flacon Pilsener is now the second most popular beer in Sweden. The beer pours a golden color with a white head. The aroma is sweet, with pale malt and honey notes. The taste is similar with a medium bitterness and metallic notes.

NILS OSCAR GOD LAGER

Country of Origin: *Sweden* • **Brewery Founded:** *1996* • **Alcohol Content:** *5.3%*

The Nils Oscar Brewery is an independent Swedish microbrewery and spirits company based in Nyköping, Sweden. The brewery was founded in Stockholm 1996. The beers of Nils Oscar Brewery have received good reviews and have been awarded several gold medals at the Stockholm Beer Festival. The raw materials for the beer (including oat, wheat, barley, and rye) are cultivated at the Tärnö Manor farm. The brewery's malting plant is also located on the farm. The beer is light amber with a thin, foamy white head. The beer is clear and has a few bubbles. The taste is quite sweet and includes touches of honey and fruit with some citrus, grain, and light hops.

PRIPPS BRYGGERIER BLÅ

Country of Origin: *Sweden* • **Brewery Founded:** *1828* • **Alcohol Content:** *3.5%*

Pripps was founded in Gothenburg, Sweden by Johan Albrecht Pripp. Pripps became a major brewery and is now a part of the Carlsberg group. The brewery's main beer is Pripps Blå. Pripps also owned the Ramlösa mineral water brand. Pripps lager was first introduced in 1959 and is said to be one of the most popular beers in Sweden. The beer is brewed with exactly 51% barley, the minimum amount required by Swedish law. A low-calorie version of the beer, Pripps Blå Light, is also available. Blå is a pale lager. It pours a golden color with some foam. It has a light grassy aroma and the taste has notes of light malt and hops.

SPENDRUPS BRYGGERI JULBRYGD

Country of Origin: *Sweden* • **Brewery Founded:** *1923* • **Alcohol Content:** *5.3%*

Spendrups Bryggeri is headquartered in Vårby, Sweden. The company was originally founded as the Grängesbergs Bryggeri, and became Spendrups Bryggeri in 1983. Julbrygd is a brown ale with a short-lived whitish head. The aroma is caramel and floral with raisins and walnuts. It is made with American hops. The beer has a light to medium body, and has quite a dry taste with a faint note of sweetness. The beer has some roasted notes in the finish, with some medium bitterness.

UNITED KINGDOM

ADNAMS BROADSIDE ALE

Country of Origin: *U.K.* • **Brewery Founded:** *1872* • **Alcohol Content:** *4.7%*

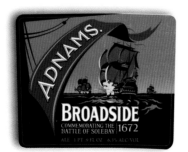

Brewed with Pale Ale malt and First Gold hops, Broadside is a dark ruby red beer rich in fruitcake aromas, almonds, and conserved fruit. In keeping with Adnams' regard for local tradition and history, the name Broadside recalls 1672's fierce naval Battle of Sole Bay, fought off the English coast at Southwold, Suffolk, against the ships of the Dutch Republic. Broadside is a strong cask ale of the Bitter variety. The brew is also available in bottles at 6.3% strength.

ADNAMS LIGHTHOUSE

Country of Origin: *U.K.* • **Brewery Founded:** *1872* • **Alcohol Content:** *3.4%*

Lighthouse is a light Pale Ale. It is a golden beer with a subtle fragrance, lovely malty flavors, and a long hoppy finish. Brewed with Pale Ale and Crystal malt, the brew has overtones of caramel and toffee provided by the use of a blend of Fuggles and Goldings hops. Lighthouse takes its name from one of the most iconic landmarks in its hometown of Southwold, England.

ADNAMS SOLE BAY CELEBRATORY ALE

Country of Origin: *U.K.* • **Brewery Founded:** *1872* • **Alcohol Content:** *10.0%*

Sole Bay Celebratory Ale is a champagne of beers. Hazy gold in color with a good carbonation, it has aromas and flavors of honey, bread, bananas, pear drops, and bubblegum. The beer is brewed with East Anglian Pilsner malted barley, Demerara, and Muscavado sugar using Nelson Sauvin hops. The brewers add a few springs of locally grown lavender at the end of fermentation to add a subtle floral. The beer is bottled in a champagne style flask. Sole Bay Celebratory Ale was first brewed in November 2009 to celebrate the Sole Bay Brewery's 350th anniversary.

ADNAMS SOUTHWOLD BITTER

Country of Origin: *U.K.* • **Brewery Founded:** *1872* • **Alcohol Content:** *3.7%*

Southwold Bitter is a beautiful copper-colored beer. It is dry-hopped with Fuggles hops for a distinctive flavor. The beer is brewed with the finest East Anglian Pale Ale malt barley, which is sourced locally. The Fuggles hops are added late in the boil to preserve the herbal flavors of this traditional English hop. The beer is sold in casks, bottles, and cans. First brewed in 1967, the beer was originally known as Adnams Best Bitter. The beer is marketed with Adnams' oldest trademark, Southwold Jack (the knight with the sword).

ARKELL'S 1843

Country of Origin: *U.K.* • **Brewery Founded:** *1843* • **Alcohol Content:** *4.2%*

Arkell's house lager was launched to celebrate the year that John Arkell started brewing beer at his brewery in Swindon, Wiltshire. 2013 was the 170th anniversary of the founding of the brewery. This is a classic craft lager brewed using Pale Malt with some wheat added for extra body and texture. The beer is also brewed with traditional lager hops and is gradually fermented at a low temperature. It is then matured for three weeks in the tank at an even lower temperature to produce a pleasant, light, refreshing beer.

ARKELL'S BALL & CHAIN

Country of Origin: *U.K.* • **Brewery Founded:** *1843* • **Alcohol Content:** *5%*

Arkell's Ball & Chain was originally brewed to celebrate head brewer Alex Arkell's wedding on January 26, 2013. Alex produced this brew to celebrate the occasion by making this innovative new beer. The brew uses four different types of malt and three hop varieties added throughout the process. The beer is a well-balanced deep amber beer with floral notes.

ARKELL'S NOEL ALE

Country of Origin: *U.K.* • **Brewery Founded:** *1843* • **Alcohol Content:** *5%*

Arkell's Noel Ale was launched in 1987. It was named in honor of the grandfather of Arkell's present Chairman, Sir Noel Arkell, who was born on Christmas Day. The brew is the strongest of Arkell's Ales. This full-bodied beer is cleverly disguised by its distinctive light color. This is a seasonal beer available in December each year.

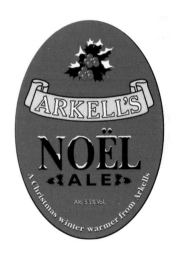

ARKELL'S 2B

Country of Origin: *U.K.* • **Brewery Founded:** *1843* • **Alcohol Content:** *3.2%*

Arkell's 2B is a light quaffable session bitter. The beer has been constantly brewed since the early 1900s. The beer was been Arkell's most popular brew until the 1970s when it was overtaken by Arkell's 3B. The beer is a soft amber color with a mild hoppy aroma and a crisp refreshing flavor.

ARKELL'S 3B

Country of Origin: *U.K.* • **Brewery Founded:** *1843* • **Alcohol Content:** *4.0%*

Arkell's 3B was originally known as Arkell's Best Bitter Beer. It was first brewed in 1910 and has been affectionately known as BBB or 3B ever since. It is a copper-colored ale with a pleasant fruity and malty nose. It has a lingering bittersweet flavor of balanced Maris Otter malt and traditional Fuggles and Golding hops.

ARKELL'S PETER'S PORTER

Country of Origin: *U.K.* • **Brewery Founded:** *1843* • **Alcohol Content:** *4.8%*

Peter's Porter is a smooth, dark and delicious brew which reflects the taste of yesteryear. The Arkell's Kingsdown Brewery celebrated 170 years of brewing in 2013 by staging an Open Day and Beer Festival for visitors to tour the brewery. It is one of the very few remaining Victorian breweries in the world that is still producing beer.

B&T BLACK DRAGON

Country of Origin: *U.K.* • **Brewery Founded:** *1982* • **Alcohol Content:** *4.3%*

Black Dragon is a dark cask beer brewed using Golding hops, Pearl Pale Malt, Crystal Malt, Black Malt, roast barley, and wheat malt. Independent brewer Banks & Taylor began brewing in the town of Shefford, Bedfordshire in 1982. The brewery aimed to produce traditional cask ales using the finest raw materials. The brewery adopted the B&T name in 1994.

B&T DRAGON SLAYER

Country of Origin: *U.K.* • **Brewery Founded:** *1982* • **Alcohol Content:** *4.5%*

Dragon Slayer was originally brewed for St. George's Day. The beer is a straw-colored bitter. It is dry, malty, and lightly hopped. The beer is brewed with Pearl Pale Malt, wheat malt, Challenger Hops, and Golding Hops for a finely tuned flavor.

B&T GOLDEN FOX

Country of Origin: *U.K.* • **Brewery Founded:** *1982* • **Alcohol Content:** *4.1%*

Golden Fox is a golden refreshing beer with fruity overtones. It is brewed using Pearl Pale Malt, Amber Malt, Golding Hops, and Cascade Hops. The overall taste is of floral and citrus balanced with biscuit malt and some bitterness in the finish.

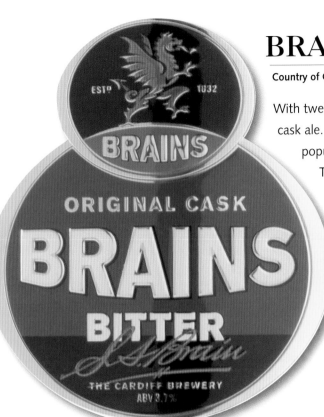

BRAINS BITTER

Country of Origin: *U.K.* • **Brewery Founded:** *1882* • **Alcohol Content:** *3.7%*

With twelve pints sold every minute, Brains bitter is the brewery's biggest selling cask ale. It is brewed in Wales. The beer's easy drinking style has proved very popular with the cask ale customer. The beer has won numerous awards. The beer was the only Welsh winning beer in the *Daily Telegraph* newpaper's Best of British Beer Awards 2007.This famous pint is a rich amber colored, well balanced, and refreshing beer. Goldings and Fuggles hops from The Welsh Marches create an appetizing and crisp aroma. This compliments the subtle flavor of fine Pale Malt. Crystal clear water combines with the unique Brains yeast to create the complete Welsh beer experience.

BRAINS SA GOLD

Country of Origin: *U.K.* • **Brewery Founded:** *1882* • **Alcohol Content:** *4.3%*

The latest shining addition to Brains cask ale range, SA Gold was launched in 2006. Its refreshing and clean taste has proved very popular with both consumers and industry experts. The beer has won several awards in the years since it was launched. SA Gold is a full-flavored, hoppy, and refreshing golden ale. Careful use of hops creates a satisfying bitterness, perfectly balanced by vibrant citrus aromas and complex hop flavors. These are derived from late hopping, using Cascade and Styrian Golding hops.

BRAINS BARRY ISLAND IPA

Country of Origin: *U.K.* • **Brewery Founded:** *1882* • **Alcohol Content:** *3.4%*

Brains Barry Island IPA is a light, copper-colored ale with a fresh, hoppy taste, and a clean bitter finish. It is brewed with two varieties of hops, combined with Pale and Crystal malts. Brains IPA is a well-balanced and easy-drinking pint of beer. It is an ideal session beer.

BRAINS THE REVEREND JAMES

Country of Origin: *U.K.* • **Brewery Founded:** *1882* • **Alcohol Content:** *3.4%*

The Reverend James beer is steeped in history. Acquired when the brewery bought the Crown Buckley brewery, The Reverend James beer is brewed to an original recipe dating back to 1885. The beer is named after one of the original owners of the Buckley Brewery, the Reverend James Buckley. Buckley was a business man with two conflicting roles, saving souls and satisfying thirsts. It is brewed to a traditional recipe and has been described as having a full-bodied and warming flavor. The Reverend James is rich, spicy, and aromatic and has a deeply satisfying finish.

BRAKSPEAR BITTER

Country of Origin: *U.K.* • **Brewery Founded:** *2002* • **Alcohol Content:** *3.4%*

Brakspear Beers are brewed at the newly established Wychwood Brewery in Witney, Oxfordshire. The brewery uses the original equipment that dates from 1779, which they moved from their original site at Henly-on-Thames, England. Brakspear are part of the Marstons Brewery Group. Crystal, Black, and Maris Otter pale malts provide the backbone of this outstanding bitter style beer. Hops are added three times to the brew to maintain a strong hoppy flavor. The brewing recipe uses Fuggles and Goldings hops combined with the original Brakspear yeast.

BRAKSPEAR OXFORD GOLD

Country of Origin: *U.K.* • **Brewery Founded:** *2002* •
Alcohol Content: *4.6% (bottle), 4% (draught)*

Brakspear Oxford Gold is a remarkably zesty brew, with a fresh, citrus aroma and a firm, fruity flavor. Pale Ale malt gives the beer its gold-gilt hue, spruced with a hatful of Crystal malts. This gives the beer body, texture, and a delicate honey taste. The blend of Fuggles, Golding, and Styrian hops delivers an aromatic brew.

BRAKSPEAR TRIPLE

Country of Origin: *U.K.* • **Brewery Founded:** *2002* • **Alcohol Content:** *6.7%*

Thanks to the two fermentations in the Brakspear Double Drop system, this highly aromatic and satisfying strong beer delivers its rich flavor with subtlety and balance. Crystal, Black, and Maris Otter pale malts are used. Target hops are added three times to provide a good balance between bitterness and fragrance. This is a triple hopped strong beer, packaged in individually numbered bottles.

CAIRNGORM GOLD

Country of Origin: *U.K.* • **Brewery Founded:** *2001* • **Alcohol Content:** *4.5%*

The Cairngorm Brewery Company is a craft brewery that was established in 2001. The brewery is situated in the village of Aviemore within the Cairngorms National Park in the Highlands of Scotland. Gold is one of the company's flagship brews. It is golden colored, light bodied, continental-style beer. Saaz hops provide an initial fresh and zesty flavor with Styrian Goldings providing late aromas. No added preservatives are used in the brew.

CAIRNGORM SHEEPSHAGGER

Country of Origin: *U.K.* • **Brewery Founded:** *2001* • **Alcohol Content:** *4.5%*

Cairngorm Sheepshagger is an exceptional continental-style beer with a good body and a refreshing aftertaste. The Cairngorms are a picturesque mountain range in the eastern Highlands of Scotland.

CAIRNGORM STAG

Country of Origin: *U.K.* • **Brewery Founded:** *2001* • **Alcohol Content:** *4.1%*

Cairngorm Stag is a mahogany-colored ale with medium to light body. Challenger and Fuggles hops are added plentifully giving initial bitterness that is then balanced by a caramel finish from the roast malts.

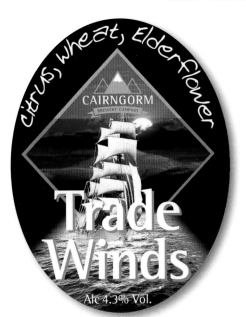

CAIRNGORM TRADE WINDS

Country of Origin: *U.K.* • **Brewery Founded:** *2001* • **Alcohol Content:** *4.3%*

Trade Winds is light golden in color, with a high proportion of wheat. This gives the beer a clean fresh taste. The mash blends together with the Perle hops and elderflower. This gives the beer a bouquet of fruit and citrus flavors.

CALEDONIAN 80 SHILLING ALE

Country of Origin: *U.K.* • **Brewery Founded:** *1869* • **Alcohol Content:** *4.1%*

This brew is made with three different varieties of hop and a multitude of malts. Caledonian 80 Shilling ale has hidden depths. The beer is satisfying and timeless. This is a definitive classic 80 Shilling ale. It is full-bodied with complex malt and hop flavors, dry and spicy. The beer is characterised by a superb creamy head and hoppy finish.

CALEDONIAN DEUCHARS IPA

Country of Origin: *U.K.* • **Brewery Founded:** *1869* • **Alcohol Content:** *3.9%*

Caledonian Deuchars is a deliciously refreshing brew. It is a fabulous balance of malt and hops. Discerning beer drinkers consider the brew to be the benchmark of quality cask beer and for those new to cask beer.

CALEDONIAN FLYING SCOTSMAN

Country of Origin: *U.K.* • **Brewery Founded:** *1869* • **Alcohol Content:** *4.0%*

Flying Scotsman is a sophisticated full-flavored premium bitter. The brew combines the best barley from the north with robust southern hops. The beer is profoundly malty in aroma but balanced with hints of raisins, spice, and toasty dryness.

CALEDONIAN GOLDEN XPA

Country of Origin: *U.K.* • **Brewery Founded:** *1869* • **Alcohol Content:** *4.3%*

Golden XPA is brewed with three distinctive hops. Cascade hops deliver enticing floral aromas, floral Hallertau Hersbrucker hops add softy fruitiness, and Northdown hops develop aromas and a light bitterness. These are balanced with a malty flavor and a satisfying bitterness. This beer has become more fashionable with the growth in popularity of golden ales.

CASTLE ROCK BLACK GOLD

Country of Origin: *U.K.* • **Brewery Founded:** *1997* • **Alcohol Content:** *3.8%*

Castle Rock Black Gold is a well-balanced dark mild ale with some bitterness. The beer is full bodied, but not too sweet. It is an award winning mild that delivers a light fresh taste to a traditional beer style. The Castle Rock brewery was originally founded in 1977 by former Campaign for Real Ale (CAMRA) chairman Chris Holmes. It was originally called the Tynemill brewery.

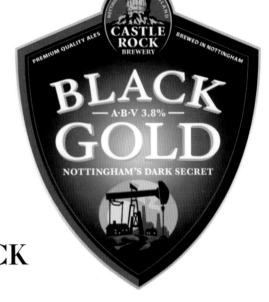

CASTLE ROCK ELSIE MO

Country of Origin: *U.K.* • **Brewery Founded:** *1997* • **Alcohol Content:** *4.7%*

Elsie Mo's name was derived from the Maris Otter malt from which it is brewed. This malt gives the beer a distinctive golden hue. A blend of hops, Challenger predominating, provides the special aroma and leaves a pleasantly crisp aftertaste. The Castle Rock brewery was established as a partnership between the Bramcote Brewery & Tynemill in 1997. Bramcote have now stopped brewing. The site opened next door to the Vat & Fiddle public house in Nottingham, England. This is now the Castle Rock Brewery Tap.

CASTLE ROCK HARVEST PALE

Country of Origin: *U.K.* • **Brewery Founded:** *1997* • **Alcohol Content:** *3.8%*

Castle Rock Harvest Pale has been described by the esteemed beer writer Roger Protz as "The finest blond beer I've drunk in many a year." Harvest Pale is brewed with gently-kilned malt, and an aromatic blend of American hops. These are added during the brewing process and give this pale beer exceptional poise. Its distinct hop flavor leads to a crisp finish. Harvest Pale has firmly established itself as Castle Rock's flagship beer. The beer was voted SIBA National Champion Bitter in 2004, the Champion Bitter of Britain 2007, and the Champion Beer of Britain in 2010.

CASTLE ROCK SHERIFF'S TIPPLE

Country of Origin: *U.K.* • **Brewery Founded:** *1997* • **Alcohol Content:** *3.4%*

Sheriff's Tipple is a great session bitter with a distinctive hop character. This is derived from the Golding hop. The name of the beer draws on the rich history of England's Nottingham Castle and its evil Sherriff, who appears in the famous legend of Robin Hood. The beer is tawny brown and slightly darker than the Nottingham Gold beer it replaced.

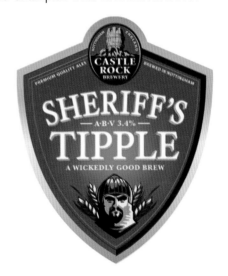

COURAGE BEST BITTER

Country of Origin: *U.K.* • **Brewery Founded:** *1787*
Alcohol Content: *4.0% (cask), 3.8% (bottle/can)*

With over two hundred years of brewing pedigree, Courage Best Bitter retains its widespread popularity in the United Kingdom. The beer is pale brown in appearance with a bitter aftertaste. Courage Best Bitter consumers enjoy its low alcohol level, which makes it an ideal session bitter. Courage is now part of the Wells & Young Brewery Group.

COURAGE DIRECTORS

Country of Origin: *U.K.* • **Brewery Founded:** *1787* • **Alcohol Content:** *4.8%*

This premium cask ale has a strong following throughout the United Kingdom. Courage Directors was originally brewed exclusively for the directors of Courage's Alton, Hampshire brewery. Following public demand, the beer was made available to the public. It is a genuine premium beer, pale brown in appearance with a deep rich taste.

EVERARDS MALTY TASKER

Country of Origin: *U.K.* • **Brewery Founded:** *1849* • **Alcohol Content:** *5.0%*

Malty Tasker was first brewed in 2012. It is a golden ale with fruity characters of citrus zest and a complex body. This is supported by a robust alcohol level. Rye malt, oats, and wheat are combined with a blend of Challenger and Saaz hops. This gives the beer a truly European flavor.

EVERARDS ORIGINAL

Country of Origin: *U.K.* • **Brewery Founded:** *1849* • **Alcohol Content:** *5.2%*

Everard's brew uses Maris Otter malt and a skilful combination of Fuggles, Challenger, and Goldings hops to produce a tasty tawny, copper-colored premium ale. Everards is an independent British regional brewery founded in Leicester in 1849. Its founders were William Everard and Thomas Hull. The brewery produces cask ales and owns over one- hundred-and-sixty tenanted pubs. These are mainly based in the county of Leicestershire. The brewery has won The Publican Pub Company of the Year Award three times. The company is one of very few businesses which have been run by the same family for over one-hundred-and-fifty years. Richard Everard is the chairman of the brewery, and is the fifth generation of his family to work in the business.

EVERARDS TIGER BEST BITTER

Country of Origin: *U.K.* • **Brewery Founded:** *1849*
Alcohol Content: *4.2%*

Tiger Best Bitter is an award winning best bitter with universal appeal. Tiger Best Bitter is a classic example of the perfect balance between sweetness and bitterness. Maris Otter malt gives the beer a rounded toffee character. It is hopped with Fuggles and Goldings.

EVERARDS SUNCHASER

Country of Origin: *U.K.* • **Brewery Founded:** *1849* • **Alcohol Content:** *4.0%*

Sunchaser Blonde is a thirst-quenching beer made in the style of a European lager. It is brewed using Hallertau,Saaz, and Tettnang hops combined with a special lager malt. The beer has subtle fruit flavors and a little sweetness. The beer is best served at two degrees below cellar temperature.

FULLER'S ESB

Country of Origin: *U.K.* • **Brewery Founded:** *1845*
Alcohol Content: *5.5% (cask), 5.9% (bottle)*

ESB has a rich mahogany appearance. In the nose, the beer is bursting with cherry and orange, balanced by soft malty toffee and caramel notes. The flavor is typical of a full-bodied ale. The unique blend of Northdown, Target, Challenger, and Goldings hops imparts grassy and peppery notes. The beer also has an intense citrus fruit character of grapefruit, orange, and lemon. The blend of Pale Ale and Crystal malts in the brew give biscuit and toffee hints to the beer.

FULLER'S HSB

Country of Origin: *U.K.* • **Brewery Founded:** *1845* • **Alcohol Content:** *4.8%*

First brewed in 1959, HSB (Horndean Special Bitter) is an award-winning, distinctive, high quality, premium bitter. HSB was the flagship brew of Horndean's Gales Brewery, which was acquired by Fullers in 2005. The brew is full bodied and silky, with a hint of Dundee fruitcake that leads to a rich, fruity taste and a silky smooth finish. Today, HSB is brewed with pride and passion at Fullers Chiswick, London brewery, where the original Gale's yeast is still alive and well. HSB has now spread from its home county of Hampshire, England.

FULLER'S LONDON PRIDE

Country of Origin: *U.K.* • **Brewery Founded:** *1845* • **Alcohol Content:** *4.1% (cask, 4.7 (bottle/can)*

Fullers London Pride is an award-winning classic beer and is the brewery's flagship bitter. It is a rich, smooth and balanced brew. It has a distinctive malty base that is complimented by a well-developed hop character. This is created by adding Target, Challenger, and Northdown hop varieties.

FULLER'S SEAFARERS ALE

Country of Origin: *U.K.* • **Brewery Founded:** *1845* • **Alcohol Content:** *3.6%*

Seafarers is another ex-Gales brew, and is a delicious, thirst quenching ale. This is an ideal session beer due to its relatively low alcohol content. The secret of the refreshing taste of this light, amber-colored beer is in the blend of finest quality English malt. This gives the beer a malty tang. The beer is brewed with Admiral hops and the unique Gales yeast. It is now made at the Fullers Chiswick, London brewery.

GOACHER'S BEST DARK ALE

Country of Origin: *U.K.* • **Brewery Founded:** *1983* • **Alcohol Content:** *4.1%*

Best Dark Ale is a rich and complex full-bodied ale. The beer is brewed with high proportions of Crystal malt and East Kent Golding hops. Goacher's is a traditional brewery that uses only malt and Kentish hops to brew its beers. Maidstone, Kent has a long tradition of commercial brewing that dates to the early part of the seventeenth century. At the beginning of the twentieth century, there were four independent brewers in the town. By 1972 the last of these had ceased production. After an interval of eleven years, Phil and Debbie Goacher opened their brewery in Kent's Loose Valley, which is just outside the town of Maidstone.

GOACHER'S GOLD STAR ALE

Country of Origin: *U.K.* • **Brewery Founded:** *1983* • **Alcohol Content:** *5.1%*

Goacher's Gold Star Ale is a true draught pale ale made with floor-malted, low-color Maris Otter malted barley. The beer is hopped with the finest East Kent Aroma hops. It is a tasty and characterful ale.

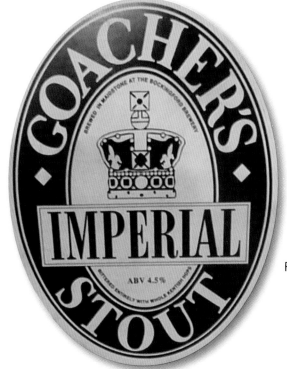

GOACHER'S CROWN IMPERIAL STOUT

Country of Origin: *U.K.* • **Brewery Founded:** *1983* • **Alcohol Content:** *4.5%*

Crown Imperial Stout is a convincing attempt to replicate the flavor and character of the true bottled Irish stout. The beer is brewed with roasted barley and extremely high levels of Kent Fuggles hops.

GOACHER'S OLD 1066 ALE

Country of Origin: *U.K.* • **Brewery Founded:** *1983* • **Alcohol Content:** *6.7%*

Old 1066 was named after the original gravity of the brew. It is a rich and fruity barley wine. 1066 has been produced in small quantities by Goacher's every winter since the brewery started brewing its own beers.

GOACHER'S REAL MILD ALE

Country of Origin: *U.K.* • **Brewery Founded:** *1983* • **Alcohol Content:** *3.4%*

Real Mild Ale is a full-flavored dark mild beer that is brewed with chocolate and black malts. It is hopped with Kent Fuggles. The beer was first brewed in 1988. Its relatively low alcohol content makes it an ideal session beer.

GRAINSTORE BREWERY COOKING BITTER

Country of Origin: *U.K.* • **Brewery Founded:** *2010*
Alcohol Content: *3.6%*

Cooking is a colloquial term for session beer. This beer is a smooth full-flavored golden bitter. The beer has a good bitter-sweet balance and drinkability. The Grainstore Brewery was founded in 2010 by Tony Davis. Davis was the former head brewer for the county of Rutland's celebrated Ruddles Brewery. His aim was to re-establish brewing in the county using the famous Rutland water. The water was fundamental to the flavor of the original Ruddles brew.

GRAINSTORE BREWERY GB BEST

Country of Origin: *U.K.* • **Brewery Founded:** *2010* • **Alcohol Content:** *4.3%*

GB Best is brewed with Golding hops, which makes the beer a strong bitter-style brew. It is lighter in taste than other Grainstore beers and has a pronounced floral flavor and aroma. The beer's graphic features a British bulldog glass, complete with a pint glass bearing an inverted version of the Ruddles horseshoe logo.

GRAINSTORE BREWERY PHIPPS IPA

Country of Origin: *U.K.* • **Brewery Founded:** *2010* • **Alcohol Content:** *4.2%*

Phipps IPA is brewed to an authentic 1930s recipe. It is a golden beer relying solely on Pale Ale malt in its grist for its color. The classic blend of Goldings and Fuggles hops gives characteristic English ale flavors to this full-bodied India Pale Ale.

GRAINSTORE RUTLAND BITTER

Country of Origin: *U.K.* • **Brewery Founded:** *2010* • **Alcohol Content:** *3.4%*

Rutland Bitter is the ale that made Rutland famous for its brews during the last century. This venerable tradition is now being carried forward by the Grainstore Brewery. Rutland Bitter has a predominately bitter taste with overtones of sweetness and a fruity, hoppy aroma. The malted barley and traditional hop varieties used to brew the beer are all sourced from the best farming areas in England and these materials are prepared to a very strict specification. It is an ideal session ale because of its relatively low alcohol content.

HALL & WOODHOUSE BADGER BREWERY BLANDFORD FLYER

Country of Origin: *U.K.* • **Brewery Founded:** *1777* • **Alcohol Content:** *5.2%*

This is an English pale ale which is light golden in color. It has a sweet scent and a fresh taste of ginger. The beer has good carbonation and a medium body. The flavor is fruity but retains the essential bitterness of a bitter style brew and with a spicy bite. Hall & Woodhouse have been independently owned and family run since 1777. The brewery is based in Blandford St. Mary in the county of Dorset. The brewery supplied the troops who were based in Weymouth Harbour during the Napoleonic wars.

HALL & WOODHOUSE BADGER BREWERY GOLDEN CHAMPION

Country of Origin: *U.K.* • **Brewery Founded:** *1777* • **Alcohol Content:** *5.0%*

Golden Champion is an award-winning beer in a typical English Pale Ale style. It is a premium strong brew and sports a light fruity flavor. It also has an underlying bitter taste. The beer is only sold in bottles.

HALL & WOODHOUSE BADGER BREWERY POACHER'S CHOICE

Country of Origin: *U.K.* • **Brewery Founded:** *1777* • **Alcohol Content:** *5.7%*

This beer is a rich, smooth brew with a softly spiced sweetness. It has dark liquorice notes and a fruity damson aroma. Poachers Choice is a dark ruby ale which makes the most of local ingredients. This is an art shared by both the Badger brewery and the wily poacher. The brew is only available in bottles.

HALL & WOODHOUSE BADGER BREWERY TANGLEFOOT

Country of Origin: *U.K.* • **Brewery Founded:** *1777* • **Alcohol Content:** *4.9% (cask), 5.0% (bottle/can)*

This is an award-winning premium bitter that is available in bottles, cans, and on tap. Tanglefoot got its name from an incident where the brewery owner's dog tangled him in his leash. It is a smooth-tasting surprisingly light beverage.

HARVEY'S COPPERWHEAT BEER

Country of Origin: *U.K.* • **Brewery Founded:** *1790* • **Alcohol Content:** *4.8%*

This brew was inspired by SIBA's (The Society of Independent Brewers) Wheat Beer challenge in 2001. Harveys make the beer with 40% Wheat Malt and 60% Malted Barley. To underline the continental heritage of the brew, it is brewed with Hallertau hops imported from Germany. This award winning brew has been described as "wheat and sweet." The beer is light in color and dry on the palate.

HARVEY'S IPA

Country of Origin: *U.K.* • **Brewery Founded:** *1790* • **Alcohol Content:** *3.5%*

Harvey's have been brewing in Lewes in the county of Sussex in England for over two hundred years. The brewery's impressive Victorian Gothic tower is landmark of the town. The building now houses a modern brewing plant that produces beer using traditional methods. Harvey's IPA has a delicate, grassy, and earthy hop aroma. The refreshing bitterness of this beer is balanced by the subtle malt flavors which make for an extremely drinkable pint. The beer is dry in flavor with a lasting aftertaste. The relatively low alcohol content makes it an ideal session beer.

HARVEY'S OLD ALE

Country of Origin: *U.K.* • **Brewery Founded:** *1790* • **Alcohol Content:** *4.3%*

Harvey's Old Ale is a Victorian-style dark winter brew produced from higher proportions of Crystal malt. This is a popular seasonal beer and is eagerly anticipated in October each year, when it returns from summer recess. Old Ale was Harvey's first beer to win a National Award in 1952 and has won many other accolades.

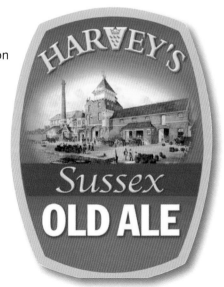

HARVEY'S OLYMPIA ALE

Country of Origin: *U.K.* • **Brewery Founded:** *1790* • **Alcohol Content:** *4.3%*

Olympia is a golden summer ale. The beer is very refreshing with a balanced complexity. It was first produced in 2005 to celebrate that summer's award at Kensington Olympia for Best Bitter. It became an instant hit and is especially appreciated when served at 55 degrees fahrenheit.

HARVEY'S SUSSEX BEST BITTER

Country of Origin: *U.K.* • **Brewery Founded:** *1790* • **Alcohol Content:** *4.0%*

Sussex Best Bitter is a superbly balanced bitter with a prominent hop character. The beer is Harvey's flagship brew and takes up over 90% of their total brewing capacity. The brew was the winner of the Champion Best Bitter of Britain title at CAMRA's Great British Beers Festival in 2005 and 2006. The beer is also sold as Blue Label when it is bottled.

HARVEY'S SUSSEX MILD

Country of Origin: *U.K.* • **Brewery Founded:** *1790* • **Alcohol Content:** *3.0%*

Sussex Mild is a dark malty mild. The beer is hearty and a sustaining ale when there is physical work to be done. Harvey's has won awards for mild-style beers for over half a century, and this type of beer enjoys a long heritage at the brewery. Sussex Mild is available throughout the year.

HOOK NORTON DOUBLE STOUT

Country of Origin: *U.K.* • **Brewery Founded:** *1849* • **Alcohol Content:** *4.8%*

A blend of malts gives Double Stout a character all of its own. Black malt enriches the color and teases the palate with an unmistakable 'toast' flavor. Brown malt gives it the dryness.

HOOK NORTON HOOKY

Country of Origin: *U.K.* • **Brewery Founded:** *1849* • **Alcohol Content:** *3.6%*

Hook Norton Hooky is a subtly balanced, golden bitter. The beer is hoppy to the nose, and malty on the palate. It is a classic session beer, and eminently drinkable.

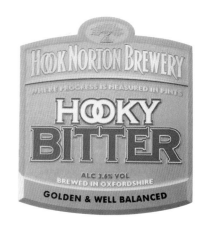

HOOK NORTON HOOKY MILD

Country of Origin: *U.K.* • **Brewery Founded:** *1849* • **Alcohol Content:** *2.8%*

Hooky Mild is a dark chestnut-colored ale, full of roast malt flavors. The beer is complemented with superb dry-hop aromas from East Kent Goldings.

HOOK NORTON LION

Country of Origin: *U.K.* • **Brewery Founded:** *1849* • **Alcohol Content:** *4.0%*

Roger Protz, a leading beer writer says that Hook Norton Lion is "A perfectly balanced bronze beer, full of fruit flavors and aromas. Complex yet refreshing, Lion has a long, bittersweet finish." The Hook Norton brewery is one of only thirty-two family-owned breweries in the United Kingdom and is one of the finest examples of a Victorian tower brewery.

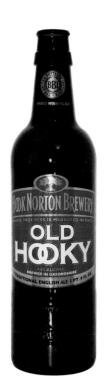

HOOK NORTON OLD HOOKY

Country of Origin: *U.K.* • **Brewery Founded:** *1849* • **Alcohol Content:** *4.6%*

Hook Norton Old Hooky is a beautifully balanced tawny red ale. It is brewed with Maris Otter Malt, which is fruity by nature. The beer has a well-rounded body and the suggestive echo of Crystal Malt. The beer was first brewed for Queen Elizabeth II's Silver Jubilee celebrations in 1977.

JENNINGS BITTER

Country of Origin: *U.K.* • **Brewery Founded:** *1828* •
Alcohol Content: *3.5%*

Jenning's Brewery was founded in the village of
Lorton, which is situated between Keswick and
Cockermouth in the English Lake District. It was
founded by John Jennings. Jenning's Bitter is the
original beer brewed by the Cockermouth brewery
and has been in production for over a hundred
years. It is a distinctively darker bitter, with a more-
ish taste. Its drinkable strength makes it the ideal
session beer. The beer is brewed with English Pale Ale and
Amber malts, to give the beer a nutty flavor, combined
with a subtle blend of English aromatic hops.

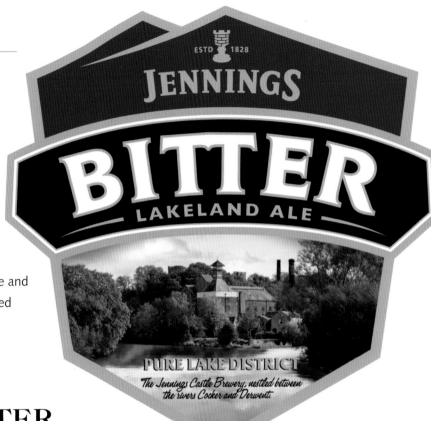

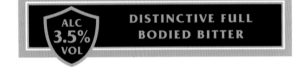

JENNINGS SNECK LIFTER

Country of Origin: *U.K.* • **Brewery Founded:** *1828*
Alcohol Content: *5.1%*

Jennings Sneck Lifter is an award winning
beer. It is a strong and satisfying ale that is
warming and full of complex flavors. This creates an intriguing beer of great character.
This dark beer has a reddish tinge, which is derived from the use of colored malts.
These are perfectly balanced with specially formulated brewing sugars and English
aromatic hops. The brew was first introduced in 1990 as a winter warmer. Jennings
Sneck Lifter has now become a firm favorite in the brewer's portfolio. In British dialect
"sneck" means a door latch and a "sneck lifter" referred to a man's last coin that
enabled him to lift the latch of a pub door and buy himself a drink. He would be
hoping to meet friends there who would treat him to one or two more.

JENNINGS COCKER HOOP

Country of Origin: *U.K.* • **Brewery Founded:** *1828* • **Alcohol Content:** *4.6%*

Cocker Hoop is an award-winning golden bitter from a malty brew. The beer is hopped with Styrian
Golding hops that are added at various stages of the fermentation to give a classic hop flavor and aroma. It
is a bitter beer of great character and appeals to beer drinkers who are looking for a brew of true quality. It
was launched in 1995 as September Ale. The brew has now become extremely popular with the many
tourists who visit England's beautiful Lake District. The brew's name is derived from the old technique of
Cock-a Hoop. This is an old custom of removing the cock (or spigot) from a barrel and resting it on the
hoop of the cask. The brewery is also located on the banks of the River Cocker.

JENNINGS CUMBERLAND ALE

Country of Origin: *U.K.* • **Brewery Founded:** *1828* • **Alcohol Content:** *4.7%*

Cumberland Ale is a superb golden colored ale, brewed with English Pale Ale malt and the finest English aromatic hops. The bee is traditionally brewed using pure Lakeland water drawn from the brewery's own well. It is a full-flavored beer with a delicate hop character and it is designed to appeal to the modern beer drinker. Cumberland Ale won a silver medal in 2009 and a bronze medal in 2010 at the International Beer Challenge.

JOULE'S BLONDE

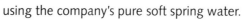

Country of Origin: *U.K.* • **Brewery Founded:** *1779/2010*
Alcohol Content: *3.8%*

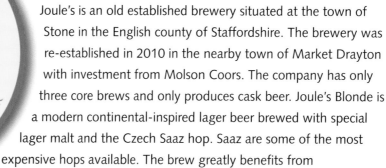

Joule's is an old established brewery situated at the town of Stone in the English county of Staffordshire. The brewery was re-established in 2010 in the nearby town of Market Drayton with investment from Molson Coors. The company has only three core brews and only produces cask beer. Joule's Blonde is a modern continental-inspired lager beer brewed with special lager malt and the Czech Saaz hop. Saaz are some of the most expensive hops available. The brew greatly benefits from using the company's pure soft spring water.

JOULE'S PALE ALE

Country of Origin: *U.K.* • **Brewery Founded:** *1779/2010* • **Alcohol Content:** *4.1%*

Joule's flagship brew is their Pale Ale. The beer is brewed with a blend of Crystal Malt for a biscuit base and Tipple Malt for a sweet caramel flavor. The brew is enhanced by the use of local mineral water.

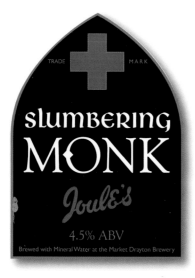

JOULE'S SLUMBERING MONK

Country of Origin: *U.K.* • **Brewery Founded:** *1779/2010* • **Alcohol Content:** *4.5%*

Slumbering Monk is Joule's premium beer. It attains its alcohol content by using a concentration of Crystal Malt which also imparts a deep copper color to the brew. The company stresses that no artificial colorings or flavors are used. The beer's name is reminiscent of a time in the sixteenth century when the monasteries brewed the best beers. The company's Red Cross logo is adapted from the one the monks used to mark their barrels, thus identifying their ales as abbey brews.

KELTEK BEHEADED

Country of Origin: *U.K.* • **Brewery Founded:** *1997* • **Alcohol Content:** *7.6%*

Keltek Beheaded is brewed in Cornwall and this range of craft ales is themed around the local Arthurian legend. They brew their award-winning ales by hand with traditional craftsmanship. The brews are made with the finest whole hop flowers, British malts, and hand-pitched yeast. Beheaded is Keltek's strongest ale. It pours a dark amber with a crimson tint and is deceptively smooth. The beer is slightly sweet and does not have a strong taste of alcohol, often associated with strong beers. The beer has a complex and indulgent flavor.

KELTEK KING

Country of Origin: *U.K.* • **Brewery Founded:** *1997* • **Alcohol Content:** *5.1%*

Keltek King is a premium bitter that is exceptionally well balanced and long-lasting on the palate. Keltek's King has won an array of awards, including Champion Bottled Beer in the SIBA National Brewing Competition, Gold in the International World of Beer Festival in Miami, America. It has also won two South West Regional Gold Medals. The brew is available in bottles and ten and twenty liter polypins.

KELTEK LANCE GOLDEN ALE

Country of Origin: *U.K.* • **Brewery Founded:** *1997* • **Alcohol Content:** *4.0%*

Lance Golden Ale is a refreshing pale ale with a fruity and malty first impression. This is followed by a hint of tangerine with a gentle bitterness. The taste is unusually long on the palate for a lower gravity beer.

KELTEK MAGIK

Country of Origin: *U.K.* • **Brewery Founded:** *1997* • **Alcohol Content:** *4.0%*

Magik is Keltek's benchmark brew. This is a traditional bitter full of hops and malt flavors with a gentle bitterness. The beer won the SIBA award of the South West Champion Best Bitter. According to Arthurian legend, the magic of the wizard Merlin helped to bring about the birth of King Arthur at Tintagel Castle in Cornwall. There remains a cavern below the castle, Merlin's Cave, which local folklore has long associated with the wizard.

MARSTON'S BURTON BITTER

Country of Origin: *U.K.* • **Brewery Founded:** *1834* • **Alcohol Content:** *3.8%*

Marston's Burton Bitter is one of Marston's oldest beers and was among the first created by John Marston when he established his brewery. The beer is crafted using only the finest, barley, hops, yeast, and the famous Burton spring water. This delivers an exceptionally clean tasting beer combining malty biscuit flavors with a delicate hop character and finish. The spring water does not come from the River Trent, it is actually rain water that has fallen on the surrounding hills and percolated down through gypsum rock beds. This water forms an underground stream on the valley floor. It is the trace elements of gypsum (calcium sulphate) which help to brew a clearer, brighter bitter. Marston's collect this natural spring water from several wells on the brewery site.

MARSTON'S EPA

Country of Origin: *U.K.* • **Brewery Founded:** *1834* • **Alcohol Content:** *3.6%*

EPA is a premium easy-drinking ale brewed as a alternative to the many lager-type beers on the U. K. market. The beer is brewed in a traditional style that reflects a time when pale ale was the most popular style of beer. EPA is brewed with a range of classic hops including Cascade and Styrian.

MARSTON'S PEDIGREE

Country of Origin: *U.K.* • **Brewery Founded:** *1834* • **Alcohol Content:** *4.5%*

Marston's Pedigree has a distinctive flavor which is due to its special blend of Burton spring water, Fuggles and Goldings hops, and the brewery's own unique strain of yeast. Marston's Pedigree is exceptional premium ale. Pedigree is Marston's flagship ale and forty-one million pints of the beer are sold every year. It is also available in cans and bottles.

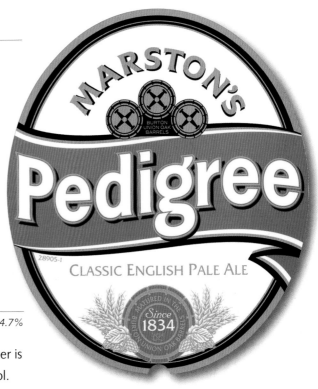

MARSTON'S RESOLUTION

Country of Origin: *U.K.* • **Brewery Founded:** *1834* • **Alcohol Content:** *4.7%*

Marston's Resolution is a full-flavored premium ale. The beer is double fermented so that all the sugar is turned into alcohol. This makes the beer relatively strong, while it remains crisp and light. The brewery claims that the beer is easy to drink and doesn't leave you feeling full and bloated.

McEWAN'S EXPORT

Country of Origin: *U.K.* • **Brewery Founded:** *1856* • **Alcohol Content:** *4.5%*

McEwan's Export is the second fastest selling premium ale in Scotland. The brand is one of the most well known in the McEwan brewery's portfolio. The brewer was acquired by Wells and Young's in 2011.

McEWAN'S IPA

Country of Origin: *U.K.* • **Brewery Founded:** *1856* • **Alcohol Content:** *4.5%*

McEwan's India Pale Ale is a English India Pale Ale (IPA) style of beer brewed by The Caledonian Brewery Company Limited. The brewery is based in Edinburgh, the capital of Scotland.

McEWAN'S LAGER

Country of Origin: *U.K.* • **Brewery Founded:** *1856* • **Alcohol Content:** *3.6%*

This mass-produced lager is a pasterized and force-carbonated keg lager. The brew is also available in cans. Production of the brew moved to Bedford, England in late 2011 following the acquisition of both the McEwan's and Younger's brands by Wells & Young's. Wells and Young's bought the trademarks from Heineken.

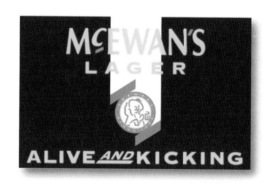

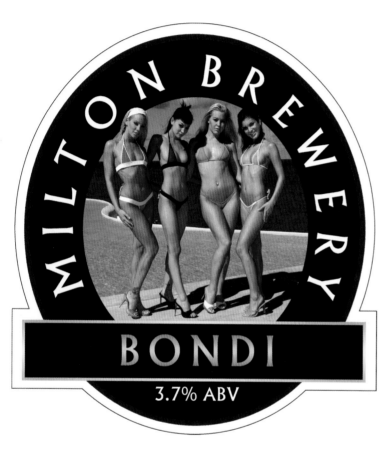

MILTON BONDI

Country of Origin: *U.K.* • **Brewery Founded:** *1999* • **Alcohol Content:** *3.7%*

Milton Bondi is a golden session bitter-style beer. It has a delicate hoppy flavor that leads to a satisfying bitter finish.

MILTON CYCLOPS

Country of Origin: *U.K.* • **Brewery Founded:** *1999* • **Alcohol Content:** *5.3%*

Milton Cyclops is a light, copper-colored ale with a rich hoppy aroma and a full body. The beer has notes of fruit and malt that develop in the finish. The beer is brewed with three different malts and four different varieties of hops. The Milton brewery is a traditional brewer of English ales, although it is located in an industrial unit from the 1950s. The brewery distributes its beers nationally and has several seasonal beers on its list. Its Nero brew is suitable for vegetarians and vegans. Most Milton beers have names with classical times. These include Seven Wonders, Imperator, and Ancient Cities. They also have an Antipodean beer list, with guest beers including their Bondi brew.

MILTON NERO

Country of Origin: *U.K.* • **Brewery Founded:** *1999* • **Alcohol Content:** *5.0%*

Milton nero is a satisfying, full-flavored black brew with a good balance of malt, roast, and fruit flavors. Its bittersweet taste carries through to a dry finish. Nero is an unrefined beer and is suitable for vegans and vegetarians. It is one of Milton's Imperator range of beers.

MILTON PYRAMID

Country of Origin: *U.K.* • **Brewery Founded:** *1999* • **Alcohol Content:** *4.4%*

Pyramid is bronze in color and is powerfully hoppy. This special beer has a wonderful complex bitter orange flavor, with a lasting bitter finish. The brew is part of Milton's Seven Wonders range of beers.

MILTON SPARTA

Country of Origin: *U.K.* • **Brewery Founded:** *1999* • **Alcohol Content:** *4.3%*

Sparta is a refreshing pale bitter. The brew is packed with hop flavors and has a crisp bitterness. The beer is part of Milton's Ancient Cities range of beers.

MOORHOUSE'S BLACK CAT

Country of Origin: *U.K.* • **Brewery Founded:** *1865* • **Alcohol Content:** *3.4%*

Black Cat is a specialty dark ruby ale from Moorhouse's brewery. The brew house is located in town of Burnley in the English county of Lancashire. The brewery is an independent company. The founding family sold the brewery in 1978. It has since passed through the ownership of several entrepreneurial private owners. Black Cat is described as a dark refreshing beer with a chocolate malted flavor and a smooth hoppy finish.

MOORHOUSE'S BLOND WITCH

Country of Origin: *U.K.* • **Brewery Founded:** *1865* • **Alcohol Content:** *4.5%*

Moorhouse name their brews in honor of the famous witches of the town of Pendle in the English county of Lancashire. Blond Witch is the company's first golden lager-style beer. Using continental ingredients the beer claims to have the lightest possible hue, but minus the bubbles that characterize most commercial lagers in the United Kingdom.

MOORHOUSE'S PENDLE WITCHES BREW

Country of Origin: *U.K.* • **Brewery Founded:** *1865* • **Alcohol Content:** *5.1%*

This beer is a full malty-tasting golden ale with a crisp fruity aftertaste and a soft citrus nose. It has a rich auburn/chestnut hue.

MOORHOUSE'S PRIDE OF PENDLE

Country of Origin: *U.K.* • **Brewery Founded:** *1865*
Alcohol Content: *4.1%*

Pride of Pendle is an award winning cask bitter. The brew has a fine balance of malt and hops to deliver a long dry and satisfying taste experience.

OAKHAM ALES BISHOPS FAREWELL

Country of Origin: *U.K.* • **Brewery Founded:** *2006* • **Alcohol Content:** *4.6%*

Bishops Farewell is a strong premium beer of structured quality. The aroma is dominated by elaborate and fruity hop notes. It has a grainy background and a dry finish. Oakham Ales new seventy-five barrel brew house officially opened on Friday 13, October 2006. Its first commissioned brew was made on April 1, 2006.

OAKHAM ALES CITRA

Country of Origin: *U.K.* • **Brewery Founded:** *2006* • **Alcohol Content:** *4.2%*

Citra is a light and refreshing beer with a pungent grapefruit, lychee, and gooseberry aroma. This leads to a dry and bitter finish.

OAKHAM ALES INFERNO

Country of Origin: *U.K.* • **Brewery Founded:** *2006* • **Alcohol Content:** *4.0%*

Inferno is a light ale that flickers complex fruits across the tongue, leaving a dry, fruity, and bitter finish. The beer is a refreshing session brew.

OAKHAM ALES JHB

Country of Origin: *U.K.* • **Brewery Founded:** *2006* • **Alcohol Content:** *3.8%*

JHB is a golden beer. Its aroma is dominated by hops that give the brew characteristic citrus notes. Hops and fruit dominate on the palate and are balanced with malt and a bitter base. The beer has a dry hoppy finish with soft fruit flavors.

OAKHAM ALES PREACHER

Country of Origin: *U.K.* • **Brewery Founded:** *2006* • **Alcohol Content:** *4.3%*

Preacher is a rich, full bodied chestnut-colored seasonal ale. It has a smooth delicate bitterness. The beer has plenty of sweet malty flavors with a powerful fruity hop tang and a rich aroma.

OTTER ALE

Country of Origin: *U.K.* • **Brewery Founded:** *1990* • **Alcohol Content:** *4.5%*

Otter Ale is the Otter brewery's first beer. It pours with a particularly stable bead. The alcohol content of this premium ale is high enough to enable a perfect balance between its flavor and aroma. Otter Ale delivers the flavors of quality floor-malted barley, and finishes with a combination of fruit and some bitterness. The beer's nose is a balance of malt and fruit.

OTTER BITTER

Country of Origin: *U.K.* • **Brewery Founded:** *1990*
Alcohol Content: *3.6%*

Otter Bitter is a beautifully light and fruity beer with good hoppy bitterness. It leaves a refreshing bitterness which makes the beer very drinkable. It is an old-fashioned session beer. It is a simple bitter style beer with no frills.

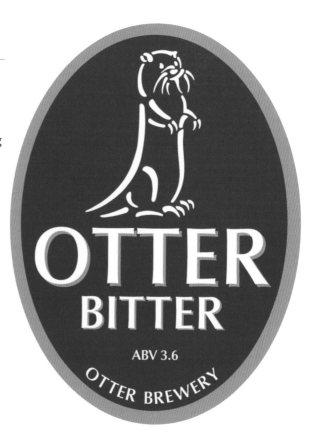

OTTER BRIGHT

Country of Origin: *U.K.* • **Brewery Founded:** *1990* • **Alcohol Content:** *4.3%*

Otter Bright was formerly brewed as a seasonal summer beer. There has been a growth of interest in cask beer and Otter Bright is perfectly positioned to appeal to this new generation of cask beer drinkers. The beer is very pale in color and could easily be mistaken for lager. The brew delivers a great bitter citrus flavor with lots of carbonation. A cool cellar temperature will add to its refreshing qualities.

OTTER HEAD

Country of Origin: *U.K.* • **Brewery Founded:** *1990* • **Alcohol Content:** *5.8%*

Otter Head is the brewery's strongest beer and it delivers a rich flavor and aroma. Otter Head has the distinctive character of an old ale or barley wine. It has a malty, fruity sweet flavor which gives way to a long bitter-sweet aftertaste. The beer a well balanced aroma that reflects its taste. It pours a deep red-brown in color.

PALMERS BEST BITTER

Country of Origin: *U.K.* • **Brewery Founded:** *1794* • **Alcohol Content:** *4.2%*

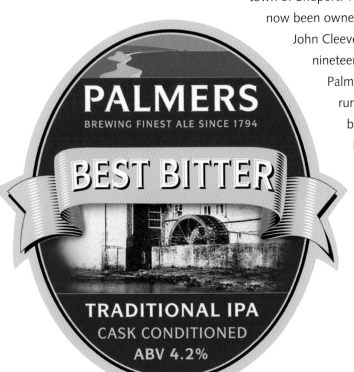

The Palmers brewery was built by the Gundry family, who were rope and net makers in the rural English county of Dorset. They built it on the banks of the River Brit in the town of Bridport. The brewery has been brewing since that time. The brewery has now been owned by several generation of the Palmer family. Two Palmer brothers, John Cleeves Palmer and Robert Henry Palmer bought the brewery in the late nineteenth century and changed the name of the brewery to J.C. & R.H. Palmer. The brothers' great grandsons, John and Cleeves Palmer, now run the company. Palmers remains among the best small independent brewers in the United Kingdom. Best Bitter has been one of the brewery's best known products for generations. It is a full-drinking, malty ale with a hoppy character. The beer is a traditional IPA from the heart of rural West Dorset.

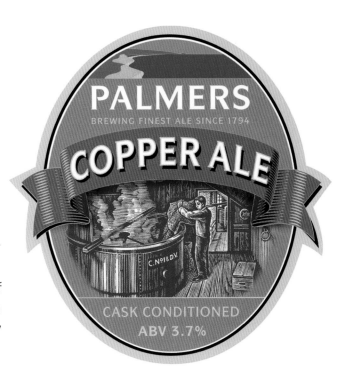

PALMERS COPPER ALE

Country of Origin: *U.K.* • **Brewery Founded:** *1794* • **Alcohol Content:** *3.7%*

Copper Ale is a well-balanced, copper-colored session ale. It has aromas of citrus fruit with a hoppy base. The beer is full-flavored, brewed with Maris Otter malt and whole leaf First Gold hops. The brew is named for Palmers' brewery copper, which is still in use in the old brewery.

PALMERS DORSET GOLD

Country of Origin: *U.K.* • **Brewery Founded:** *1794* • **Alcohol Content:** *4.5%*

Dorset Gold is a lightly hopped, golden premium ale. It is a refreshing, zesty, and thirst-quenching beer from the heart of Dorset's heritage Jurassic Coast. The beer was originally brewed as a summer ale but it proved to be so popular that it is now available all year.

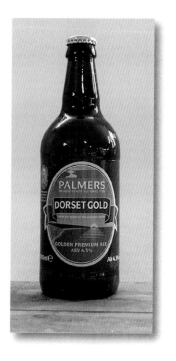

PALMERS TALLY HO!

Country of Origin: *U.K.* • **Brewery Founded:** *1794* • **Alcohol Content:** *5.25%*

Tally Ho! is strong, complex, and full of deep flavors. The beer has a taste of rich fruitcake from its roasted malt. The beer was first brewed in the 1940s. This prize-winning dark and strong old ale now has a loyal following among real ale connoisseurs.

RINGWOOD BEST BITTER

Country of Origin: *U.K.* • **Brewery Founded:** *1978* • **Alcohol Content:** *3.8%*

Ringwood Best Bitter is the perfect session beer. The beer is Ringwood's original brew and is still a favorite. The beer has a tempting hop aroma with fruit notes and a good malt feel in the mouth. It also has a dry, tangy, and fruity finish.

RINGWOOD BOONDOGGLE

Country of Origin: *U.K.* • **Brewery Founded:** *1978* • **Alcohol Content:** *5.0%*

Ringwood's blonde Boondoggle is a deliciously fruity ale that is crafted to savor and to satisfy. It delivers a hoppy aroma with a citrus punch, and has a well balanced fruity taste. Boondoggle is a blonde and luscious ale brewed with the finest English Pale Malt, First Gold, and Fuggles Hops.

RINGWOOD FORTY NINER

Country of Origin: *U.K.* • **Brewery Founded:** *1978* • **Alcohol Content:** *4.9%*

As the name suggests this is a strong premium golden ale. The beer is golden in hue and strong brewed. Ringwood has been brewing this Golden full bodied malted beer since the brewery began in 1978. Despite its strength, the beer exhibits a light, fresh hop bouquet. The brew has rounded malt in the mouth with a strong hop balance. It has a deep bitter-sweet finish.

RINGWOOD OLD THUMPER CRAFT ALE

Country of Origin: *U.K.* • **Brewery Founded:** *1978* • **Alcohol Content:** *5.1%*

Old Thumper Craft Ale is a deep brown strong ale. The beer is peppery, with a spicy aroma that has a hint of apples. The beer provides a tantalizing balance of grain and hop in the mouth. The brew has a bitter-sweet finish with delicate fruit notes. This is a warm, rounded and yet surprisingly delicate strong beer.

ROOSTERS BUCKEYE

Country of Origin: *U.K.* • **Brewery Founded:** *1993* • **Alcohol Content:** *3.5%*

Roosters Buckeye is named after a rare breed of chicken that originates from the state of Ohio in the United States. It is an easy-drinking session ale. Buckeye is a well-hopped pale ale that is brewed with a blend of American and New Zealand hops. This produces an orange, citrus fruit aroma and a refreshing level of bitterness.

ROOSTERS FORT SMITH

Country of Origin: *U.K.* • **Brewery Founded:** *1993* • **Alcohol Content:** *5.0%*

This brew is named after the town in which Rooster Cogburn lived. Fort Smith is a big and bold India Pale Ale, which is brewed using Citra and Chinook hops imported from the United States. These create tropical and passion fruit aromas and a lasting bitter finish.

ROOSTERS LONDINIUM

Country of Origin: *U.K.* • **Brewery Founded:** *1993* • **Alcohol Content:** *5.5%*

Londinium is a dark beer with a hint of coffee on the finish. It is brewed using four malts, English hops, and the addition of Taylors of Harrogate After Dark coffee. Londinium is a nod to the beer of yesteryear and a beer style made popular by the street and river porters of London in the eighteenth century.

ROOSTERS YANKEE

Country of Origin: *U.K.* • **Brewery Founded:** *1993* • **Alcohol Content:** *4.3%*

Yankee is one of the new-style, pale ales to be brewed in the United Kingdom. Yankee is a modern classic. Light and easy-drinking, it's a beer that showcases the floral and citrus fruit aromas of the Cascade hop. These are grown in the Yakima Valley, Washington State, United States of America. These hops are projected against a backdrop of soft Yorkshire water and Golden Promise pale malt.

SHARP'S CHALKY'S BARK

Country of Origin: *U.K.* • **Brewery Founded:** *1994* • **Alcohol Content:** *4.3%*

International chef Rick Stein and the award winning Sharp's Brewery have collaborated to create this unique new beer. Chalky's Bark, which is a triple fermented brew, is made with ginger and continental hops. It is a light, fruity, and refreshing beer. In is named in honor of Chalky, Rick Stein's famous Jack Russell Terrier. Sharp's Brewery was founded at the town of Rock in the English county of Cornwall. The success and growth of this young Brewery has been phenomenal. Sharp's is now the largest brewer of cask conditioned beer in England's South West (according to industry sources). Sharp's flagship brand, Doom Bar, is now the number one cask beer in the United Kingdom.

SHARP'S CORNISH COASTER

Country of Origin: *U.K.* • **Brewery Founded:** *1994* • **Alcohol Content:** *3.6%*

With its low level of alcohol, Sharp's Cornish Coaster is a perfect session ale. It has a generous measure of refreshing flavor and a light golden hue. Cornish Coaster is the perfect beer to enhance a hot summer day.

SHARP'S DOOM BAR

Country of Origin: *U.K.* • **Brewery Founded:** *1994* • **Alcohol Content:** *4.0%*

Doom Bar bitter is named after an infamous sandbank at the mouth of the Camel Estuary in North Cornwall. Doom Bar beer embodies many characteristics that reflect the grandeur of the natural landmark. Its distinctive aroma and balanced flavor make the beer very recognizable. Doom Bar has achieved international cult status and is one of the fastest growing beer brands in the United Kingdom. It is also the best-selling cask beer in the South West counties of England.

SHARP'S SPECIAL

Country of Origin: *U.K.* • **Brewery Founded:** *1994*
Alcohol Content: *5%*

Special is one of the strongest beers in Sharps' cask range. It is brewed with a higher quantity of premium English malted barley. Malted barley adds a distinctive sweetness to the flavor profile. The beer has delicious aromas of over-ripe fruit that blend with inviting roasted notes. As Head Brewer Stuart Howe says "The mouth feel is succulent with dried fruit, malt and generous hop bitterness. The finish is lingering and warm with fruit and malt notes. For a strong ale Special is subtle and dangerously drinkable."

SHEPHERD NEAME 1698 BOTTLE CONDITIONED ALE

Country of Origin: *U.K.* • **Brewery Founded:** *1698* • **Alcohol Content:** *6.5%*

Shepherd Neame is Britain's oldest brewer. While 1698 is the brewery's official founding date, there is clear evidence that its heritage pre-dates even this. The brewery was the first brewer in the Kentish town of Faversham. It was then acquired by the Shepherd and Neame families and has now become a successful, award-winning business. 1698 was originally brewed to celebrate the tercentenary of Britain's oldest brewer. 1698 is a characteristic hoppy Kentish ale and has Protected Geographical Indication. This is the same unique regional protection afforded to Champagne and Parma Ham. The ale matures naturally in the bottle and can be enjoyed fresh or it can be allowed to settle for a few months to mellow. The natural effervescence produced by bottle-conditioning , from the interaction of yeast and brewing sugars, gives 1698 fine, champagne-like bubbles. These enhance the fragrance, flavor, and overall drinking experience of the beer.

SHEPHERD NEAME BISHOPS FINGER

Country of Origin: *U.K.* • **Brewery Founded:** *1698* • **Alcohol Content:** *5.0% (cask), 5.4% (bottle)*

The beer is brewed with a firm, fruity foundation of Crystal Malt. It pours a rich ruby-color. This Kent classic belies its burly appearance with a complex of flavor. It is characterized by mouth-filling fruit, including prunes, plums, and dried apricot spiked with pepper and cinnamon. The beer has a bitter blood-orange finish. The beer takes its name from the finger-shaped signposts which directed pilgrims on their way to the tomb of Thomas a Becket in the cathedral city of Canterbury. The beer was the first strong ale to be brewed by Shepherd Neame when malt rationing was eased in the late 1950s. Bishops Finger is one of the United Kingdom's oldest bottled beers, having been brewed since 1958.

SHEPHERD NEAME MASTER BREW

Country of Origin: *U.K.* • **Brewery Founded:** *1698*
Alcohol Content: *3.7% (cask), 4.0% (bottle)*

Master Brew is made using only the finest Kentish barley and hops. It is Shepherd Neame's flagship beer in the brewery's Kentish heartland. This local hero brew is a distinctive, mid-brown bitter ale, with lots of hoppy aroma. No surprise from a beer brewed in the very heart of England's hop country. The beer is hand-crafted by the Faversham brewery's talented team of experienced brewers. Master Brew is a well-balanced traditional ale, with a taste that has been described as "wonderfully aggressive, tinged with sweetness". The Faversham Steam Brewery motto was originally adopted in the late eighteenth century, when Shepherd Neame became one of the first steam-powered breweries outside London.

SHEPHERD NEAME SPITFIRE

Country of Origin: *U.K.* • **Brewery Founded:** *1698* • **Alcohol Content:** *4.2%*

An infusion of three Kentish hops has been used to brew this beautifully balanced British bitter. It pours with a blood-orange tint and has an aromatic character. The aroma has hints of marmalade, red grapes, and pepper balanced with warm, mellow malts. This Kentish ale was first brewed in 1990 to celebrate the fiftieth anniversary of the Battle of Britain. This was fought in the skies above Kent fifty years earlier. The beer is named after the legendary Spitfire aeroplane designed by R.J. Mitchell. The versatility of the aircraft and the courage of its pilots were essential to victory in World War II and were an iconic symbol of that time.

SHEPHERD NEAME WHITSTABLE BAY ORGANIC ALE

Country of Origin: *U.K.* • **Brewery Founded:** *1698* • **Alcohol Content:** *4.5% (bottle)*

The Whitstable Bay Collection is named after the traditional Kentish fishing village of Whitstable. The village is renowned for its annual Oyster Festival, village life, and beautiful beaches. Organic Ale is light-colored and brewed using only organic ingredients. The beer blends citrusy hops with nutty malt flavors to create a flavorsome golden ale.

SKINNER'S BETTY STOGS

Country of Origin: *U.K.* • **Brewery Founded:** *1997* • **Alcohol Content:** *4.0%*

Skinner's Flagship ale was named after a Cornish woman of loose morals who also enjoyed her ale. This best-selling beer has won many awards both nationally and locally, more than any other Cornish beer. It is known as the Queen of Cornish Ales. The beer has a light hop aroma with underlying malt. It is an ideal session ale that is brewed in traditional copper with a superb balance of citrus hops, malt, and bitterness. The bitter finish is slow to develop but long to fade.

SKINNER'S CORNISH TRAWLER

Country of Origin: *U.K.* • **Brewery Founded:** *1997* • **Alcohol Content:** *3.6%*

Skinner's Cornish Trawler is the brewery's new golden ale. It is a beautifully hoppy session ale with hints of citrus and bitter sweet malts. The beer is available on draught.

SKINNER'S HELIGAN HONEY

Country of Origin: *U.K.* • **Brewery Founded:** *1997* • **Alcohol Content:** *4.0%*

Skinner's Heligan Honey is a light and refreshing bitter. It is pale amber in color with distinct hoppy overtones. The subtle addition of real Cornish honey gives the beer an interesting character and flavor. It is a SIBA National Champion Speciality Beer and has been voted one of the best speciality beers in the United Kingdom.

SKINNER'S SKINDOG CORNISH LAGER

Country of Origin: *U.K.* • **Brewery Founded:** *1997* • **Alcohol Content:** *4.4%*

Using the finest Cornish barley, wheat malt, English, and American hops, this is Cornwall's own stunning surf beer. The brew is light and zingy while being beautifully balanced. The aroma has a hint of citrus.

JOHN SMITH'S BITTER

Country of Origin: *U.K.* • **Brewery Founded:** *1847* • **Alcohol Content:** *3.6% (can), 3.8% (cask)*

John Smith's bitter has a malty, bitter sweet ale with a slight fruitiness and a bitter aftertaste. It is currently the United Kingdom's best-selling bitter beer. The original John Smith founded his brewing empire in 1847, when he started brewing ale for mill workers and factory hands. The company's motto is that it brews "No-Nonsense" ales. The brewery is now owned by Heineken.

JOHN SMITH'S EXTRA SMOOTH

Country of Origin: *U.K.* • **Brewery Founded:** *1847* • **Alcohol Content:** *3.6%*

John Smith's Extra Smooth was launched in 1993. It is a nitrogenized version of the company's famous bitter. It is now one of the United Kingdom's best selling ales. The beer has a distinct cereal character, with malty, caramel notes complimented by some fruitiness. Extra Smooth is available on draught or in cans.

JOHN SMITH'S MAGNET

Country of Origin: *U.K.* • **Brewery Founded:** *1847* • **Alcohol Content:** *4.0%*

Magnet has a subtle balance of bitter-sweet flavors including caramel and a hint of liquorice. It is an easy-drinking, full-flavored, and full-bodied brew. The beer was brewed by Cameron's of Hartlepool, a town in northern England.

SAMUEL SMITH'S EXTRA STOUT

Country of Origin: *U.K.* • **Brewery Founded:** *1758* • **Alcohol Content:** *4.3%*

This beer is a foreign export stout. This means that is has been brewed to survive transportation overseas. The brew has been favorably compared to Guinness, the main proponent of this type of beer.

SAMUEL SMITH'S OLD BREWERY BITTER

Country of Origin: *U.K.* • **Brewery Founded:** *1758* • **Alcohol Content:** *3.9%*

The Old Brewery at Tadcaster was established in 1758. It is Yorkshire's oldest brewery. Old Brewery Bitter is fermented in stone Yorkshire squares. These are fermenting vessels made of solid slabs of slate that give the beer a fuller-bodied taste. The beer has been brewed using the same strain of yeast since the nineteenth century. It pours an amber golden color. It has a malty taste redolent of toffee apple and vanilla. The beer has a dry and mild bitter aftertaste. The beer has a medium body with very low carbonation.

SAMUEL SMITH'S ORGANIC LAGER

Country of Origin: *U.K.* • **Brewery Founded:** *1758* • **Alcohol Content:** *5.0%*

Organic Lager is brewed with great care using only organic malted barley, organic hops, medium-soft water, and bottom-fermenting yeast. The beer is matured at low temperatures to bring out its delicate flavor and soft hop character and finish. The cold maturation period allows the bottom-fermenting yeasts to have a secondary fermentation. This improves the lager's flavor, purity, and condition.

SAMUEL SMITH'S TADDY LAGER

Country of Origin: *U.K.* • **Brewery Founded:** *1758* • **Alcohol Content:** *3.7%*

Taddy Lager is a European-style pale lager. It is a filtered and pasteurized lager that is served under pressure from a keg. It is brewed with barley malt, hops, yeast, and water. The beer has a simple grassy aroma with a hint of apple. It is relatively light on alcohol with a lively mouth feel.

ST. AUSTELL KOREV

Country of Origin: *U.K.* • **Brewery Founded:** *1851* • **Alcohol Content:** *4.8%*

The beer is named for the traditional Cornish Korev, meaning beer. Korev is craft brewed at the brewery in St. Austell. Korev is a relatively recent addition to the St. Austell range. It is made using the finest lager malt from barley grown in Cornwall. This is combined with a variety of continental hops including Perle, Hersbrucker, and Saaz. Korev has a pale color and a clean, crisp taste. It is bottled in amber glass to protect its freshness.

ST. AUSTELL PROPER JOB

Country of Origin: *U.K.* • **Brewery Founded:** *1851* • **Alcohol Content:** *5.5%*

Proper Job is an authentic IPA brewed with Cornish spring water and a blend of malts including Cornish Gold. The beer is made with Willamette, Cascade, and Chinook hops. The beer was first brewed in 2006 as a seasonal beer. Proper Job proved so popular that it is now a permanent part of the St. Austell Brewery portfolio and has become the brewery's second best selling cask ale.

ST. AUSTELL TRELAWNY

Country of Origin: *U.K.* • **Brewery Founded:** *1851* • **Alcohol Content:** *3.8%*

Trelawny Ale invokes the best Cornish traditions, heritage, and innovation. Locally grown barley is roasted to give this beer a classic burnished copper color and a robust full body that belies its modest strength. The beer is a unique blend of traditional English Golding and specially imported Galaxy hops from South Australia. These harmonize to give the beer a distinctive character of the old and new worlds. Peach and apricot notes dominate the aroma, with hints of butterscotch and toffee apple. The taste is full, with toasted biscuit and jam being balanced by the mellow, yet assertive bitterness of tangy hops.

ST. AUSTELL TRIBUTE

Country of Origin: *U.K.* • **Brewery Founded:** *1851* • **Alcohol Content:** *4.2%*

Tribute is the Supreme Champion Ale of Cornwall as voted for by CAMRA (The Campaign for Real Ale). It is also the favorite cask beer in England south west counties. Tribute is a favorite with locals and visitors to Cornwall, as well as being widely distributed in the rest of the United Kingdom. The beer is brewed using specially grown Cornish Gold Malt. The St. Austell Brewery Company Limited was founded in 1851 by Walter Hicks, who mortgaged his farm for 2,450 dollars to establish the business in St. Austell, Cornwall.

TENNENT'S LAGER

Country of Origin: *U.K.* • **Brewery Founded:** *1885* • **Alcohol Content:** *4.0%*

Tennant's Lager was first produced by Hugh Tennent at the Wellpark brewery in 1885. This flagship brand has long been established as one of Scotland's best-selling brews. Tennent's Lager is brewed to high standards using exceptional ingredients. It is characterized by its clean taste and refreshingly crisp finish. The beer has maintained its popularity in the face of changing tastes and fashions.

TETLEY'S CASK

Country of Origin: *U.K.* • **Brewery Founded:** *1822* • **Alcohol Content:** *3.7%*

This full-flavored hoppy Yorkshire bitter is amber colored with a white foam head. Tetley's Cask beer is easy to drink and refreshing with its balance of biscuit malts and floral hops.

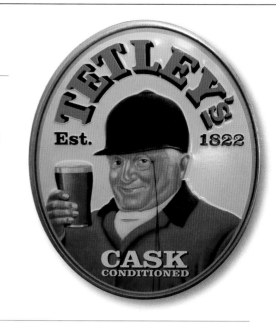

TETLEY'S GOLD

Country of Origin: *U.K.* • **Brewery Founded:** *1822* • **Alcohol Content:** *4.1%*

Pale yet full of flavor, Tetley's Gold is a unique and contemporary beer. It is a balance of refreshing citrus and floral hops. Tetley's is now part of the Carlsberg Group of brewers. Tetley's Gold is produced in several beer plants at Wolverhampton, Tadcaster, and Hartlepool.

TETLEY'S IMPERIAL

Country of Origin: *U.K.* • **Brewery Founded:** *1822* • **Alcohol Content:** *4.1%*

This strong bitter is fermented in a Yorkshire Square System. Tetley's Imperial has an amber hue with a slight head. It has a deep, well-rounded body, a tangy edge, and a lingering bitterness.

TETLEY'S ORIGINAL

Country of Origin: *U.K.* • **Brewery Founded:** *1822* • **Alcohol Content:** *4.1%*

Tetley's Original is the second most popular ale in the United Kingdom. The beer has been brewed in Leeds since 1822 using traditional brewing methods, including the dry hopping of cask ales and the use of Yorkshire Square fermenting vessels. Tetley's Original is a traditional style ale with a full-bodied hoppy flavor and a refreshing crispness on the palate.

THEAKSTON OLD PECULIER

Country of Origin: *U.K.* • **Brewery Founded:** *1827* • **Alcohol Content:** *5.6%*

Two hundred years ago in the early years of the modern brewing era, many brewers produced a dark, strong "stock" beer in the winter months. This was brewed to provide a base of fermented beer to add to beers brewed in the warm months of the summer. This is probably where Old Peculier gets its rather bizarre name. Old Peculier is a simple beer, brewed with a blend of Pale, Crystal and roasted barley malts. These are combined with two varieties of bitter hops combined with the majestic and noble Fuggles hop. This produces a beer of full-bodied flavor with subtle cherry notes and rich fruit overtones.

THEAKSTON BEST BITTER

Country of Origin: *U.K.* • **Brewery Founded:** *1827* • **Alcohol Content:** *3.8%*

When Robert Theakston founded his brewery his range of ales was limited to just two or three brews. It is almost certain that one of these was a bitter beer. Consequently Theakston assert that their Best Bitter is one of the longest established session ales brewed in Yorkshire.

THEAKSTON MASHAM ALE

Country of Origin: *U.K.* • **Brewery Founded:** *1827* • **Alcohol Content:** *6.5%*

"Not for the faint hearted!" is the shout line on Theakston's website. It is certainly a robust brew. Masham Ale is a full, rounded, great tasting ale, and a fine example of the best of English cask ales. The use of fresh Fuggles hops gives the beer a subtle fruitiness. Masham Ale is brewed in late November as a Christmas treat. Because the beer is so strong, the brewery recommends that the beer should be drunk in half pint measures.

THEAKSTON XB

Country of Origin: *U.K.* • **Brewery Founded:** *1827* • **Alcohol Content:** *4.5%*

XB is a described as a connoisseur's masterpiece. It is a strong and full-bodied ale with a subtle blend of two types of bitter and three fruit hop varieties. XB was first brewed in 1982 to celebrate the purchase of the Carlisle Brewery by Theakstons. The beer is brewed in Masham. XB was designed as a tribute to the classic border style of beer. These are strong in gravity and low with complex hop notes.

THWAITES LANCASTER BOMBER

Country of Origin: *U.K.* • **Brewery Founded:** *1807* • **Alcohol Content:** *4.4%*

Lancaster Bomber is an award winning full-bodied bitter ale. It pours chestnut colored and has an inviting malty aroma and warming aftertaste. The beer has won two Gold Medals in the European Beer Star Awards in 2007 and 2011. It was the silver medallist in the 2012 International Beer Challenge.

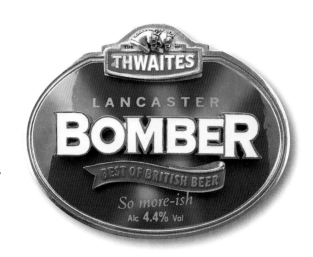

THWAITES NUTTY BLACK

Country of Origin: *U.K.* • **Brewery Founded:** *1807* • **Alcohol Content:** *3.3%*

Nutty Black is a dark ruby mild with a hint of nuttiness, combined with unmistakable roasted and bittersweet flavors. The brew is one of only four beers to have won the Champion Beer of Britain award twice. Thwaites uses only the finest dark kiln roasted malts, English barley, with Fuggles and Golding hops to create a smooth dark mild beer with a dry finish

THWAITES ORIGINAL

Country of Origin: *U.K.* • **Brewery Founded:** *1807* • **Alcohol Content:** *3.6%*

Original is exactly the same as it was back in 1807 when Daniel Thwaites began brewing the beer. It is a clean, dry tasting session bitter with a glowing amber appearance. The beer is brewed with premium grade Maris Otter malt and a blend of traditional English hops including Goldings and Fuggles. This gives the beer a malty flavored taste with a delicate dry finish.

THWAITES WAINWRIGHT

Country of Origin: *U.K.* • **Brewery Founded:** *1807* • **Alcohol Content:** *4.1%*

Thwaites Wainwright is a refreshing golden ale from Daniel Thwaites, the Lancashire brewers. The beer was named in honor of the famous fell walker, author, and fellow Lancastrian Alfred Wainwright. The beer was originally brewed as a seasonal beer with a special combination of hops. This gives the brew a fruity scent and citrus flavor. It is made with 100% Marris Otter, the king of real ale malts.

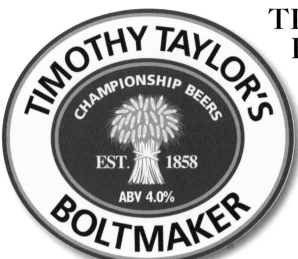

TIMOTHY TAYLOR BOLTMAKER

Country of Origin: *U.K.* • **Brewery Founded:** *1858* • **Alcohol Content:** *4%*

Boltmaker is a well-balanced, genuine Yorkshire Bitter. It has a full measure of maltiness and a hoppy aroma. It pours a clear copper golden with a good sized head. The nose is of light caramel, dough malt, and light fruit overtones. It has a very pleasant aroma. The beer is medium bodied with soft carbonation. It is smooth on the palate with bitter notes at the finish.

TIMOTHY TAYLOR GOLDEN BEST

Country of Origin: *U.K.* • **Brewery Founded:** *1858*
Alcohol Content: *3.5%*

Golden best is a light-colored mild ale in the Pennine style. The ale pours an amber color. The low alcohol content makes this an ideal session ale. The beer has a distinctive smooth and creamy flavor.

TIMOTHY TAYLOR LANDLORD

Country of Origin: *U.K.* • **Brewery Founded:** *1858* • **Alcohol Content:** *4.3%*

Landlord is a classic strong pale ale. The brew has won more national awards than any other beer. These awards include four titles as the Champion at the Brewers' International Exhibition. The beer has also been CAMRA's beer of the year on four different occasions.

TIMOTHY TAYLOR RAM TAM

Country of Origin: *U.K.* • **Brewery Founded:** *1858* • **Alcohol Content:** *4.3%*

Ram Tam is a dark, strong beer that has a reputation as a winter warmer. The beer is wholesome and satisfying and has good body and depth. The brew has a pleasant fruity afterglow. Timothy Taylor established the Brewery in the center of the town of Keighley in Yorkshire in 1858, moving to The Knowle Spring, the brewery's current site in 1863.

TITANIC ANCHOR

Country of Origin: *U.K.* • **Brewery Founded:** *1985* • **Alcohol Content:** *4.1%*

Titanic uses names inspired by maritime themes for its beers. Anchor is an impressive russet gold beer that has a strong fruity aroma. Bitterness in the initial taste allows the full impact of the hops to burst through.

TITANIC LIFEBOAT

Country of Origin: *U.K.* • **Brewery Founded:** *1985* • **Alcohol Content:** *4.0%*

Lifeboat is a dark ruby old-style ale. It is fruity and malty with a full bodied bitter-sweet flavor. It has a serene caramel character and a dry finish.

TITANIC CAPTAIN SMITH'S

Country of Origin: *U.K.* • **Brewery Founded:** *1985* • **Alcohol Content:** *5.2%*

Captain Smith's is a red-brown and full bodied beer. It has a hoppy and bitter-sweet character with roast malt flavor and a good strong finish. The beer was named after the captain of the Titanic, Captain Edward Smith, who was born in Stoke on Trent.

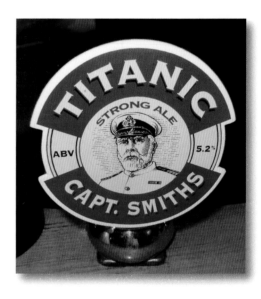

TITANIC WHITE STAR

Country of Origin: *U.K.* • **Brewery Founded:** *1985* • **Alcohol Content:** *4.8%*

This golden hoppy bitter has won four beer awards. It is a light refreshing beer with a fresh and a bitter aftertaste that belies its strength. The Titanic Brewery was founded in Burslem Stoke on Trent in 1985 by brothers Dave and Keith Bott.

VALE BEST BITTER

Country of Origin: *U.K.* • **Brewery Founded:** *1995* • **Alcohol Content:** *3.7%*

This light copper session bitter is heavily hopped with traditional varieties. This produces a thirst quenching beer with a pronounced and pleasant hop aroma.

VALE SPECIAL

Country of Origin: *U.K.* • **Brewery Founded:** *1995* • **Alcohol Content:** *4.5%*

Brothers Mark and Phil Stevens drew on their previous experiences with brewers such as Morrells and Allied Breweries and their love of traditional real ales to create the Vale Brewery. Vale's beers have always been brewed with natural ingredients. These include malted barley, hops, live yeast, and water. The beer has no additional additives, preservatives, or chemicals. The brewer was originally situated in Haddenham, Buckinghamshire in a large village in the Aylesbury Vale. The Vale Brewery Company was formed in January 1995 and their first brew became available in March 1995. Vale Special is a premium bitter brewed with Maris Otter, Crystal, and chocolate malts blended with the choicest hops.

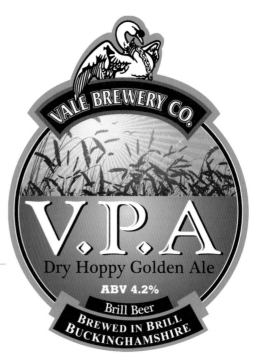

VALE PALE ALE

Country of Origin: *U.K.* • **Brewery Founded:** *1995* • **Alcohol Content:** *4.2%*

Vale Pale Ale is brewed with hops imported from the United States combined with Kent's finest produce. The beer has is an assertive dry hoppy ale with a pronounced malt background.

VALE GRUMPLING OLD ALE

Country of Origin: *U.K.* • **Brewery Founded:** *1995* • **Alcohol Content:** *4.6%*

Vale Grumpling Old Ale is an award winning premium ale with complex malt and hop flavors. The beer is named after the base plinth stones of the Wychert wall, a well known Haddenham landmark.

VALE BLACK SWAN DARK MILD

Country of Origin: *U.K.* • **Brewery Founded:** *1995* • **Alcohol Content:** *3.9%*

Vale Black Swan Dark Mild is an award winning mild ale. The beer is dark and smooth with an impressive full roast flavor that belies its strength.

WADWORTH 6X

Country of Origin: *U.K.* • **Brewery Founded:** *1875* • **Alcohol Content:** *4.3%*

Wadworth have been brewing beer in Devizes since 1875. The brewery was founded by Henry A. Wadworth. The business then passed to his founding partner John Smith Bartholomew. The brewery is now run by the fourth generation of the Bartholomew family. Wadworth's Victorian tower brewery is a landmark in the center of Devizes. The brewery site combines a tradition of craft with modern production techniques and systems. Full bodied and distinctive, 6X remains one of the South of England's most famous beers. The beer is mid-brown in color, malty, and fruity with a balancing hop character.

WADWORTH FARMERS GLORY

Country of Origin: *U.K.* • **Brewery Founded:** *1875* • **Alcohol Content:** *4.7%*

Farmers Glory is one of Wadworth's seasonal beers and is available from May to October each year. It is a classic English ale that celebrates the hard work and fruits of the local agricultural industry. It is a rewarding brew after a hard day's work.

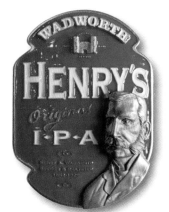

WADWORTH HENRY'S IPA

Country of Origin: *U.K.* • **Brewery Founded:** *1875* • **Alcohol Content:** *3.6%*

This golden brown beer, named after Henry Wadworth, has a good balance of flavor and a long lasting aftertaste, which becomes increasingly biscuity. It is a good session beer.

WADWORTH HORIZON

Country of Origin: *U.K.* • **Brewery Founded:** *1875* • **Alcohol Content:** *4.0%*

Wadworth Horizon is an easy-drinking all year round beer and is robust enough to accompany most foods. Horizon is light in color, but is full flavored and best enjoyed cool.

WELLS & YOUNG'S BOMBARDIER

Country of Origin: *U.K.* • **Brewery Founded:** *1875* • **Alcohol Content:** *4.1% (cask), 4.7 (bottle)*

Roger Protz, the editor of The Good Beer Guide said of Bombadier, the beer has "A burnished copper color, it has a rich, tempting aroma of peppery hops and raisins, while the palate is dominated by more dark fruit, juicy malt and tangy hops." Wells & Young is firmly placed as the UK's largest private brewing company, it is fiercely independent, and with an enviable portfolio of some of the UK's most popular cask beers and speciality lager brands.

WELLS & YOUNG'S YOUNG'S BITTER

Country of Origin: *U.K.* • **Brewery Founded:** *1875* • **Alcohol Content:** *3.7% (cask), 4.5% (bottle)*

Young's Bitter one of the fastest growing standard cask beers in England and Wales. It is a refreshing session ale, golden in color, with a light, dry palate, a fresh, fruity aroma, and a long, satisfying bitter finish.

WELLS & YOUNG'S YOUNG'S RAM ROD

Country of Origin: *U.K.* • **Brewery Founded:** *1875* • **Alcohol Content:** *5.0% (bottle)*

This beer is named for the Dorset Horn Ram that lived in the brewery stables in Wandsworth. Young trademark is a also a design based on the animal. The beer is a proven symbol of Young's brewing heritage and has been a firm favorite with drinkers for over thirty years. Ram Rod is a 100% malt brew with Maris Otter and Crystal Malts combined with Fuggles and Golding hops.

WELLS & YOUNG'S YOUNG'S SPECIAL

Country of Origin: *U.K.* • **Brewery Founded:** *1875* • **Alcohol Content:** *4.5% (cask)*

Young's Special is a classic premium bitter with cult status amongst cask beer aficionados. The brew is amber in color. The beer is a 100% malt brew combining Maris Otter and Crystal malts with locally sourced British Fuggles and Goldings hops.

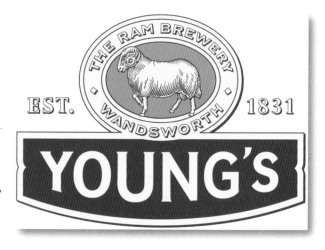

WYCHWOOD DR. THIRSTY'S

Country of Origin: *U.K.* • **Brewery Founded:** *1983* • **Alcohol Content:** *4.1% (bottle)*

This premium blonde beer is brewed with pale lager malt combined with a blend of four hops; Styrian, Cascade, Sovereign, and Chinook to produce a refreshingly crisp brew with a bitter finish. Wychwood's Brewery is noted for its intricate, fantasy-based label artwork. This is inspired by the myths and legends surrounding the ancient medieval Wychwood Forest. The brewery is now part of Marstons.

WYCHWOOD GOLIATH

Country of Origin: *U.K.* • **Brewery Founded:** *1983* • **Alcohol Content:** *4.2%*

Goliath is a traditionally craft-brewed ale made with Pale and Crystal Malts for an intense ruby color and rich malty taste. The brew uses Fuggles and Styrian Goldings hops for a classic refreshing bitterness. The beer is brewed by Wychwood and is only available in bottles.

WYCHWOOD HOBGOBLIN

Country of Origin: *U.K.* • **Brewery Founded:** *1983* • **Alcohol Content:** *5.2% (bottle), 4.5% (cask)*

Hobgoblin is the Wychwood's flagship beer. It is brewed at the Wychwood Brewery and was created by brewer Chris Moss. The beer is described by Wychwood as a ruby ale. Jeremy Moss, Wychwood's head brewer, describes the drink as "full bodied and well balanced with a chocolate toffee malt flavor, moderate bitterness and a distinctive fruity character with a ruby red glow." The beer was the first bottled beer in the United Kingdom to feature an illustrated label, as opposed to a simple text-based one. The beer is currently the fifth best-selling bottled ale in the UK.

WYCHWOOD KING GOBLIN

Country of Origin: *U.K.* • **Brewery Founded:** *1983* • **Alcohol Content:** *6.6%*

King Goblin is essentially a stronger and more flavorful variety of the brewery's Hobgoblin beer. It is a Special Reserve ale. It is currently available in bottles in the United Kingdom in Morrisons and Tesco supermarkets, and Draegers supermarkets in the United States. It is served on draught during real ale festivals at Britain's Wetherspoons public houses.

YOUNGER'S TARTAN ALE

Country of Origin: *U.K.* • **Brewery Founded:** *1778* • **Alcohol Content:** *3.7%*

Younger's make a range of quality ales in Scotland that have a long tradition and heritage. Younger's Tartan Special has recently been re-launched in cans by the brewery's new owners, Wells & Young. The beer is a medium gravity, dark Scottish ale whose sweet and slightly fruity character is balanced by a fine roast barley flavor. The beer is now brewed in Bedford, England.

UNITED STATES OF AMERICA

3 STARS BREWING COMPANY THE MOVEMENT

Country of Origin: *United States* • **Brewery Founded:** *2008* • **Alcohol content:** *5.9%*

3 Stars Brewing Company is based in Washington D.C. and was founded in 2011. It was launched by Dave Coleman and Mike McGarvey. The pair began as home brewers and worked out their own recipes for their brews, including the brewery's Syndicate Saison. This brew won a silver medal at the 2011 Maryland Governor's Cup competition. The pair is particularly interested in using rye as a brewing ingredient. The brewery has around twelve year-round offerings. The Movement is an American pale ale made with 2-row and Caravienna malts combined with Centennial and Cascade hops. The beer has an aroma of hops and flowers with subtle hop bitterness and a smooth clean finish.

49TH STATE BREWERY BAKED BLONDE

Country of Origin: *United States* • **Estate Founded:** *2010* • **Alcohol content:** *5.6%*

The 49th State Brewery is based in Denali Park, Alaska. It is the town's meeting point for sustainably-produced food, award-winning hand-crafted beers, and an energetic atmosphere right in the heart of Alaska. The brewery makes small-batch hand-crafted artisan ales and lagers, which are brewed on the premises. The brewery draws its inspiration from the great brewing cultures of the world, including those of Belgium, Great Britain, and the United States. The brewery combines the best malt, hops, water, and yeast to produce beers that are only served on tap. It has twelve core beers and several specialty beers. Baked Blonde is an unfiltered golden ale with fruit, floral, and honey notes in the aroma. The taste has malt sweetness and a clean hop flavor. The beer is brewed with 2-row and Munich Malts, Cascade, and Zythos Hops.

612 BREW SHERE KHAN

Country of Origin: *United States* • **Estate Founded:** *2013* • **Alcohol content:** *8.0%*

612 Brew was founded by Robert Kasak. The brewery is located in Minneapolis, Minnesota. Shere Khan (Tiger King) is a gorgeous orange color. Green cardamom and saffron are added at the five-minute mark of the brew. These unusual ingredients provide a strong peppermint aroma and a soft and delicate saffron flavor. The Topaz hops balance the Indian spices from the dry hopping addition. The brew is available in 612's taproom and other local bars and restaurants.

A. C. GOLDEN BREWING COMPANY COLORADO NATIVE

Country of Origin: *United States* • **Brewery Founded:** *2008* • **Alcohol Content:** *5.5%*

The A.C. Golden Brewing Company is a subsidiary of MillerCoors, a joint venture between SABMiller and Molson Coors Brewing Company. It is located in Golden, Colorado. Its purpose is to serve as a specialty brewing arm of MillerCoors. The A.C. Golden Brewery operates in the former pilot brewery of the Coors Brewery. The brewery launched its first beer, Herman Joseph's Private Reserve, in 2008. The company began brewing its seasonal beer, a Vienna-style lager called Winterfest, in 2009. In April 2010, A.C. Golden introduced Colorado Native lager. It is an amber lager made with 100% Colorado ingredients. The beer pours crystal-clear and copper-colored with a long-lasting head. It has a rather faint aroma of light biscuit scent and a wisp of hops. The taste is of toasted bread with evenly balanced light hop bitterness throughout. The beer has a crisp, clean, dry mouth feel with a lively carbonation.

ALASKAN BREWING COMPANY ALASKAN IPA

Country of Origin: *United States* • **Brewery Founded:** *1986* • **Alcohol Content:** *6.2%*

The Alaskan Brewing Company is a regional craft brewery located in Juneau, Alaska. The company's beers have won numerous awards at regional, national, and international beer competitions. The brewery was founded by Marcy and Geoff Larson. Alaskan Brewing currently produces five year-round beers, four limited release seasonal ales and several specialty beers with limited distribution each year. The beers are currently available in fifteen states. Their beers include Alaskan Amber, Alaskan Stout, Alaskan Winter Ale, and Alaskan Black IPA. Alaskan IPA is honey gold in color with a fruity, citrus aroma. A blend of hops and dry hopping (in which hops are added directly to the tanks during fermentation), give this brew a complex, aromatic character with a refreshing hop finish.

ALE INDUSTRIES GOLDEN STATE OF MIND

Country of Origin: *United States* • **Brewery Founded:** *1990s* • **Alcohol Content:** *4.4%*

Ale Industries was founded in Concord, California by brewers Morgan Cox and Steven Lopez. Cox and Lopez are now considering a move to Oakland, California. It is now planned to re-start the brewery in the former Norton bucket factory. One of Ale Industries best-known brews is the Golden State of Mind. This is a California native ale brewed with locally grown barley, oats, and wheat. Local and organic chamomile, orange peel, and coriander are added to the finish, which gives this beer an amazingly level of refreshment.

ALESMITH BREWING COMPANY X EXTRA PALE ALE

Country of Origin: *United States* • **Brewery Founded:** *1995* • **Alcohol Content:** *5.25%*

AleSmith Brewing Company was founded by Skip Virgilio and Ted Newcomb in San Diego, California. In 2002 the brewery was purchased by the company's brew master, Peter Zien. AleSmith produces a variety of beers, many of which have high alcohol content and are strongly hopped beers. The brewery is consistently rated among the best brewers in the world. In 2008, AleSmith was awarded the title of Small Brewing Company and Small Brewing Company Brewer of the Year at the Great American Beer Festival. AleSmith's beers are inspired by the brewing styles of Great Britain and Belgium and many of their beers are known for their depth of character. AleSmith X Extra Pale Ale is a clean, light-colored, light-bodied ale. The beer has a good dose of dry hops balanced by a gentle sweetness, giving an almost sweet-and-sour effect. The beer pours a light golden color, with a white head. The flavor is of citrus and pine, balanced by malty sweetness. This fades to a dry finish with a lingering hoppiness. The aroma has a strong lemon and citrus character, with sweet malt and pine in the background.

ALLAGASH BREWING COMPANY ALLAGASH BLACK

Country of Origin: *United States* • **Brewery Founded:** *1994* • **Alcohol Content:** *7.5%*

Allagash Brewing Company is located in Portland, Maine. It was founded by Rob Tod to offer a wide range of Belgian-style beers. Tod established a small fifteen-barrel brewery and began by brewing Allagash White, modeled after Belgian Wit beer. His beer gets its flavor from the use of wheat in place of barley as well as the addition of Curaçao, orange peel, coriander, and other spices. All of the beers the brewery produces are bottle conditioned. The technique calls for two fermentations, the first in the fermenting tanks and the second in the bottle itself (a process known as the methode champenoise). A coolship is then used to cool the wort. Before the beer is bottled, a small amount of yeast and sugar is added and a second fermentation occurs. Today, Allagash has six year-round beers in its portfolio, seven yearly releases and numerous one-offs and keg only releases. Allagash Black is a Belgian-style stout brewed with 2-row barley, torrified wheat, oats, roasted malt, and chocolate malt blended with a generous portion of dark caramelized candy sugar. The silky mouth feel balances the roasted character of the brew, which has coffee and dark chocolate notes.

AMHERST BREWING COMPANY GONE POSTAL IPA

Country of Origin: *United States* • **Brewery Founded:** *1997* • **Alcohol Content:** *7.0%*

The Amherst Brewing Company is a full-service brewpub located in Amherst, Massachusetts. The brewery was established by a small group of investors and originally occupied the lower level of the former First National Bank Building off North Pleasant Street. Gone Postal IPA is a collaboration brew, made with Ed Malachowski of the Amherst Post Office. The beer is Amherst's hoppiest ever brew, made with over two pounds of hops per barrel. The brew has big notes of citrus and pine with just enough malt flavor to provide good balance.

BARE HANDS BREWERY MAIL ORDER BRIDE

Country of Origin: *United States* • **Brewery Founded:** *2010* • **Alcohol Content:** *10.2%*

The Bare Hands Brewery is located in Granger, Indiana. It was founded with a simple ethos. The brewery is passionate about great beer and wants to share it with others. Their brews are hand-crafted in small batches with the highest quality ingredients. Bare Hands brews are only available on tap. Mail Order Bride is a Russian Imperial stout. It is a strong beer with a prominent chocolate, coffee, and malt aroma. It pours black with a moderate head. The flavor notes are of sweet chocolate, coffee grounds, and barley malt. The brew has a moderately bitter herbal finish.

BARLEY MOW BREWING COMPANY GOLDEN EXTRAVAGANZA!

Country of Origin: *United States* • **Brewery Founded:** *2000s* • **Alcohol Content:** *5.0%*

The Barley Mow Brewing Company is a nano brewery and tavern located in the downtown shopping district of Largo, Florida. Similar to a micro brewery, a nano brewery is a federally licensed brewery on an even smaller scale. Nano breweries are the fastest growing portion of the craft beer industry and have already begun producing award winning beers all over the United States. The Barley Mow Brewing Company is a two barrel brew house (a barrel is equal to thirty-one gallons). Barley Mow's Golden Extravaganza! is a blonde ale and is one of the brewery's lightest beers. It has light malt, light hops, and light alcohol and is a particularly refreshing beer.

BARREL HOUSE BREWING COMPANY POOR MAN'S BLONDE

Country of Origin: *United States* • **Brewery Founded:** *2000s* • **Alcohol Content:** *5.0%*

The Barrel House Brewing Company is nestled in the rolling hills of San Luis Obispo County in the heart of California's wine country. Barrel House's Poor Man's Blonde Style Ale is a smooth beer with aromas of hop and peach. This Blonde Style Ale is pumped full of delicious flavor. This is a craft beer drinker's blonde. Barrel House brew the beer with Mosaic hops. This beer imparts huge citrus and fruit character while it finishes slightly sweet and clean.

BARRIO BREWING COMPANY BARRIO IPA

Country of Origin: *United States* • **Brewery Founded:** *1995* • **Alcohol Content:** *7.2%*

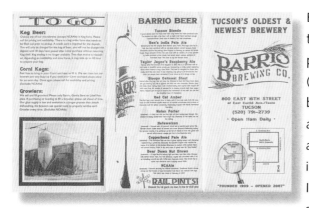

Barrio was founded by Dennis Arnold. It is based in Tucson, Arizona. At the time, Arnold had no brewing experience of any kind. Barrio is now in a new purpose-built brewing facility. The brewer's top sellers are Tucson Blonde (Arnold's original beer), the Barrio IPA, and Redcat Amber (which has also been brewed since the beginning). Barrio's Nolan's Porter and TJ Razzberry are named after Arnold's son and daughter. The brewer's Copperhead Ale and Oatmeal Stout date back to the 1990s. The Hefeweizen is the only beer in the regular line-up that has been created in the twenty-first century. Barrio IPA is brewed like the original IPA made at England's Burton-upon-Trent. This style calls for a high hop rate combined with an elevated alcohol content, because it was brewed to survive the journey from England to Bombay for the British troops stationed there. The beer is made with 2-row pale malt, specialty malts, and Columbus hops.

BAYOU TECHE BREWING BIERE ACADIE

Country of Origin: *United States* • **Brewery Founded:** *2009* • **Alcohol Content:** *6.0%*

Bayou Teche Brewing was founded to craft beers that compliment the cuisine and lifestyle of Cajuns and Creoles. With that mission, the Knott brothers decided to convert a discarded railroad car into a farmhouse brewery in Arnaudville, Louisiana. The old railroad car is now the home of several innovative ales. As a bière de garde, Acadie offers the style's prominent malty aroma. A freshly poured beer is highly carbonated and bronze-colored with a thick off-white head. The brew is malty with an underlying caramel sweetness, and finishes medium-dry. The restrained use of continental hops provides its balanced hop bitterness. Acadie offers the smooth roundness of an artisanal farmhouse ale. It is brewed year-round with the restrained use of Strisselspalt and Saaz hops.

BAXTER BREWING COMPANY PHANTOM PUNCH

Country of Origin: *United States* • **Brewery Founded:** *2000s* • **Alcohol Content:** *6.8%*

Baxter Brewing Company is based in Auburn, Maine. The brewery distributes its canned craft beers in six-packs and on draught. The brewery cans all of its beers because it believes that cans are better for the beer and the environment. Phantom Punch is Baxter's winter stout. It is a foreign extra stout with a hearty alcohol level. Its deep black hue and rich tan head compliment the full, but not overly-heavy body. Roasted and toasted malts dominate the flavor, with hints of caramel and strong notes of chocolate. Roasted organic cocoa nibs reinforce the malty chocolate flavors, while real vanilla beans suggest a touch of sweetness without weighing down the brew. Phantom Punch has just enough British hops to balance the stout's maltiness, but this is Baxter's least hoppy beer to-date. The beer pairs well with Mexican mole dishes, barbecue, grilled meats, rich creamy cheeses, and chocolate.

BEER ENGINE CAP EXPERIMENT

Country of Origin: *United States* • **Brewery Founded:** *2011* • **Alcohol Content:** *Variable%*

Beer Engine is Kentucky's smallest brewery and beer bar. It is located in Danville, Kentucky. The brewery sources its ingredients with the utmost care and develops unique beers that challenge the most experienced palate. CAP Experiment is a classic American pilsner, and the brewery makes a series of versions of this light, crisp, moderately-hopped lager. The bitterness and alcohol levels vary from batch to batch.

BELL'S BREWERY LAGER BEER

Country of Origin: *United States* • **Brewery Founded:** *1983* • **Alcohol Content:** *4.5%*

Bell's Brewery is based in Kalamazoo, Michigan, and has a second brewing facility in Comstock, Michigan. Bell's Brewery produces several different Bell's brand of beers. They also own the Eccentric Cafe brewpub. The brewery was founded by Larry Bell who made his first brews in a fifteen-gallon soup kettle and fermented the beer in open fermenters covered with saran wrap. Bell's flagship summer beer is now known as Oberon. Bell's Lager Beer is crafted with pilsner and Munich malts. It has a pronounced hop character. The beer pours a clear light pale straw color with a thin white head. The aroma is lightly grassy and the flavor is similar.

BIER BREWERY COMPANY SANITARIUM

Country of Origin: *United States* • **Brewery Founded:** *2011* • **Alcohol Content:** *13%*

Bier Brewery and Taproom is located in Indianapolis, Indiana. This brewery and taproom is committed to high quality. Its small size allows Bier to have the utmost control over the many variables that go into each hand-crafted batch. The results have been successful at various beer competitions. Bier won the Indiana State Fair Champion Brewery award in 2011 and 2012. The brewery also won a silver medal in the 2012 World Beer Cup in the Belgian Dubbel category and took silver at the Great American Beer Festival for its Belgian Quadruple, Sanitarium. The beer is a seasonal brew only available in the winter. It won a silver medal at the 2012 Great American Beer Fest in the Belgian-style Abby Ale category.

BIG ISLAND BREWHAUS LOOKING GLASS WHEAT ALE

Country of Origin: *United States* • **Brewery Founded:** *2011* • **Alcohol Content:** *5.0%*

Thomas Kerns began home-brewing for fun in 1988 and went on to found the Big Island Brewhaus in Kamuela, Hawaii. Within six months of opening the brewery's Overboard IPA won a gold medal at the U.S. Open Beer Championships with silver medals going to Big Island's White Mountain Porter and Red Giant Ale. Big Island brews up to fifteen distinct beers at any one time. The brewery's current beer list includes Looking Glass Wheat ale. This is Belgian-style wheat (wit) beer is crystal clear, but unfiltered. It is crisp and refreshing while also being flavorful with nuances of plum, bubblegum, and spice imparted by the special Belgian yeast. The beer also has flavors of subtle wheat and barley. Big Island also brews Malama Lager (a helles lager), Graham's Pilsner (a Bohemian-style pilsner), Pau Hana Pale Ale (an American style pale ale), Paniolo Pale Ale, Irie Irish Stout, Mele Mai Bock (a helles bock), White Mountain Porter, Overboard IPA, Red Giant Ale, Hoptopias IPA, Golden Sabbath, and Dark Sabbath (Belgian abbey ale).

BIG SKY BREWING COMPANY SCAPE GOAT

Country of Origin: *United States* • **Brewery Founded:** *1995* • **Alcohol Content:** *5.0%*

Big Sky Brewing Company was started by Neal Leathers, Bjorn Nabozney, and Brad Robinson. Brad and Neal had been home brewers in Michigan since the mid 1980s. The brewery is located in Missoula, Montana. Their first step was to produce and star in a series on MCAT, Missoula's local cable access television station. The program was called Beer Talk and consisted of Brad and Neal tasting various beers and commenting on them. The show was a big hit. Big Sky's first beer was Whistle Pig Red Ale. Big Sky's Scape Goat is a classic British pale ale beer, brewed with Montana flair. It is made from East Kent Goldings and Crystal hops. It is a crisp and thirst-quenching beer with citrus tasting notes.

BIG WOODS BREWING COMPANY HARE TRIGGER IPA

Country of Origin: *United States* • **Brewery Founded:** *2012* • **Alcohol Content:** *6.5%*

Big Woods Village is a micro brewery destination located in the heart of Brown County, Indiana. The village is home to Big Woods Brewing Company, Big Woods Pizza Company, & Big Woods Gallery. Big Woods Hare Trigger IPA is brewed to be traditional to the style. It is made with caramel and Pale Malts combined with Warrior & Cascade Hops. Its slightly higher alcohol content means that the beer lasts well.

THE BREWHOUSE SANTA BARBARA NIRVANA PALE ALE

Country of Origin: *United States* • **Brewery Founded:** *2002* • **Alcohol Content:** *5.5%*

Brewhouse
Santa Barbara, CA

The Brewhouse Santa Barbara's brews are hand-crafted to be enjoyed on its premises in Santa Barbara. This ensures that their customers enjoy the freshest possible beer that has never traveled more than a few feet. Their beers are brewed in small, seven barrel batches in two large copper vessels. The brewer's beers include Nirvana Pale Ale, West Beach IPA, Honey Brown Ale, Condor Pilsner, Montecito Street Wheat, Apricot Wheat, Saint Barb's Ales, Vow of Blindness, Baseball Saison, Breakwater Wit, and Habanero Pilsner. Nirvana Pale Ale is a West Coast pale ale. It is made from pale and crystal malts, and a generous amount of Cascade hops.

BRIDGE BREW WORKS BELGIAN BLONDE DUBBEL

Country of Origin: *United States* • **Brewery Founded:** *2010* • **Alcohol Content:** *6.1%*

Bridge Brew Works was founded by Ken Linch and Nathan in Fayetteville, West Virginia. It is a small craft brewery that specializes in Belgian-style brews. Its beers are sold in bottles and on draught throughout West Virginia. Belgian Blonde Dubbel pours an opaque ruby chestnut and had a medium tan-colored head. The aroma has significant dark fruit, of fig, raisin, and plum. The flavor follows suit and also has lightly roasted and earthy hop notes. The mouth feel is medium and the finish is fruity and earthy.

BROKEN TOOTH BREWING BEAR TOOTH ALE

Country of Origin: *United States* • **Brewery Founded:** *2000* • **Alcohol Content:** *6.0%*

Broken Tooth Brewing is based in Anchorage, Alaska. Clarke Pelz is the brewer there. Broken Tooth's beers include Bear Tooth Ale, Fairweather IPA, Hard Apple Ale, Hefeweizen, Northern Lights Amber, Pipeline Stout, Polar Pale Ale, Prince William Porter, and Wild Country Raspberry Wheat. Broken Tooth's Bear Tooth Ale is an American brown ale. It is light brown in color, with a tan head and slight haze. The beer is more assertively hopped than many brown ales, it has a clean and citrus aroma with subtle malty sweetness. Malt and hops dominate the flavor of the brew.

BRONX BREWERY BRONX PALE ALE

Country of Origin: *United States* • **Brewery Founded:** *2011* • **Alcohol Content:** *6.3%*

The Bronx Brewery is a small, craft brewery in the Port Morris section of the South Bronx. It was launched by a small team with two things in common: a maniacal focus on creating high-quality beer and a passion for the Bronx and New York City. Its traditionally-crafted pales ales use only premium and minimally-processed materials to create fresh, bold beer from a borough known for its bold character. Bronx beers can now be found throughout New York. Bronx Pale Ale is the brewery's flagship beer. This deep amber, American pale ale is brewed with five different barley malts, generous additions of Cascade and Centennial hops, and a unique strain of yeast. The British, German, and American malts used provide a blend of caramel, biscuit, and nutty malt flavors. The kettle and whole leaf dry hops provide a gentle, pleasant bitterness with an intense floral and citrus aroma. The beer is available year-round.

BROOKLYN BREWERY BROOKLYN LAGER

Country of Origin: *United States* • **Brewery Founded:** *1988* • **Alcohol Content:** *5.2%*

Brooklyn Brewery aspires to make flavorful beers that enrich the life, tradition, and culture of the communities it serves. It has an award-winning roster of year-round, seasonal, and specialty beers. Brooklyn now has the reputation of being one of the top craft beer producers in the world. The brewery claims to export more beer than any other American craft brewery. Brooklyn's brew master Garrett Oliver is widely acknowledged as the world's foremost scholar on beer. He is the author of *The Brew master's Table: Discovering The Pleasures of Real Beer with Real Food*. Brooklyn Lager is amber-gold in color and displays a firm malt character supported by a refreshing bitterness and floral hop aroma. Caramel malts show in the finish. The aromatic qualities of the beer are enhanced by dry-hopping. This is the centuries-old practice of steeping the beer with fresh hops as it undergoes a long, cold maturation. The result is a flavorful beer, smooth, and refreshing. Brooklyn has used a Viennese beer style to create an American original.

THE BRUERY ORCHARD WHITE

Country of Origin: *United States* • **Brewery Founded:** *2008* • **Alcohol Content:** *5.4%*

The Bruery is a brewing company based in Placentia, California. It was founded by Patrick Rue and named as a fusion between his family name and the word brewery. The brewery produces an average of 2,500 barrels of beer annually at their fifteen-barrel brew house. The Bruery's year-round collection includes Saison Rue, Mischief, Loakal Red, Seven Grain Season, and Orchard White. Orchard White is an unfiltered, bottle conditioned Belgian-style witbier. This hazy, straw yellow beer is spiced with coriander, citrus peel, and lavender, which are added to the boil. A spicy, fruity yeast strain is used to add complexity, and rolled oats are added for a silky texture. Orchard White was named one of the top twenty-five beers of 2008 by *Draft* Magazine.

BUCKET BREWERY THIRTEENTH ORIGINAL MAPLE STOUT

Country of Origin: *United States* • **Brewery Founded:** *2011* • **Alcohol Content:** *6.4%*

The Bucket Brewery was incorporated in June 2011. It found a home in the Lorraine Mills in Pawtucket, Rhode Island in September. The brewery was founded by two avid home brewers. Thirteenth Original Maple Stout was the result of a brewing accident, where maple syrup was added to a ruined brew. The beer combines a complex malt base, a healthy dose of maple syrup, and an unusual blend of hops. This beer is truly original.

BULL & BUSH BREWERY
MAN BEER

Country of Origin: *United States* • **Brewery Founded:** *1997* • **Alcohol Content:** *6.5%*

Dean and Dale Peterson founded the Bull & Bush Brewery. The business started out as a pub, but became a brewery in 1997. The Bull & Bush brewing operation has become world renowned for its great-tasting and innovative creations. Master brewer Gabe Moline's brews have earned multiple accolades including the Best Beer in a Brewpub award at Westword's Best of Denver, and multiple awards at the annual Denver-hosted Great American Beer Festival. Man Beer is an IPA that has an aroma of malt and hops. The taste is of slightly roasted malt and is nicely balanced with hops, and a hint of pine. It has a bitter finish and is not overly hoppy or malty.

BUNKER BREWING COMPANY
MACHINE CZECH PILS

Country of Origin: *United States* • **Brewery Founded:** *2011* • **Alcohol Content:** *5.2%*

Bunker Brewing Company is a small artisan brewery located in the East Bayside neighborhood of Portland, Maine. Its passion is to create the best experimental, traditional, and seasonal brews, three and a half barrels at a time. The brewery was found by Chresten Sorensen and Jay Villani. The brewery's flagship beer is its Machine Czech Pils. The beer has old-world charm. Its biscuity German malt meets Saaz hops to create a classic Czech-style pilsner.

BURNT HICKORY BREWERY
FIGHTING BISHOP

Country of Origin: *United States* • **Brewery Founded:** *2011* • **Alcohol Content:** *8.5%*

The Burnt Hickory Brewery is located in Kennesaw and Georgia. The brewery made its first beer on April 1, 2012. Burnt Hickory operates as a self-financed nano brewery (the brewery produces under two-hundred barrels of beer a year). The brewery makes a range of colorfully-named beers including Ezekiel's wheel, Cannon dragger, Big Shanty, Fighting Bishop, and Old Wooden Head. Fighting Bishop is a Belgian-style Trippel is made with green peppercorns. It is a strong Belgian ale with a golden color and spicy taste.

BURLEY OAK BREWING COMPANY BUNKER C

Country of Origin: *United States* • **Brewery Founded:** *2011* • **Alcohol Content:** *6.6%*

The Burley Oak Brewing Company is located in the town of Berlin, Maryland. The town is situated in the Burley Plantation, a 300-acre land grant dating back to 1677. The brewery is based in a building that was originally a cooperage. Burley is now bringing barrels back to the building to age their hand-crafted ales. Burley Oak's Bunker C is available year-round. It is a robust porter, pitch black in color with notes of baking chocolate, fresh coffee, and a distinct umami character. The beer is named after the term for crude oil and shares its rich dark color.

CANTERBURY ALEWORKS CANTERBURY ALE

Country of Origin: *United States* • **Brewery Founded:** *2000s* • **Alcohol Content:** *5.5%*

Canterbury AleWorks is a one-barrel, water-powered, and wood fired nano brewery that handcrafts world-class ales with local flare. The brewery was founded by Steve Allman and is located in Canterbury, New Hampshire. Canterbury Ale is available on tap. It is an American Pale Ale with an excellent balance. Citrusy Cascade hops and crisp subdued malt ensure that this golden all-American Pale Ale will become a refreshing home-town classic.

CAPE COD BEER BEACH BLONDE ALE

Country of Origin: *United States* • **Brewery Founded:** *2004* • **Alcohol Content:** *4.9%*

In its first year of operation, Cape Cod Beer had twelve customers and one employee. The brewery delivered its first beers in a minivan. The brewery grew and its Beach Blonde Ale is now described as a "holiday in a glass." The brew is one of Cape Cod's year-round brews, and is an American golden ale. Light and refreshing, it is a very drinkable golden ale with a hint of toasted malt character and a clean finish. This refreshing light bodied and golden colored American blonde ale is smooth and easy drinking.

CAPE MAY BREWING COMPANY CAPE MAY IPA

Country of Origin: *United States* • **Brewery Founded:** *2010* • **Alcohol Content:** *6.0%*

Cape May Brewing Company is located in Rio Grande, New Jersey. The brewery set out to create fresh, delicious beer for South Jersey. Cape May was the first micro-brewery at the Jersey Shore. Cape May IPA is the brewery's flagship beer. It is a decidedly hoppy, bitter, and moderately strong American Pale Ale. It is brewed with Cascade hops. These give floral and citrus notes to the brew. This IPA emphasizes the hop aroma and flavor, while muting the hop bitterness.

CAPITAL BREWERY WISCONSIN AMBER

Country of Origin: *United States* • **Brewery Founded:** *1984* • **Alcohol Content:** *5.2%*

Capital Brewery is located in Middleton, Wisconsin. It was founded by Ed Janus, and works out of a former egg processing plant. The company produces over 30,000 barrels of beer annually. It produces nineteen distinct beers, of which eight are annuals, five are seasonals, and six are limited release brews. Most are made using the strict Reinheitsgebot guidelines. The company's beers have won individual awards at a number of competitions, including the Great American Beer Festival, and The Great Taste of the Midwest. Capital Brewery won the title of America's #1 Rated Brewery at the World Beer Championships in 1998. Capital was named the Grand National Champion in the 2013 US Open Beer Championship. The brewery's beer list includes Wisconsin Amber, Mutiny, Capital Dark, Capital Pilsner, US Pale Ale, Island Wheat, and Supper Club. Capital Wisconsin Amber pours a clear light amber with a finger of head. The beer tastes of caramel, toffee, sweet corn, candied apple, bready malts, and fruit.

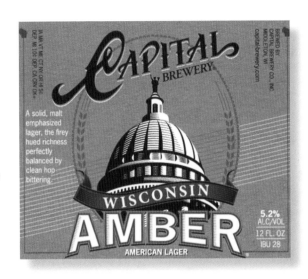

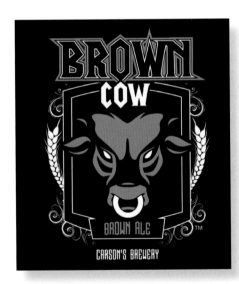

CARSON'S BREWERY BROWN COW

Country of Origin: *United States* • **Brewery Founded:** *2012* • **Alcohol Content:** *5.0%*

Carson's Brewery was founded in 2012 in Evansville, Indiana and is now Southern Indiana's premier micro brewery. Carson's started with barrel-sized brews that were used to test, improve, and perfect many different types of beer. The best became their core offerings, a range of American ales, wheats, brown ales, IPAs, and seasonal brews. Brown Cow has a complex biscuit and dark toast aroma. A beige head tops this copper-brown beer. The beer has tasting notes of nutty malt with balancing hops and a medium dry finish.

CAUTION BREWING COMPANY HONEY MATRIMONY BROWN ALE

Country of Origin: *United States* • **Brewery Founded:** *2009* • **Alcohol Content:** *5.9%*

Caution is located in Denver, Colorado. The brewery makes a good selection of four different flagship beers. Caution's Honey Matrimony Brown Ale is made with wildflower honey from Clark's Honey Farm in Evans, Colorado, and base malts from the Colorado Malting Company in Alamosa. By starting with a well balanced American brown ale, Caution's proprietary techniques allows the delicate aroma and flavors of honey to come through perfectly. The beer is the perfect marriage of Colorado ingredients.

CELLARMAKER BREWING COMPANY
CELLARMAKER HOP KILLAH

Country of Origin: *United States* • **Brewery Founded:** *2007* • **Alcohol Content:** *7.1%*

Cellarmaker is a San Francisco, California brewery producing beers in small batches one beer at a time. The brewery's limited output and choice allows them to experiment with different hops, barrels, and yeasts. They make highly aromatic hoppy beers featuring the following hops: Nelson Sauvin, Galaxy, Motueka, Simcoe, Citra, Amarillo, Mosaic, Centennial and more. Cellarmaker Hop Killah is an India Pale Ale with a deep golden color and white head. It has a lightly resinous aroma. The flavor is of malt and light caramels with light toast and a trace of biscuit.

CENTRAL COAST BREWING CATCH 23

Country of Origin: *United States* • **Brewery Founded:** *1998* • **Alcohol Content:** *7.5%*

Central Coast Brewing is based in San Luis Obispo, California. Unusually, this craft brewer cans most of its brews. Central Coast's Catch 23 beer is a Black IPA. The beer pours quite dark brown/black and has a medium beige head. Its aroma is of citrus and grapefruit forward, with some roasted malt notes in the background. The flavor is about the same, with some pine resin and molasses. The rye presents as a bit of a bite.

CIGAR CITY BREWING CUBANO-
STYLE ESPRESSO BROWN ALE

Country of Origin: *United States* • **Brewery Founded:** *2008* • **Alcohol Content:** *5.5%*

Cigar City Brewing is an award-winning brewery in Tampa, Florida. The brewery also has an outlet in the Tampa International Airport. The brewery's Cubano-Style Espresso Brown Ale is a rich brown ale redolent with Cuban-style roasted espresso beans. The flavor also has sweet caramel, toffee, and hints of dry nuttiness. Cuban Espresso is a popular drink in the Cigar City of Tampa owing to its many Sicilian and Cuban immigrants. The beans for Cubano-Style Espresso Brown Ale are roasted locally by

Mazzaro's Italian Market and Deli in St. Petersburg, Florida to the brewery's exact specifications. The beer pours brown in color.

DC BRAU THE PUBLIC PALE ALE

Country of Origin: *United States* • **Brewery Founded:** *2011* • **Alcohol Content:** *6.0%*

Owned by Brandon Skall and Jeff Hancock, DC Brau is the first beer brewer to open in Washington DC since 1956. The brewery ranked fifth in 2013's list of The Ten Fastest-Growing Craft Breweries in the United States. DC Brau has grown from producing 1,698 barrels of beer in 2011 to 5,002 barrels in 2012. DC Brau's The Public Pale Ale is brewed in the classic American pale ale style. Its assertive bitterness is backed by C-60 and Vienna malts, which lend notes of rich, yet semi-dry caramel. The aroma is of white grapefruit and citrus. It pours a crimson copper color and is available year-round. The Public is DC Brau's most popular offering.

DARK HORSE BREWERY THE CROOKED TREE IPA

Country of Origin: *United States* • **Brewery Founded:** *1997* • **Alcohol Content:** *6.0%*

The Dark Horse Brewery is a micro brewery and tap room in Marshall, Michigan. It was founded by Aaron Morse. The Dark Horse brews a variety of beers and beer styles, including Crooked Tree India Pale Ale, Amber Ale, Raspberry Ale, Sapient Trip Ale, Boffo Brown Beer, and Black Bier. Several seasonal and experimental brews are also produced. Dark Horse hand-folds and stocks every six-pack produced. Dark Horse has won several medals at various brewing competitions. Crooked Tree IPA was inspired by West Coast IPAs but is brewed with Michigan style. The Crooked Tree is heavily dry hopped to give it a big aroma of pine and citrus. The flavors are big, yet very balanced between fresh hops and malt. The hops give the brew a fruit flavor that finishes dry, crisp, and clean. It pours a deep copper color with a bit of haziness.

DESCHUTES BREWERY MIRROR POND ALE

Country of Origin: *United States* • **Brewery Founded:** *1988* • **Alcohol Content:** *5.0%*

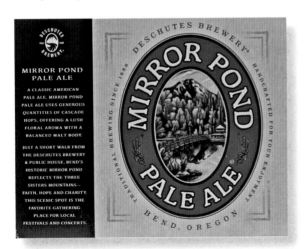

Deschutes is a craft brewery located in Bend, Oregon. The company, founded by Gary Fish, produces a range of beers which it distributes to twenty-one states. As of 2012, it was the fifth-largest craft brewery in the United States. In June 2013 Ernst & Young recognized Gary Fish as a Pacific Northwest Entrepreneur of the Year. Deschutes produces a range of beers including Black Butte Porter, Mirror Pond Pale Ale, Chainbreaker White IPA, Deschutes River Ale, Obsidian Stout, Red Chair NWPA, Twilight Summer Ale, Jubelale, Hop Henge, Fresh Squeezed IPA, Hop Trip, Chasin' Freshies, The Dissident, Mirror Mirror, and the highly acclaimed The Abyss. Mirror Pond has consistently won awards in the pale ale category at various brewing competitions, including the gold medal at the 2010 Great American Beer Festival and the World's Best Premium Pale Ale in 2010. Deschutes's Black Butte is the best-selling craft porter in the United States. The company's spring seasonal, Red Chair Northwest Pale Ale, was named the World's Best Beer in 2012. Deschutes uses an in-house, proprietary yeast strain resembling Wyeast Laboratories' Ringwood Ale yeast.

DEVIL'S CANYON BREWING COMPANY CALIFORNIA SUNSHINE RYE IPA

Country of Origin: *United States* • **Brewery Founded:** *2001* • **Alcohol Content:** *7.1%*

Devil's Canyon Brewing Company, located in the heart of the San Francisco Bay area peninsula, produces award-winning, hand-crafted beers and root beer brewed with premium ingredients. Prior to the 1780s the canyon portion of Belmont and San Carlos was known as the Devil's Canyon. Since opening their doors in 2001, Devil's Canyon Brewery has won over thirty-five awards for its craft beers and received the 2009 People's Choice award at the San Francisco International Beer Festival. In 2013 Devil's Canyon was voted the favorite brewery in the Bay Area. California Sunshine Rye IPA is one of Devil's Canyon's core products. It is exceptionally well balanced with assertive hop bitterness, a toasty and bready malt mouth feel, and a grassy, dry finish. It is the brewery's re-interpretation of a traditional unfiltered English-style IPA.

DOGFISH HEAD BREWERY 90 MINUTE IMPERIAL IPA

Country of Origin: *United States* • **Brewery Founded:** *1995* • **Alcohol Content:** *9.0%*

Dogfish Head Brewery is based in Milton, Delaware and was founded by Sam Calagione. Dogfish Head grew nearly 400% between 2003 and 2006. The brewery takes its name from Dogfish Head, Maine where Calagione spent summers as a child. The brewery makes several extreme beers, such as Liquor de Malt, a bottle-conditioned malt liquor. Dogfish Head products often use non-standard ingredients, such as green raisins in "Raison D'Être". Some beers, including the WorldWide Stout, 120 Minute India Pale Ale, and the raspberry-flavored strong ale Fort, are highly alcoholic, reaching 18% to 20% alcohol by volume. One of Dogfish Head's most notable beers was a green beer called Verdi Verdi Good, produced in 2005. Its green color was derived from brewing the beer with blue-green algae. 90 Minute Imperial IPA has been described as one of the best IPA's in America. It is a big beer with a great malt backbone that stands up to the extreme hopping. The beer tastes of brandied fruitcake, raisins, and citrus.

DRAGOON BREWING COMPANY DRAGOON IPA

Country of Origin: *United States* • **Brewery Founded:** *Mid-1990s* • **Alcohol Content:** *9.0%*

The Dragoon Brewing Company was founded by Bruce Greene when he brewed his first batch of beer in his kitchen. Right then he decided to start saving to open his own brewery. Within a few years, Bruce's son Eric had also been bitten by the brewing bug. Dragoon is located in Tucson, Arizona. In 2009 Dragoon started to brew Dragoon IPA. This is a classic West Coast IPA. It is pale in color, with bracing bitterness, and a high alcohol content. It has fruity, floral, citrus hop aroma. It is made from a simple malt bill with North American malt base and pale caramel malt. Dragoon use copious amounts of Northwest hops throughout the boil. After fermentation is complete, Dragoon dry hop the beer with Crystal 15, Crystal 60, Columbus, Zythos, and Magnum hops.

FOUR FRIENDS BREWING QUEEN CITY RED

Country of Origin: *United States* • **Brewery Founded:** *2007* • **Alcohol Content:** *6.0%*

The Four Friends brewery is located in the heart of Charlotte, North Carolina to fulfill a growing demand for hand-crafted quality beer. Four Friends crafts the finest possible beer in small batches. Head brewer Jonathan Fulcher makes brews with complex aromas, silky bodies, and an explosion of flavor. Queen City Red is an Irish Red Ale. The beer pours a deep mahogany red. It is created with six malts blended in perfect harmony. The beer is smooth and subtle yet robust and rich with flavors of coffee, malt, chocolate, and toffee.

FOUR PEAKS BREWERY KILT LIFTER

Country of Origin: *United States* • **Brewery Founded:** *1996* • **Alcohol Content:** *8.0%*

Four Peaks Brewery is an Arizona brewery and restaurant. The original and main location is in an old creamery and warehouse on 8th Street in Tempe, Arizona. The building was built in 1892 as an ice plant and served as a creamery until 1953. Its selection of beers varies, but several favorites (including Kilt Lifter and 8th Street Ale) are available on tap, in bottles, in cans at local bars and restaurants throughout the South western United States. The brewery usually also has one or more real ales ready to serve, and depending on the season, cult favorites like Pumpkin Porter may also be available. Four Peaks has gained nationwide fame in recent years as a result of earning numerous awards at the annual Great American Beer Festival in Denver, Colorado. Categories in which Four Peaks brews were recognized and awarded medals include Scottish Style Ale, American-Style Strong Pale Ale and English-Style Bitter, just to name a few. Kilt Lifter pours a clear light brown color. The beer has a creamy aroma and the taste is also creamy with sharp malty notes.

FRANCONIA BREWERY
FRANCONIA LAGER

Country of Origin: *United States* • **Brewery Founded:** *2008* • **Alcohol Content:** *4.8%*

Dennis Wehrman is the brew master and owner of the Franconia brewery. Franconia is located in McKinney, Texas. Dennis studied brewing at the University of Munich, Germany. His family brewing history dates back to 1800. Franconia focuses on environmental sustainability and is in the process of becoming 100% energy independent. Its Franconia Lager is a full-bodied southern German-style lager. It is deep golden in color and contains a malty sweetness throughout the pint. The brew is made with traditional Bavarian lager yeast and aged for at least six weeks. This maturation makes the beer smooth to drink. It is made with 2-row pale malt and Munich malt.

FROTHY BEARD BREWING COMPANY LOWCOUNTRY LIBATIONS BRACKISH BROWN

Country of Origin: *United States* • **Brewery Founded:** *2007* • **Alcohol Content:** *5.91%*

Frothy Beard is located in North Charleston, South Carolina. The brewery grew out of a passion for creativity, culinary arts, and beer. The three owners, Michael Biondi, Steve McCauley and Joey Siconolfi have been friends for over a decade and have been brewing together for the last six years. The brewery's Lowcountry Libations Brackish Brown is an American Brown Ale. The brew is a Frothy Beard collaboration with Low Country Libations winner Braden Haragen.

FULLSTREAM BREWERY FULLSTREAM LAGER

Country of Origin: *United States* • **Brewery Founded:** *2010* • **Alcohol Content:** *5.5%*

Fullsteam is based in Durham, North Carolina. Its beers are inspired by the food and farm traditions of the South and their mission is to pioneer the art of distinctly Southern beer. Fullsteam brews both traditional and experimental beers with Southern produce, including heirloom grains and seasonal botanicals. The brewery also runs a dog-friendly tavern in Durham. Fullstream lager is the brewery's best-known brew. It was also their first beer. It is an American common lager, a hoppy amber beer. The brew won a gold medal at the 2012 U.S. Beer Open in the American Amber/California Common category.

GENESEE BREWING COMPANY GENESEE BEER

Country of Origin: *United States* • **Brewery Founded:** *1878* • **Alcohol Content:** *4.5%*

Genesee Brewing Company is located on the Genesee River in Rochester, New York. Local brewery Reisky and Spies changed hands and was renamed as the Genesee Brewery in 1878. Genesee Beer is an American lager. The beer pours a clear light golden with a fluffy white head. It has average visible carbonation. The beer smells of malt with very mild hops. The flavor is light with pale malts and a touch of hopping. It is quite sweet. The beer has a light body with a good amount of carbonation. The beer has a crisp and refreshing finish.

GENEVA LAKE BREWING COMPANY WEEKENDER WHEAT

Country of Origin: *United States* • **Brewery Founded:** *2011* • **Alcohol Content:** *4.6%*

Geneva Lake was founded by father and son team Pat and Jonathan McIntosh who co-own the brewery. It is located in Redmond, Wisconsin. The pair brews Geneva Lake's beers to original recipes developed by Jonathan McIntosh. The brewery currently has five year-round brews. One of these is Weekender Wheat. This classic wheat beer offers classic thirst quenching refreshment. The beer is very smooth and drinkable, a great beer for the warmer months. It pours yellow with a white head. Geneva Lake's brews are served in the brewery's taproom.

GHOST RIVER BREWING GOLDEN ALE

Country of Origin: *United States* • **Brewery Founded:** *2008* • **Alcohol Content:** *4.0%*

Ghost River Brewing knows that great water makes great beer and that some of the greatest drinking water on earth is available in west Tennessee. The brewery is located in Memphis. Brewing locally guarantees that every hand-crafted, full-flavored Ghost River brew is the freshest beer available. Ghost River Golden Ale is a Kolsch-style beer brewed with Munich and caramel malts and German hops. It is a mellow and refreshing brew. The beer is available all year.

GLACIER BREWHOUSE BAVARIAN HEFEWEIZEN

Country of Origin: *United States* • **Brewery Founded:** *1996* • **Alcohol Content:** *5.0%*

The Glacier BrewHouse is based in Anchorage, Alaska. The brewery specializes in English and American West Coast-style beers and has an elaborate oak aging program. In 2012, the brewery produced 4,500 barrels of beer. All Glacier's brews are created and brewed on the premises. Head Brewer Kevin Burton has been brewing beer in Alaska for over sixteen years. The brewery has fourteen beers on tap including Raspberry Wheat, Imperial Blonde, and Eisbock. Glacier's Bavarian Hefeweizen has fruity aromas of banana and clove. The beer is made with premium German pilsner malt and German Tettnang hops. The brew has a low bitterness and is refreshing and smooth.

GOLDEN ROAD BREWING POINT THE WAY IPA

Country of Origin: *United States* • **Brewery Founded:** *2011* • **Alcohol Content:** *5.9%*

Golden Road Brewing aims to create a range of craft beers that reflect the way people live in dynamic Los Angeles. Golden Road Brewing's ethos is to make session beers that people can enjoy every day. The brewery also makes limited release beers and custom-brewed IPAs. Golden Road's Point The Way IPA is made with 2-row, Golden Promise, and Cara malts and Cascade, Chinook, HBC 342, Galena, and Warrior hops.

GOOSE ISLAND BREWERY 312 URBAN WHEAT ALE

Country of Origin: *United States* • **Brewery Founded:** *1995* • **Alcohol Content:** *4.2%*

Goose Island Brewery is located in Chicago, Illinois. It began as a single brewpub, established by John Hall. The brewery was bought by Anheuser-Busch in 2011. Goose Island produces several year-round and seasonal styles of craft beer, the best-known of which are 312 Urban Wheat Ale and Honker's Ale. Goose Island's beers are distributed across the United States and Britain. Goose Island's 312 Urban Wheat Ale has a spicy aroma of Cascade hops. This is followed by a crisp, fruity ale flavor delivered in a smooth, creamy body. The beer pours a hazy straw. It is brewed with a selection of hops, including First Gold, Liberty, and Cascade combined with 2-row and torrified wheat malt.

GORDON BIERSCH BREWERY CZECH STYLE PILSNER

Country of Origin: *United States* • **Brewery Founded:** *1988* • **Alcohol Content:** *5.3%*

Gordon Biersch Brewery was founded by Dan Gordon and Dean Biersch. Gordon (a graduate of the five-year brewing engineering program at Weihenstephan, Germany) and Biersch opened their first brewery restaurant in Palo Alto, California in July 1988. In 1999, the restaurants were sold to what ultimately became CraftWorks Restaurants & Breweries. Gordon Biersch currently brews beer for Costco and Trader Joe's under contract. The Gordon Biersch brewery and bottling plant is located in San Jose, California. The brewer makes bock, hefeweizen, kolsch, marzen, and a Czech-style pilsner. Gordon Biersch's pilsner pours a clear straw with a thick white head. The aroma is of grain and grass. The taste has a balance of sweetness, Noble hops, and some grassiness. The beer has a medium body and carbonation.

GRAND TETON BREWING BITCH CREEK

Country of Origin: *United States* • **Brewery Founded:** *1988* • **Alcohol Content:** *6.0%*

Grand Teton Brewing is the original brewery of Grand Teton and Yellowstone National Parks. The brewery is located in Victor, Idaho, at the base of the Teton Mountains. The brewery uses glacial run-off water in its brews. This unique resource surfaces at a spring a half mile from the brewery. The Teton Valley also grows good malting barley, and their hops come from Southern Idaho. Bitch Creek beer is named for a local landmark. The creek is spring fed and flows out of the west side of the Grand Tetons. This extra special brown ale balances big malt sweetness and robust hop flavor for full bodied mahogany ale. The beer is brewed with Idaho 2-row malted barley, German Melanoidin, CaraAmber, CaraAroma, and CaraMunich malts with Galena,

HANGAR 24 CRAFT BREWERY
ORANGE WHEAT BEER

Country of Origin: *United States* • **Brewery Founded:** *2007* • **Alcohol Content:** *4.6%*

Ben Cook, Founder and master brewer fell in love with beer and its culture. Wanting to learn more, he attended and graduated from the Master Brewers Program at the University of California, Davis. Following graduation, Ben found a great location for his brewery, adjacent to California's Redlands Airport. Aptly, he named his brewery Hangar 24. Hangar 24 Orange Wheat beer is one of the brewery's year-round offerings. It is crisp, tangy, and refreshing. The citrus aroma, light mouth feel, and tangy finish are this unfiltered beer's trademarks. This is accomplished by adding whole locally grown oranges throughout the brewing process, which perfectly coalesce with the wheat and barley base. The beer won a gold medal at the 2012 Los Angeles International Commercial Beer Competition.

HARLEM BREWING COMPANY
SUGAR HILL GOLDEN ALE

Country of Origin: *United States* • **Brewery Founded:** *1920s/1996* • **Alcohol Content:** *4.0%*

The Harlem Brewing Company was first established in the Prohibition era. Its beer was served in speakeasies and was said to be the brew of choice for the many of the famous artists and performers who worked in Harlem during this era. The brewery floundered, but was re-established in 1996 with the launch of Sugar Hill Golden Ale. This has an unusually rich and smooth character with a well-balanced taste and artisanal quality. The beer has a subtle citrus accent with a hoppy finish.

HARPOON BREWERY HARPOON IPA

Country of Origin: *United States* • **Brewery Founded:** *1986* • **Alcohol Content:** *5.9%*

The Harpoon Brewery is a micro brewery, with plants in Boston, Massachusetts and Windsor, Vermont. The brewery was the first company to obtain a permit to manufacture and sell alcohol in the Commonwealth of Massachusetts in over twenty-five years and has played an important part in the rebirth of the American micro brewery system. It is now the ninth-largest craft brewery and sixteenth-largest brewery in the United States. The brewery is best-known for its Harpoon IPA. The brewery also brews multiple other year-round beers including the award-winning Dark, UFO Hefeweizen, UFO Raspberry Hefeweizen, UFO White, Leviathan IPA Rich, and Dan's Rye IPA. Harpoon also has four seasonal beers, an Octoberfest Marzen style ale and Celtic Red, a beer made in the style of an Irish red for St. Patrick's Day. Harpoon IPA was first brewed in 1993 and has now become a New England classic. It began as a summer seasonal but is now Harpoon's bestselling beer and their flagship ale. The beer finds harmony in the combination of hops, malt, and yeast so that no single ingredient dominates the drinking experience. The blend of malt provides depth in body and color, and is balanced by a pleasantly hoppy finish. The citrus and pine of Cascade hops complement a sturdy malt backbone and the floral aromas of Harpoon's yeast.

HARVEST MOON BREWERY & CAFÉ PIGS ASS PORTER

Country of Origin: *United States* • **Brewery Founded:** *1996* • **Alcohol Content:** *5.0%*

Harvest Moon is located in Belt, Montana. It was founded by Stan Guedesse and John Ballantyne. Pigs Ass Porter was first brewed by Harvest Moon in 1997. It is a multiple award-winning dark ale brewed in the Burton-on-Trent English style. This was due to the similarity of water chemistry in Belt compared to this classic English porter producing area. The brew has plenty of body without a sharp bite. The ale is brewed with pale, caramel, chocolate, and black malts to create a creamy, smooth, roasted, slightly chocolate tasting ale that has a touch of hops in the finish. This ale can be enjoyed in every season and is best when served cool, not cold. Why Pigs Ass Porter? While drinking this new brew one evening back in 1997, the local hog farmer showed up to collect Harvest Moon's spent mash.

HEATHEN BREWING RIP PORTER

Country of Origin: *United States* • **Brewery Founded:** *2011* • **Alcohol Content:** *5.2%*

Heathen Brewing is a small craft brewery created from the soul of home brewing. It is located in Vancouver, Washington. Sunny Parsons founded the brewery and co-brews Heathen's beers with Rodney Striker. The brewery's remit is to use local ingredients in small craft batch brewing. Heathen Brewing makes small batches of progressive ales. RIP Porter is really intense porter. The pale, chocolate, Crystal 80, and Carapils malted barley give this beer a rich chocolate and coffee flavor. This rich porter is full of Willamette hops.

HELLTOWN BREWING PEVERSE STOUT

Country of Origin: *United States* • **Brewery Founded:** *2011* • **Alcohol Content:** *6.5%*

Helltown is named in honor of its historical roots. The brewery was founded by a small group of home brewers. Several years, and countless batches later it was decided to push a weekend hobby to the next level and in the spring of 2011 operations officially began. Helltown's beers range from the classic to the contemporary. Each style is brewed with the finest and freshest ingredients possible. Perverse Stout pours black. It is brewed with Maris Otter, Chocolate malt, Black malt, Cara-malt 15, and roasted barley combined with East Kent Goldings hops.

HIGH POINT BREWING COMPANY RAMSTEIN BLONDE

Country of Origin: *United States* • **Brewery Founded:** *1994* • **Alcohol Content:** *5.4 to 5.5%*

The High Point Brewing Company is the first exclusive wheat beer brewery in America. The founder and driving force of High Point is award-winning home brewer, Greg Zaccardi. After working as a brewer in southern Germany, Greg returned to Butler, New Jersey. His Ramstein-branded beers are made with wheat, barley, hops, and yeast imported from Bavaria. The German town of Ramstein surrounds the United States Ramstein Air Force Base. High Point wanted the name of its beers to reflect a marriage of German tradition and American innovation. Ramstein Blonde is an unfiltered traditional German weiss beer. It has a malty wheat bouquet brimming with clove and apple aromas. Wheat and barley are balanced by imported German Tettnanger hops.

HOG HAUS BREWING COMPANY FAT WOODSTOCK WHEAT

Country of Origin: *United States* • **Brewery Founded:** *2004* • **Alcohol Content:** *4.5%*

Julie Sill opened the Hog Haus brewery in Fayetteville, Arizona. It is the only operating brewery in the Northwest Arkansas area. It has a fantastic location at the corner of Dickson and West Streets. Hog Haus makes several beers including Fat Boy Blue, Curly Tail Ale, Ruby Red Ale, Pale Rider, Java Porter, Scout Stout, Abbey Road Pale Ale, Black Hole Imperial Stout, Pumpkin Ale, and Wheel Sucker Wit. Woodstock Wheat is a German style hefeweizen and is Hog Haus's most popular beer. It is brewed with 60% white wheat malt, and 40% pilsner malt. A special yeast strain contributes the characteristic fruity, spicy, clove, and banana flavors that make this brew unlike any other. Just a touch of German hops provides enough balance to make it an extremely smooth beer to drink. Woodstock Wheat is unfiltered giving it a cloudy appearance.

HOLLISTER BREWING COMPANY BEACHSIDE BLONDE

Country of Origin: *United States* • **Brewery Founded:** *2007* • **Alcohol Content:** *4.8%*

Hollister Brewing Company was established with a vision of creating hand-crafted beer to compliment hand-crafted food. Hollister is a locally-owned and operated brewpub. It was born of a devotion to quality, craft, and community. Hollister Brewing Company takes pride in having up to fifteen different beers on tap at any given time. The brewery's Beachside Blonde is a German style Kolsch ale. It is Crisp and clean with an earthy hop bite. Hollister also brews a hefeweizen, American IPA, pumpkin beer, extra pale ale, American brown ale, India red ale, golden pale ale, Scottish heavy ale, Belgian saison, West Coast IPA, Belgian blonde ale, and an Imperial IPA.

HORSEFLY BREWING COMPANY BUG-EYED BLOND

Country of Origin: *United States* • **Brewery Founded:** *2009* • **Alcohol Content:** *5.4%*

Horsefly Brewing Company is based in Montrose, Colorado. The founders decided they wanted the brewery name to represent something local. They couldn't spell Uncompahgre so they settled on Horsefly. Horsefly Mountain is a 10,000 feet high peak on the Uncompahgre Plateau west of Montrose. Horsefly's Bug-Eyed Blond is an American blonde ale. It pours a bright gold and has a frothy white head. The beer is made with Cara pilsner malt and has an aroma of biscuit, shortbread, and vanilla. It has a faint hint of wheat, but no hops. The taste is sweet and malty with a nice bitter finish. The beer has a light body and medium carbonation.

HUDEPOHL-SCHOENLING BREWING COMPANY LITTLE KINGS ORIGINAL CREAM ALE

Country of Origin: *United States* • **Brewery Founded:** *1986* • **Alcohol Content:** *5.5%*

Hudepohl-Schoenling Brewing Company is the last of the great Cincinnati breweries. Unlike the dozens of hometown breweries that faltered during Prohibition, Hudepohl, which was founded in 1885, survived. Schoenling Brewing Company was created in 1933. The two breweries merged in 1986, and in 1999 the company was sold to Snyder International Brewing Group. The old Schoenling bottling plant was sold to the Sam Adams Boston Beer Company. The plant now bottles Hudepohl-Schoenling brands including Little Kings Original Cream Ale. The beer is brewed with the same tried and tested recipe that has delighted beer drinkers since 1958.

It's Good To Be King.

HUDEPOHL-SCHOENLING BREWING COMPANY SCHOENLING LAGER

Country of Origin: *United States* • **Brewery Founded:** *1986* • **Alcohol Content:** *4.0%*

The Hudepohl-Schoenling Brewing Company is a wholly owned subsidiary of Christian Moerlein Brewing. Schoenling's Lager is known as "Cincinnati's Finest." Although it is no longer available in bottles or cans, the beer is available in kegs in Greater Cincinnati, Dayton, and Northern Kentucky. There are still a few bars that carry this beer on tap and many people serve it at home. The beer is golden in color and deliciously refreshing. Schoenling Lager was first brewed in Cincinnati, Ohio in 1934.

I & I BREWING BITTER ORANGE BLOSSOM

Country of Origin: *United States* • **Brewery Founded:** *2012* • **Alcohol Content:** *4.8%*

I & I Brewing is a very small brewery located in Chino, California. I & I brew in very small batches and currently the only place to get their beer is directly from the brewery. This allows the brewery a great deal of freedom in the variety of styles and recipe selection. The brewery has six beers on tap, including their Bitter Orange Blossom brew. This is an amber ale. The addition of a large amount of bitter blossom water gives the beer a floral aroma and a bitter orange flavor.

IDAHO BREWING COMPANY IDAHO PALE ALE

Country of Origin: *United States* • **Brewery Founded:** *2009* • **Alcohol Content:** *5.6%*

Idaho Brewing Company is located in Idaho Falls, Idaho. The brewery is known across Eastern Idaho for its award-winning, hand-crafted ales and lagers. The brewery's tasting room overlooks the scenic Snake River. The brewery always has twelve beers on tap, including eight year-round brews. Their signature beer, Idaho Pale Ale is an American pale ale. It has a caramel, malty backbone showcasing Cascade, Columbus, and Falconer's Flight hops. The beer is dry hopped with citrus and floral notes.

IECHYD DA BREWING COMPANY BOXCAR BROWN

Country of Origin: *United States* • **Brewery Founded:** *2011* • **Alcohol Content:** *5.9%*

Iechyd Da is a brewpub located in Elkhart, Indiana. It offers hand-crafted ales, lagers, pizzas, sandwiches and soda. The brewery makes a range of beers from English-style session beers to hoppy American pale ales and barrel aged beers. "Iechyd da" is a Welsh toast which literally means "Good Health." Iechyd Da's Boxcar Brown is a slightly sweet and malty American brown ale with a little caramel and roast. The beer finished with notes of hops.

INTUITION ALE WORKS PEOPLE'S PALE ALE

Country of Origin: *United States* • **Brewery Founded:** *2010* • **Alcohol Content:** *6.75%*

The Intuition Ale Works is a Jacksonville, Florida-based craft brewery established by owner and brewer Ben Davis. Intuition specializes in small-batch hand-crafted ales and their mission is to create quality, flavorful, and creative beers in a wide range of styles. In February of 2012, Intuition became the first craft brewery in the state of Florida to can their beers and the brewery currently cans three of its brews. These include People's Pale Ale and Jon Boat Coastal Ale. Intuition also brews a host of draught-only small batch specialties. People's Pale Ale is the brewery's flagship beer. It is an American-style pale ale inspired by the hoppy pale ales of the West Coast. It features 2-row malted barley and two caramel malts. The beer is brewed with Magnum hops for bittering and the traditional pale ale hops of Williamette and Cascade for flavoring and citrus aromas.

IPSWICH ALE BREWERY IPSWICH ALE

Country of Origin: *United States* • **Brewery Founded:** *1991* • **Alcohol Content:** *5.4%*

Residents of Boston's North Shore were first introduced to Ipswich Ale during the spring of 1991. With nearly twenty years of history, the Ipswich Ale Brewery has been in existence longer than nearly every other craft brewer in New England. The Ipswich Ale portfolio of beers is now distributed across New England. Ipswich Ale is the brewery's flagship beer. The beer has been named one of the World's Ten Best Beers by *Wine Spectator* Magazine, and has been in production since 1991. A North Shore classic, Ipswich Ale is a medium-bodied, unfiltered English-style pale ale with subtle hoppiness and a smooth malty flavor.

IRON FIST BREWING COMPANY RENEGADE BLONDE

Country of Origin: *United States* • **Brewery Founded:** *2000s* • **Alcohol Content:** *5.2%*

Iron Fist Brewing Company is a family-owned brewery located in Vista, California, in the middle of the exciting San Diego craft beer scene. The brewery's passion for hand-crafted beer prompted them to make enough beer to sell. Renegade Blonde is a Kölsch-style blonde ale. When the beer is young, it has a crisp, malty flavor with a refreshingly bitter finish, not unlike a lager. With age, it develops a mild, fruity character, like an ale. It is crisp, mild, and refreshing.

IRON SPRINGS PUB & BREWERY ALTMANS ALT

Country of Origin: *United States* • **Brewery Founded:** *2004* • **Alcohol Content:** *4.5%*

Iron Springs is a locally-owned and operated pub and brewery located in Fairfax, California. Everything is hand-crafted on the premises. Restaurateur Mike Altman and brewer Christian Kazakoff craft beer to pair with food and to reflect the seasons. Iron Springs strives to provide the finest craft ales using only the best ingredients from around the world, including their own proprietary house yeast. Iron Springs always have at least twelve beers pouring at all times. These include everything from pilsner and kolsch to Imperial IPAs and barley wines. Altman's Alt is made from a traditional Alt recipe that was handed down from Mike's great, great uncle, Jebidiah Altman.

IRONFIRE BREWING COMPANY SYNNER PALE ALE

Country of Origin: *United States* • **Brewery Founded:** *2011* • **Alcohol Content:** *5.0%*

Ironfire Brewing Company was founded by John Maino and Gregory Webb. For the Webbs, brewing the highest quality ales and lagers is a way of life. The beers they produce are painstakingly modified time and time again. Every one of their ales and lagers has its own unique brand. Sometimes this leads to Ironfire's beers not fitting into neat categories. Synner Ale is more than a pale ale. Synner is slightly bitter with a punchy hop aroma and flavor. Brewed in the tradition of a So-Cal session IPA, it's copper in color with a medium malt body. This ale is brewed to be dry on the palate and to have a distinctive fruitiness in the aroma.

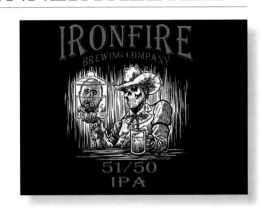

JAILHOUSE BREWING COMPANY BREAKOUT STOUT

Country of Origin: *United States* • **Brewery Founded:** *2008* • **Alcohol Content:** *7.8%*

The Jailhouse Brewing Company is located in Hampton, Georgia, where it operates from the old town jailhouse that was built in the 1920s. The brewery's beers are named in the spirit of law breaking; Slammer Wheat, Misdemeanor Ale, Mugshot IPA, Breakout Stout, and Conjugal Visit West Coast Inspired Red Ale. Breakout Stout is a robust blend of dark roasted malts. It is a bold American Stout with sturdy hop bitterness, a hint of chocolate from chocolate malt and a pleasing finish. Breakout Stout compliments desserts and lends a surprising depth when paired with savory dishes. It is brewed with malted 2-row barley, caramel malt, chocolate malt, and roasted barley. Chinook and Cascade hops bitter the beer. The beer is particularly tasty with cheesecake, brownies, chili, black beans, steak, and cheddar.

JEKYLL BREWING BIG CREEK KOLSCH

Country of Origin: *United States* • **Brewery Founded:** *2013* • **Alcohol Content:** *5.0%*

Jekyll Island, Georgia was the location of the first brewery of the Deep South in 1738. Jekyll Brewing, located in Alpharetta, Georgia commemorates this tradition. The brewery was founded by Mike Lundmark and Josh Rachel. They brew a line-up of brew styles derived from global craft beers. Jekyll's Big Creek Kolsch is a delicately balanced beer style originating from the Cologne region of Germany and brewed according to the Reinheitsgebot purity law. It is brewed from only barley, hops, water, and yeast. The beer is made at a cold temperature to give the style a dry quality. Big Creek Kolsch is made from ale yeast, which gives the beer's flavor hints of pear and bread. Big Creek pairs well with simple foods like cheese and sausages.

JESTER KING BREWERY LE PETIT PRINCE

Country of Origin: *United States* • **Brewery Founded:** *2010* • **Alcohol Content:** *2.9%*

Located in the beautiful Texas Hill Country, Jester King is an authentic farmhouse brewery committed to making artisan ales of great depth and character. The brewery seeks to embrace nature and local terroir in its brewing. It draws water from the brewery well and uses naturally occurring yeast. Jester King uses as many organic ingredients as possible and the majority of its beer is certified as organic. Le Petit Prince is a farmhouse table beer. It is light-bodied, well-hopped, low alcohol table beer. It is a dry, un-spiced, highly attenuated table beer. It is an unfiltered, unpasteurized, and naturally conditioned ale.

JOLLY PUMPKIN ARTISAN ALES LA ROJA

Country of Origin: *United States* • **Brewery Founded:** *2004* • **Alcohol Content:** *7.2%*

Jolly Pumpkin Artisan Ales is a micro brewery located in Dexter, Michigan. It was founded by Ron Jeffries and produces a variety of unfiltered and unpasteurized rustic country beers. Jolly Pumpkin ages its beers in wine barrels which contain naturally occurring microbiological cultures. These cultures produce a complex flavor profile that has been described as being like farmhouse ale or American wild ale. La Roja is an artisan amber ale brewed in the Flanders tradition. The beer is deep amber with earthy caramel, spice, and sour fruit notes developed through natural barrel aging. It is unfiltered, unpasteurized, and blended from barrels. The beer is produced year-round.

JUBILEE CRAFT BEER COMPANY RANDY'S IPA

Country of Origin: *United States* • **Brewery Founded:** *2010* • **Alcohol Content:** *5.5%*

Jubilee Craft Beer Company was founded by Nashville native Mark Dunkerley. Mark got into craft beer on a family trip to Oregon in 2004. The Oregon Brewers Festival opened his eyes to a whole new world of beer and he's been hooked ever since. Randy's IPA is the brewery's newest beer. It is a well-balanced IPA that delivers plenty of hop character with a smooth finish. Randy's IPA is brewed at the Mayday Brewery in Murfreesboro, Tennessee. The brew is composed of East Kent Goldings, Cascade, and Zythos hops to deliver a bold flavor. Pale, caramel, biscuit, and Munich malts provide balance with the hops. The wheat gives the beer a big mouth feel with a smooth finish.

LAKE SUPERIOR BREWING COMPANY SPECIAL ALE

Country of Origin: *United States* • **Brewery Founded:** *1994* • **Alcohol Content:** *6.0%*

The Lake Superior Brewing Company began as the dream of Bob Dromeshauser. It is located in Duluth, Minnesota. The brewery's current owners are Don and Jo Hoag, John Judd III, and Karen Olesen. Today, Lake Superior Brewing Company remains the only commercial micro brewery in the Northland. The brewery continues to focus on making distinctive, hands-on brews. Lake Superior Brewing Company makes four beers year-round: Special Ale, Kayak Kolsch, Sir Duluth Oatmeal Stout, and Deep Water Black IPA. Special Ale pours an orange-gold hue. The beer has piney hop aromas, a medium-bodied feel on the palate, and toasty malt flavors. These give way to a hoppy and bitter finish. The brew is an assertive and rich India Pale Ale. The beer earned the silver medal at the World Beer Championship.

LATROBE BREWING COMPANY ROLLING ROCK

Country of Origin: *United States* • **Brewery Founded:** *1939* • **Alcohol Content:** *4.6%*

Rolling Rock is an iconic American pale lager brewed by the Latrobe Brewing Company of Pittsburgh, Pennsylvania. The brand was sold to Anheuser-Busch of St. Louis, Missouri, in 2006, which transferred brewing operations to New Jersey. The final batch of Rolling Rock was shipped from the Latrobe brewery in 2006. The beer is brewed with only the finest malted barley, rice, corn, and blend of hops. Rolling Rock is a classic lager well-known for its distinctive, full-bodied taste and its craftsmanship. The beer is full-flavored, with a subtle bite. It has a light-to-medium body and color.

LAUGHING DOG COLD NOSE WINTER ALE

Country of Origin: *United States* • **Brewery Founded:** *2005* • **Alcohol Content:** *6.9%*

The Laughing Dog Brewing is located in Sandpoint, Idaho. The brewery began with an intention to brew beers with more hops. The brewery now makes craft beers of interesting flavors. Laughing Dog has now brewed over fifteen distinct beers, including seasonals like its Huckleberry Ale and Winter Ale together with award-winning IPA's and stouts. Cold Nose Winter Ale is a strong English ale with an American twist. Laughing Dog brews the beer with plenty of malt and hops then dry hops the beer for an American-style winter brew.

LAZY MAGNOLIA BREWERY SOUTHERN PECAN

Country of Origin: *United States* • **Brewery Founded:** *2003* • **Alcohol Content:** *9.7%*

Lazy Magnolia is Mississippi's oldest packaging brewery, and the first one founded since prohibition was enacted in 1907. It is located in Kiln, Mississippi. The brewery offers locally brewed beer to Mississippians but its brews can now be found throughout the South. According to Lazy Magnolia, Southern Pecan is the first beer in the world to be made with whole roasted pecans. The pecans are used like grain and provide a deep and nutty character to the flavor profile. The beer is very lightly hopped to allow the malty, caramel, and pecan flavors to shine through. The beer pours dark mahogany. Southern Pecan won a bronze medal in the 2006 World Beer Cup in the Specialty Beer category.

LEFT COAST HOP JUICE DOUBLE IPA

Country of Origin: *United States* • **Brewery Founded:** *2004* • **Alcohol Content:** *4.39%*

Left Coast Brewing Company is an independent brewery, based in San Clemente, California. The company began operations in a 5,000 square foot warehouse. In their first year Left Coast produced just over 3500 barrels of beer. This is equal to approximately 7000 kegs of beer. Left Coast produces five full-time beers. Their flagship beer is Hop Juice Double IPA. The other four are Asylum Belgian-style Tripel Ale, Trestles IPA, Voo Doo American Stout, and Una Mas Amber Alger. Left Coast also offers four seasonal beers throughout the year. These are Red Tide Belgian-Style Red Ale during spring, Board Walk Saison during summer, Ale Epeteios Imperial Stout in the fall, and The Wedge Black IPA in the winter. Hop Juice is brewed with CTZ, Cascade, Mount Hood, Centennial, Amarillo, and Simcoe hops.

LEFT HAND BREWING COMPANY SAWTOOTH ALE

Country of Origin: *United States* • **Brewery Founded:** *1994* • **Alcohol Content:** *5.3%*

Left Hand Brewery was founded by Dick Doore and Eric Wallace. Left Hand was named in honor of Chief Niwot (the Arapahoe word for left hand) whose tribe wintered in the local area of Longmont, Colorado. The brewery's first batch of beer was Sawtooth Ale, which has since become their most popular brew. In their first year of operation, Left Hand took home two medals at the Great American Beer Festival, a Gold Medal in the bitter category for Sawtooth Ale, and a bronze medal in the Robust Porter category for Black Jack Porter. In 1995, the brewery was able to start putting their logo on bottle caps. Sawtooth Ale is an English-style Extra Special Bitter. It is a well balanced beer, with significant hop character, medium body, and a maltiness which increases as the beer warms.

LEXINGTON BREWING AND DISTILLING COMPANY KENTUCKY ALE

Country of Origin: *United States* • **Brewery Founded:** *1999* • **Alcohol Content:** *8.19%*

Lexington Brewing and Distilling Company was revived by Dr. Pearse Lyons when the old Lexington brewery closed its doors in 1999. Lyons thus resurrected the brewing and distilling tradition of Lexington, Kentucky, a tradition that dates back to the 1790s. His ambition was to brew the best possible beers. The brewery's first beers were Kentucky Ale and Kentucky Kölsch. Capitalizing on Kentucky's position as producer of 98% of the world's bourbon, Kentucky Ale is matured in Kentucky bourbon barrels for six weeks. This gives the beer a distinctive taste, color, and fragrance. The brew is an American strong ale and is Lexington's flagship beer. It has won many awards including medals at the Great American Beer Fest. Lexington's master brewers describe the beer as a marriage between two classic beer styles; Irish Red Ale and English Pale Ale. Light amber in color, Kentucky Ale owes its body and character to imported malts and a pinch of wheat malt for a rich, smooth taste. The unique body and character of Kentucky Ale is heavily influenced by the water used to brew the beer. This is drawn from aquifers in the limestone rock under the state's Bluegrass region.

THE LONE PINT BREWERY 667 NEIGHBOR OF THE BEAST

Country of Origin: *United States* • **Brewery Founded:** *2012* • **Alcohol Content:** *6.6%*

The Lone Pint Brewery is a grassroots brewery dedicated to creating distinctive local Texas ales that are tasty, hoppy, and quaffable. The brewery uses raw whole cone hops to bitter and flavor their brews. Lone Pint's 667 Neighbor of the Beast American India Pale Ale uses bountiful amounts of American 2-row malted barley and a sprinkle of Maris Otter malt in combination with three different whole cone American hops. The hops are individually transitioned throughout the boil to highlight each hop's characteristics. Post-fermentation, 667 is dry hopped with vast amounts of the same three hops. The beer is orange nectar in color with a frothy white head and light malt body. It is full of hop flavor and aroma with notes of grapefruit, peach, and honey.

LONE TREE BREWING COMPANY ARIADNE'S BLONDE

Country of Origin: *United States* • **Brewery Founded:** *1878* • **Alcohol Content:** *5.7%*

Lone Tree Brewing Company is a European-style craft brewery and tasting room based in Lone Tree, Colorado. The brewery specializes in small hand-crafted batch brews and sharing the experience with fellow beer lovers. Opening Lone Tree Brewing Company means much more to partners John Winter and Jason Wiedmaier than just serving beer. To them, it is about creating a community atmosphere where people who share their excitement about hand-crafted beer feel right at home. Ariadne's Blonde is a blonde ale, with sweet malt and coriander. A pinch of magnum hops balances the beer.

THE LOST RHINO BREWING COMPANY RHINO CHASERS PILSNER

Country of Origin: *United States* • **Brewery Founded:** *2011* • **Alcohol Content:** *5.6%*

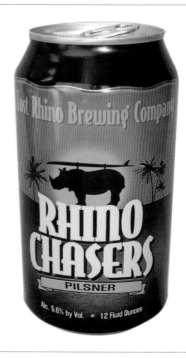

The Lost Rhino Brewing Company is a micro brewery located in Ashburn, Virginia. The company produces both beer and root beer. Their flagship pilsner-style beer is Rhino Chasers Pilsner. Lost Rhino was founded by Matt Hagerman and Favio Garcia, two veterans of the Northern Virginia brewing community. The brewery now brews 5,000 barrels of beer each year. In addition to three core brands and four seasonal brews, the brewery produces special limited release beers. Rhino Chasers Pilsner is a Bohemian Pilsner. It is a crisp golden lager with a rich and dense creamy head. Premium Pilsner and Munich malts generate a malty-sweet backbone, but the hops really make this brew stand out. American Hallertau and Saaz hops give rise to the beer's spicy hop flavor and fresh aromas.

LUCKY BUCKET BREWING COMPANY LUCKY BUCKET LAGER

Country of Origin: *United States* • **Brewery Founded:** *2008* • **Alcohol Content:** *4.5%*

Lucky Bucket is located in La Vista, Nebraska. After several stops and starts, the brewery launched its first beer, Lucky Bucket Lager. The brew is a pre-Prohibition-style lager that salutes a time when lagers had greater character and more distinct flavours. Lucky Bucket's lager is also devoid of the additives found in many of today's mainstream lagers. Lucky Bucket's lager has a light, malty flavor that's easy on the palate. Filtered twice, the subtle maltiness nicely balances floral hop notes. The beer is dry-hopped with a fresh blend of aromatic West Coast hops. Lucky Bucket Lager is a great session beer.

MAC & JACK'S BREWERY AFRICAN AMBER

Country of Origin: *United States* • **Brewery Founded:** *1993* • **Alcohol Content:** *5.2%*

Mac & Jack's objective is to make the finest ales in America's Northwest. Most of the brewery's ingredients come from the region, including its malted barley and Yakima hops. Located in Redmond, Washington, Mac & Jack's currently produces six beers, including African Amber. This is the Northwest's original, unfiltered, and dry hopped amber ale. The beer has a floral, hoppy taste, followed by well-rounded malt. It finishes with an organic hop flavor. Locally sourced 2-row grain and a blend of specialty malts give this amber ale its rich taste. Further complexity is achieved by leaving the beer unfiltered, which gives the beer its cloudy appearance. Mac & Jack's place a bag of fresh, locally-grown Yakima Valley hops in each keg of this cult classic.

MACK HOUSE BREWERY PSYCHO PHISH

Country of Origin: *United States* • **Brewery Founded:** *Recent* • **Alcohol Content:** *9.0%*

The Mack House Brewery is based in Florida. It brews a wide variety of experimental beers, including Psycho Phish. This is the micro brewery's best-selling beer and it is made on the premises. The beer is a blend of Mack House's Panic Attack (a strong Belgian-style amber ale) and Special Golden Ale (infused with Florida navel oranges). Mack House also brews Mack In Black (an Imperial black ale), Panic Con Pablo (Panic Attack infused with roasted coffee), Holy Mole (a chocolate oatmeal stout), and Friends From Florida (a Floridian-style IPA).

MAD RIVER BREWING COMPANY STEELHEAD EXTRA PALE ALE

Country of Origin: *United States* • **Brewery Founded:** *1990* • **Alcohol Content:** *5.6%*

Mad River is based in Blue Lake, California. Now in their third decade Mad River is committed to producing fine ales. The brewery combines the most traditional brewing methods with an environmentally sound approach. Mad River Brewing Company hand craft their ales. Their award-winning brews have become renowned for their unique flavor profile and consistent quality. Steelhead Extra Pale Ale and John Barleycorn barley wine have received gold medals at The Great American Brew Festival. Mad River is perhaps best-known for its Steelhead brand ales, including their flagship Extra Pale as well as an Extra Stout, a Scotch Porter, and Steelhead Double IPA. They also produce the popular Jamaica beer brand, originally produced for North California's legendary Reggae On The River Festival. Steelhead Extra Pale Ale is a bright golden-hued ale of medium body with a spicy, floral hop character and a very mild bitterness. The beer goes well with poultry, fish, sushi, and spicy foods.

MADHOUSE BREWING COMPANY HONEY PILSNER

Country of Origin: *United States* • **Brewery Founded:** *2010* • **Alcohol Content:** *5.0%*

The Madhouse Brewing Company is a production-only micro brewery located in the historic Maytag buildings of Newton, Iowa. All brewing, fermentation, and packaging of the beer occurs onsite, and it is then distributed. Light and crisp, Madhouse's Honey Pilsner has a full flavor for an easy drinking beer. It is golden in color, with subtle fruit-like flavors balanced with Noble hops. It has a delicate floral aroma that is achieved with the addition of honey. This is sourced from the Ebert Company, an Iowa-based apiary. The beer is hopped with Hallertau hops.

MADISON RIVER BREWING COMPANY BAETIS BELGIAN ORANGE

Country of Origin: *United States* • **Brewery Founded:** *2004* • **Alcohol Content:** *5.4%*

Madison River Brewing Company is situated in Southwestern Montana's Gallatin Valley, in the town of Belgrade. The area is an outdoorsman's paradise. The Madison River has earned the reputation as one of the best places to fly-fish in the world. Howard McMurry started the brewery and chose its name. The brewery's first brew was Hopper Pale Ale. It now offers a variety of tasty brews including Salmon Fly Honey Rye, the brewery's flagship brew. Baetis Belgian Orange is a Belgian Wit beer. It is brewed for drinkers that want a lighter wheat beer with low hops and low alcohol. The brew has a strong, sweet orange peel influence. The hops used in this brew are used to develop flavor and aroma rather than bitterness. The brew is light in color and body. It is crisp, refreshing, sweet, and easy-drinking.

MAGIC HAT BREWING COMPANY G-THING!

Country of Origin: *United States* • **Brewery Founded:** *1994* • **Alcohol Content:** *5.7%*

Magic Hat Brewing Company is located in South Burlington, Vermont. The brewery brews three year-round beers and several seasonal products and one-off batches. The company is now owned by Cerveceria Costa Rica. Magic Hat's year-round beers are #9 Not Quite Pale Ale, Circus Boy Hefeweizen, and Single Chair Pilsner. G-Thing! is a Ginger Spice Ale with a fresh ginger zing and bready

malt backbone. Its subtle roasty notes and mild hop bitterness slowly give way to a serene cinnamon spiciness as the malt tones melt away. The beer is made with pale, Caramel Vienna, Caramel Munich, Victory, chocolate, and wheat malts combined with Magnum and Northern Brewer hops. Ginger juice and cinnamon are added to the brew.

F. X. MATT BREWING COMPANY SARANAC PALE ALE

Country of Origin: *United States* • **Brewery Founded:** *1853* • **Alcohol Content:** *5.5%*

F.X. Matt Brewing Company is an American family-owned brewery at the foothills of the Adirondack Mountains in Utica, New York. It is the second oldest family-owned brewery in the United States, as it has been brewing beer since 1853. Its most popular product is the Saranac line of beers, and also it produces root beer and ginger beer. Matt Brewing ranked as the sixth largest craft brewing company in the United States based upon 2011 beer sales volume. The brewery has produced thirty different Saranac beers. These include Adirondack Lager (a German amber lager), Black & Tan (a stout/amber lager blend), Pale Ale (an English pale ale), Black Forest (a Bavarian Schwarzbier), India Pale Ale, Lager (a traditional American lager), and a seasonal Belgian White. Saranac beers have been awarded several honors. In 1991, Saranac Amber Lager (today known as Adirondack Lager) was named the top premium lager at the Great American Beer Festival. Saranac Pale Ale is a classic English Pale Ale brewed with six specialty malts and aggressively-hopped with hand-selected English Kent Goldings & Fruggles hops. Inevitably, the beer has a rich and fruity hop bouquet. It pours a copper amber color and has a smooth, full-flavored taste with a crisp finish that comes from a genuine top-fermented ale.

MAYFLOWER BREWING COMPANY MAYFLOWER PORTER

Country of Origin: *United States* • **Brewery Founded:** *2007* • **Alcohol Content:** *5.2%*

Mayflower Brewing Company is a craft beer micro brewery located in historic Plymouth, Massachusetts. The brewery was founded by a tenth great grandson of John Alden, the beer barrel cooper who came to America on board the Mayflower. It is dedicated to celebrating the history and legacy of the Pilgrims by creating unique, high-quality ales for the New England market. Mayflower brews and packages its beer in Plymouth. The brewery uses only traditional brewing methods and ingredients. Their product line includes a set of year-round beers that honor traditional English ales, seasonal beers that celebrate the New England weather, and small batch releases to try out new ideas. Mayflower Porter is a rich, complex brew that is smooth and full-flavored. Five varieties of malted barley provide notes of roasted coffee beans and bittersweet chocolate with a hint of smokiness. It is brewed with 2-row pale, Caramel Munich, chocolate, peated, and brown malts combined with Pilgrim and Glacier hops, and Mayflower's House Yeast. The beer pours black.

MAZANITA BREWING KENTUCKY COMMON

Country of Origin: *United States* • **Brewery Founded:** *2010* • **Alcohol Content:** *4.5%*

Manzanita Brewing is a home-grown maker of fine craft beers based in San Diego, California. Founders Garry Pitman and Jeff Trevaskis set out to brew excellent ale and have now made more than 3,500 barrels of good beer. With their 2012 expansion into a new thirty-barrel brew house, the guys from Manzanita look forward to sending their beer throughout Southern California and the rest of the United States. Their Kentucky Common is a sessionable spring beer made using whiskey techniques and ingredients. Mazanita let the sour-mash rest for twenty-four hours before the boil, which allows the souring bacteria to flavor the brew. Kentucky Common was a 2013 Los Angeles International Beer Competition bronze medal winner.

MIKE HESS BREWERY INTREPIDUS INDIA PALE ALE

Country of Origin: *United States* • **Brewery Founded:** *2010* • **Alcohol Content:** *8.5%*

The Mike Hess Brewery started out as the smallest production brewery in San Diego, California with a hand built stainless steel three vessel system (mash/lauter, boil, and whirlpool) along with four sixty gallon food grade plastic conical fermenters. They now brew in a 12,500 square foot facility in the heart of North Park. This area is the home of San Diego's craft brew industry and was recently named one of America's hippest neighborhoods by Forbes magazine. The brewery's Intrepidus India Pale Ale is one of their flagship brews. It pours light golden-orange with a white head. Tangerine, star fruit, and other citrus aromas fill the nose. The taste is of floral hops with a lingering bitter finish.

MILLER BREWING COMPANY MILLER 64

Country of Origin: *United States* • **Brewery Founded:** *1855* • **Alcohol Content:** *2.8%*

Miller 64 is a lighter version of the regular Miller Genuine Draft Light. It is a low alcohol, low calorie pale lager beer with sixty-four calories per bottle. Until recently, no other beer on the market had fewer calories. Miller launched this beer in the summer of 2007 in Madison, Wisconsin. The beer pours a golden straw hue and a light, thin white head. The taste is mildly sweet with an average carbonation. It is light bodied and quite watery.

MILLER BREWING COMPANY MILLER BEER

Country of Origin: *United States* • **Brewery Founded:** *1855* • **Alcohol Content:** *4.7%*

Frederick Miller founded the Miller Brewing Company in 1855 when he bought the small Plank Road Brewery. The brewery's location in the Milwaukee's Menomonee Valley meant that it had good access to raw brewing materials from the nearby farms. In 2002, Miller was acquired by South African Breweries in a deal worth $5.6 billion. The new company became SABMiller. Miller Genuine Draft was introduced in 1985 as the original cold filtered (unpasteurized) draft beer. The brew won the gold medal in the American-style Premium Lager category at the 1999 World Beer Cup. The beer was originally introduced as Miller High Life Genuine Draft.

MILLER BREWING COMPANY MILLER HIGH LIFE

Country of Origin: *United States* • **Brewery Founded:** *1855* • **Alcohol Content:** *4.6%*

Miller High Life dates from 1903 and is Miller's oldest brand. High Life is a pilsner and is described by the manufacturer as "The Champagne of Beers." The beer is noted for its high, champagne-like level of carbonation. It was originally available in miniature champagne bottles and was one of America's high-end beers for many years. High Life bottles have always been distinctive, with their bright gold labels, tapered-necks, and Girl in the Moon logo. Legend has it that the image was painted in the early 1900s and was based on company founder Frederick Miller's granddaughter. High Life won the gold medal in the American-style Lagers category at the 2002 World Beer Cup. Recently, High Life has enjoyed increasing popularity with its "Take Back the High Life" campaign, which markets the brew as "a good honest beer at a tasty price."

MOERLEIN LAGERS & ALES ZEPPELIN BAVARIAN STYLE PALE ALE

Country of Origin: *United States* • **Brewery Founded:** *1853* • **Alcohol Content:** *5.0%*

Moerlein was founded by Christian Moerlein, an apprentice brewer from Bavaria, Germany. His brewery was established in Cincinnati, Ohio. Christian Moerlein's Zeppelin Bavarian Style Pale Ale. It is the latest addition to the Christian Moerlein range of craft beers. The beer is brewed with Noble German hops, pilsner, and Munich malts. It has delicate floral and fruity notes from the late addition of hops to the kettle and the dry-hopping process.

MONKEY PAW PUB & BREWERY MONKEY PAW SATANIC CHIMP

Country of Origin: *United States* • **Brewery Founded:** *2011* • **Alcohol Content:** *6.0%*

Monkey Paw is located in San Diego, California. The brewery handcrafts a wide range of beers in various styles. Their style line-up includes an American brown ale, American red ale, American lager, witbier, American double IPA, milk stout, tripel, Russian Imperial stout, American pilsner, Belgian strong pale ale, Bohemian pilsner, American porter, and a rauchbier. Monkey Paw Satanic Chimp is an American amber ale. It is a dry beer with notes of roast and caramel. The taste has mild hop bitterness and a touch of citrus.

MONKISH BREWERY OBLATE

Country of Origin: *United States* • **Brewery Founded:** *2011* • **Alcohol Content:** *6.3%*

The Monkish Brewery is located in Torrance, Los Angeles, California and is a brewery with a tasting room. The brewing area houses a fifteen-barrel brewing system with fermentation and conditioning tanks. The tasting room is a space where guests may come to purchase and sample beers created at the brewery. Oblate is one of Monkish's flagship beers. It is a Belgian-style blonde ale spiced with chamomile. This smooth, approachable beer reveals golden hues and has fruity, floral, spicy flavors and aromas. An oblate is a person who has devoted his or her life to a monastic way of living but has not taken full monastic vows. Monkish also brews Crux, Moira, Red Table, Pour Toi, Vigil, Lumen, Tripelist, and Magnificat.

MOTHER EARTH BREWING
SISTERS OF THE MOON

Country of Origin: *United States* • **Brewery Founded:** *2008* • **Alcohol Content:** *6.9%*

Mother Earth Brewing is a craft beer brewery located in Kinston, North Carolina. It was founded by owners Stephen Hill and Trent Mooring. Mother Earth currently produces four different styles of beer in bottles, an India Pale Ale called Sisters of the Moon; a Kolsch-style ale called Endless River; a Belgian Wit beer called Weeping Willow Wit, and a Munich-style dunkel lager called Dark Cloud. Mother Earth also can two beers; a pale ale called Second Wind and a hefeweizen called Sunny Haze. Sisters of the Moon IPA is an American-style India Pale Ale. The beer is brewed using a variety of hops including Centennial, Amarillo, and Saaz hops. Mother Earth uses a hopback in the brewing process.

MOTHER ROAD BREWERY AND TAP ROOM
ROADSIDE AMERICAN ALE

Country of Origin: *United States* • **Brewery Founded:** *2004* • **Alcohol Content:** *5.0%*

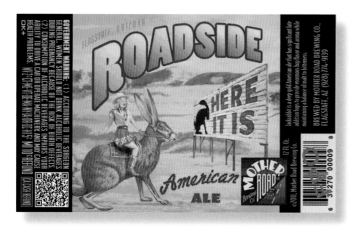

The Mother Road Brewery and Tap Room is located in the Southside of Flagstaff, Arizona. The Mission of Mother Road is to hand craft distinguished beers with respect for history, community, and the environment. Mother Road's vision is to become a Southwest regional brewery by utilizing local products whenever possible. They seek green and innovative technologies to aid their beer production. Roadside American Ale is a pale ale that is extremely hoppy in flavor and aroma, but not bitter. The beer is a showcase of American hops with a medium body and excellent malt balance. Roadside was the gold medal winner at the American Beer Awards for American Pale Ales for 2012. The beer was inspired by the many roadside attractions of Route 66.

MOTHER'S BREWERY TOWHEAD
AMERICAN BLONDE

Country of Origin: *United States* • **Brewery Founded:** *2010* • **Alcohol Content:** *5.2%*

Mother's Brewery is located in Springfield, Missouri. It was founded by local man Jeff Schrag who wanted to launch a Midwest brewing company. Mother's is committed to artistic craftsmanship and brewing craft beers. Mother's loves to brew beers that push creative boundaries. The brewery employs proven, traditional brewing techniques while exploring new flavors and new flavor combinations. Many of Mother's beers are stylistic mash-ups. Towhead American Blonde marries traditional German golden ale and classic Midwestern wheat ale. It is refreshingly light-bodied with a lasting flavor. The beer starts slightly sweet with hints of fruit. It finishes with a faint hop flavor.

MOTOR CITY BREWING WORKS BOHEMIAN LAGER

Country of Origin: *United States* • **Brewery Founded:** *1994* • **Alcohol Content:** *5.2%*

Motor City Brewing Works is located in Detroit, Michigan. The brewery is committed to producing hand-crafted superior quality beer. This is unfiltered and unpasteurized to assure maximum freshness and natural flavor. The brewery's equipment was custom fabricated from salvaged equipment and scrap metal from Detroit's great industrial era. Motor City Motown Bohemian Lager is one of the brewery's flagship brews. It is an original Detroit beer style brewed with Noble hops and pure Detroit water to bring out the crisp, clean flavor.

MYSTERY BREWING ROSALIND

Country of Origin: *United States* • **Brewery Founded:** *2011* • **Alcohol Content:** *6.6%*

Mystery Brewing was founded by Erik Lars Myers. After a decade of home brewing, Myers started writing about the craft beer industry in his blog *Top Fermented*. With help from the North Carolina Brewers Guild he finally decided to venture into the brewing business. Rosalind is Mystery's fall saison beer. It is a drier, hoppier version of the brewery's summer saison beer, Evangeline. Apple, pear, and pineapple flavors from the brewery's yeast strain harmonize with the floral character of European hops for a refreshing fall saison.

NEBRASKA BREWING COMPANY FATHEAD BARLEY WINE

Country of Origin: *United States* • **Brewery Founded:** *2005* • **Alcohol Content:** *11.3%*

The Nebraska Brewing Company is located in Papillion, Nebraska. It is a relaxed dining destination complemented by the brewery's fresh hand-crafted ales. Founded by local man Paul Kavulak, the brewery offers a great range of strong and character brews. These include Fathead Barley Wine, Black Betty Russian Imperial Stout, Chardonnay French Oak Hop God, Chardonnay French Oak Melange A Trois, Procrastinator Doppelbock, NE Blonde, Infinite Wit, EOS Hefeweizen, Brunette Nut Brown Ale, Cardinal Pale Ale, India Pale Ale, and Hop god IPA. Nebraska's Fathead Barley Wine is a rich, full-bodied barley wine with a wonderfully warming character from its malts and dark brown sugars. It pours a burgundy color. The beer is

somewhat sweet from the molasses used in the brew. The non-barrel-aged version of this beer took a silver medal in the 2009 U.S. Open Beer Championships. Using Stranahan's whiskey barrels, Nebraska age the beer for six months to impart a small amount of oak tannin and whiskey character.

NEW BELGIUM BREWING COMPANY FAT TIRE AMBER ALE

Country of Origin: *United States* • **Brewery Founded:** *1991* • **Alcohol Content:** *5.2%*

New Belgium Brewing Company is located in Fort Collins, Colorado. It was founded by home brewer Jeff Lebesch. As of 2010, it was the third-largest craft brewery and the seventh-largest overall brewery in the United States. Fat Tire, an amber ale, is the company's flagship beer. Fat Tire was inspired by Lebesch's bicycle trip through Belgium, as he cycled from brewery to brewery. The company promotes its Fat Tire by placing colorful vintage bicycles outside its brewery. This is located next to the public bike path along the Cache La Poudre River. *Esquire* magazine selected Fat Tire Amber Ale as one of the "Best Canned Beers to Drink Now" in February 2012. Fat Tire reflects the broader palette of ingredients (fruits, spices, and esoteric yeast strains) used in Belgian beers. Jeff created Fat Tire and Abbey Belgian Ale. He assumed that Abbey would be his big gun beer, but Fat Tire quickly became more popular. The beer has good balance, and has toasty, biscuit-like malt flavors steadied with hoppy freshness.

NEW ORLEANS LAGER & ALE BREWING COMPANY FLAMBEAU RED ALE

Country of Origin: *United States* • **Brewery Founded:** *2008* • **Alcohol Content:** *5.7%*

New Orleans Lager & Ale creates refreshing high-quality beer in the heart of New Orleans, Louisiana. The brewery was founded by Kirk Coco & Peter Caddoo. Flambeau Red is the brewery's spring seasonal ale. The creation of Flambeau Red Ale starts with the selection of seven unique malts, to give this seasonal beer its distinctive flavor. The malt is complemented by three hop varieties to achieve a well-balanced American-style red ale. The beer is brewed with American ale yeast which produces a bright and warm beer to drink on Mardi Gras nights.

NO LABEL BREWING COMPANY DON JALAPENO ALE

Country of Origin: *United States* • **Brewery Founded:** *2009* • **Alcohol Content:** *6.0%*

The No Label Brewing Company was founded by the Royo family. No Label's first home was an old rice silo. The brewery is located in Katy, Texas. Don Jalapeno Ale is based on the brewery's Pale Horse Ale. It is brewed with sixty pounds of jalapeños, thirty pounds raw and thirty pounds roasted (seeds included). The beer is a seasonal beer, available every spring.

NOTCH BREWING COMPANY NOTCH SESSION ALE

Country of Origin: *United States* • **Brewery Founded:** *2010* • **Alcohol Content:** *4.5%*

Notch is the first brewing company to focus exclusively on session beer and is now on the front edge of a trend. Notch was launched by Chris Lohring, a professional brewer since 1993, most notably at the Tremont Brewery in Boston, Massachusetts. Notch loves session beer for its unique ability to extend the good times. Notch Session Ale is an American session ale. It is a pale copper color with a firm malt body and a dry, hoppy finish. The beer is well balanced and finishes dry. Notch Session Ale is unfiltered and hopped throughout the brewing process with three American hop varieties, resulting in a complex depth of hop flavor.

OAK CREEK GOLD LAGER

Country of Origin: *United States* • **Brewery Founded:** *1995* • **Alcohol Content:** *4.5%*

The Oak Creek Brewery is located at Sedona, Arizona. The brewery makes American Ales, Belgian Ales, English, Irish & Scottish Ales, Lagers, Wheat Ales, Stouts, and Porter. They have eight beers on tap at any one time. Oak Creek Gold Lager is a richly gold-colored Bohemian Pilsner style beer. It is fresh and malty with a good balance of hops and malt and a dense, white rocky head of foam. The beer maintains its zest and balance of hops and malt from start to finish. It is a cold-lagered, naturally carbonated, all-malt beer.

OAKSHIRE BREWING O'DARK: 30

Country of Origin: *United States* • **Brewery Founded:** *2006* • **Alcohol Content:** *6.3%*

Oakshire was established by brothers Jeff and Chris Althouse. It is now a fifteen-barrel production brewery based in Eugene, Oregon. Oakshire is dedicated to making fine craft beer. What began as a home-brewing hobby and a love of beer has turned into award-winning beer on draft and in bottles. Their brews are now available throughout the Pacific Northwest. The name Oakshire represents the company's core values: strength, independence, and community. Cascadian O'Dark:30 is brewed with dark malt, Cascade, and Centennial hops. It is a spring seasonal beer.

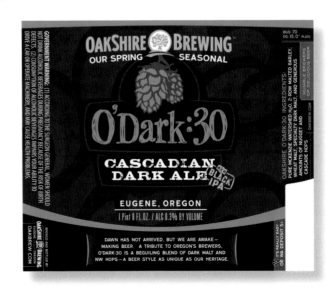

ODELL 90 SHILLING ALE

Country of Origin: *United States* • **Brewery Founded:** *1989* • **Alcohol Content:** *5.3%*

Odell Brewing Company was founded by Doug Wynne and Corkie Odell in a converted grain elevator located on the outskirts of downtown Fort Collins, Colorado. Doug had spent ten years refining his beer recipes until he settled on the brewery's first two recipes, 90 Shilling (a Scottish ale) and Easy Street Wheat. After brewing and kegging his beer, Doug would deliver it, pick up empties, and make sales calls out of his old mustard-colored Datsun pickup. In 1994 the brewery constructed a more conventional brewery and brewed 8,300 barrels of beer. In 1996 Odell added a bottling line to their facility. Odell's brews several classic beers including 90 Shilling Ale, Cutthroat Porter, an IPA, 5 Barrel Pale Ale, Levity Amber Ale, and Easy Street Wheat. 90 Shilling Ale is the brewery's flagship beer. It is a Scottish ale and is richer than most amber ales. The beer is smooth and satisfying, with a crisp, clean Colorado taste. The name comes from the old Scottish method of naming a brewery's beer, based on its original gravity and the resulting tax rating. The beer has a light copper pour with an off-white head, and a sweet caramel aroma. The taste has sweet malts along with caramel, and some resinous hop notes.

OLD DOMINION BREWING COMPANY DOMINION LAGER

Country of Origin: *United States* • **Brewery Founded:** *1989* • **Alcohol Content:** *5.3%*

The Old Dominion Brewing Company was founded by Jerry Bailey, a former federal government employee. The brewery is currently located in Dover, Delaware and produces a variety of beers. In 2006, the brewery sold the equivalent of 27,000 barrels of beer, making Old Dominion the fiftieth-largest brewery in the country. About half of Old Dominion's beer is sold on tap and the other half in bottles. The brewery makes around seven year-round beers and four seasonals. Old Dominion's Dominion Lager is a Dortmunder-style beer. It is brewed using four types of malted barley to produce a smooth, flavorful and complex beer.

ONE TRICK PONY BREWING KENTUCKY MOUNTAIN

Country of Origin: *United States* • **Brewery Founded:** *2000s* • **Alcohol Content:** *11.3%*

One Trick Pony is a small micro brewery located south of Chicago, in Lansing Illinois. Their tasting room serves eight different selections of our hand-crafted beer. Kentucky Mountain is a barrel-aged old ale. It is named for a gaited horse bred and developed in Kentucky and is aged for more than four months in bourbon barrels. The beer is inspired by the traditional British ales of the 1700s, and One Trick Pony brew the beer with all-British malts combined with pale, roasted, smoked, and British yeast. It is given a dash of hops for character and balance and some late-added vanilla bean for a full but mellow mouth feel.

ORLANDO BREWING ORGANIC BLONDE ALE

Country of Origin: *United States* • **Brewery Founded:** *2004* • **Alcohol Content:** *4.5%*

John Cheek founded Orlando Brewing, which is located in Orlando, Florida. Ed Canty, the founder of the Florida Brewer's Guild and professional brewer, then joined John in the business. Orlando Brewing decided to brew their beer in accordance with the German Purity Law of 1516 (the Reinheitsgebot) and decided that they would only use organic ingredients. The purists at Orlando, Brewing knew that it takes great ingredients to make great beer, and decided to stick to the time-tested tradition. They use organic 2-row barley. Orlando's beers became the first to be declared "Fresh from Florida." In 2006 the brewery was certified organic, making it the only U.S.D.A. certified organic brewery south of Vermont and east of Colorado. Florida's craft beer industry has boomed and the organic movement has taken root. Orlando beers can now be found in over one hundred locations in Florida. Orlando's Organic Blonde Ale is a flavorful, light-bodied beer. This is made possible by the use of carefully selected organic malts; only the best imported New Zealand organic hops, pure water, and a house blend of yeasts. The fermentation has a crisp, dry finish and fewer carbohydrates than any other Orlando Brewing beer.

ORLISON BREWING COMPANY IPL INDIA PALE ALE

Country of Origin: *United States* • **Brewery Founded:** *2009* • **Alcohol Content:** *6.6%*

Orlison Brewing is located in Airway Heights, Washington. Orlison is a small craft lager brewery dedicated to making the best craft beers in the Pacific Northwest. Orlison is the first inland Northwest brewery to can its beer. Orlison's company motto is "Brew No Evil." Orlison's IPL India Pale Ale was designed by Orlison founder and brew master Bernie Duenwald. Duenwald crafts the beer with nine different hops (added in three separate stages) and a hefty dose of malt. The beer has the flavorful features of an IPA and the clean finish of a lager.

OSKAR BLUES BREWERY DALE'S PALE ALE

Country of Origin: *United States* • **Brewery Founded:** *1997* • **Alcohol Content:** *6.5%*

Oskar Blues is located in Longmont, Colorado. The company cans craft-brewed beer and is owned by Dale Katechis. Dale launched the canning operation in a sixty-year-old barn next door to his pub in the fall of 2002. Oskar Blues was the first American Craft Brewery to brew and can their beer. The original crew used a hand-canning line on a table-top machine that sealed one can at a time. The brewery has now expanded considerably and the Longmont brewery packaged 59,000 barrels of beer in 2011. Oskar Blues makes six year-round brews, including Dale's Pale Ale, Old Chub, G'Knight, Ten FIDY, Gubna, and Mama's Little Yella Pils. Dale's Pale Ale was Oskar Blues' first beer. It is a cross between an American pale ale and an India Pale ale, brewed with European malts and American hops.

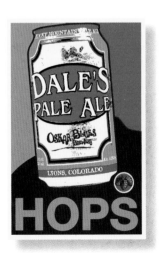

OXBOW BREWING COMPANY FARMHOUSE PALE ALE

Country of Origin: *United States* • **Brewery Founded:** *2011* • **Alcohol Content:** *6.0%*

Oxbow is an American farmhouse brewery specializing in traditional Belgian-style ales with contemporary American influence. They brew small batches of beer in a renovated barn in rural Newcastle, Maine. Oxbow's Farmhouse Pale Ale is the brewery's signature brew. It is brewed with American hops and fermented with Oxbow's famous saison yeast and its own well water.

OYSTER BAY BREWING COMPANY AMBER ALE

Country of Origin: *United States* • **Brewery Founded:** *2012* • **Alcohol Content:** *6.0%*

Oyster Bay Brewing Company is in the business of making great beers locally on Long Island. Since it opened, the brewery has been committed to producing unconventional ales and lagers that defy styles and categories. Its hand-crafted brews utilize only the best ingredients. Oyster Bay's products are thoroughly New York at heart. The brewery blends old and new world techniques with creativity and style. Oyster Bay's Amber Ale is one of the brewery's current offerings. Amber ales range from bland, caramel-flavored beers to products with a healthy malt and hop balance. This quality amber pours a hazy, burnt orange brown with a white head. The aroma has light toasted bread, whole coffee bean, earth, and tobacco leaf. The flavor has plenty of coffee with some brown sugar sweetness and brown bread. It has a dry, coffee finish.

PABST BREWING COMPANY GENUINE DRAFT

Country of Origin: *United States* • **Brewery Founded:** *1844* • **Alcohol Content:** *4.5%*

The Pabst Brewing Company was founded by Jacob Best. In 1889, the company was named for Frederick Pabst. It currently brews over two dozen brands of beer and malt liquor from various defunct brewing companies. Pabst is now is headquartered in Los Angeles, California. Pabst Genuine Draft pours a pale golden color with a big white head. The aroma has lots of sweet corn notes and a fair amount of apple juice flavor. There are hints of metal and a subtle grassy character. The taste is of corn and grain with some noticeable metal. It is lightly bitter with some hints of malt. The beer's body is light with a high level of carbonation.

PEARL BREWING COMPANY PEARL

Country of Origin: *United States* • **Brewery Founded:** *1883* • **Alcohol Content:** *4.73%*

The Pearl Brewing Company was established in San Antonio, Texas. The company is now owned by Miller. Pearl beer is still in production at Miller's Fort Worth, Texas facility, but the Pearl Brewery in San Antonio was closed in 2001. Pearl, Pearl Light, and Country Club are still available, but only in small volumes and in selected markets such as Texas and Oklahoma. Today's distribution is a far cry from the forty-seven state coverage Pearl's beers once had. Pearl pours a pale gold with a thin head. The beer has a lively carbonation with a clean flavor profile. The taste is of sweet grain with hops.

PEOPLE'S BREWING COMPANY AMAZON PRINCESS IPA

Country of Origin: *United States* • **Brewery Founded:** *2000s* • **Alcohol Content:** *6.8%*

The People's Brewing Company is located in Lafayette, Indiana. It has a 6,000 square foot brewing facility and taproom. The brewery specializes in small batch recipes and generally has six beers on offer in the taproom at any one time. Amazon Princess IPA is an American-style India Pale Ale. The beer is brewed with an American base malt with additional Crystal malt that gives the beer its orange hue. It is hopped with Simcoe hops, which give the beer a tropical flavor and aroma. Passion fruit and grapefruit dominate the flavor and aroma. The beer was originally brewed one year after the brewery's first brew day.

PHILADELPHIA BREWING COMPANY KENZINGER

Country of Origin: *United States* • **Brewery Founded:** *2000s* • **Alcohol Content:** *4.5%*

Philadelphia brews its beers in the oldest and largest brewing facility in Philadelphia. The brewery is fiercely independent. It brews fresh beer daily and delivers the fresh beer daily. Philadelphia believes that there is more than just great beer behind a successful brewery and is deeply involved in the local community. Kenzinger is a crisp, light-bodied, golden beer that is very refreshing. The combination of premium German pilsner malts and American Noble hops makes a pleasing and refreshing brew.

PIG MINDS BREWING COMPANY BUILT TO LAST IIPA

Country of Origin: *United States* • **Brewery Founded:** *2000s* • **Alcohol Content:** *8.2%*

Pig Minds is a brew pub located in Machesney Park, Illinois. Pig Minds specializes in hand-crafted ales in a variety of styles. The micro brewery uses the finest barley, wheat, malts, and hops to produce its tasty beers. The brewery serves several beers on tap, including its Blake Hoffman American Wheat, Southy Bitch Slap Irish Red, Meredith Road! (a sour cherry and guajillo pepper ale), Mother Superior American Porter, Crazy Eyes IPA, and Built to Last IIPA. Built to Last IIPA is brewed with Zythos hops and dry hopped with Citra and Galena hops.

PITTSBURG BREWING COMPANY IRON CITY BEER

Country of Origin: *United States* • **Brewery Founded:** *1861/2000s* • **Alcohol Content:** *4.7%*

From the brewery's beginnings in 1861, Pittsburgh Brewing Company has always been committed to its deep roots in the Pittsburgh community, its strong traditions, innovation, and brewing great beer. Iron City Beer is Pittsburgh's flagship brand. It is a traditional American lager brewed in classic Pittsburgh style. Iron City Beer is a classic American lager and an icon of Pittsburgh's culture. The beer boasts scents of sweet corn and wheat and a smooth crisp pale malt flavor. The beer has a dry finish with very little bitterness. Iron City Beer is lightly-hopped and carbonated and is very easy to drink.

POWER HOUSE BREWING COMPANY DIESEL OIL STOUT

Country of Origin: *United States* • **Brewery Founded:** *2005* • **Alcohol Content:** *6.6%*

Doug Memering and Jon Myers formed the Power House Brewing Company and bought the famous Columbus Bar in 2006. It is located in Columbus, Indiana. The pair added twenty draft brews to this brewpub's offering, and updated their brewing equipment. The Columbus Bar celebrated seventy years of continuous operation in 2009. The brewery's Diesel Oil Stout is a black stout beer with a firm brown head. Power House adds a little bit of lactose for ballast. Columbus is home to Cummins Incorporated who manufacture diesel engines. This beer is dedicated to the hard working men and women that work there.

PRETTY THINGS BEER AND ALE PROJECT JACK D'OR

Country of Origin: *United States* • **Brewery Founded:** *2008* • **Alcohol Content:** *6.5%*

Dann and Martha Paquette brew Pretty Things beers. They are tenant brewers, meaning that they work in rented brewery space around Massachusetts. Their flagship beer is Jack D'Or. It is an American saison beer, brewed with Nugget, Styrian, Goldings, Columbus, and Palisade hops blended with Pils, Vienna, Wheat, oats, and rye malts. The beer pours a bright gold. Jack D'Or is the kind of beer Martha and Dann like to drink before, after, and during a great meal. The beer was inspired by some of the Paquettes's favorites like Saison DuPont, DeRanke's XX Bitter, and De Dolle's Arabier. Bitterness is the real backbone of Jack D'Or. Despite all of the spicy flavors in this beer it contains no actual spices or citrus.

PRODIGAL BREWERY PRODIGAL OKTOBERFEST

Country of Origin: *United States* • **Brewery Founded:** *2009* • **Alcohol Content:** *5.6%*

The Davis family purchased the abandoned Meloon farm in 2009 and planted certified organic hops. The farm is located in Effingham, New Hampshire. The Prodigal Brewery is now located in an outbuilding on the family farm. Prodigal runs its brewery in an environmentally friendly way. The brewery's spent grain feeds the farm goats, its yeast and hops are composted, and any excess water irrigates the hopyard. Prodigal Oktoberfest is an American version of the German festbier style. The beer is a full-bodied but quaffable amber lager. It is cool-conditioned for an extended time to yield a smooth and rich tasting brew that is never heavy. It is made with Hallertau, Spalt, and Tettnang hops.

PROSPECTORS BREWING COMPANY REFUGEE TRIPEL

Country of Origin: *United States* • **Brewery Founded:** *2012* • **Alcohol Content:** *9.8%*

Prospectors is currently set up to brew 310 gallons of beer at a time. The brewery is located in Temecula, California. Brewing on this relatively small scale allows Prospectors to maintain quality at a finite level that would be increasingly difficult on a larger system. Their five fermentors allow the brewery to keep a variety of beers on tap year-round. The tasting room is situated in the middle of the brewery and allows people to experience beer and what goes into producing it. Patrons of the tasting room get a front row seat to the brewing process. Prospectors specializes in brewing hand-crafted ales in the traditional Belgian-style. Refugee Tripel is a great showcase of Belgian brewing techniques in balanced strong ale. Illusion IPA blurs the line between a California IPA and a Belgian ale. Mystique Strong is a Belgian-style strong ale with a sweet, spicy, malty taste.

RAPP BREWING COMPANY OMG

Country of Origin: *United States* • **Brewery Founded:** *2012* • **Alcohol Content:** *20%*

The Rapp Brewing Company was founded by brew master Greg Rapp. Rapp is a nano brewery in the heart of Pinellas County, Florida. The brewery specializes in small batch, hand-crafted, artisanal ales and lagers. Rapp explores beer styles and variations on them. The brewery also recreates lost beer styles. Rapp is located in the brewery-rich Tampa Bay area, adding to Tampa's reputation as a destination for craft beer lovers. Rapp's OMG is a high alcohol American strong ale. It is oily black in appearance with no head and no sign of carbonation. The aroma is of chocolate and the taste is of vanilla, caramel, and dark fruits. The body is a little thinner than expected.

REUBEN'S BREWS AMERICAN RYE

Country of Origin: *United States* • **Brewery Founded:** *2012* • **Alcohol Content:** *5.4%*

Adam Robbings and Grace Kim Robbings co-founded Reuben's Brews, and brew nearly all their beer with brother-in-law Mike Pfeiffer. The brewery and brewpub is located in Ballard, Seattle. Adam Robbings left his job in telecommunications to open this successful, small brewery after he learned to love brewing at home. Reuben's Brews offerings include American Rye. This is a clean, crisp, and refreshing rye-based brew. Light in color and hazy, this brew has an aroma of citrus and tangerine that compliment a smooth body and a crisp finish. The brewer also makes Reuben's Roggenbier (a rye hefeweizen), Reuben's Imperial Rye IPA, Imperial IPA, Robust Porter, Roasted Rye PA, and Balsch (a kolsch beer).

REVOLUTION BREWING COMPANY COLORADO RED ALE

Country of Origin: *United States* • **Brewery Founded:** *2008* • **Alcohol Content:** *6.2%*

Revolution is a family-owned and family-run business. The brewery tries to source its ingredients locally. It is co-owned by Mike King and Gretchen King. Revolution is a craft brewery that takes its brewing water directly from Mount Lamborn springs. The brewery does not filter or pasteurize its beers, or use chemical additives. Each batch is hand-stirred. Revolution's Colorado Red Ale is a true, robust red, generously hopped beer. It is a bright and malty brew.

RIVER NORTH BREWERY RIVER NORTH WHITE

Country of Origin: *United States* • **Brewery Founded:** *1988* • **Alcohol Content:** *5.0%*

River North Brewery is located just north of downtown Denver. The brewery focuses on brewing Belgian-style ales and American style ales with a Belgian twist. The brewery was founded by Matt Hess (with a lot of help from his wife Jess). Matt is a former engineer who now spends his time engineering the latest recipes for his brewery. River North White is a white ale, a Belgian-style Wit. It has a subtle spicy, citrus aroma and a delicate, dry finish. It is a sessionable and refreshing beer.

WWW.CRAFTCANS.COM

RHINELANDER BREWING COMPANY RHINELANDER EXPORT LAGER

Country of Origin: *United States* • **Brewery Founded:** *1882* • **Alcohol Content:** *5.0%*

The original Rhinelander brewery was founded by Otto Hilgermann and Henry Danner. The current Rhinelander brewery is located in Rhinelander, Wisconsin. The company acquired the Rhinelander and Rhinelander Light beer brands and all related assets from the Minhas Craft Brewery in 2009. The new company now brews Rhinelander Export Lager, Rhinelander Original, and Rhinelander Light Lager. Rhinelander Export Lager is made with the original recipe. It is a refreshing and malty beer made with the finest 2-row malted barley and sun-ripened hops. It has a light and smooth finish with crisp carbonation.

ROGUE ALES DEAD GUY ALE

Country of Origin: *United States* • **Brewery Founded:** *1988* • **Alcohol Content:** *6.6%*

Rogue Ales is an American craft brewery located in Ashland, Oregon. The company is now headquartered in Newport, Oregon. Rogue operates brewpubs in Oregon, Washington, and California and exports their beers throughout the United States and internationally. The company is owned by Jack Joyce, Rob Strasser, and Bob Woodell. Rogue makes a very wide range of different beers of several styles. The brewery's Dead Guy Ale is one of their best-known brews. It pours a deep honey color and has a malty aroma, rich hearty flavor, and a well balanced finish. Dead Guy is a heller bock brewed with Northwest Harrington, Klages, Maier Munich, and Carastan malts along with Perle and Saaz hops. The beer was created to celebrate the Mayan Day of the Dead (November 1, which is also known as All Souls Day). The Dead Guy label design proved popular and was incorporated into a bottled product a few years later.

ROUGH DRAFT AMBER ALE

Country of Origin: *United States* • **Brewery Founded:** *2000s* • **Alcohol Content:** *7.5%*

Rough Draft likes to reward forward thinking with hand-crafted beers that are as unique in character as those who drink it. They favor style over perfection and take joy in sharing their great-tasting creations with those who love to try new beer. The beers that prove to be winners in their tasting room will be the ones the brewery puts into distribution. Rough Draft's Amber Ale is a well-balanced and full-flavored ale. It has a roasty, malty taste with hints of caramel and chocolate. The beer has a full body and a balanced profile.

ROUGHTAIL BREWING COMPANY RED REPUBLIC

Country of Origin: *United States* • **Brewery Founded:** *2012* • **Alcohol Content:** *5.7%*

Roughtail Brewing is located in Oklahoma City, Oklahoma. The brewery was founded by Blaine Stansel and Tony Tielli. Red Republic is a subversive take on the classic red ale style of beer. The beer has a deep red hue, and a rich maltiness supporting a powerful citrus hop aroma. It is brewed with Cascade hops and is only available on draft.

ROUND BARN BREWERY BRAHMAN BLACK IPA

Country of Origin: *United States* • **Brewery Founded:** *2007* • **Alcohol Content:** *5.4%*

Round Barn Brewery is based in Baroda, Michigan. Owned by the Moersch family, the company began making wine and spirits and opened a micro brewery in 2007. The brewery learned the art of micro-beer production and released a line of full-bodied beers. Round Barn beers are now offered in twelve ounce bottles. Brahman is a curry-infused Black IPA. The beer has slightly roasted flavor notes with an obvious and upfront hop character. The light addition of Maharaja curry is apparent in the beer. This adds complexity while balancing the acidity of the roasted malts.

RUBY MOUNTAIN BREWING COMPANY ANGEL CREEK AMBER ALE

Country of Origin: *United States* • **Brewery Founded:** *1994* • **Alcohol Content:** *5.0%*

Ruby Mountain Brewing Company is located on Angel Creek Ranch in Clover Valley, at the base of the East Humbolt range of Nevada's Ruby Mountains. Ruby Mountain Brewing is Nevada's only micro brewery brewing and packaging beer for off-premise sale in kegs, bottles, and party pigs. The brewery's unique location on a working ranch came about as the result of owners Steve and Maggie Safford's quest to diversify their ranch economy. Their beers are based on recipes perfected during twenty-five years of home brewing. They are brewed from malted grains, hops, yeast, and pure Ruby Mountain water. Angel Creek Amber Ale is reddish copper in color. It is brewed with a blend of pale, Crystal, and Munich malts. The slightly roasted flavor of the malts is balanced with ample additions of Cascade and Centennial hops. The beer is a classic American-style amber ale.

RUSSIAN RIVER BREWING COMPANY PLINY THE ELDER

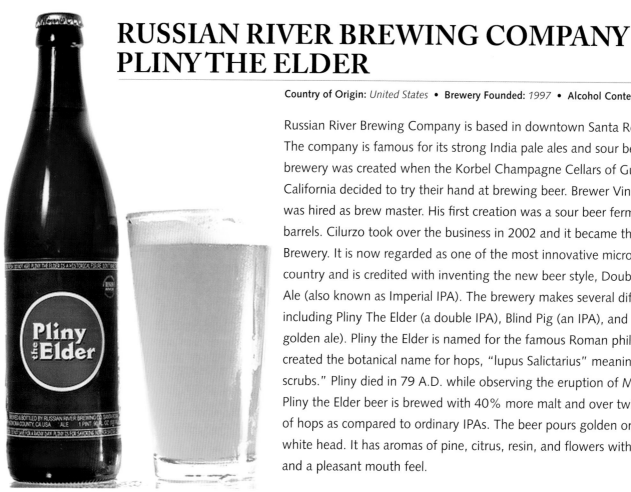

Country of Origin: *United States* • **Brewery Founded:** *1997* • **Alcohol Content:** *8.0%*

Russian River Brewing Company is based in downtown Santa Rosa, California. The company is famous for its strong India pale ales and sour beers. The brewery was created when the Korbel Champagne Cellars of Guerneville, California decided to try their hand at brewing beer. Brewer Vinnie Cilurzo was hired as brew master. His first creation was a sour beer fermented in wine barrels. Cilurzo took over the business in 2002 and it became the Russian River Brewery. It is now regarded as one of the most innovative microbrewers in the country and is credited with inventing the new beer style, Double India Pale Ale (also known as Imperial IPA). The brewery makes several different brews including Pliny The Elder (a double IPA), Blind Pig (an IPA), and Damnation (a golden ale). Pliny the Elder is named for the famous Roman philosopher who created the botanical name for hops, "lupus Salictarius" meaning "wolf among scrubs." Pliny died in 79 A.D. while observing the eruption of Mount Vesuvius. Pliny the Elder beer is brewed with 40% more malt and over twice the amount of hops as compared to ordinary IPAs. The beer pours golden orange with a white head. It has aromas of pine, citrus, resin, and flowers with great bitterness and a pleasant mouth feel.

SADDLEBOCK BREWERY DIRTY BLONDE PALE ALE

Country of Origin: *United States* • **Brewery Founded:** *2000s* • **Alcohol Content:** *5%*

The Saddlebock Brewery is the first production brewery located in Northwest Arkansas. The company has built a state-of-the-art environmentally-conscious brewery on a farm in Springdale, Arkansas. The brewery is committed to brewing fine, European-style beers with the best ingredients, brewed with care in small batches, without artificial ingredients or preservatives. Saddlebock doesn't rush their fermentation process; they know that great-tasting beer takes time. The brewery's core brews are Dirty Blonde, Hefeweizen, Dunkelweiz, and IPA. Saddlebock Dirty Blonde Ale was inspired by the great German-brewed kolsch beer. It is a true hybrid beer, brewed with ale yeast, but fermented like a lager. The cold temperatures give Dirty Blonde a refreshing dry quality, while the ale yeast contributes a complex fruity flavor and bread-like aroma not normally found in a lager. This is a more subtle brew, with a light malt flavor and a touch of fruit, giving it a unique and refreshing quality. It is the perfect beer to pair with food.

SALMON RIVER BREWERY UDAHO GOLD

Country of Origin: *United States* • **Brewery Founded:** *2008* • **Alcohol Content:** *4.7%*

Salmon River Brewery is a partnership between two married couples: Matt and Jennifer Hurlbutt and Matt and Ellen Ganz. Their vision was to create excellent craft beer and serve it in a fun and comfortable atmosphere. The brewery is located in McCall, Idaho. Salmon River makes four flagship beers including Udaho Gold. This is a crisp and refreshing golden ale that is golden in color with minimal hop presence. It is brewed with Premium Brewer's and Vienna malts combined with Nugget and Mount Hood hops. They also serve a rotating selection of seasonal beers.

SANTE ADAIRIUS RUSTIC ALES

Country of Origin: *United States* • **Brewery Founded:** *1984* • **Alcohol Content:** *7.3%*

Sante Adairius Rustic Ales is a small brewery located in the coastal city of Capitola, California. The brewery's focuses on producing well-constructed beers with an eye towards simplicity and character. Its approach to beer making is one of whimsy, highly inspired by the Belgian tradition. Its beers are often barrel-aged in French oak Pinot Noir wine barrels with various yeast and bacteria. The brewery is owned and operated by Adair Paterno and Tim Clifford and makes a range of beers including West Ashley. The flavor of this Saison beer is orange, lactic, and bursting with apricot aroma.

SAWTOOTH BREWERY KETCHUM CREAM ALE

Country of Origin: *United States* • **Brewery Founded:** *2011* • **Alcohol Content:** *4.9%*

Sawtooth Brewery is located in Ketchum, Idaho. The brewery makes five year-round brews, and four seasonal beers. Ketchum Cream Ale has a smooth mouth feel and clean ale flavors. The brew has a crisp malt profile and a delicate hop bitterness. The beer is brewed with a combination of 2-row pale malt, biscuit malt, honey malt, American lager yeast, House Cream Ale yeast, flaked barley, and cluster hops.

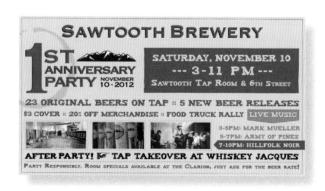

JOSEPH SCHLITZ BREWING COMPANY SCHLITZ

Country of Origin: *United States* • **Brewery Founded:** *1848* • **Alcohol Content:** *4.6%*

Schlitz's roots were in August Krug's Milwaukee restaurant in 1848. Krug was an immigrant from Bavaria. Two years later Krug hired Joseph Schlitz, another German immigrant, from Mainz to be his bookkeeper. When Krug died in 1856, Schlitz took over the management of the brewery. He married Krug's widow, Anna two years later and changed the name of the business to his own. In 1902, Schlitz became the largest producer of beer in the world. Its iconic brew became known as "The beer that made Milwaukee famous" and was advertised with the slogan "When you're out of Schlitz, you're out of beer." Schlitz is now owned by the Pabst Brewing Company. The beer pours clear pale golden with a frothy white head. The aroma has malt, corn, herbs, and hops. The taste is sweet and slightly bitter with a medium body and average carbonation.

SEBAGO BREWING COMPANY SADDLEBACK ALE

Country of Origin: *United States* • **Brewery Founded:** *1998* • **Alcohol Content:** *3.9%*

Sebago Brewing Company offers a line of year-round craft beers, five seasonal beers, and several highly-anticipated limited edition beers. These include their Bourbon Barrel Aged Stout, Hop Swap, Barleywine, and Patersbeir. They are all brewed with the finest malt, hops, and crisp water from Maine's Sebago Lake. Sebago's Saddleback Ale is a light, crisp American ale with a clean finish that is available year-round. The Czech hops balance the pale malt, revealing the beer's natural drinkability. Saddleback Ale is the perfect session beer. It pours a light straw color.

SELKIRK ABBEY BREWING INFIDEL BELGIAN-STYLE IPA

Country of Origin: *United States* • **Brewery Founded:** *1999* • **Alcohol Content:** *8.2%*

Selkirk Abbey is based in Post Falls, Idaho. It is a Belgian-themed brewery, inspired by the founders' interest in these brews. Belgian brewers make every kind of beer from refreshing saisons, to sours and malty Trappists. Selkirk has made its own version of several of these brews. Selkirk's Infidel Belgian Style IPA challenges the notion of beers fitting into established style guidelines. The beer unites the assertive, citrus hoppiness of an American IPA with the traditional spicy notes of a Belgian pale ale. As well as serving beer on tap in its Abbey-themed taproom, Selkirk Abbey is also now bottling its beers to be sold in stores.

SHADES OF PALE BREWING COMPANY READY TO FLY

Country of Origin: *United States* • **Brewery Founded:** *2000s* • **Alcohol Content:** *4.0%*

Shades of Pale is a family-owned production brewery in Park City, Utah. The brewery now makes several distinctive brews. The brewery's Ready to Fly beer is a medley of specialty malts and hops brewed to evoke its Utah origins. This amber ale has a refreshing profile of medium bitterness. It's a little more hoppy than the brewery's Publican Pale Ale but not as hoppy as an IPA. The taste has hints of raisin and plum, and has a graham cracker finish at the back of the palette.

SHEBEEN BREWERY CANNOLI BEER

Country of Origin: *United States* • **Brewery Founded:** *2013* • **Alcohol Content:** *5.2%*

Shebeen Brewery is based in Wolcott, Connecticut. The brewery was founded by avid home brewer Rich Visco. Originally from Northern Ireland, Visco named the brewery Shebeen from a Gaelic word meaning "speakeasy" or "illegal brew house." Shebeen's brews range from a German Cerveza (a Kölsch style beer brewed with agave nectar), Concorde Grape Saison (slightly bitter and complex Belgian-style beer), Bacon Kona Stout, and Wasabi Cucumber (a Japanese rice style beer). Perhaps the brewery's most notorious creation is their Cannoli Beer. This is brewed with spices and lactose. It is served with a powdered sugar rim on the beer glass and chocolate shavings floating on the beer.

SHIPYARD BREWING COMPANY
BATTLEGROUND ALE

Country of Origin: *United States* • **Brewery Founded:** *1994* • **Alcohol Content:** *4.8%*

Shipyard Brewing Company is a micro brewery and soft drink manufacturer based in Portland, Maine. Shipyard is the fifteenth largest micro brewery in the United States and owns several other brands including the Sea Dog Brewing Company and Casco Bay Brewing Company. Shipyard first began at Federal Jack's Restaurant and Brew Pub in Kennebunk, Maine. Within two years, demand for Shipyard beer outpaced the small operation and, in April 1994, businessman Fred Forsley and brewer Alan Pugsley opened the Shipyard Brewing Company in the heart of the waterfront in Portland, Maine. The brewery is on the site of the former Crosby Laughlin Foundry. Shipyard's Battleground Ale is a smooth, traditional American wheat beer that has an inviting golden color. The beer has a mellow malted wheat flavor, with a pleasurable mild zing. The beer has a clean, crisp refreshing taste. The beer works

well with a wedge of lemon or lime. It is brewed with Hallertau hops and 2-row, British, Munich, pale ale, and malted wheat malts. The brewery brews several beers including Export Ale, Old Thumper Extra Special Ale, Shipyard Light, Fuggless India Pale Ale, Bluefin Stout, Chamberlain Pale Ale, Shipyard Brown Ale, and Capt'n Eli's Soda.

SHMALTZ BREWING COMPANY
HE'BREW HOP MANNA IPA

Country of Origin: *United States* • **Brewery Founded:** *1996* • **Alcohol Content:** *6.8%*

Shmaltz Brewing Company is an American craft brewing company based in Clifton Park, New York. Schmalz owns HE'BREW Beer and Coney Island Craft Lagers. The company was founded as American Jewish Celebration Beer by proprietor Jeremy Cowan. The brewery's company's beers now are distributed in over thirty-one states, Canada, and England. Shmaltz is known for blurring beer styles and using puns, art, history, and pop culture in every aspect of their products. After sixteen years as a contract brewer, Shmaltz officially opened their own brewery in Clifton Park, New York in May 2013. HE'BREW Hop Manna IPA is the brewery's first single IPA. It is brewed with specialty 2-row, wheat, Munich, Vienna, and CaraMunich 40 malts combined with Warrior, Cascade, Citra, Amarillo, Crystal, and Centennial malts.

SIERRA NEVADA BREWING COMPANY PALE ALE

Country of Origin: *United States* • **Brewery Founded:** *1980* • **Alcohol Content:** *4.0%*

Sierra Nevada was established by home brewers Ken Grossman and Paul Camusi. Located in Chico, California, Sierra Nevada Brewing is one of the top craft breweries currently operating in America. Sierra Nevada's Pale Ale is the second best-selling craft beer in the United States, behind the Boston Beer Company's Samuel Adams Boston Lager. The company is now the sixth-largest brewing company in the United States and was named Green Business of the Year by the United States Environmental Protection Agency in 2010. Sierra Nevada's year-round offerings include its Pale Ale, Porter, Stout, Torpedo Extra IPA, and Kellerweis Hefeweizen. Sierra's flagship Pale Ale is a careful balance between aggressive hops and hearty malt flavor. It is brewed with Cascade hops that give the beer a grapefruit aroma and fruity palate. Like several other Sierra Nevada offerings, this brew is bottle-conditioned. It is the best-selling American pale ale in the United States.

SIN CITY BREWING COMPANY SIN CITY LIGHT

Country of Origin: *United States* • **Brewery Founded:** *2000s* • **Alcohol Content:** *3.75%*

Sin City Brewing Company is a Las Vegas-based micro brewery launched by Richard Johnson. Sin City's brews are produced to satisfy micro brewery beer drinkers who prefer traditional domestic styles. Sin City beers accentuate the indulgent nature of Las Vegas. The beers are brewed in small batches (one hundred kegs at a time) using traditional methods, premium raw materials, and a strict adherence to the Rheinheitsgebot purity laws. Sin City beers are brewed and distributed exclusively in Las Vegas. Sin City Light is a refreshing and crisp light beer. The beer is a premium product brewed with imported malted barley. It is lightly hopped with a satisfying degree of carbonation.

SKULL COAST BREWING COMPANY GALLOW'S POINT DEAD MAN'S PORTER

Country of Origin: *United States* • **Brewery Founded:** *2011* • **Alcohol Content:** *7.0%*

The Skull Coast Brewing Company brand was born in a Charleston, South Carolina library. Its founder, Dave Fox, named the brewery after a 1700s map with the words "Skull Coast" etched along the Carolina coastline. Gallow's Point Dead Man's Porter is from the brewery's list of fall and winter seasonals. Gallows Point is an Imperial porter made with real chocolate and macadamia nuts. It was recently named one of the Top Twenty American Porters in the United States.

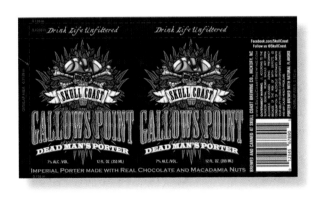

SMUTTYNOSE BREWING COMPANY OLD BROWN DOG

Country of Origin: *United States* • **Brewery Founded:** *1994* • **Alcohol Content:** *6.7%*

Smuttynose is the one of the Granite State's leading craft breweries. It is located in the historic seaport city of Portsmouth, New Hampshire. Smuttynose beers are now distributed from Maine to Florida and as far west as Wisconsin. The brewery's Old Brown Dog has been cited as a classic example of the American brown ale. Compared to a typical English brown ale, Old Brown Dog is fuller-bodied and more strongly hopped. The beer was first brewed in 1988 at the Northampton Brewery. In 1989 it won a silver medal in its category (American Brown Ale) at the Great American Beer Festival in Denver. The beer pours deep reddish brown. It is made with North American, 2-row, Munich 10L, C-120, and chocolate malts combined with Cascade, Galena, and Willamette hops.

SOCIETE BREWING COMPANY THE BUTCHER

Country of Origin: *United States* • **Brewery Founded:** *2011* • **Alcohol Content:** *9.8%*

Societe Brewing Company was founded by Travis Smith, formerly of Russian River Brewing Company and The Bruery, and Doug Constantiner, formerly of The Bruery. Societe Brewing Company is a production brewery and tasting room occupying a 16,000 square foot building centrally located in San Diego, California. Societe focuses specifically on IPA's, Belgian-inspired brews, and wine-barrel aged sours. These are all hand-crafted in a twenty barrel brew house. The brewery's beers are available throughout San Diego and at their newly built and customized facility. This showcases a tasting room with an unobstructed view of the barrel room and brewery. The Butcher

is a Russian Imperial stout. It pours pitch black and opaque with a dark mocha head. The beer has a roasted malt aroma with sweet chocolate notes. It is well-balanced with dark and milk chocolate notes, gourmet coffee bean, and oatmeal countered by baker's chocolate and fudge-like sweetness. It is a medium bodied brew. Societe's other brews include The Apprentice, The Dandy, and The Pupil.

SOLEMN OATH BREWERY RAVAGED BY VIKINGS

Country of Origin: *United States* • **Brewery Founded:** *2011* • **Alcohol Content:** *9%*

Solemn Oath is a hometown brewers based in Naperville, Illinois. The brewery was co-founded by John and Joe Barley and has Tim Marshall as its head brewer. Solemn Oath doesn't have a flagship beer but the brewery is constantly tinkering with its beer formulas and coming up with new brews. Barley says that Solemn Oath plans on experimenting with new concoctions for the first couple of years. The brewery wants to see how popular its individual brews are before they choose a line-up. Solemn Oath focuses on traditional Belgian-style beers with American flare. During the summer months, Solemn Oath usually attends at least one craft beer festival every weekend. Solemn Oath's Ravaged by Vikings is an American Double IPA. The beer has a rich caramel malt sweetness and bright American hop flavors of grapefruit citrus, pine, and tropical fruit.

TALLGRASS BREWING COMPANY PUB ALE

Country of Origin: *United States* • **Brewery Founded:** *2007* • **Alcohol Content:** *4.4%*

Tallgrass was founded by husband and wife team Jeff and Tricia Gill. It is located in Manhattan, Kansas. Manhattan is a town nestled in the Flint Hills and surrounded by the Tallgrass Prairie. The area's pure water is an excellent choice for brewing beer. Pub Ale was the brewery's first beer, launched in 2007. In 2010 Tallgrass declared its "canifesto" and began packaging its beers exclusively in cans instead of bottles. The beers brewed by Tallgrass are now sold in cans and on tap in fourteen states. Pub Ale is a rich and mild brown ale in the tradition of great English pub beers. It is brewed with a blend of four specialty grains and malted 2-row barley. These give the beer its smooth character and lightly sweet flavor, with just a hint of chocolate. The brewery offers seven year-round brews and three seasonals.

TAMPA BAY BREWING COMPANY OLD ELEPHANT FOOT IPA

Country of Origin: *United States* • **Brewery Founded:** *1996* • **Alcohol Content:** *7.0%*

The Doble family founded the Tampa Bay Brewing Company to satisfy Tampa Bay's thirst for better beer. The brewery is still a family affair, with mother and son serving as general manager and brew master. Tampa Bay always has nine beers on tap, brewed in their twelve-barrel system. Tampa's Old Elephant Foot IPA is a traditional India Pale Ale that is brewed with Northern Brewer, Centennial, and Cascade hops.

TEXAS BIG BEER BREWERY TEXAS CRUDE

Country of Origin: *United States* • **Brewery Founded:** *2010* • **Alcohol Content:** *7.0%*

The Texas Big Beer Brewery is a small brewery located in Buna in southeast Texas. It is situated out in the woods of the Big Thicket. The brewery is owned and operated by John and Tammy McKissack. Texas Big Beer likes to make brews with a rich malty flavor and a nostalgic feel. Texas Crude is a very dark robust porter. It is close to black in color and has a very roasty flavor. For such a dark beer, the flavor is also clean. It is the brewery's most popular brew and is highly drinkable and not too heavy.

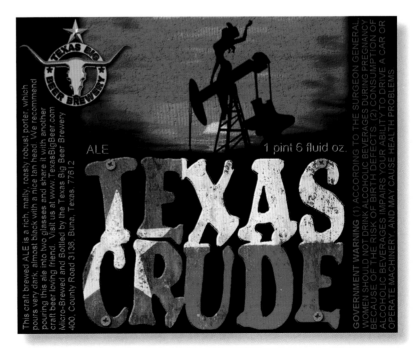

THIMBLE ISLAND BREWING COMPANY AMERICAN ALE

Country of Origin: *United States* • **Brewery Founded:** *2010* • **Alcohol Content:** *5.0%*

The Thimble Island Brewing Company is located in Branford, Connecticut. It was founded by beer enthusiasts who wanted to share their love of craft beer. Prior to Prohibition, the United States was home to over two thousand craft breweries. By the 1980s, barely one hundred remained. Thimble Island seeks to recreate the American tradition of local brewing. Their American Ale pours copper with an off-white head. The beer smells earthy with some crisp, notes of sage. The beer tastes mildly spicy and has a full bodied finish. The brew is easy to drink and enjoyable.

THORN STREET BREWERY ABBEY WALL

Country of Origin: *United States* • **Brewery Founded:** *2012* • **Alcohol Content:** *6.9%*

Dennis O'Connor teamed up with avid home brewers and fellow San Diego natives Dan Carrico and Eric O'Connor to start the Thorn Street Brewery in San Diego, California. The renovated space has been transformed into a beautiful tasting room with a seven barrel brew house. One of the Thorn Street brews is Abbey Wall, a Belgian-styled Abbey Dubbel.

THUNDER CANYON BREWERY ARROYO BROWN ALE

Country of Origin: *United States* • **Brewery Founded:** *1997* • **Alcohol Content:** *5.2%*

Thunder Canyon has specialized in brewing the finest craft beer. This micro brewery is located in Tucson, Arizona.   The brewery has won more awards than any other local brewery and has now crafted over sixty beers. They also brew seasonal beers. Thunder Canyon's beers include Arroyo Brown Ale, Blackout Stout, Cuppa Joe Porter, Skyline Dunkel, Warhead Stout, and Peacemaker Imperial Stout. The beer pours a clear deep amber color with a small off white head. The aroma and flavor is caramel malt with faint esters. There is a light hop presence. The beer has a medium body.

TIGHTHEAD BREWING COMPANY
SCARLET FIRE RED ALE

Country of Origin: *United States* • **Brewery Founded:** *2010* • **Alcohol Content:** *5.6%*

Tighthead Brewing Company is based in Mundelein, Illinois. The brewery is dedicated to crafting quality beer for all seasons. It is nestled in a small community in Northern Illinois. Tighthead provides fresh, quality craft beer to Lake County and the Chicago area. It was founded by owner and brew master Bruce Dir. The name Tighthead was derived from the name of the rugby position of tighthead prop. Bruce Dir played this position for most of his thirteen-year rugby career. The brewery makes around eleven brews. Scarlet Fire is an American style red ale. The beer has a balance of malt sweetness from caramel malt and subtle toasty notes from roasted barley. The beer is brewed with American Ale yeast, and the hops are East Kent Goldings.

TIN ROOF BREWING COMPANY
PERFECT TIN AMBER ALE

Country of Origin: *United States* • **Brewery Founded:** *2010* • **Alcohol Content:** **4**.*5%*

Tin Roof Brewing Company was started by two childhood friends with a passion for beer and a desire to create their own Southern, hand-crafted brand. Tin Roof's Perfect Tin Amber Ale is an American-style amber ale brewed with a variety of specialty malts. These malts combine to form a distinct flavor profile with hints of toffee and chocolate. The beer's mild bitterness doesn't linger. The final product is a malty, medium-bodied, and easy drinking session beer. It pairs well with most grilled or roasted meats, chilis, and stews. The beer is made with pale, Munich, Extra Special, pale chocolate, special roast, and caramel malts. These are combined with Chinook, Cascades, Columbus, and Kent Goldings hops.

TITANIC BREWING COMPANY
CAPTAIN SMITH'S RYE ALE

Country of Origin: *United States* • **Brewery Founded:** *1995* • **Alcohol Content:** *6.0%*

Miami, Florida's Titanic Brewing Company was conceived, developed and registered by Kevin Rusk. Based on the fact that Miami is the cruise capital of the world, Kevin wanted the concept of his hostelry to reflect the city's maritime tradition. The Titanic claims to be Miami's "oldest and finest brewpub." The brewery always has six Titanic beers on draft, whose names also echo the famous liner. These include Triple Screw Light Ale, Captain Smith's Rye Ale, White Star India Pale Ale, Britannic Best Bitter, Boiler Room Nut Brown Ale, and Shipbuilders Oatmeal Stout. Captain Smith's Rye Ale is German-styled amber ale brewed with American 2-row pale malt and malted rye. Rye produces a complex flavored beer that is malty, fruity, and spicy, but slightly cereal in character. It finishes light clean and spicy. The beer pours amber in color.

TWIN LAKES BREWING COMPANY GREENVILLE PALE ALE

Country of Origin: *United States* • **Brewery Founded:** *2006* • **Alcohol Content:** *5.5%*

The Twin Lakes Brewing Company aims to preserve the art of American brewing, by producing premium American ales and lagers. The brewery is based on a farm in Greenville, Delaware. Twin Lakes uses 100% natural ingredients including whole flower hops, the best grains, cultured brewer's yeast, and fresh local water. Twin Lakes Greenville Pale Ale is now available in cans. Local distributors all over the state of Delaware and many in Pennsylvania and Maryland can now sell cases of the beer. Greenville Pale Ale is a traditional, American-style pale ale that is rooted in the Pacific Northwest brewing tradition. Twin Lakes uses whole flower Cascade hops and American 2-row barley malt to produce a light amber ale that is medium bodied with a significant floral-citrus hop essence and aroma that makes it extremely drinkable and refreshing. This is the brewery's signature brew.

TWISTED CREW BREWING COMPANY DIRTY BLONDE

Country of Origin: *United States* • **Brewery Founded:** *2010* • **Alcohol Content:** *6.8%*

Twisted Crew Brewing Company offers eight beers on tap. The brewery is located in Seymour, Indiana. Visitors can sample beers on tap and buy a growler of beer. This is a half gallon glass container. Dirty Blonde is a Belgian pale ale. The brew is a smooth easy drinking beer with numerous characteristics of a typical Belgian. It has distinct malty sweetness from the honey malt that is well balanced by moderate dosing of cluster hops. The flavor finishes with the unmistakable banana and clove notes found in beers of this style.

TWISTED PINE BREWING COMPANY'S ROCKY MOUNTAIN WHEAT

Country of Origin: *United States* • **Brewery Founded:** *1995* • **Alcohol Content:** *5.0%*

Twisted Pine Brewing Company's first pints were brewed by craft beer industry legend Gordon Knight in 1995. The brewery's original line-up consisted of American Amber Ale, Honey Brown Ale, and Raspberry Wheat Ale. Twisted Pine is located in Boulder, Colorado. Today, Twisted Pine is driven by experimentation in brewing and strong community involvement. The brewery's Rocky Mountain Wheat has aromas of sweet malt and clean wheat. It has a light body, lively carbonation, with clean malt and hop flavors.

WORTH BREWING COMPANY FIELD TRIP IPA

Country of Origin: *United States* • **Brewery Founded:** *2007* • **Alcohol Content:** *6.5%*

The Worth Brewing Company was founded by the husband-and-wife team of Peter Ausenhus and Margaret Bishop. It is located in Northwood, Iowa. The aim of the brewery is to reintroduce the tradition of a locally owned brewery serving hand-crafted, high-quality, distinctive beers. The nation's small and mid-sized towns were once dotted with such breweries. Typically, Worth has six of their own beers on tap. The brewery's Field Trip IPA was first brewed in 2009. It is a bronze-colored ale with a balance of malt and hops. Centennial and locally grown Cascade hops provide a viny, citrus flavor and aroma. American and Belgian malts provide a firm sweet backbone to the hops. The brew finishes with firm hop bitterness. Field Trip IPA is brewed with several malts, including 2-row malted barley; Belgian Carapils, and Special B, blended with Worth County honey. The beer is hopped with Worth County Chinook, Worth County Magnum, Worth County Cascade, and West Coast Centennial hops.

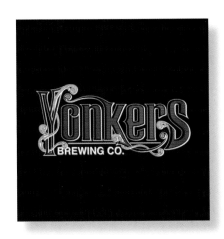

YONKERS BREWING COMPANY LAGER

Country of Origin: *United States* • **Brewery Founded:** *2010* • **Alcohol Content:** *5.2%*

Yonkers Brewing Company was founded by two Yonkers natives, John Rubbo and Nick Califano. The pair founded the brewery to create a great beer for a great city. Yonkers Lager is the brewery's flagship beer. It is an easy-drinking, accessible Vienna-style lager with a balance between the rich malt character and refreshing hop presence. It is copper in color, and not too sweet or bitter.

D.G. YUENGLING & SON TRADITIONAL LAGER

Country of Origin: *United States* • **Brewery Founded:** *1829* • **Alcohol Content:** *4.4%*

D. G. Yuengling & Son is the oldest operating brewing company in the United States. It was initially called the Eagle Brewery. By volume of beer brewed, Yuengling is now one of the largest breweries in the country and the joint largest American-owned brewer. This family-owned company is headquartered in Pottsville, Pennsylvania. The brewery is named after the anglicized last name of its German founder, Jungling. Yuengling's Traditional Lager is an American amber or red lager. The beer pours light amber with lots of bubbles and a medium white head. The beer smells of apple juice, cracker malt, and Noble hops. The taste is light with hints of apple juice, cracker malt, and almost no hop bitterness.

INDEX

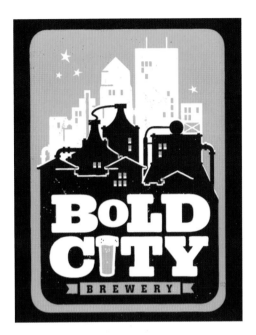

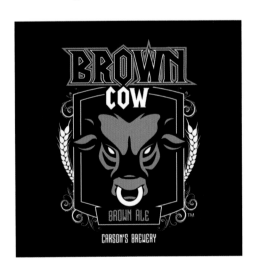

F. X. Matt Brewing Company Saranac Pale Ale 376

Mayflower Brewing Company Mayflower Porter 377

Mazanita Brewing Kentucky Common 377

Mike Hess Brewery Intrepidus India Pale Ale 377

Miller Brewing Company Miller 64 378

Miller Brewing Company Miller Beer 378

Miller Brewing Company Miller High Life 378

Moerlein Lagers & Ales Zeppelin Bavarian Style Pale Ale 379

Monkey Paw Pub & Brewery Monkey Paw Satanic Chimp 379

Monkish Brewery Oblate 379

Mother Earth Brewing Sisters of the Moon 380

Mother Road Brewery and Tap Room Roadside American Ale 380

Mother's Brewery Towhead American Blonde 380

Motor City Brewing Works Motown Bohemian Lager 381

Mystery Brewing Rosalind 381

Nebraska Brewing Company Fathead Barley Wine Ale 381

New Belgium Brewing Company Fat Tire Amber Ale 382

New Orleans Lager & Ale Brewing Company Flambeau Red Ale 382

No Label Brewing Company Don Jalapeno Ale 382

Notch Brewing Company Notch Session Ale 383

Oak Creek Gold Lager 383

Oakshire Brewing O'Dark: 30 Cascadian Dark Ale 383

Odell 90 Shilling Ale 384

Old Dominion Brewing Company Dominion Lager 384

One Trick Pony Brewing Kentucky Mountain 384

Orlando Brewing Organic Blonde Ale 385

Orlison Brewing Company IPL India Pale Ale 385

Oskar Blues Brewery Dale's Pale Ale 385

Oxbow Brewing Company Farmhouse Pale Ale 386

Oyster Bay Brewing Company Amber Ale 386

Pabst Brewing Company Genuine Draft 386

Pearl Brewing Company Pearl Lager Beer 386

People's Brewing Company Amazon Princess IPA 387

Philadelphia Brewing Company Kenzinger 387

Pig Minds Brewing Company Built to Last IIPA 387

Pittsburg Brewing Company Iron City Beer 387

Power House Brewing Company Diesel Oil Stout 388

Pretty Things Beer and Ale Project Jack D'Or 388

Prodigal Brewery Prodigal Oktoberfest 388

Prospectors Brewing Company Refugee Tripel 389

Rapp Brewing Company OMG Ale 389

Reuben's Brews American Rye 389

Revolution Brewing Company Colorado Red Ale 390

River North Brewery River North White 390

Rhinelander Brewing Company Rhinelander Export Lager 390

Rogue Ales Dead Guy Ale 391

Rough Draft Amber Ale 391

Roughtail Brewing Company Red Republic 391

Round Barn Brewery Brahman Black IPA 391

Ruby Mountain Brewing Company Angel Creek Amber Ale 392

Russian River Brewing Company Pliny The Elder 392

Saddlebock Brewery Dirty Blonde Pale Ale 393

Salmon River Brewery Udaho Gold 393

Sante Adairius Rustic Ales West Ashley 393

Sawtooth Brewery Ketchum Cream Ale 394